Marketing Research

Measurement, Method and Application

Raymond Kent
University of Stirling

INTERNATIONAL THOMSON BUSINESS PRESS

I(T)P® An International Thomson Publishing Company

London • Bonn • Johannesburg • Madrid • Melbourne • Mexico City • New York • Paris
Singapore • Tokyo • Toronto • Albany, NY • Belmont, CA • Cincinnati, OH • Detroit, MI

Marketing Research

Copyright © 1999 Raymond Kent

I(T)P® A division of International Thomson Publishing Inc.
The ITP logo is a trademark under licence

British Library Cataloguing-in-Publication Data
A catalogue record for this book is available from the British Library

First published 1999 by International Thomson Business Press

Typeset by J&L Composition Ltd, Filey, North Y[...]
Printed in the UK by Clays Ltd, St Ives plc

ISBN 1-86152-2155-3

International Thomson Business Press
Berkshire House
168-173 High Holborn
London WC1V 7AA
UK

http://www.itbp.com

Contents

Preface

In 1964, Cicourel published a book entitled *Method and Measurement in Sociology*. In it he stated that 'The typical problem of measurement in sociology is, on the one hand, one of implicit theories with vague properties and operations tied in unknown ways to measurement procedures which, on the other hand, have explicit quantitative properties wherein the operations permitted can be defined concisely'. The typical problem of measurement in marketing is fundamentally the same in 1998 as it was when expressed by Cicourel for sociology over thirty years ago. We, as marketers, tend to think in terms of theories and concepts with vague properties, but take measurements of variables with precise mathematical characteristics. But how do we get from one to the other? How do we or can we operationalize our concepts? Some concepts like sex and age of respondents can be translated into precise measures very easily. For others it may not be that difficult, but there are many ways in which it might be accomplished, for example measuring a person's social class. Do we base it on personal or family or household incomes, on the occupation of the head of the household, or on perceived or self-defined class, and what sorts of categories of social class should we use? For yet other concepts, their measurement is entirely problematic, for example measuring a customer's loyalty to a brand, or his or her level of satisfaction with a product or service. This book is about the principles and methods that may be used in the measurement of marketing variables and about the range of measurement applications adopted by the larger market research agencies in the UK. It is based on the author's earlier book *Marketing Research in Action* (1993), but develops the theme of how we generate good measures of marketing concepts to a far greater extent.

All the chapters have been rewritten to reflect the new focus on measurement, but also to reflect the idea of approaching research from different perspectives. Wherever possible, the use of recent computer software is emphasized, particularly SPSS for Windows. However, other packages are introduced as appropriate, for example Logotron's Pinpoint for questionnaire design.

The book will be of value to students, both undergraduate and postgraduate, who are taking courses in marking research as part of a marketing qualification, or for the Diploma of the Market Research Society. The businessman and the marketing manager will also find much of interest if he or she wants to discover what marketing research may have to offer them.

At the end of each chapter there is a summary of the key points, there are suggestions for further reading, a list of the key concepts used and questions for further discussion. There are also some interesting Web sites that can be usefully surfed and a number of suggestions are made at the end of some of the chapters. For lecturers adopting the book there is a *Teachers' Manual* that contains suggested answers to the questions for further discussion plus a selection of Powerpoint slides that may be used or adapted for lectures.

Raymond Kent
University of Stirling

Acknowledgements

I am grateful for permission given by SPSS, St Andrews House, West Street, Surrey, to produce screen shots of a range of SPSS windows. I would also like to thank the following people for their generous help in producing this text:

Julie Anderson, Research Services Ltd
Andy Brown BMRB
Anita Emery, Taylor Nelson AGB
Tim Farmer, Research Services Ltd
Jane Grimes, Research International
Richard Holloway, Taylor Nelson AGB
Gareth Jones, BEM
Harriet Penrose, Research Services Ltd
Chrisine Purves, BMRB
Michael Roe, Research International
Jim Stone, Maritz Inc.

List of Tables

List of tables

List of Figures

1

Marketing research in perspective

Elida Faberge (formerly Elida Gibbs) manufacturers and markets a wide range of toiletries and fragrances including bodysprays for men (Lynx) and women (Impulse) and unisex (Addiction), deodorants (Sure), hand and body lotions (Vaseline), shampoos (Organics and Timotei), toothpaste (Gibbs SR and Mentadent), soaps (Pears) and hairspray (Harmony). Each brand needs to be right in terms of the marketing mix and acceptability to the retail trade. According to the sales and customer development director, Tracey Rogers, 'selling' to customers is no longer appropriate. The Company has to market itself and its brands 'so customers are predisposed to buy from us'. Lynx, Impulse, Sure and Vaseline are each market leaders in their categories. Organics is number two behind Proctor and Gamble's Pantene. Other brands, however, are further down the league including Harmony, Pears, Gibbs SR and Mentadent. Astral skin cream and Hero male frangrances have already been dropped from the Elida Faberge range. The Company faces difficult decisions about what to do with the products that are lagging behind in their respective markets (Barnard, 1996).

How can marketing research help Elida Faberge to make these decisions? The answer is that it can do so in a number of different ways that should become clear as you read this chapter. In particular, this chapter will consider:

- the nature and scope of marketing research,
- the role of marketing research in the organization,
- the different types of marketing research,
- the different perspectives from which research may be approached,
- the role of theories and models,
- the market research industry,
- some ethical issues.

The nature and scope of marketing research

It is often said that marketing is an approach to business that is based on the idea that the most important person to the company is the customer. The company adopting the marketing concept is, according to marketing wisdom, customer-oriented; it must make what it knows it can sell, not attempt to sell what it knows it can make. If this were true (and if only life were that simple) then marketing research would be concerned largely with collecting data on customer requirements and anticipating their future needs.

As always, reality is not quite so simple. Companies offering goods and services in commercial transactions are constrained to be 'customer-oriented' with what they have – with their existing plant, machinery, workforce, location, company reputation, and with their own particular strengths and weaknesses. Furthermore, they must operate in an immediate, 'micro' or 'task' environment which consists not only of customers, but also includes competitors, suppliers, distributors, trade unions, shareholders, financial institutions, government departments and so on. In the wider general or 'macro' environment there will be general economic, technological, social, political and legal factors that, to varying degrees, all need to be taken into account. In addition, not all organizations are business organizations that need to make a profit to survive. Some may be staffed not by employees but by volunteers. If marketing is to be applied to these organizations as well, it must be concerned with the rather broader notion of matching whatever are the objectives of the organization with, on the one hand, the problems, characteristics and resources of the organization itself, and on the other with the target market, audience, beneficiaries, members and so on, taking into account the various 'publics' with a stake in the organization.

If marketing research is to help with this 'matching' process, it must be concerned with more than simply collecting data on markets and customers. Certainly, in the early days of marketing research, this was what most market researchers did. Even today, there are 'field and tab' agencies that restrict their activities to collecting survey data and tabulating the results. Most marketing research, furthermore, still includes, at some stage, data collection and data analysis. However, clients or internal users of marketing research data increasingly look for some interpretation of the data, perhaps even going so far as to ask for recommendations for marketing action. Sometimes managers are unclear about the nature of the problem facing them or about the kind of research that is needed. In this situation, market researchers may become involved in diagnosing company problems, analysing organizational strengths and weaknesses, or identifying threats and opportunities in the environment. Some organizations look for assistance in choosing or evaluating alternative marketing strategies and tactics. Some ask for help in ensuring that such actions are being implemented. In brief, market researchers may become involved in helping organizations to formulate their marketing plans and to monitor the progress in their implementation. Some managers seek help with only some of these activities; others may want help with them all, in which case the market researcher may well, in effect, become part of the client's marketing team.

Marketing research, then, is concerned with the collection, analysis and interpretation of data both on organizations and on their environments, so that information can be provided to assist management in diagnosing, deciding and delivering marketing strategies and tactics.

This definition of marketing research is illustrated in Figure 1.1, which emphasizes the important point that research activity must be related to problems that organizations face, to issues that they must consider or to decisions they need to take.

The term 'marketing research' is sometimes used synonymously or interchangeably with 'market research'. Some market researchers, however, see the latter term as being limited to the process of researching markets. Curiously, many textbooks on the subject, both in the UK and in the USA, use the

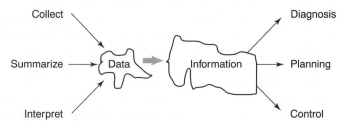

Figure 1.1 Marketing research defined.

word 'marketing' in their titles, but between the covers, lapse into the more colloquial use of the term in such phrases as 'market research activity', 'market researchers' or the 'market research industry'. To avoid confusion, and to avoid the punctiliousness of carefully changing all phrases like the ones just mentioned to 'marketing researchers' or the 'marketing research industry', this book will use the term 'market analysis' to refer to the process of researching markets. 'Marketing research' will be used to describe the whole enterprise which is the subject of this book, and 'market research' to refer to the activities of those people involved in the market research industry who buy and sell data or research services.

Another peculiarity of some textbooks on marketing research is that, having defined it as going beyond simply researching markets, they proceed to ignore precisely what researching markets (market analysis) involves. Market analysis is, however, a key component of most marketing research, and it includes the activities of measuring the size, composition and structure of a market, analysing purchasing behaviour, product usage and attitudes towards products and brands, segmenting markets, market tracking, and sales volume and brand share prediction. These topics are taken up in detail in Chapter 8.

The role of marketing research in the organization

Marketing research can be used by business and other types of organization in several different ways:

- to help tackle or resolve 'one-off' problems or issues,
- to assist in making plans and setting objectives for the future,
- to monitor changes in the environment as they occur,
- to build up a database or marketing information system that can become a resource for a growing range analyses or database marketing techniques,
- to use as a common 'currency' with which organizations can negotiate with media owners, advertising agencies, distributors, suppliers or other agents whose services they require.

A typical one-off problem may be how to react to a threat from a new product or new technology being introduced by competitors, or to a sudden or persistent decline in sales or in market share. If a competitor introduces a new product, marketing research may be called upon to examine consumer perceptions of the advantages and any limitations of the new product and how it compares with existing products available. Explaining the decline in sales may mean undertaking desk research to collect information on recent trends in the industry and in the structure of the market to show whether the company is unique in its problems or whether competitors are experiencing a similar problem. Various hypotheses about why the decline is taking place can then be tested.

Alternatively, the problem may, like the situation for Elida Faberge, be one in which a 'best' course of action needs to be determined. Marketing research can measure the extent of customer satisfaction or dissatisfaction with the range of products offered by Elida Faberge. It can study the awareness of its brands, how the brands are used and what attitudes users and non-users have of the brands. Tastes and fashions may be changing, so research may be needed to determine in what ways the products may need to be modified or how adjustments may be required in the way they are promoted.

Proactive, marketing-oriented companies like Elida Faberge will be concerned with making plans for the future. Marketing planning entails diagnosing the current situation, setting objectives, generating potential alternative strategies for achieving them, selecting the best strategies, and undertaking implementation. Marketing research can help with all the various stages of planning, not only by diagnosing the current situation, but also providing background data for determining what are reasonable or feasible quantitative targets, for example, for market penetration, market development or product development.

Monitoring changes in the environment clearly requires continuous research (see Chapter 4). However, such research can be used in two different contexts: to generate 'advance notice' of changes so that they can be reacted to immediately before they become a major problem, or to keep track of the progress of a strategy that has already been implemented, Thus advertising tracking studies may be used to measure the 'success' of Elida Faberge in raising awareness of its brands or recall of its advertisements.

While ad hoc research results can be added to a database, it is usual to make regular updates from continuous research. Such a database could be used to show, for example, that although sales of a brand have been fairly steady over the year, there may nevertheless have been considerable changes in the kinds of people purchasing, the quantities they buy and the frequency with which they buy them. This is particularly true for products like toiletries and fragrances.

Finally, if a company wishes to persuade a retailer to give shelf-space to its brands, it may need data from retail panels to show that a given increase in such space will generate a particular quantity of extra sales. Tracey Rogers of Elida Faberge comments that store managers do not always understand the importance of health and beauty to the consumer. While stores would not be out of stock of baked beans, they 'often are for major drivers like Lynx because they do not give enough support and facings'. Market research data could be used to show the effects of being out of stock.

Marketing research, then, can be used for a variety of purposes. However, the undertaking or commissioning of marketing research does not, by itself, guarantee success or that the problem or problems to which it is addressed will be solved. There are many examples of companies ending up in trouble after extensive research has been carried out; some highly successful companies have never undertaken marketing research of any kind. There are many other factors apart from the information derived from marketing research that determine the success or failure of a company or of its brands. Furthermore, there are circumstances in which undertaking marketing research can be a waste of time.

- Marketing research may, for example, have been designed without reference to any decisions that depend on, or at least will be strongly influenced by, the results of the research.
- The research results may be ignored, misused, misunderstood or misinterpreted by managers.
- The research may be poorly designed or carried out.
- The results of the research may be inconclusive, giving rise to different opinions about the significance of the findings.

In short, to be of any value, marketing research must relate to key issues or decisions within an organization, it must be properly executed, and the results must be fully understood and used.

It needs to be clear at the outset, furthermore, that marketing research is no substitute for decision-taking. Like any tool, well used it helps managers to do a better job. It helps to reduce the risks in business decisions, but will not make the decision for them. Even if action standards *are* defined before the research begins (for example, 'We'll launch the product provided at least 40 per cent of respondents give it a rating of six out of ten or more'), it is the manager, not the researcher, who defines these standards. Good marketing requires flair and creativity along with sound judgement and experience. Marketing research is no substitute for these either; but good information can help reduce the area in which hunch, gut feeling or simply good luck have to operate.

Types of marketing research

You should now have a feel for what marketing research is and how it may be used, but, clearly, there are many different kinds of marketing research. The bases for identifying the different types will, however, vary according to whether you consult textbooks on marketing research, ask market research executives in market research agencies, or enquire of academics and researchers in universities and colleges.

Textbook categories

Most textbooks distinguish different types of marketing research according to two key dimensions: the *objectives* that the research is designed to achieve on the one hand and the *source* of data on the other. Research objectives tend to be classified into three main kinds:

- exploratory,
- descriptive,
- causal (or experimental or explanatory).

Exploratory research, according to the majority of the textbooks, is research aimed at generating insights, ideas and hypotheses rather than measuring or testing them. According to Chisnall (1997) exploratory research designs attempt to identify the real nature of research problems and, in some cases, to formulate hypotheses or generate explanations for testing in later research. Crimp (1990), by contrast, argues that the research planner undertakes exploratory research in order to generate an adequate basis for designing research, and she includes searching for data that are already available both within the company and from external sources, consulting experts, conducting observational studies, consulting people in the marketplace, and buying into an omnibus survey.

However, exploratory research does not necessarily imply the use of specific methods of data collection (or, indeed, that such methods are limited to exploratory purposes); rather it implies that whatever style of research is used, the end product of the research is the generation rather than the testing of ideas. Such research, furthermore, needs to be distinguished from the notion that nearly all research has an exploratory *phase* which is preliminary to the main research and which goes beyond exploration and includes descriptive elements.

Descriptive research is usually characterized as being concerned with measuring or estimating the sizes, quantities or frequencies of things. Market research reports are often descriptive, for example, they measure market size, market structure, and the behaviour and attitudes of consumers in the marketplace. Churchill (1995) emphasizes that descriptive research is not just a fact-gathering exercise; it presupposes prior knowledge about the issues being studied, and will be designed to secure specific kinds of information. The variables being measured and the mode of their analysis will be spelled out in advance. Churchill, however, then proceeds to include practically all types of marketing research except experimental research as types of 'descriptive' study, as if such research was necessarily limited to being descriptive and could not be used for either exploratory or explanatory purposes. It would be more sensible to reserve the term 'descriptive' for research that measures and presents variables one at a time, and does not attempt to analyse the relationships between them.

Causal research is typically seen as being concerned with establishing cause-and-effect relationships in an attempt to explain *why* things happen. Such research is often equated with experimental procedures since, so it is argued, only when some form of experimental control is exerted, can causality be demonstrated. The implication here is that other forms of research, such as survey research, cannot be used to establish causes or offer explanations. As is explained later in Chapter 6, many different types of research can, with varying degrees of success, attempt to establish the extent to which one or more factors or variables exercise some degree of influence over others. It would be more helpful instead to distinguish between investigative research that does measure the extent to which variables are related together, but without necessarily implying that some are 'dependent' and others are 'independent', and 'causal' research that does make these distinctions.

The difficulty with the textbook distinctions is that most research in practice will be some combination of exploration, description, investigation and causal analysis. Most research projects will have an exploratory phase, will produce descriptive data in the main research stage, and will go on to analyse the nature of relationships between variables. Each stage will shade into the next with exploratory research becoming the basis for description, and description forming the first part of an investigative analysis and so on. Only research that *limits* itself to generating ideas can be legitimately characterized as 'exploratory' and only research that *limits* itself to univariate analysis is purely 'descriptive'.

The other dimension along which textbooks tend to distinguish different types of marketing research is according to the two main sources of data:

■ secondary sources,
■ primary sources.

Secondary sources refer to any materials that already exist and may include:

■ published articles in journals, books, newspapers or magazines,
■ data that have been published in various statistical sources, for example government statistics or trade association statistics,
■ data that may be available for purchase from a business publishing house, a market research agency or an advertising agency,
■ data that the company already possesses as a result of its everyday operations.

The term 'secondary' refers to the idea that the data are being used for a secondary purpose. The original material may well have been collected and used in other ways. Such data are commonly looked at while sitting at a desk, and such activities are often referred to as 'desk' research. These sources are considered in more detail in Chapter 4. Secondary sources should be distinguished from secondary analysis, which is a process in which secondary data are used as inputs to further statistical analysis rather than just being gathered together and re-presented in more or less their original or in condensed form.

Primary sources refer to research that has been undertaken specifically for the problem or project at hand. Most of this book is about different ways of collecting primary data. It is often forgotten, however, that secondary data were originally collected using the same methods. The corollary is that different researchers need to bear in mind how the data were collected in the first place along with their associated strengths and limitations. Many government statistics, for example, are collected using questionnaire surveys, sometimes for whole populations of individuals or organizations, but quite often only for samples, in which case the figures produced are only estimates. The topic of estimation is taken up in detail in Chapter 6.

As with making distinctions between types of marketing research based on research objectives, so distinctions based on data source and calling it 'secondary research' or 'primary research' are of limited value since in practice, once again, these sources are usually combined. Secondary data collection is more likely to be just a stage in a research project, probably exploratory, but possibly descriptive, investigative or even causal. Only research that *limits* itself to the use of secondary data can be characterized as 'secondary research'.

Agency distinctions

Nearly all research undertaken by market research agencies is commissioned, although a number of individuals working in such organizations do sometimes contribute to academic, scholarly seminars, conferences or journals. The dimensions that such companies use to categorize different types or styles of research may often be deduced from the way they are structured. Different departments, teams, or even different subsidiary companies may specialize in a particular type of research. Five common dimensions may be distinguished:

- the kind of data collected,
- the duration of the research,
- client focus,
- the amount of value added,
- the type of customer.

Some market research agencies categorize their activities according to the kind of data collected: qualitative or quantitative. Qualitative research is geared primarily to the collection of qualitative data, the main features of which are outlined in the next chapter. Some agencies specialize in this type of research, which consists mainly of 'depth' interviewing or group discussions. These activities are explained in Chapter 4. The larger organizations may well have a department, or a whole subsidiary, devoted to qualitative research.

Quantitative research is focused primarily on the collection of quantitative data, and will consist of research that uses formal questionnaire techniques at some stage, whether for face-to-face interviews, telephone research, postal research, or it may involve various forms of experimental or quasi-experimental research. Again, these are described in Chapter 4.

Other market research agencies will make a distinction in terms of the duration of the research: whether it is ad hoc or continuous. Ad hoc research is a 'one-off' piece of research that has a beginning point, and concludes with a final report of the results. It will go through a number of stages from an initial brief or analysis of the problems to be investigated, to data collection, data analysis, and presentation of the findings.

Continuous research, by contrast, takes measurements on a regular basis in order to monitor changes that are occurring in the marketplace. Such research goes through cycles of data production which, in many respects, resemble a production line that has to meet given deadlines by scheduling its activities, and has to achieve agreed standards of quality control. There is no envisaged 'end' to the research process. The data are normally fed into some kind of management or marketing information system where they are added to a database and used as a core asset for a variety of analyses.

Overlapping with the distinction between ad hoc and continuous research is the slightly different distinction between customized and syndicated research. Customized research is tailor-made for a particular client to meet the needs of that client. Syndicated research means that either the research process or the research data are shared between a number of clients. The word 'syndicated' arose when manufacturers got together as a syndicate to supply data that they all required. This function has now largely been taken over by the market research agencies, who use the term 'syndicated' to mean either that the data are sold to a number of clients, or that several clients share a survey. Such research has sometimes been called 'off-the-peg' research since it is not customized for any one particular client.

There is a tendency for ad hoc research to be customized, and for continuous research to be syndicated, particularly since continuous research requires a lot of investment and other resources, and is usually too expensive for one client to afford. However, some ad hoc research may nevertheless be syndicated, while some continuous research is commissioned by one client and may be thought of as ad hoc. Some research, such as advertising tracking studies, may take place over time, so is continuous, but for a fixed period. Some agencies, however, use the term 'ad hoc' to denote a survey carried out for a single client.

Another basis on which some market research agencies structure their activities is by the amount of value that is added. In some cases the client requires only contract research – the agency is contracted only to collect data, or to collect and analyse them, according to specification. At the other extreme, the agency may be involved in a considerable degree of consultancy work before the research even begins. Such consultancy research may:

■ assist in the diagnosis of the problem or problems facing a client organization,
■ help to draft a research brief,
■ make recommendations for actions that need to be taken,
■ monitor their implementation.

Such research is, clearly, going to cost the client a lot more, but a recent trend is towards greater involvement of the market research agency in the business of its clients. Some agencies have set up special teams or offer a special service when such involvement is wanted.

There is a growing trend for market research agencies to separate out different kinds of research according to the kind of customer. Some may distinguish broadly between *consumer research* and *business research*. Consumer research takes the end user – private individuals or households – as the point of data collection. Business research takes other organizations who use the client's products or services in the provision of a further product or service as the point of data collection. Again, there may be a separate division or company that specializes in each type of research. Some go further and divide up the markets in a little more detail, for example they may have teams devoted to food and drink, home and personal care, finance, leisure and tourism, medical products, and agriculture.

Academic approaches

Academics are likely to see a basic distinction between:

■ commissioned research,
■ scholarly research.

Commissioned research is research undertaken on behalf of clients on a fee-paying basis. Clients will determine the problems or issues that the research is to address. The timescale for its completion is usually agreed and strictly limited, while the end-product will normally be a management report that is not to be published, since the results are confidential to the client. The success of the research is judged by how pleased the client is with the results, not by whether the researcher has followed the 'correct' scientific procedures or has developed or tested a new theory. Virtually all of the research undertaken by market research agencies will be commissioned of this kind.

Scholarly research, on the other hand, is research that the academic has decided he or she wishes to do for his or her own ends – so the topic is decided by the researcher. This may well be for publication as an article in a journal, as material for a book or book chapter, a result of a successful application to a funding body or as a basis for making such an application. The research will be judged by scholarly standards that give a central role to the development or testing of theory, and the use of systematic, justifiable and transparent methods of research. The timescale for the research tends to be relatively flexible and the results are always publicly available.

Academics are usually driven to making a choice between these two types of research. They cannot usually be mixed because of the confidentiality of the results of commissioned research and because the results of such research, in any case, may well be of interest only to one company. Furthermore, academics, who nowadays are increasingly pressurized for time, often find they are unable to do both commissioned research and scholarly research. The recent research assessment exercises in the universities means that academics have to declare themselves as 'research active', and what counts are their publications, not the consultancy they may have done. Academics who devote most of their time to consultancy are likely to find themselves in separate institutes or groupings within the university and may well have to earn their salaries from such activities.

Perspectives on marketing research

A perspective is a particular vantage point from which some phenomenon may be viewed. It is a way of perceiving some problem, puzzle, issue or event. The 'truth' or 'reality' that emerges is always relative to the particular position of the observer or researcher. The profit made by an entrepreneurial organization is a just reward for effort, initiative, taking risk or enterprise from one perspective: it is a mode of exploitation of the weaker members of society from another.

While marketers may agree that their discipline includes the application of systematic methods of inquiry to the problems and puzzles of facilitating or managing exchanges between individuals and organizations, consensus soon breaks down when they begin to consider choices between and commitments to different versions of 'inquiry', contrasting perceptions about the nature of 'reality', varied agendas of 'problems' and 'puzzles' to be solved, and discordant ideas about the objectives that research is meant to achieve.

There are certainly many perspectives in marketing – in the last analysis as many as there are marketers! There will, however, be points of overlap as well as points of difference. It is helpful to group these perspectives together into contrasting 'ideal-types' even though any one individual perspective may not fit uniquely or obviously into one particular type. Three perspectives will be suggested below, each making different basic or 'meta-theoretical' assumptions about the process of systematic inquiry, about the nature of reality, about the kinds of problems addressed, the puzzles to be solved, and the uses to which the findings of research should be put. Each perspective goes by many different names, but here we shall call them positivist, activist and interpretive. In explaining them, it will probably be helpful to use a metaphor to characterise each. The first (positivist), it will be suggested, views the market researcher as a kind of marketing physicist, the second (activist) as a marking physician, and the third (interpretive) as a marketing psychiatrist.

The marketing physicist

The marketing physicist sees markets and organizations as *systems* with structures of components that are interrelated, and which can be independently observed, measured, analysed and predicted. The search is for patterns and regularities that may be explained in terms of theories that apply in a range of different contexts. The model is very much that of the natural sciences. The validity of the research is judged by asking whether the correct scientific procedures were followed. These procedures are based on a set of underlying principles.

■ Only phenomena that can be observed can be used to validate knowledge. This rules out all forms of subjective experience.
■ Scientific knowledge is arrived at through the accumulation of verified facts derived from systematic observation or record-keeping.
■ Scientific theories are used to describe patterns of relationships between these facts and to establish causal connections between them.
■ The process is neutral and judgement-free. Observations are uncontaminated by the scientist's own predilections. Thus ethical issues can be included only if they are included as part of the research.

The steps involved in undertaking this kind of research are fairly standard:

1   begin with the theory that relates to the issue or problem to be studied,
2   deduce from the theory what you would expect to find in reality,
3   generate hypotheses that can be tested,
4   decide how the variables in the hypotheses are to be measured,
5   decide what other variables need to be controlled,
6   collect the data,
7   analyse the data,
8   report the results,
9   relate the findings back to the theory.

The objective is to produce scientifically verified knowledge. Personal values are sources of bias and must be eliminated from the process of inquiry. The proper relationship between the marketing physicist and the organizations and individuals that are the object of inquiry is one of emotional, professional and judgemental detachment. The desired state is one of value-neutrality. Ethical and social problems are translated into technical issues. Their resolution is a matter of applying appropriate techniques of observation, measurement and analysis.

   The marketing physicist has his or her own rhetoric that includes reference to dependent and independent variables, hypotheses, correlation, sampling, statistical significance, experiment, testing, validity, reliability, causality, generalization and replication. These are the stuff of language to which scientific nostrils are attuned.

The marketing physician

A physician is a specialist in medical diagnosis and treatment. The marketing physician sees the market or the organization as the 'patient' whose ailments and symptoms need to be identified before remedies can be sought. In place of detachment and neutrality is intervention and open partisanship. The physician cares about what happens – the aim is to make the patient well again. There is no pretence at being neutral – the physician takes sides, usually on the side of the organization in the battle against the competition. The goal is not to *study* an organization's problems, it is to *do* something about them, to find solutions or make changes.

Markets and organizations do not, from this perspective, constitute some kind of balanced and integrated system of mutually interdependent parts, but a vast arena or *battlefield* where struggles between competitors takes place. Thus, according to Kotler (1997), there are strategies for market leaders that include attack, pre-emptive, counter-offensive and mobile defence, there are strategies for market challengers that include frontal attack, encirclement attack and guerrilla attack, and so on. Marketing as a form of medical practice is very much an activist discipline. It is about finding means to achieve ends, or what some sociologists would call 'functionalist'. The concern is as much with what ought to be as with what is. The ultimate goal is not the acquisition of scientifically validated knowledge for its own sake, but the achievement of profits or other organizational goals. The marketing physician is personally involved in prescribing treatments and monitoring their effects. At the end of the day, it is the results that count and which underpin the validity of an idea or an action.

The marketing psychiatrist

From this perspective, reality is in the mind. It is a subjective, constructed reality. There is no 'objective' reality 'out there' to be observed and measured. People construct multiple realities so it is necessary to empathize with them if we wish to understand them. Marketing phenomena need to be studied from the perspective of those being researched. To do this the researcher must build up a picture of the realities people construct from the ground up, from specimens of behaviour, from careful observation, and above all by asking people about themselves. Markets and organizations are neither an organized system of interrelated parts, nor a battlefield, but an immense *gallery* of exhibits, of specimens of consumer and organizational behaviour. The goal of the marketing psychiatrist is not the accumulation of verified knowledge nor the pursuit of organizational goals, but of understanding. The researcher is neither detached from values nor engaged in them; rather the researcher examines the role values play in the construction of reality. Validity is sought neither in objective analysis nor in the effects of active intervention, but in the views and perspectives of participants in marketing exchanges. The marketer is also, of course, a participant. His or her reflexivity is not just an open admission of values and biases, but rather an awareness of self in the act of studying exchange behaviour.

The interpretive perspective comes in a number of sub-varieties, some of which have very impressive-sounding names like phenomenology, ethno-methodology, semiotics and ethnography. But what they have in common is that they focus on how people construct, communicate, negotiate and renegotiate meanings. They are concerned with attitudes, perceptions and interpretations.

There are, however, some fundamental problems associated with the perspective of the marketing psychiatrist. First, there is the problem of interpretation. How feasible is it to perceive as others perceive? Will not different researchers come up with different interpretations? Second, there is the problem of induction. Concepts, hypotheses, theories, models are all likely to emerge *from* the research rather than be imposed beforehand. While 'grounded theory' may have its advantages, the fact that it can never be disproven by the same data that suggested it in the first place means that the data can be consistent with many different interpretations with no 'objective' way of distinguishing between them. Lastly, there is the problem of generalization. If each piece of research is being treated holistically, the findings are unique to the particular case or set of cases under observation.

A perspective on the perspectives

The physicist, the physician and the psychiatrist are all scientists, each performing their discipline in an objective manner, that is, in a way that is uncoloured by the emotions and feelings of the researcher. They see themselves as engaged in the application of systematic methods of inquiry to the problems and puzzles of managing marketing exchanges. It is just that there are different versions of 'science', one empirical-analytic, with the aim of making predictions and controlling the path of future progress; another diagnostic-prescriptive, which aims at success and liberation from ailment; and a third empathetic-interpretive, which aims at complete understanding by seeking to enter the life-world of others and imaginatively experiencing their experiences.

It is often assumed that the various perspectives are mutually exclusive or incompatible, and that the researcher must choose between them. It could be argued, however, that each is appropriate to different kinds of research problem, so the choice becomes a technical or pragmatic consideration based on a thorough diagnosis of the problem.

Alternatively, it is possible to consider how the perspectives might be combined, adding the strengths of each together. From the physicist, for example, we get a focus on what, how and how many; from the physician we investigate means and ends; and from the psychiatrist we get a focus on why and how it is perceived. Any topic or problem may be studied from each of these perspectives. Take brand loyalty. From the perspective of the physicist, the marketing researcher would be concerned to study the factors that are conducive to brand loyalty, to generate and then test theories and hypotheses about these factors. He or she would then investigate brand-switching behaviour, changes and trends in market structures and market shares in order to predict the outcomes in terms of loyalty of a range of marketing strategies. From the perspective of the physician, the market researcher will seek to make recommendations to a client organization on the most effective ways of enhancing brand loyalty. He or she will look at schemes operated by competitors, find out what constitutes 'best practice' and what action to avoid. The advantages and limitations of a range of measures for enhancing brand loyalty will be studied. Finally, from the perspective of the psychiatrist, the market researcher will seek to understand why consumers are loyal or disloyal to brands. He or she will be concerned with how consumers perceive brands, what images they hold of brands and of the companies that make them.

It is tempting to argue that the researcher should, ideally, do all of these to get a complete and richer picture. In practice there will be competing demands and conflicts of interest. Only the physician takes sides, abandoning neutrality and becoming partisan. Finding the 'best' course of action for a client may do little to advance theoretical and empirically substantiated knowledge. The physician is bound by confidentiality – the findings of marketing research must not be revealed to competitors. The physicist, by contrast, is interested in publication.

It must be remembered, furthermore, that the suggested perspectives are analytic constructs that are intended to reflect major divisions and overlaps in ideas and in practices. Marketing researchers, of course, do not call themselves 'marketing physicists' or 'marketing physicians', but by many other names and labels. Nor should they be treated as categories to 'put' particular individuals into. Individuals do, after all, change their minds over the course of their careers. What these 'ideal-type' perspectives reflect are tendencies to do marketing or marketing research in a particular way. Nor are they pursued in isolation from one another; rather they form the basis for serious debate, even heated controversy, within the discipline. The marketing psychiatrist is likely to argue that the marketing physicists (whom they often actually call 'positivists') are blinkered by their arrogance in believing that they have access to privileged knowledge, that they 'know better' than those being studied what their 'real' problems are and what the future consequences of their actions will be. They will argue that the physicists and the physicians manufacture their data using the same processes of reality construction that everybody else uses, but that they nevertheless continue to behave as if their data reflected some kind of reality external to their own perceptions of it. The creations of marketing academics and marketing consultants are but a pale reflection of the complexity, the sophistication and the wonder of everyday commonsense reality and the process of its creation.

On the other hand, the marketing physicists and the physicians will retort that subjective impressions are worthless and amount, in effect, to no more than sophisticated journalism. Any study that is based on the subjective impressions of the researcher cannot be 'scientific' as that term is commonly understood. Subjectivism is a moral cop-out. To pretend that validity is ultimately with the social actor or the consumer is a fraud, since the market researcher cannot avoid the responsibility for deciding who inquiries are to be made about, what they are to focus on, how many people are to be involved and when 'enough' information has been gathered. Physicians accuse both the other perspectives of transforming serious organizational issues into technical problems or into semantic debates about definitions. The physicists, in turn will accuse the physicians of being partial, or working on behalf of organizations without any clear goals for the betterment of society. So the debate goes on.

The role of theories and models

Theories

Believe it or not, we all use theory in our everyday lives, although we probably do not call it 'theory', but a 'hunch' or an 'idea'. We speculate about the world around us, we make generalizations based on past experience, and we use these generalizations to make predictions about what usually happens when certain contingencies arise or to help us understand and explain things. Theory, in short, consists of ideas that work or may work in more than one context. To marketing academics 'theory' is an exposition of abstract principles that are seen to lay behind events or situations like the 'product life cycle theory', 'consumer behaviour theory' or 'the theory of the five competitive forces'.

Philosophers have tended to define theories more formally as sets of logically interrelated propositions – or words to that effect. They tend to emphasize the deductive nature of these interrelationships and some may include testability as a further criterion. One of the few books on marketing theory (Hunt, 1983) follows a similar line by suggesting that theory is 'a systematically related set of statements, including some law-like generalizations, that is empirically testable'.

A theory, then, at its simplest is an integrated set of statements about the relationships between variables, for example: 'I have a theory that the main factors affecting accurate price recall are the presence of on-pack pricing, frequency of purchase and age of customer.'

Theory is often contrasted with practice. Students often complain that a course is 'too theoretical' and that it should be 'more practical'. Such sentiments, while understandable, nevertheless miss the point: that *any* human behaviour which is meaningful is underpinned by theory. What varies is the degree of attention we pay to such underpinnings in an attempt to make the theory explicit. Only when it is rendered explicit, however, can we hope to understand the behaviour concerned. Good theories correspond with reality, they enable us to predict with some degree of accuracy, and they help us to understand. *There is, in fact, nothing so practical as a good theory.*

Models

Reality is inherently complex, and one way of coping with this complexity is to deliberately oversimplify in order to focus on the essentials. Models in the everyday sense are representations of physical objects on a smaller scale. To the academic, they are simplified descriptions of a system or a structure that are devised to assist the process of making calculations concerning the relationships between key variables and of making predictions.

Simplifications may be achieved in a number of different ways, for example:

- ignoring variables that are of lesser importance and just concentrating on the key variables,
- holding potentially confounding variables constant using statistical methods,
- assuming that the variables other than those in the model do not change,

■   making simplifying assumptions that enable the researcher to make deduc-
    tions or inferences about what would happen if the postulates were true.

Market researchers tend to prefer one or both of the first two. They will focus
on just the key variables in a situation, or use multivariate statistics to hold
chosen variables constant. Economists are more likely to use the third and
fourth techniques, for example, by arguing that certain relationships hold
ceteris paribus – all other things being equal, or assuming a two-person three
good economy with perfect knowledge and no transport costs – so-called
'desert-island' economics.

Formally, we can define a model as a set of variables and specifications
about the relationships between them that are deemed to hold among a
population of cases (individuals, groups or organizations). As such models
have three main components:

■   a set of cases,
■   a set of variables,
■   one or more statements about the relationships between the variables.

'Cases' and 'variables' are explained in detail in Chapter 2. For the moment,
suffice it to emphasize that models are *representations* of a structure or a
system, not the structure or the system itself. Thus while I can say, 'I have a
theory that this is the case . . . ', I do not say, 'I have a model that this is the
case . . . ', rather 'I have a model of a situation . . . ' or, 'I have a model that
represents . . . '. Models provide the link between the theory and the data.
While theories may be testable, they may be testable in a number of different
ways. Models are what we *actually* test in terms of specified variables
amongst specified cases.

We can distinguish several different types of model according to how
specific they are, for example:

■   conceptual models,
■   graphical models,
■   quantitative models.

The least specific are conceptual models which are models of ideas and will
be stated in words. Graphical models are more specific in that they give a
graphical representation of the relationships between variables, for example, in a flow chart, a line graph or a scatterplot. Quantitative models relate
variables by way of mathematical formulae. A fully specified mathematical
model will enable calculations to be made of changes in one or more
output variables that are a consequence of adjustments to one or more
input variables.

The market research industry

The market research industry in the UK may be considered as consisting of
three main groups of 'players':

■   the research suppliers,
■   the research buyers,
■   the market research profession.

The research suppliers

The UK is widely regarded as a major leader, if not the world leader, in the development and practice of marketing research. Why such talent should be associated with an economy whose performance since 1945 has, in many respects, been disappointing, is an open question. Perhaps the market research industry's main shortcoming is its reluctance to market itself. Certainly, the industry enjoyed a sustained boom during the 1980s, with turnover more than doubling in that period. Only during the early 1990s were there signs that the steady annual expansion in market research turnover was beginning to falter.

Client companies in the past have tended to commission research when they were optimistic and expansion-minded, and to chop it from their budgets as an easy cost saving when profits were threatened. More recently, however, many manufacturing and service organizations have regarded research as a vital component of their marketing plans, and as a supplier of data, information and analyses on which to make investment decisions in bad times as well as in good. This bodes well for the health of the market research industry even in times of relative recession.

The largest market research agencies in the UK have formed themselves into a trade association – the Association of Market Survey Organisations (AMSO). This was established in 1964 and initially it focused on its role as a support group for those running its member companies. It collected reliable statistics about the industry and sought to clarify and improve the status of market research interviewers. It set out a code of standards outlining responsibilities of members towards both clients and the public. During the 1980s membership doubled and in 1997 it stood at 38 agencies, including most of the largest UK organizations. AMSO has, with growing membership, become more outward-looking and now represents the industry on a range of bodies such as the Confederation of British Industry, the Advertising Association and the Data Protection Tribunal. To qualify for membership market research agencies must be equipped to undertake full-scale national surveys and be committed to the highest standards of quality and professionalism in their work.

In 1996, AMSO members had a turnover of £446.4 million, which represents about 70 per cent of the estimated total industry turnover. Together they employ over 4000 permanent salaried staff in their UK agencies. Members vary from the largest agencies with turnovers in excess of £60 million down to those with less than £1 million and employing fewer than 20 people. Some of the agencies are multi-national public limited companies or are owned by such companies, and do not like to think of themselves any more as 'agencies' (although they will continue to be called 'agencies' here in order to distinguish them from client 'companies'). Table 1.1 shows the top ten AMSO companies. The three largest – Taylor Nelson AGB, NOP (National Opinion Polls) and Research International – together account for nearly 40 per cent of total AMSO member turnover. During the 1980s AMSO turnover increased by an average of 10 per cent per annum in real terms. By 1991 the recession had begun to bite and the increase over 1990 was only 1.7 per cent – in real terms a decline in just under 4 per cent. However, by 1994–96, annual growth was averaging 12 per cent with some agencies achieving over 30 per cent growth.

Agency	1996 Turnover (£ million)	Growth (% 1995–96)
Taylor Nelson AGB	68.4	8.2
NOP Research Group	54.8	10.4
Research International	50.2	17.0
Millward Brown	44.7	10.1
BMRB International	25.2	18.5
Research Services Ltd	24.7	18.4
MORI	16.5	16.0
Research Business	13.8	8.3
MBL Group	13.3	16.1
IRI Infoscan	11.1	16.6

AMSO members regularly carry out 15 million interviews annually, excluding retail panels and consumer panels. Personal interviews still dominate UK data collection, representing over 40 per cent of fieldwork turnover (see Table 1.2). However, this technique has continued to decline in relative importance, while telephone interviewing is on the increase and now represents over 20 per cent of turnover. In terms of the actual numbers, however, more interviews are now conducted by telephone (4.9 million) than face-to-face in home (4.1 million) with almost as many by post (3.6 million).

Besides the big agencies, there are hundreds of smaller organizations in the UK. The Market Research Society Yearbook for 1994 lists over 500 companies, but over 80 per cent of these are businesses employing 12 or fewer professional staff (Bryson *et al.*, 1990). Only 6 per cent of agencies employ more than 30. The market research industry is thus in many ways a classic small-business industry. This is an industry in which anybody can start up on their own, and the number of agencies doubled in the 1980s. Together, small firms have about 20 per cent of the total industry turnover (Bryson *et al.*, 1990). As with other industries with a high proportion of small new companies, there is a rapid turnover of small firms. One half of all market research firms existing in 1980 had disappeared by 1990 (Bryson *et al.*, 1990). Both large and small companies are predominantly located in London and the South East of England. Nearly 50 per cent of MRS listed companies are in inner London, while nearly 90 per cent are somewhere in the South East.

Data collection method	% turnover
Personal interviews	41.3
Telephone interviews	20.3
Hall tests	10.6
Group discussions	9.6
Post/self-completed	8.6
Street interviews	3.7
Depth interviews	2.6
Mystery shopping	2.6

The main trends in the market research industry are:

- restructuring through acquisitions and mergers to create larger conglomerates of companies,
- large groups of companies now offer a complete range of services,
- a growth in the development of proprietary research techniques,
- continuing segmentation into consultants and data handlers.
- growing internationalizaton of research,
- moves into high technology.

Until 1992, AGB (Audits of Great Britain) had been market leader for three decades when it was bought out by Taylor Nelson and became part of Taylor Nelson AGB. Until 1994 the number two was always Nielsen, a subsidiary of A. C. Nielsen, the world's largest market research agency based in the US. However, in 1994 it withdrew from AMSO, officially because membership no longer provided useful benefits, but allegedly to avoid disclosure of disappointing figures (Kleinman, 1996). Research International, Millward Brown and BMRB (British Market Research Bureau) have all been acquired by Martin Sorrell's WPP advertising agency and run by Kantar, the research wing of WPP. These agencies, however, are run independently, although their combined turnover is in fact larger than that of Taylor Nelson AGB.

During the 1980s the large market research companies tended to specialize in different segments of the market. Thus AGB concentrated on consumer panels, Nielsen on retail panels, Millward Brown on advertising research and so on. However, competition in the late 1980s grew fierce. AGB bought up the National Market Research Association (NMRA), a retail panel operator and Nielsen's main rival in that area. At the same time, Nielsen set up its own consumer panel, Homescan, in direct competition with AGB's Superpanel. Both are illustrations of the trend towards full-service suppliers who can offer the complete range of research to all clients.

The market research industry has, in 25 years, moved from a cottage to a high-tech, computer-dominated industry in which companies have now packaged their services so that clients can buy 'off-the-peg' services with standardized, proprietary techniques, each claiming to offer 'unique' advantages over the competition. Some of these services are described in Chapter 8.

Another trend is towards segmentation of the industry into those who provide high value-added consultancy and complete customer care, and those who handle enormous databanks, all captured electronically. The existing trend towards globalization of markets and the needs of transnational consumers will also mean that multi-country research will be increasingly important in the next few years.

Finally, there has been a trend for the market research companies themselves to segment their business more by type of market and type of customer than by type of research. This is part of the trend towards increased value-added research in which the market research company is expected to become part of the client company marketing team so research executives need to become expert in particular markets.

The research buyers

The areas which AMSO clients commissioned research are shown in Table 1.3. The table also indicates the per cent change from 1994 to 1995. Food

Table 1.3
Source of AMSO member
turnover
Source: AMSO

Area of business	Turnover 1995 (£m)	% change from 1994
Food and non-alcoholic drinks	48.4	+10
Media	36.0	+14
Public services and utilities	31.4	+2
Financial services	27.1	+4
Motor vehicles	25.5	+37
Pharmaceuticals	23.5	+9
Business and industrial	21.4	+7
Health and beauty	21.0	+14
Government and public bodies	18.3	+9
Retailers	18.2	+18
Household products	16.6	+21
Alcoholic drinks	15.8	+12
Travel and tourism	13.7	+25
Advertising agencies	9.7	−3
Household durables	5.2	+35
Oil	3.8	−19
Tobacco	2.8	−23
Other direct clients	37.3	+23

and non-alcoholic drinks companies are the biggest spenders on marketing research, followed by the media and public services and utilities. Growth was positive across all the markets covered by AMSO companies' research activities except for oil and tobacco. The greatest increases came from Motor Vehicles and Household Durables.

The market research profession

The UK is well-served with professional associations. It has a professional body based on individual membership – the Market Research Society – which is the largest body of its kind in the world. It was founded in 1947, and now has over 7000 members, about half of whom are women. The Market Research Society seeks to ensure the maintenance of professional standards in the practice of marketing research of all kinds, to provide its members with an educational, information and social forum, and to represent the interests of the UK market research profession in the world at large. It offers the only UK academic qualification solely covering market research – the Diploma of the Market Research Society. Members of the society subscribe to a code of conduct that puts a premium on confidentiality, so that the anonymity of respondents is carefully protected.

Practitioners in the non-consumer field may belong to the Industrial Marketing Research Association (IMRA), whose members also subscribe to the same code of conduct binding upon MRS members. The trade association AMSO has already been mentioned, but there is also the Association of British Market Research Companies (the ABMRC). This was founded in 1982 and consists of the smaller research companies and consultancies and in 1996 had 150 members. In 1981 the Association of Qualitative Research Practitioners (the AQRP) was formed and now comprises over 500 individual members who work variously in research companies, advertising and major client organizations. It provides a forum for all those interested in the conduct and development of qualitative research.

Most of the large market research companies are members of the Interviewer Quality Control Scheme (IQCS). This is an offshoot of the original Market Research Society Interviewer Identity Card Scheme. To be a member of the IQCS a company has to meet specified market research fieldwork standards that cover recruitment, training, supervision and back-checking. Members are audited every year and a report goes to the full Council of the IQCS.

Besides those individuals in companies buying or selling research, there are academics and researchers in universities and colleges, mostly in departments of marketing, business or management, who undertake commissioned market research, consultancy or scholarly research. In addition, there are those employed in large organizations that have their own in-house market research departments or capabilities. Some of these individuals may be responsible for actually conducting research; others may oversee the commissioning of research, or of certain parts or stages of the project, like data processing, from agencies, some of whom may specialize in that kind of activity. Not a lot is known about the nature and value of the research conducted in-house, since reports remain confidential, and the value of the labour and resources involved may be difficult to estimate. In-house research, while not 'commissioned' in the sense of being a result of a client–agency transaction, is very similar to commissioned research in terms of the characteristics described above.

Ethical issues

Ethics are moral principles or standards that guide the ways in which individuals treat their fellow human beings in situations where they can cause actual or potential harm whether economic, physical or mental. Ethics in marketing research are concerned with professional standards of conduct and with the use of techniques in ways that avoid harm to respondents, to clients or to other parties. Marketing researchers depend for the effective practice of their profession on the goodwill and participation by the public. At the same time members of society are becoming increasingly aware of their rights and sensitive about invasions of their privacy. Any individual, company or agency that violates the implicit trust of participants in a study makes it more difficult and more costly for *all* market researchers to approach and recruit survey respondents or participants to group discussions. Good ethical standards are good business. In consequence various associations whose members are involved in marketing research have developed codes of conduct to guide the behaviour of its members. In the UK the Market Research Society has developed its own code of conduct, the main principles of which are summarised in Box 1.1.

The main ethical issues that arise concern:

- privacy,
- confidentiality,
- deception,

Code of Conduct

This was introduced in 1954 as a self-regulatory code and has been amended several times since. The Code is agreed by the Market Research Society and the Industrial Market Research Association and is designed to support all those engaged in marketing or social research in maintaining professional standards, and to ensure that research is conducted in an ethical manner. It also has to ensure that research is conducted in accordance with the principles (and spirit) of the Data Protection Act.

Below is a summary of the main provisions of the Code. The summary was derived from the Web page of the Market Research Society, the address of which is given at the end of the chapter. Have a browse.

Responsibilities to informants

■ Informants' identities must not be revealed to anyone not directly involved in the reserach without their consent, nor used for any other than research purposes.
■ Nobody should be adversely affected or embarrassed as a direct result of participating in a research study.
■ Interviewers must always show proof of identity to informants, giving the name, address and phone number of the research agency conducting the study.
■ Informants must not be coerced or subjected to unwelcome intrusion and must have the rights both to respected privacy and to withdraw their co-operation at any time.
■ No child under 14 should be interviewed without parent's/guardian's/responsible adult's consent, nor any young person aged 14-17, if the subject of the interview is sensitive.

Responsibilities to the general public and business community

■ Other activities, e.g. selling, opinion-moulding and collection of personal data, should not under any circumstance be misrepresented as market research.
■ Market research should be honest and objective and neither research methods nor findings may be used to mislead.

Responsibilities to clients

■ Client's identity, information about their business, and their commissioned market research data and findings should remain confidential to the clients unless both client and agency agree details of any publications.
■ Full methodological details of each project undertaken must be supplied to the client.

General

■ All written or verbal assurances made by anyone involved with or commissioning or conducting a study must be factually correct and honoured.
■ Everyone subject to the Code of Conduct must adhere to its full provisions, protect and enhance the ethical and professional reputation of market research and
■ ensure, whenever possible, that all others connected with studies are aware of, and abide by, the provisions of the full Code.

Box 1.1   The Code of Conduct

■   imposition,
■   integrity,
■   misrepresentation.

If a market researcher telephones a respondent to obtain an interview late on a Sunday evening, or if a researcher observes a customer's behaviour in a shop without the customer's knowledge, are these instances of invasion of privacy? It might be argued that since anybody can observe behaviour in public places then the latter example is not unethical, particularly since no harm is involved. In the former case there may be mental harm if the outcome is the annoyance of the householder.

The issue of confidentiality might affect both respondents and, if commissioned research, clients. If respondents are told or reassured that their replies will be treated with confidentiality, then it will be unethical for the research to pass this information on to other parties, for example selling mailing lists. If a client does not wish to be identified to respondents, then it would be unethical for interviewers to pass this information on. If the researcher is working on behalf of a particular client, then confidential information about the business should not be passed on to competitors.

Deception may come in many forms. Misleading a respondent into thinking that an interview will take five minutes when the researcher knows in will take 20 is unethical. Covertly numbering questionnaires that are meant to be 'anonymous' so that the researcher can determine who has and who has not returned them could also be seen to be deception.

Respondents' rights to be able to refuse to grant an interview need to be respected and they should not be pressurized. There should be no adverse effects that result from participating in research, like receiving unsolicited sales material or price rises that result from questions about what maximum prices people would accept for a product.

Integrity includes both the technical and administrative integrity of the research so that the results are not 'doctored' or 'massaged' in any way or tied up in jargon just to baffle the client. Lack of integrity shades into misrepresentation in which research results are presented in a way likely to mislead readers or clients. This might include deliberately withholding information, misusing statistics or ignoring relevant data.

Marketing physicists, in considering ethical issues, are likely to emphasize the greatest good of the greatest number in deciding 'correct' courses of action and will argue that a social cost/benefit analysis needs to be conducted for any contemplated action. The marketing physician will evaluate ethical behaviour in terms of fairness and justice in the operation of relationships between competitors. The marketing psychiatrist will focus on individual rights and the principles of universality – that every act is based on reasons that the actor would be willing to have others use, and compensation – that injured parities are restored to their original position.

Summary

Marketing research is nowadays no longer just the collection of data on markets and consumers. Increasingly it is part of the marketing function within an organization and has extended itself backwards to providing data for the diagnosis of organizational problems, and forwards to the generation, selection, implementation and monitoring of solutions to these problems. It is, furthermore, no longer restricted to the provision of data, but includes the analysis and interpretation of the results. In short, marketing research is concerned with the collection, analysis and interpretation of data that may be used for the diagnosis, planning and control of organizational marketing objectives and strategies.

Although market analysis is still an important, if not crucial, ingredient in marketing research, and a great deal of research that is commissioned from market research companies is limited to researching markets, such activities will be a waste of time unless they are designed and executed in the context of marketing decisions that need to be taken or specific issues that need to be resolved. Marketing research, whether commissioned or carried out in-house, can help with all stages of the marketing planning process.

Textbook categorizations of types of marketing research have their limitations; market research agency distinctions are perhaps a better guide to the differing approaches to marketing research. It must also not be forgotten that, apart from research whose purpose is to further the objectives of a particular organization, there is also research carried out for academic purposes.

The UK market research industry is a world leader with research suppliers who have an international reputation, ably supported by a range of professional and trade associations. That UK organizations have not always seen fit to make full use of the services offered by market research agencies is perhaps testimony to a reluctance, until recently, of those agencies to apply their expertise to their own back yard and market themselves.

Key concepts

marketing research	secondary research	continuous research
exploratory research	primary research	customized research
descriptive research	qualitative research	syndicated research
investigative research	quantitative research	contract research
causal/exploratory research	ad hoc research	consultancy research
consumer research	positivist perspective	
business research	activist perspective	
commissioned research	interpretive perspective	
scholarly research	theory/model	

Further reading

■ The notion of the three perspectives and the use of metaphor to characterize them has been adapted from Boughey, H (1978) *The Insights of Sociology: An Introduction*, Boston, Mass.: Allyn and Bacon.

■ On the nature of theory and the role of marketing models see Hunt, S (1983) *Marketing Theory: The Philosophy of Marketing Science*, Homewood, Ill.: Richard D Irwin.

■ On perspectives, have a look at Brown, S (1995) 'Postmodern marketing research: no representation without taxation', *Journal of the Market Research Society*, Vol 37, No 3, pp 287–310.

■ For keeping ahead of developments in the market research industry there is no better place than the excellent official journal of the Market Research Society, *Journal of the Market Research Society*.

Further reading

- For keeping up to date on the market research industry the best source is the journal *ADMAP*.
- For a more in-depth discussion of marketing ethics and many more references in that area, see Appendix 2A, 'Marketing Research Ethics', in Churchill, GA (1995) *Marketing Research. Methodological Foundations*, Fort Worth, Texas: The Dryden Press.

Questions for further discussion

1   Consider how the various types of research are suited to the range of uses to which marketing research can be put.
2   An anti-smoking organization wants advice on the best ways of getting across to the general public the dangers of smoking. Consider how the marketing physicist, the marketing physician and the marketing psychiatrist would approach this task.
3   Will the major trends in the market research industry make it easier or more difficult for the inexperienced research buyer?
4   Now that the advertising of cigarettes has been banned in the UK and in a number of other countries, a cigarette manufacturer is seeking advice on how to promote its products without using advertising or sponsorship of sport. Outline some of the ethical issues faced by a market researcher who is considering taking on this commission.

Useful Web sites

Try 'surfing the Web' to find out more about the market research industry. Here are some useful sites to look at:

http://www.mori.com
http://www.cim.co.uk
http://www.amso.co.uk
http://www.esomar.nl
http://www.marketresearch.org.uk

2

The nature of data and the measurement of variables

In Chapter 1 it was explained that marketing research is concerned with the collection, analysis and interpretation of data that are useful in the diagnosis, planning and control of marketing strategies. However, before considering how data are collected and analysed it is essential to understand what 'data' are in the first place, and what types of data emerge from research activity. This chapter will consider the nature and types of data that market researchers collect, showing in particular how quantitative data are a result of the process of measurement.

What are data?

The *Pocket Oxford Dictionary* defines 'statistics' as 'numerical facts systematically collected on a subject', where 'facts' are taken to be 'things known to be true'. The term 'data' – often used to denote statistical material – derives from the Latin word which translates literally as 'things given'. The statistical products of quantitative research – the data – are often called 'findings'. Data are thus portrayed as a form of knowledge, of things known to be true – sheer, plain, unvarnished and unchallengeable. They are, apparently, untainted by social values or ideology, untouched by human hand. Data, in short, are commonly regarded as 'the facts'.

In reality, data are created, not discovered. They arise as a result of human activity. They are a product of systematic record-keeping, for example in parish registers, hospital records, invoices, questionnaires, electronic meters, tape recordings or video recordings. But the record-keeper captures data for his or her own purposes. Data may be collected in many different ways, using different data capture instruments and employing different definitions of what is being recorded. Sometimes mistakes are made in the data capture process. Different researchers are likely to produce very different results, apparently from observing the 'same' things or events. Even government statistics are often based on questionnaires, and, as we shall see, there are many things that can go wrong with this process (see Figure 2.1).

This does not imply that data are meaningless artefacts, but it must be remembered that the particular concepts, techniques of measurement and methods of data collection used in each piece of research are chosen and developed within a structure of interests that encompasses not only the

'Molly! How many kids have we now?'

Figure 2.1 Collecting nice hard facts: finding out how many people there are.

individual commitments of the researcher, but also of the organizations involved in marketing activities, the consumers, the respondents or subjects, and the clients, funding or sponsoring agencies. In short, data are not 'the facts' or 'things given'. They are social products that are manufactured, not collected.

Marketing research can play many different roles in an organization and may be approached, as was explained in Chapter 1, from different perspectives. Research – and data collection as part of it is no exception – is a messy business. There is no such thing as a 'perfect' piece of research. Data produced by research activity will vary considerably in terms of quality from one piece of research to another. We, both as data producers and as data users, need to judge this quality; but bear in mind that we probably cannot give any particular set of data a 'score out of 10' for quality. We would at least wish to give the data different 'ratings' on different dimensions. Furthermore, we have seen that the quality of marketing research products is judged in different ways according to the perspective being adopted. According to one perspective, 'good' data have been collected using the correct scientific procedures; according to another, 'good' data help to solve problems whatever procedures were used; and according to the third perspective, 'good' data allow for complete sympathetic emotional participation.

It also needs to be kept in mind that data not only come in different qualities, judged according to different criteria, and with a range of different interests in mind, but that the data themselves may be of very different types.

Types of data

The historian likes to think of parish registers, diaries of famous people, or transcripts of what was said in the House of Commons as 'data'. A sociologist with a tape recorder studying 'street corner society' likes to think that he or she is collecting 'data'. An anthropologist looking at some unusual, remote tribe of people, considers that he or she is collecting 'data' by making records of experiences and observations. The archaeologist uses physical traces or remains as evidence or data on past events, conditions or social behaviour. The manager of a business organization may think more in terms of sales data or information on balance sheets and profit and loss statements. The market researcher may think of the results of a telephone survey or the recording of a focus group discussion as 'data'. In short, there are many different types of data, but we can put them into two broad categories: qualitative and quantitative.

Qualitative data

Qualitative data are non-numerical records and arise as words, phrases, statements, narrative, text or pictures. The words may be spoken or they may be written or printed text. The spoken words may have been recorded in writing or captured electronically. Printed text merely needs to be accessible, which may mean taking a photocopy or making notes from the text. Pictures need to be captured either as a snapshot by drawing, painting or taking photographs, or monitored over a period of time using film or video.

Market researchers often collect qualitative data, mostly in the form of words. These may arise as some kind of narrative or text, for example, a story, account or description of what happened or what 'normally' happens in particular circumstances. Alternatively, they may be isolated statements made by respondents or participants and could be in response to a series of open-ended questions. Such statements will reflect respondents' knowledge, beliefs, attitudes, opinions or aspirations, very often in respect of products or services that they buy, or in respect of their reactions to attempts made by business organizations to communicate with customers or potential customers through advertising, publicity, sponsorship, personal selling or sales promotions.

Most qualitative data in marketing arise from informal or 'depth' interviews or from group discussions. Such research is usually called 'qualitative research' and this is considered in detail in Chapter 4 along with the procedures used for the analysis of the narrative or text that arise from that form of research. However, qualitative data may also emerge in the course of formal, quantitative research such as in surveys or experiments when respondents are asked to give some of their answers in their own words in response to open-ended questions. Such data may also arise from unstructured observation carried out by researchers. The analysis of this kind of qualitative data involves procedures that are a little different from the analysis or narrative and text, and these are considered in detail in Chapter 6 on data analysis.

Quantitative data

Quantitative data are numerical records that result from a process of measurement. The literature on measurement is largely in psychology and it relates mostly to the measurement of attitudes. Most texts on marketing research relate measurement only to attitude measurement, but it is important to realize that all quantitative research relies on a process of measurement for all its variables, not just attitudes. Measurement is commonly defined as the assignment of numbers to represent properties of objects according to rules. Thus if we record a person's age as '45' then we have assigned the number 45 to represent the property age of an individual. The problem with this formulation is that it does not cover all situations that we would wish to include as 'measurement'.

First, not everything we want to measure pertains to the properties of an 'object'. We may wish to measure the properties of people – as individuals or as groups – or the properties of organizations or events. In marketing research we call the focus of the measurement process the 'case'. Second, we do not always assign numbers in the measurement process. Thus if we wish to record the sex of a respondent in a survey, we would assign them to one of two categories – male or female. If we want to measure the social class of a respondent we might assign them to one of the categories A, B, C1, C2, D or E according to the occupation of the chief wage earner of the household. What we assign, then, are not necessarily numbers, but values from a scale of values. Third, simply to 'assign' a scale value does not complete the measurement process – we need to make a systematic record. These records might take various forms like questionnaires, diaries, tape recordings, video recordings or some form or electronic data capture. Finally, the 'properties' or 'characteristics' of the cases we measure are usually referred to in all the sciences as 'variables' – things that vary.

In short, when we measure we make a systematic record of a *value* from a *scale* of values in respect of a *variable* for a particular *case*.

Each of these concepts will now be explained in turn.

Value

It is unfortunate that the word 'value' has many different connotations in everyday use: worth, goodness, usefulness, esteem, price, price in relation to quality or quantity, moral principles, standards. In most sciences 'value' stands for the exact amount of a variable quantity in a particular case. In the social sciences it would include, besides an exact amount, a precise category or classification of an object, person, organization or group. A value is what we actually record in the process of record-keeping. We might, indeed, record an exact amount, like 56,743 employees; alternatively, we might record as a value a category like 'yes', 'male', 'very dissatisfied' or 'strongly agree'. It is possible, of course, to assign a number to these categories, so we allocate 1 = yes, 2 = no and 3 = don't know. Most survey analysis packages such as SPSS, which is explained in Appendix 3, require that all values are given a number before they can be entered. The verbal descriptions of the allocated numbers are usually referred to as 'value labels', thus making it clear that we are using the numbers only as labels, not as an exact amount of a variable quantity.

Scale

A scale is a set of values which represents a continuum on which the cases to be measured can be located and is constructed in such a way that all observations of interest to the researcher can be assigned unambiguously to a particular scale value. This implies that a set of scale values must meet three criteria:

■ they are exhaustive of all the possibilities,
■ they are mutually exclusive, that is, non-overlapping,
■ they refer to a single dimension.

The first criterion means that all the observations that we make must fit somewhere on the scale. To make a set of values exhaustive, it is sometimes necessary to have an 'other' category for observations that do not fit into any of the scale values specified, for example, the answers to the question, 'For which of the following purposes do you mostly use cooking fat?' may be categorized into:

Deep frying	[ ]
Shallow frying	[ ]
Roasting	[ ]
Pastry making	[ ]
Other uses	[ ]
(please specify)	

By adding the 'other uses' category, the set of values is now exhaustive of all the possibilities and there is no answer that cannot be put into a category.

The second criterion means that all observations should fit into one and only one category. If the set of categories is overlapping, then the value of measurements taken is severely limited. Consider the following set of categories for Region of Head Office:

■ England,
■ Wales,
■ Scotland,
■ Northern Ireland,
■ London and the South East.

An office in or around London will be counted twice, making analyses of head office location statistics dubious, to say the least.

The third criterion – that the set of scales values should relate to only one dimension – is sometimes ignored. To say that the categories 'baby', 'telephone', 'railway ticket' and *Coronation Street* do not refer to a single dimension is fairly obvious. However, many marketing people make a distinction between different types of consumer goods into:

■ convenience goods,
■ shopping goods,
■ speciality goods.

Quite apart from the fact that these categories may be overlapping for many products, there are two very different dimensions implicit here. One refers to the degree of search behaviour involved in selecting a brand (convenience goods versus shopping goods), while the third category, speciality goods, has more to do with brand loyalty. That more than one dimension is being referred to is not always obvious.

Scales are of different types, as we shall see in a moment, but all of them need to meet each of the above three criteria to be useful. In addition, scales vary in terms of the ways in which they define the relationships between scale values. Those scales that meet just the three specified criteria define the relationships between scales values in terms of *equivalence*. This means that all the cases assigned to a scale value are seen to be equivalent in terms of the property being measured. The simplest of such scales are where there are just two categories, one for cases that possess a characteristic and one for cases that do not. These are *binary* scales and there are many examples in marketing: yes/no to a question; bought/did not buy a product; watched/did not watch a television programme; made a profit/did not make a profit last year. All computer codes are based on binary scales. A binary code assigns a value of 1 for cases that possess a characteristic and 0 for those that do not. If you are familiar with the binomial distribution you will recognize that this requires a binary scale of successes or failures, heads or tails.

Sometimes the scales refer to sets of three or more categories that are exhaustive, mutually exclusive and refer to a single dimension, but where the relations between the scale values are still solely in terms of equivalence. The uses of cooking fat scale above is a good example of a *nominal* scale where the categories may be listed in any order without changing the sense of the data being presented. For some questions a simple yes/no answer may not be exhaustive if some people say 'sometimes' or 'don't know' or 'cannot remember', so a nominal scale with several categories needs to be developed.

Some sets of scale values define the relationships between the scale values not only in terms of equivalence, but also in terms of *order* – whether a case possesses or manifests more or less of a characteristic. Thus there is an implied order in 'heavy', 'medium', 'light' and 'non-user' of a product. There is a sense in which such sets of categories could be written 'out of order'. Sets of scale values ordered in this way may are *ordinal* scales. The standard social class groupings used by market researchers (see Table 2.1) form such an ordinal scale that goes from high to low. Some measures are based on degrees of agreement or disagreement with statements that refer to an attitude being measured or degrees of satisfaction or dissatisfaction with a product or

Social class	Social status	Head of household's occupation
A	Upper middle class	Higher managerial, administrative or professional
B	Middle class	Intermediate managerial, administrative or professional
C1	Lower middle class	Supervisory or clerical, and junior administrative or professional
C2	Skilled working class	Skilled manual workers
D	Working class	Semi and unskilled workers
E	Those at lowest level of subsistence	State pensioners or widows (no other earner), casual or lowest-grade workers

Table 2.1
Social class definitions
Source: National Readership Surveys Ltd

service. The scale values, however, do not indicate how much more or less is possessed by the cases in one category compared with another. Thus we do not know how many pints of beer a 'heavy' drinker drinks compared with a 'medium' or a 'light' drinker.

One particular version of an ordinal scale is a *rank ordered* scale where either each case being measured is given its own ranking, or each of a number of objects, products or services is given a rank ordered position. Thus a class of 30 students may be ranked 1–30 following a class test, or seven brands may be ranked 1–7 by customers. Such scales have special numerical characteristics which mean that particular kinds of statistics may be applied to them.

All scales that are just sets of categories, whether ordered or not, do not give any measure of the 'distance' between one category and the next. There is no measure or metric with which to calibrate such distances. We cannot, for example, compare the 'distance' between social class B and social class C1 with the 'distance' between classes C2 and D. All such scales may be referred to jointly as *non-metric* scales – that is, they do not possess a metric with which to measures distances between scales values.

For some scales, however, there *is* a metric with which we can define distances between scale values. We may do this either in terms of numbers of occurrences, or in terms of some process of calibration. As a measure of size, magnitude or extent we sometimes count up how many occurrences constitute that size, magnitude or extent. Thus we could count up the number of people in a group as a measure of group size, the number of employees in an organization as a measure of organizational size, or the number of checkouts in a supermarket as a measure of shop size. In this situation we must necessarily arrive at a whole number – an integer. We cannot have a fraction of a person or part of a checkout. The implication of this is that the number of scale values is finite. Thus household size will have a very limited number of scale values – one-person, two-person, three-person household and so on. Where the scale values are a result of counting whole occurrences, then the scale is usually said to be 'discrete', so we can call these *discrete metric* scales.

For a characteristic like age there is a calibrated measure or metric in units of time. We can say by how much one person is older or younger than another in units of time since birth. Using a ruler to measure length, a pair of scales to measure weight, units of currency to measure wealth or income or profit or costs will result, if we take a lot of measurements, in a very large number of scale values. Potentially, the number of scale values is infinite, but they are limited, in practice, either by the accuracy and precision of the measuring instrument or by the wish of the researcher to round off measurements, for example to age at last birthday.

The difference between continuous and discrete scales is sometimes a little difficult to draw. For example, in the case of money, it is not possible to have a fraction of the smallest unit of currency, but the number of scale values can, nevertheless, be very large. Only when the number of scale values is very limited does it have any statistical consequences, for example, for the 'smoothing' of a graph, which should really be done only for continuous metric variables.

The different types of scale are summarized in Figure 2.2. Notice that we can think of these scales as constituting different 'levels' of measurement from the lowest level of binary scale up through increasing levels of sophistication

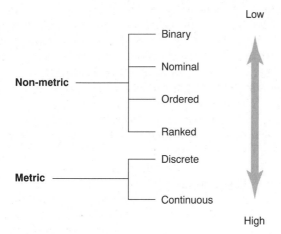

Figure 2.2 Summary of scale types.

to continuous metric. As we move up the levels of measurement the kinds of statistical operation we can perform on the data become more sophisticated. What kinds of statistics we can perform on what kinds of scale will be explained later in Chapter 6.

Variable

A variable relates to a property of the case that is being recorded. Variables have the obvious characteristic that they vary – at a minimum between two scale values (for binary scales), up to potentially an infinite number of scale values for continuous metric scales. Variables can be classified according to two key dimensions: the focus of the property to which they refer, and their role in the research. Properties may focus on characteristics that are:

- demographic,
- behavioural,
- perceptual.

Demographic variables measure 'factual' properties that the researcher ascribes, attributes or assigns to cases. They are features that tend to be fixed, slow to change or beyond the ability of the individual to change at will, for example, a person's sex or educational background. Some may change slowly, for example age, social grade or income. Some may be subject to sudden changes interspersed with periods of stability, for example, marital status, family size or area of residence. While 'demographics' are normally thought of as pertaining to individuals or groups of individuals, organizations, too, can be measured in terms of a range of demographic features like the type of industry, size, age, profitability, growth and so on.

Geodemographics are based on the demographic composition or structure of a small local area – a neighbourhood. All households and all individuals in a neighbourhood are given the 'average' characteristics for that area, characteristics that may be used as a basis for market segmentation, targeting, drawing samples, the planning of store locations, or, more recently, for database marketing.

CACI Limited, an international firm of management consultants, was the first agency to develop a classification of residential neighbourhoods in a system it called ACORN (A Classification of Residential Neighbourhoods). Other competing systems of neighbourhood classification have been subsequently generated, and the use of such procedures has become known as 'geodemographics'. The various systems of classification are based on the principle that knowing where people live enables them to be defined as living in a certain type of area, and hence are likely to have certain social characteristics, lifestyles, or buying habits that are of interest to marketers.

Behavioural variables may relate to what people actually did in the recent past, to what they usually or currently do, or to what they might do in the future. Typical measures of behaviour taken in the analysis of consumer markets relate to the purchase and use of products and brands, for example, purchase/non-purchase of a product or brand over a specific time period, brand variant purchased, quantity/size of pack, price paid, source of purchase, other brands bought, nature of purchase, and use/consumption of the product. These measures may, in turn, be used to generate calculations of brand loyalty, brand-switching behaviour and frequency of purchase. If the research is a product test or product concept test, consumers may be asked about future behaviour, for example, likelihood of trial of a new product and likely frequency of purchase.

Perceptual variables include attitudes, opinions, beliefs and images. Attitudes are relatively enduring likes or dislikes, preferences or other positive or negative evaluations of objects, persons, organizations, events or situations. Their measurement is central to many marketing decisions, for example, in market segmentation, evaluating the effectiveness of advertising campaigns, or making predictions of product purchases. While attitudes do not always correspond directly with behaviour, they are, by definition, 'predispositions' to act in particular ways, and hence strongly influence behaviour. This means that when attitudes of a large number of people are measured or estimated, then predictions about future behaviour, particularly purchase decisions, can usually be made with some degree of accuracy.

Opinions are somewhat different from attitudes. They do not necessarily have a directional quality and may express feelings or views about what other people should or should not do in the world. Beliefs refer to what people think they know about situations, products or communications, but which cannot usually be underscored by factual evidence, while knowledge refers to awareness or memory of such factual knowledge. Images are somewhat vaguer than beliefs, being representations in the mind of the character or attributes of a person, object or organization. The measurement of perceptual variables is thus very complex and will usually require a process called scaling, which will be explained later in the chapter.

In terms of the various roles demographic, behavioural and perceptual variables may play in research, we can distinguish variables being used as:

- descriptors,
- independent variables,
- dependent variables.

Variables used as descriptors in a piece of research make no implications as to their relationships to other variables. Demographics in particular are often used structurally to provide a framework for defining and describing the population of cases, to serve as a basis for sample design, or to act as weights or controls to ensure that the results represent the population correctly. Behaviours and perceptions, however, may also be used for structural purposes.

Alternatively, variables may be used analytically to explore the relationships between variables. Variables treated as causes or influences are known as independent variables. Such variables may be seen as necessary preconditions for some outcome to happen, they may be regarded as sufficient by themselves to bring such an outcome about, or they may be treated as just one influence among many. Variables treated as the effects or outcome are the dependent variables. These are the variables the researcher is trying to explain, understand or predict. Behaviours, perceptions and some demographics may be used in any of the three roles in research. Some demographic variables are difficult to conceive as being used as dependent variables – trying to 'explain' a person's sex or age for example! Some variables may be used in more than one role in a piece of research. Thus some demographics may be used for both structural and for analytic purposes, for example using age both to describe the population of cases and also using it to see how far it explains variation in one or more of the dependent variables. Some variables may be used as both dependent and independent variables in the same piece of research, for example, customer satisfaction may be seen as a result of a customer's prior expectations about the product or service (i.e. it is a dependent variable) and at the same time as causing or influencing repeat purchase behaviour (i.e. it is also an independent variable). The combinations of different types of variable attribute and their roles in the research are shown in Figure 2.3.

Case

A case is the type of object, person, group of people, organization, situation or event whose characteristics are being measured and recorded in the process of data capture. The cases may be objects, people, groups and so on of a particular kind, for example, 'motorists' or 'mothers with babies', or even 'motorists with a driving conviction who have held a licence for over 15 years'. In any one particular piece of research there may be more than one type of case, for example, a study may measure characteristics of both organizations and the individuals within them. Most research will be concerned with a set or 'population' of cases, although a case study as such may involve only one case or perhaps comparing two or three cases. If there are many cases it may be necessary to take a sample of cases and use the sample to make estimates for the total set. The topic of sampling is considered in detail in Chapter 5.

Attribute	Role in research		
	Descriptor	Independent variable	Dependent variable
Demographic			
Behaviour			
Perception			

Figure 2.3 Variable attributes and roles.

Frequencies

A single measurement, then, involves making a systematic record of a value from a scale of values in respect of a variable for a particular case. However, in most marketing research the researcher is interested in more than just one case - one individual or one organization - so there will be a separate value recorded for each case. If the scale is continuous metric each scale value may be a unique number, each having a frequency of one and perhaps measured to several decimal places. We could, however, round off, round down or round up each scale value, for example to the nearest whole number, in which case a scale value may happen more than once. Thus in a group of 130 people, there may be six persons aged 23 (age in years rounded down to age last birthday). For each of the 130 cases there will be a recorded scale value. The number of times a scale value happens is the *frequency*; in this example the frequency of people aged 23 is six. If the scale is discrete metric the scale values will be whole numbers anyway and we could record the number of times each value occurs. The result, however, may still be a very large number of scales values. For age, for example, there may be up to 100 scale values if we record people's ages year by year. One way of reducing the number of scale values, but keeping an overall view of the distribution, is to group scale values together. Thus the individual ages of respondents to a survey may be grouped into categories of 15-19, 20-24, 25-29 and so on. The number of shops selling Brand X at various prices may be grouped into under 40p, 41-45p, and over 50p. We can then produce a frequency for each grouping.

For non-metric scales there will usually be a limited number of scale values anyway, so it makes sense to report the frequency of each. The results will often be laid out as a table, the scale values forming the rows, and the frequencies (and perhaps relative frequencies) the columns. Tabular analysis is considered in detail in Chapter 6.

Where the research involves a large or relatively large number of cases then it becomes possible to talk about metric or non-metric data, binary data, ordinal data and so on, rather than ordinal scales or nominal scales, which refer to the characteristics of the measurement processes used for any one particular case.

Data transformations

Besides reporting the frequencies attached to scale values, it is usually feasible, sensible and meaningful to make a number of transformations to the data. For both discrete and continuous metric scales we can add up the scale values to obtain a total, for example the total amount of money possessed by 50 individuals. In doing so, while we loose information on the frequencies for each scale value, we can divide by the total number of cases to give an average quantity, in this example of money, possessed by each person. We can also calculate a measure of the extent to which, on average, the values depart from the mean.

For non-metric scales, by contrast, it is not possible to add up scale values. Thus while it is possible to add up 45p and 30p to obtain 75p, you cannot add up brown, green and white into some total and obtain an 'average' colour! However, since *frequencies themselves are discrete metric*, it is always possible to add them up. Thus if we have 15 men and 20 women in a group we can say we have 35 people in total.

Other data transformations might involve upgrading scales so that they may be treated as at a 'higher' level. Researchers may do this in order to apply the more sophisticated statistical techniques that thereby become available. The most usual transformation is for sets of ordered categories to be upgraded to metric scales. There are two main ways in which this may be accomplished. The researcher may allocate numerical scores to ordinal categories, and then treat the scores as if they referred to metric qualities. Thus the level of interest in a television programme may be recorded on a 5-point scale:

	Allocate score
Extremely interesting	5
Very interesting	4
Fairly interesting	3
Not very interesting	2
Not at all interesting	1

A score is allocated to each individual response and the total for all respondents can be added up and divided by the number of respondents to give an average score. A number of assumptions, however, are being made in this process, the main one that the 'distances' between each point on the scale are equal so that, for example, the distance between 'very interesting' and 'fairly interesting' is the same as the distance between 'fairly interesting' and 'not very interesting'. Such an assumption may well be unwarranted, and it would certainly be unwise to treat total scores in any absolute sense. However, for measuring change, for example from one week to the next, then changes in the average scores *are* likely to reflect real changes in people's level of interest. Error, provided it is constant, does not affect measures of change.

The other way to create metric scales is to define categories of an ordinal scale in numerical terms. Thus a distinction between 'small', 'medium' and 'large' organizations is only an ordinal distinction. However, if the researcher defined 'small' organizations as having fewer than 50 employees, 'medium' as having between 50 and 200 employees, and 'large' as having over 200 employees then a discrete metric scale has been created, the 'metric' in this case being size measured by the number of employees. With a larger number of categories, more precisely defined, with upper and lower limits, it becomes possible to calculate an average size. This procedure is fine provided there is accurate information, for example in the situation above, on the number of employees in each organization of interest.

There are some circumstances when a researcher may downgrade a scale and treat it as at a lower level. Thus a metric scale may be treated as a ranked scale by ignoring the distances between categories. A class test out of 100 may be used to create ranks of first, second, third and so on. This may be undertaken by the researcher either because he or she feels that the assumptions of the original metric are unwarranted, or because the variable is to be correlated with another ranked scale and a special statistic that requires two ranked scales may be applied. Another example of downgrading is when a researcher wishes to cross-tabulate a nominal with an ordinal scale. An appropriate measure of association may be chosen that treats both variables as nominal, thereby ignoring the ordering of the categories in one of the variables. A more extreme example is when a researcher takes a continuous metric scale like age and groups cases into a binary scale of 'old' and 'young' or an ordinal scale of 'old', 'middle aged' and 'young'. This may be done if the researcher wishes to cross-tabulate age with another binary, nominal or ordinal variable, for example, 'purchased' and 'did not purchase' Brand B in the last seven days. The age split would normally be done in a way that creates two (or three or more as required) roughly equal groups.

A final example involves the researcher taking a set of nominal categories and transposing them into a set of binary variables. Suppose a question in a questionnaire is as follows: 'To which of the following countries have you been on holiday in the last five years? Tick as many as appropriate.'

France	[ ]
Germany	[ ]
Spain	[ ]
Greece	[ ]
Portugal	[ ]
Other EU countries	[ ]

Many survey analysis packages cannot handle more than one response to a question so the question is converted into a set of binary items each with two scale vales: ticked and not ticked. One other use that may be made of this procedure is for what is usually called 'dummy variable' analysis. Here the value of 1 is given to ticked items and 0 to unticked ones. This then enables the set of items to be used in quite sophisticated statistical analyses.

The process of operationalization

In the physical world, objects and the relationships between phenomena exist independently of the researcher's perception of them. In the social world, many phenomena do not exist except as the perceptions of individuals, and relationships of causality or influence between them may have no reality other than in the objectives and motives of social actors. Furthermore, such phenomena and the relationships between them do not become manifest unless it is through the presence of and procedures used by the researcher to produce what he or she calls 'data'. Data, as we have seen, are no more than systematic records. Their significance derives only from what we might call a 'theory of instrumentation' that confirms that the data do indeed measure or signify the concepts we have in mind.

An operational definition specifies the procedures to be used to measure a concept. The theory of instrumentation to be offered in this book suggests that the process of 'specification' can be:

■ direct,
■ indirect,
■ derived.

For some measures the record itself *is* the value of the variable we want to measure. We observe the sex of a respondent and one of two values will be recorded; we ask a respondent his or her age, or a manager how many employees in the company, and a number will be recorded; we ask a respondent: 'How satisfied are you with the quality of the food in this café, very satisfied, somewhat satisfied or dissatisfied?' and one of three categories will be recorded. These are examples of *direct* measurement in which we assume:

- there is a 'true' or 'correct' answer, let's call it Xt,
- the observation or record, Xr, corresponds with the true value, i.e. $Xt = Xr$.

In the case of observed sex of respondent, the only danger is that the record-keeper makes a mistake. In the case of enquired age, besides the danger of the record-keeper making a mistake there is the additional danger that the respondent tells a lie. For enquired number of employees we can add the danger of misinformation or incorrect recall. With all three, however, it is possible, at least in principle, to check out the observations or records from other information. In the case of measuring customer satisfaction, however, we cannot do this. We have no way of knowing that Xt even exists, or for how long it remains stable, and if it does exist (or we assume it does), Xt may not equal Xr because:

- the person is unwilling to express his or her true feelings,
- the person may be in a bad mood,
- the answer is affected by situational factors,
- the answer is affected by the wording of the question or the way it was addressed,
- the respondent did not understand the question.

In these circumstances, direct measures are problematic because what we are trying to measure are concepts, ideas or abstractions that have no immediate observable referent. We cannot 'see' a person's degree of satisfaction or 'observe' their social class, so unless the researcher specifically wants to measure perceived satisfaction or perceived social class rather than some objective measure of each, then he or she will need to take an indicator – an *indirect* measurement – of the concept, for example: 'Has your washing machine needed any repairs since you purchased it? ' or 'Can you please tell me the occupation of the chief wage earner in the household?' In the first case the researcher is taking the need for repair as an indicator of customer dissatisfaction, and in the second the occupation as an indicator of social class (see Box 2.1 on the measurement of social class in the UK).

With concepts as complex as customer satisfaction or brand loyalty, asking just one question of respondents or taking just one measure may be insufficient. Such concepts will have several if not many aspects or facets. It may be necessary in respect of many perceptual variables to ask several questions, each relating to a slightly different aspect of the item or items being evaluated. Measures are then derived from the responses. At this stage it would be appropriate to consider which of four different approaches to such *derived* measurement is appropriate.

- We could decide that there is a single dimension going from high to low or positive to negative. In this case we need a way of combining answers together to produce an overall score. These are usually called *summated rating* scales.

The measurement of social class has always been very difficult. Along with age it is commonly used as a control in the selection of quota samples (which are explained in Chapter 5), and therefore has to be assessed before the interview begins. This requires an easy and simple system for the interviewer to apply in the field with a reasonable degree of reliability and validity. Most measurements are based on the system developed for the National Readership Survey (which is explained in Chapter 8). The categories (see Table 2.1) are determined by the occupation of the head of household. Unfortunately, a considerable amount of probing on the part of the interviewer is sometimes necessary to establish which class the occupation falls into. These probes vary according to type of job and whether the respondent is self-employed or not, and it is often difficult to elicit the necessary information without using half a page of questionnaire space. Usually the interviewer actually makes the classification, but details of the occupation of the head of household on which it is based are normally required for checking purposes. Details of the National Readership Survey system are given in a manual to interviewers that runs to 19 pages. Not all agencies, however, adhere to the system, and in consequence measures of social class by different agencies may not be strictly comparable.

There have been many criticisms of the NRS classification system. It was developed at a time when lifestyle, income and status were all reflected in occupation, and when there were few working wives. Nowadays, these conditions no longer hold. The classification ignores the impact of multiple household incomes, and it fails to reflect changes in attitudes and behaviour that have affected the consumption of many products. However, in spite of attempts to find a system of measuring social class that is manifestly better, none has, so far, been generated.

In 1981 a working party representing the advertisers, the advertising agencies, the television companies and the Market Research Society published a report which concluded that:

- Social grade provided satisfactory discriminatory power (that is, individuals or households in the six social grades showed different patterns of consumer behaviour across a wide range of variables from product purchasing to going on holidays, and varying patterns of possessions, disposible income, lifestyle and so on).
- No alternative standard classification variables were found to provide consistently better discriminatory power.
- There was no evidence to show a decline in the discriminatory power of social grades over the previous decade.

However, more recent evidence suggests that while social class *is* a good discriminator, gradings made by interviewers in the field or based on details collected by such interviewers, may be unreliable, which certainly makes social grade problematic when used for structual as opposed to analytic purposes.

Box 2.1   The measurement of social class

- We could decide that there are several separate dimensions that it would be unwise to attempt to add together so we generate a profile of scores on each item. This is a process called *profiling*.
- We could decide that the items varied in the degree of relative importance attached to them by respondents, in which case we might ask respondents to rank them – a process called *ranking*. This might be done directly, but more likely a ranking will be derived from one or more of several procedures like conjoint (or trade-off) analysis, which is explained in Chapter 6.
- We could decide that the key variable is 'produced' by a number of factors each of which adds something to it. A common technique will be multiple regression analysis which tries to 'explain' as much of the variance in a

dependent variable from the variance on two or more independent variables. This process of *statistical explanation* may be seen as an alternative to scaling when the researcher feels that the variable is single dimensional.

Summated rating scales and profiling are considered in more detail below. The particular techniques used for ranking and statistical explanation need to wait until we come to data analysis in Chapter 6.

Summated rating scales

Summated rating scales are created by allocating numerical scores to ordinal response categories for each aspect of the item being measured. These scores are then totalled for each case. Suppose 150 respondents in a survey are asked to rate their level of satisfaction with five aspects of a service from very satisfied to very dissatisfied and scores are allocated as illustrated in Figure 2.4. Total scores can now be added up. The maximum a customer can give is 5 on each aspect, totalling 25. The minimum is 5. These totals can then be divided by 5 to give an average score for each case.

A particular version of a summated rating scale developed to measure attitudes is the Likert scale published by Likert in 1932. These scales are based on getting respondents to indicate their degree of agreement or disagreement with a series of statements about the object or focus of the attitude. Usually, these are on 5-point rating scales from strongly agree, through agree, neither agree nor disagree, disagree to strongly disagree. Likert's main concern was with unidimensionality - making sure that all the items would measure the same thing. Accordingly, he recommended a series of steps.

1 A large list of attitude statements, both positive and negative, concerning the object of the attitude is generated, usually based on the results of qualitative research.
2 The response categories are assigned scores, usually 1-5, but some researchers prefer -2, -1, 0, $+1$, $+2$. These may need to be reversed for negative statements.
3 The list is tested on a screening sample of 100-200 respondents representative of the larger group to be studied and a total score is derived for each respondent.
4 Statements that do not discriminate (i.e. everybody gives the same or similar answers) or that do not correlate with the overall total score, are discarded. This is a procedure called item analysis and it avoids cluttering

How satisfied were you with the performance of our staff on each aspect of service when you last telephoned us?

	Very satisfied	Fairly satisfied	Neither	Fairly dissatisfied	Very dissatisfied
Speed of getting through	5	4	3	2	1
Getting the right person	5	4	3	2	1
Politeness	5	4	3	2	1
Staff knowledge of products	5	4	3	2	1
Efficiency	5	4	3	2	1

Figure 2.4 A summated rating scale – customer satisfaction with service provided.

Below is a series of statements that people have made about the ABC Club. Please indicate to what extent you agree or disagree with each statement by putting a circle around the appropriate number

	Strongly agree	Agree	Neither	Disagree	Strongly disagree
I get through very quickly	5	4	3	2	1
I always get the right person	5	4	3	2	1
The staff are not very polite	5	4	3	2	1
Staff know their products well	5	4	3	2	1
The staff are not very efficient	5	4	3	2	1

Figure 2.5 A Likert scale.

up the final scale with items that are either irrelevant or inconsistent with the other items. Correlation is considered later in Chapter 6.

5   The remaining statements, such as the ones in Figure 2.5, are then administered to the main sample of respondents, usually as part of a wider questionnaire survey. Usually the statements will be randomly ordered to mix positive and negative ones. The items in Figure 2.5 were generated by 'converting' the items in Figure 2.4 into a set of Likert items.

6   Totals are derived for each respondent.

The problem with Likert scales is that the totals for each respondent may be derived from very different combinations of response. Thus a score of 15 may be derived either by neither agreeing nor disagreeing with all the items or by strongly agreeing with some and strongly disagreeing with others.

Consequently, it is often a good idea also to analyse the patterns of each response on an item-by-item basis. It must also be remembered that the derived total scores are not absolute, so that somebody scoring 20 is not 'twice' as favourable as somebody scoring 10. Strictly speaking, the scores should be used to generate ordinal data. Some researchers, however, have argued that little error arises if we treat such ordinal scales *as if* they were metric. For example, some researchers will calculate an average score for groups of respondents or for particular items. It must also be said that the screening sample and subsequent item analysis are often omitted by market researchers who just generate the statements, probably derived from or based on previous tests, and go straight to the main sample. This is in many ways a pity, since leaving out scale refinement and purification will result in more ambiguous, less valid and less reliable instruments. In fact, whether such a collection of Likert-type items represents true Likert scaling is an open question.

Profiling

It would be possible to use Likert-type items for profiling by calculating an average across cases separately for each item, so that, for Figure 2.4, there would be an average score for *speed of getting through* and another for

Please put an X at a point between the two extremes which
indicates your view about the service you received from the Club

Fast to get through	:___:___:___:___:___:___:	Slow to get through
Get the right person	:___:___:___:___:___:___:	Get the wrong person
Staff are polite	:___:___:___:___:___:___:	Staff are impolite
Staff know products	:___:___:___:___:___:___:	Staff do not know products
Staff are efficient	:___:___:___:___:___:___:	Staff are inefficient

Figure 2.6 A semantic differential.

getting the right person, and so on. There would be no attempt to add up
scores for the five items. A more common way of obtaining a profile is to use a
semantic differential scale. These scales were developed by Osgood *et al.*
(1957) and were designed originally to investigate the underlying structure of
words, but have subsequently been adapted to measure images of stores,
companies or brands and attitudes. They present dimensions as a series of
opposites, which may be either bipolar, like 'sweet . . . sour', or monopolar,
like 'sweet . . . not sweet'. Respondents may be asked to indicate, usually on a
7-point scale, where between the two extremes their views lie, as illustrated in
Figure 2.6. In most scales there are three groups of adjective pairs:

- an evaluation dimension such as 'good . . . bad' or 'sweet . . . bitter'.
- a potency dimension such as 'strong . . . weak', or 'deep . . . shallow',
- an activity dimension such as 'fast . . . slow', or 'noisy . . . quiet'.

Unlike Likert items, which may be classified into positive and negative statements, semantic differentials may not be classifiable in this way, for example
'bitter . . . sweet' – which is the 'positive' one? For this reason there may be no
attempt to add the items together, but to present them as a 'snake' diagram as
in Figure 2.7. The seven positions on the scale will be scored 1–7 (or $-3 - +3$)
and an average taken separately for each item across the cases. It is then
possible to compare profiles of two or more brands, stores or companies.

If the items *are* to be added up, they must be clearly classifiable into positive
and negative and subject to an item analysis procedure on a screening sample

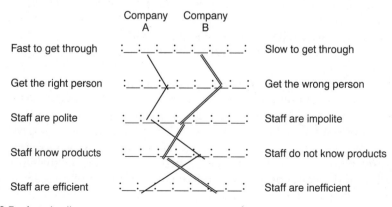

Figure 2.7 A snake diagram.

as for Likert scales. In practice this is often not done, which, again, is a pity because the validity and reliability of the scale may then be in considerable doubt. It is to the topics of validity and reliability that we now turn.

Validity

The problem with all forms of derived measurement is that, precisely because it is derived, it is possible that:

■ the resulting values do not reflect what the concept was intended to measure,
■ changes in measures between one attempt and another at a later date may be a result of either changes in the phenomenon being measured or of fluctuations in the way the measurement instrument works.

The first problem is concerned with issues of *validity* and the second with issues of *reliability*.

A measurement is said to be valid if it measures what it is intended to measure. This, in practice, means looking for evidence that the instruments, techniques or processes used to measure a concept do indeed give a true reflection of what was intended. A valid measurement is one that is accurate and correct so that differences on scores reflect true differences among cases on the characteristic the researcher seeks to measure and not systematic or random error. The problem is that without knowing the 'true' score we have no way of measuring whether or not there are errors. All we can do is infer validity from whatever evidence we can muster. Such inference may come from three sources:

■ pragmatic validity,
■ content validity,
■ construct validity.

The first approach focuses on the usefulness of the measuring instrument as a predictor of some other characteristic of behaviour of the case. This approach is sometimes called predictive validity or criterion validity. If a particular measure of customer satisfaction enables us to predict with some accuracy whether or not a consumer will repeat purchase then we could say that it has pragmatic validity. The focus is purely on the size of the correlation between the measure and what it is predicting. It does not really address the issue of what in fact is being measured.

Content validity focuses on the adequacy with which the domain of the characteristic is adequately sampled by the measure. Thus measuring customer satisfaction with a new car by asking a series of questions about speed and acceleration would not adequately sample the domain of characteristics or features that determine customer satisfaction. It would, in other words, lack content validity. Content validity is sometimes known as 'face' validity because the measure is reviewed on the basis of whether or not it seems to be reasonable 'on the face of it'. The key to content validity lies in the procedures that we use to develop the instrument. Such a procedure would begin with a clear definition of the concept, perhaps relating this to how the concept has been defined in the past. The next step is to formulate a large number of items that broadly represent the concept as defined. In the last stage the items will be pruned and refined so that items that do not discriminate between respondents or cases are excluded, and any items that overlap to too great an extent with other items are avoided.

Construct validity is most directly concerned with the question of what the instrument is in fact measuring. Constructs, by their very nature, cannot be observed so must be operationalized in terms of a set of aspects that are observable. Content validity is a necessary precondition for construct validity; without an adequate sampling of the domain of the concept, construct validity cannot be achieved. Beyond this it is necessary, as part of construct validity, to establish:

- internal consistency,
- convergent validity,
- discriminant validity.

Internal consistency is a matter of the extent to which the items used to measure a concept hang together. Statistically that means that they need to correlate one with another. Convergent validity looks at the extent to which the measure relates to other constructs to which it is theoretically related. Thus a good measure of social class based on the occupation of the head of households should, if it has convergent validity, also relate to things like lifestyle, leisure pursuits, holiday-making, purchasing behaviour and so on. However, measures should have not only convergent validity, but also discriminant validity. This is the extent to which the measure is indeed new and not simply a reflection of some other variable. Scales that correlate too highly with tests from which they are intended to differ may suggest that it lack discriminant validity. Discriminant validity is indicated by low correlations between the measure of interest and other measures that are supposedly not measuring the same concept.

Reliability

Whereas validity is represented by agreement between attempts to measure the same concept or trait through methods that are as *different* as possible, reliability is represented by agreement between methods that are as *similar* as possible. Reliability is the extent to which measurements are repeatable. A scale lacking reliability cannot be valid, although, of course, reliability is no proof of validity – a scaling procedure can produce consistently misleading results. Reliability is, therefore, a necessary but not sufficient condition for validity.

So, how is reliability to be measured? There are three approaches. The first measures scale *stability* over time and depends on one or more retests at a later date. A key problem here is how long to wait between tests. The second measures scale *equivalence*, showing how two equivalent indexes given at virtually the same time are in agreement. The third measures the *internal consistency* of a set of items used as indicators. If these are intended to reflect an underlying, unobservable characteristic (a 'construct'), the items should be substantially correlated with one another.

An increasingly popular measure for establishing internal consistency is Cronbach's alpha. This takes the average correlation among items in a scale (where each item is a rating scale like a Likert scale or a semantic differential), and adjusts for the number of items. Reliable scales are ones with a high average correlation and a relatively large number of items. The coefficient varies between zero for no reliability to unity for maximum reliability. Alphas of 0.7 or higher are usually taken to be acceptable, but the purpose of the research needs to be kept in mind. Appendix 1 explains the statistic in more detail.

Datasets

Most quantitative marketing research projects will collect data not just on a large number of cases, but for each case a number, sometimes a large number, of variables will be measured for each case. Some of these variables will be metric, some will be non-metric. A dataset consists of all the values for all the variables for all the cases in a piece of research (or data collection phase in continuous research). Thus an inquiry that has 200 respondents to a questionnaire survey with 100 questions will produce a dataset that contains 200 × 100 or 20,000 pieces of information.

A dataset may be stored in many different formats, but the most useful is as a data matrix, since this interlaces each case with each variable to produce a 'cell' containing the appropriate value, as illustrated in Figure 2.8. The cases form the rows and the variables the columns. The size of the matrix is, therefore, a product of the number of cases and the number of variables. Where there are many cases and many variables such as in a large-scale survey, the data matrix will be very large. Data matrices will have different shapes depending on the nature of the research. Intensive research will have relatively few cases but many variables; extensive research will have many cases and few variables. An opinion poll is a good example of the latter where a large sample (of 1000 or so) are asked a few questions about voting intentions and party support. Usually, data matrices are rectangular – all the rows are of the same length and all the columns are of the same length. Some cells may be empty where data are missing or where some of the questions are not appropriate for some of the cases.

In order to be able to use survey analysis or spreadsheet packages it will usually be necessary to convert the non-metric scale values into numbers – numbers which are used just as labels to identify the response categories. Thus Figure 2.8 may need to be transposed into Figure 2.9. Appendix 3 shows you how to enter a data matrix into a particular survey analysis package, SPSS

Variables

Cases	Sex	Age	Class	Nationality
1	Male	26	C2	British
2	Female	32	C1	French
3	Male	19	B	Spanish
.	.	.	.	.
n	Female	33	C1	British

Figure 2.8   A case by variable data matrix.

Variables

Cases	Sex	Age	Class	Nationality
1	1	26	4	1
2	2	32	3	2
3	1	19	2	3
.	.	.	.	.
n	2	33	3	1

Figure 2.9 A generalized data matrix.

(Statistical Package for the Social Sciences). Chapter 6 will show you how to analyse a data matrix and how SPSS can be used to help.

Summary

Provided it is approached systematically, any record of narrative, text, physical objects, behaviour, observations or responses to a question will constitute data. Qualitative data are non-numerical, whereas quantitative data result from a process of measurement to produce frequencies of categories, metric assessment of quantities, or frequencies of groups of metric quantities. Sets of categories may be ordered or non-ordered; metric assessment may be discrete or continuous.

A single measurement consists of a record of a value from a scale of values for a case in respect of a given variable. Where there is a set of cases then the potential for recording frequencies arises. Where there are not only many cases but also many variables, then a dataset is produced. This may be laid out in the form of a data matrix.

Key concepts

data	descriptors
qualitative data	independent variables
quantitative data	dependent variables
measurement	frequencies
value	data transformation
scale	datasets
variable	data matrix
case	operationalization
binary scales	direct measurement
nominal scales	indirect measurement
rank ordered scales	derived measurement
discrete metric scales	summated rating scales
continuous metric	profiling
metric data	Likert scales
non-metric data	semantic differential scales
demographic variables	validity
behavioural variables	reliability
perceptual variables	

Further reading

■   Albaum, A (1997) 'The Likert scale revisited: an alternate version', *Journal of the Market Research Society,* Vol 39, No 2, pp 331–48.
■   Churchill, GA (1969) 'A Paradigm for Developing Better Measures of Marketing Constructs', *Journal of Marketing Research*, February, pp 64–73.
■   Oppenheim, AN (1996) *Questionnaire Design and Attitude Measurement*, London: Heinemann.
■   Spector, PE (1991) *Scale Development: Theories and Applications*, London: Sage.

Questions for further discussion

1   Fill in two or three examples of each type of scale and its associated values in Table 2.2.
2   How would you measure, and on what sort of a scale, each of the following?
   ■   how many times someone reads a newspaper in a week,
   ■   customer satisfaction with a restaurant,
   ■   attitudes to Radio 1,
   ■   brand loyalty to Nescafé Gold Blend over the course of a year.
3   What sort of scale will consumer responses to the following questions generate?
   ■   Have you purchased a magazine in the last few days?
   ■   Would you say you were satisfied, fairly satisfied or dissatisfied with the video you have just hired?
   ■   On a scale of 1–10 how would you rate the university course you have just completed?
   ■   Would you please put these six brands in order of your preference?
   ■   How many brothers and sisters do you have?
   ■   What size of pack did you last purchase – 0.5 kg, 1.0 kg or 1.5 kg?
   ■   Where did you go on holiday last year?
4   Why are Likert scales so popular?

Table 2.2
Examples of types of scale

Scale type	Variables	Values
Customers		
Binary		
Nominal		
Ordinal		
Ranked		
Discrete metric		
Continuous metric		
Organizations		
Binary		
Nominal		
Ordinal		
Discrete metric		
Continuous metric		

3

The instruments of data capture

In Chapter 2 it was suggested that data arise from any form of systematic record-keeping. This chapter will explore the different ways in which various data capture instruments may be used by market researchers to create such records. The focus is on the instruments themselves, not on the social or organizational contexts in which they are used. Such contexts involve the various data collection techniques which are considered in detail in Chapter 4. Most marketing researchers use questionnaires at some stage, and the questionnaire as a data capture instrument is the focus of the first major section below. Later sections consider diaries and devices, manual and electronic, for recording observations, events and discussions.

Questionnaires and questionnaire design

Questionnaires in marketing research

Asking people questions and systematically noting their responses has been a method of conducting social research in Britain since the 1790s (see Kent, 1981, for an historical account of social research in Britain). Questionnaires in marketing, certainly in the textbook literature, tend to be associated exclusively with survey research, but in practice they may be used in a number of different data collection contexts, as we shall see in the next chapter. Some market researchers, furthermore, refer rather loosely to any documents used for the purpose of data collection as 'questionnaires', although we will be distinguishing questionnaires from diaries, manual recording sheets and interview guides, which are also used 'in the field'.

A questionnaire may be defined as any document that is used as an instrument with which to capture data generated by asking people questions and which, furthermore:

- lists all the questions a researcher wishes to address to each respondent,
- provides space or some mechanism for recording the responses,
- puts questions in a logical sequence,
- draws accurate information from respondents,
- standardizes the format of the questions,
- facilitates data processing.

Questionnaires may be of different kinds, as we shall see later, but for the moment it is convenient to consider the different types of question that may be used in designing questionnaires.

Types of question

We can classify types of question in many different ways, but two key dimensions are in terms, first, of the kind of variable being measured and, second, in terms of the format of the responses offered. We saw in the previous chapter how variables may be classified according to the type of property on which they focus – demographic, behavioural or perceptual. Accordingly, it is possible to think of questions in questionnaires as measuring demographic, behavioural or perceptual variables. The most commonly used demographic variables relate to:

■ sex of respondent (male/female),
■ age of respondent (either age in years at last birthday or in class intervals),
■ social grade (see Box 2.1),
■ marital status (single, married, widowed, divorced, separated),
■ occupational status (employed full time, employed part time, unemployed),
■ income (usually in broad bands),
■ terminal education age (16, 18, 21),
■ size of household (numbers of adults and children),
■ household composition (e.g. two adults and three children),
■ type of accommodation (owner occupied, rented privately, local authority housing),
■ area (ITV Region or the Registrar General's Standard Regions).

Most agencies have lists of standard questions to include in the demographic sections of their questionnaires. A committee of the Market Research Society attempted in 1971 and again in 1984 to generate a more universal set of standard questions (reported by Wolfe, 1984). However, many agencies have continued to approach the design of classification sections in accordance with their own inclinations or 'house styles'.

Apart from social class, household status is another classification variable that has caused some problems. The usual categorization is into head of household, housewife and other adult. The head of household is the chief wage earner or the person responsible for the accommodation. Where there are two equal candidates the male is taken to be the head of household, and the older of two people if both are of the same sex. A housewife is usually the person most directly concerned with shopping and cooking in the household. Problems arise, however, if we ask, 'Can such a person be male?' and 'Can a household have no housewife, or more than one?' Usually the housewife is assumed to be female, but some agencies do allow for male housewives.

These difficulties with the traditional demographic variables have prompted some market research agencies to use life-cycle, lifestyle or geodemographic variables instead of social class and household status.

Family life-cycles are usually defined into a number of stages that families typically undergo. Thus respondents may be classified according to whether they are:

- dependants,
- single, but independent,
- married, but no children,
- married with young children,
- married with older children,
- retired.

People tend to have different aspirations, opinions and needs as they go through the various stages, exhibiting changing patterns of consumer behaviour in the process. Different market research agencies will have their own particular classifications and may combine these stages with other demographic characteristics. Thus Research Services Limited in 1981 developed a system it called SAGACITY, which generated 12 groups combining life-cycle (dependent, pre-family, family and late) with income (better off, worse off), and occupation (ABC1 and C2DE). This, claims Cornish (1981), provides better discrimination than any single dimension on its own. Life-cycle stages may be used either to classify individuals, as above, or to classify households. In both cases, questions will need to be asked about marital status, presence (and perhaps ages) of children, plus some measure of individual and/or household income.

Lifestyle analyses tend to include any variables that are not demographics and may relate to the activities, interests, attitudes and opinions of respondents. Activities might include hobbies, entertainment, club membership and sports. Interests may concern the home and family, the community, fashions, or the media, while opinions may be about themselves, social issues, politics, education and so on.

Statistical analysis like factor analysis and cluster analysis (explained in Chapter 6) are then used to identify groups or categories of people who tend to have similar characteristics. The typologies generated, however, tend to be specific to particular classes of product. Attempts to develop more generalized classifications have not been widely accepted. Thus Baker and Fletcher (1989) generated six clusters using data from British Market Research Bureau's Target Group Index, which includes nearly 200 lifestyle statements on a regular basis. The system, which the authors called 'Outlook', defines the groups as:

- trendies – people 'into' current fads, demographically up-market, affluent and concentrated in the 25–44 age group,
- pleasure-seekers – people who want things now. They are against long-term planning and have a low sense of responsibility,
- the indifferent, who do not react in any particular way,
- working-class puritans who are 'anti-fun', parochial and traditional,
- social spenders who like to go out and enjoy themselves, be lavish and sociable,
- moralists who are against everything that it enjoyable.

This system, the authors claim, maintains its validity across sub-samples and over time, is a powerful discriminator and is independent of the social class components of attitude and behaviour patterns. Ward (1987) argues, however, that such systems are uni-dimensional and cannot compete with interlaced demographics for discrimination and predictive ability. Product, or, rather, market specific studies are usually more helpful than generalized systems. Furthermore, attitude-based systems are difficult to apply in the field and are thus not easy to utilize for structural purposes, for example to apply quota controls. Finally, they provide too simple a view of humanity – people may change category depending on their mood or on the social context; they may be 'trendy' about some things and 'moralists' about others.

Geodemographics were mentioned as a particular type of variable in Chapter 2. CACI's ACORN is based on a classification of 38 neighbourhood types derived from a multi-variate analysis of Census data. Each Census enumeration district is classified into one of the types, for example, 'cheap modern private housing' or 'recent council estates'. Each district is then matched against postcodes, so that any list of customer addresses (with postcodes) can be readily analysed by ACORN criteria. Working this the other way round, it is possible to pull out all the postcodes that cover neighbourhoods with specified characteristics.

Other companies such as Pinpoint Analysis Limited, CCN Systems, and Credit and Data Marketing Services Limited, have produced refinements to this technique, as has CACI itself. Most of these refinements entail adding more information to the classification system, for example, on lifestyles, household composition and likely ages of respondents (which, using a system CACI calls MONICA, is derived from the first names of people on the electoral registers). Some systems use more than 38 types, for example, CDMS offers Super Profiles, which has 150 neighbourhood types based on details from Census data.

O'Brien and Ford (1989) report from a study commissioned by Granada Television in 1987 that both social class and lifestyle remained powerful discriminators. While lifestyle was better for some variables, it could not be used for quota control since it depended on administering a large number of attitude statements. The use of post codes to identify geodemographic characteristics remains the most powerful potential alternative to social class. It has considerable discriminatory power and can be applied robustly for structural purposes. More research is needed, however, on which geodemographic systems work best in a range of different circumstance.

The measurement of behavioural and attitudinal questions was explained in Chapter 2. However, in terms of question format, two main formats may be distinguished: fixed-choice and open-ended questions. Fixed-choice questions give respondents a list of possible answers from which to choose. Some of these questions allow the respondent to pick only *one* response from a list. The simplest result in a binary scale, for example, a yes/no answer to a question like, 'Do you own or rent a freezer?' However, many questions of this kind also require 'don't know', 'no response' or 'cannot recall' categories, so they result in a nominal scale. Some questions ask respondents to pick a category that applies to them where the categories themselves are in some kind of order, as illustrated in Figure 3.1. The result is, of course, an ordinal scale. The summated rating scales and semantic differential scales that we considered in Chapter 2 have ordered single-response categories of this kind. For metric variables, the scale values will need to be grouped as in Figure 3.2 if the researcher wishes to create a fixed choice question. The alternative is to get the respondent to write in the appropriate value, like the actual age in years. Which of these is advisable depends on how the researcher wishes to

How important is it to you that the
leisure centre has up-to-date equipment?

Very important ☐ 1
Fairly important ☐ 2
Not important ☐ 3

Figure 3.1 A single-answer ordinal scale.

In which of the following age groups are you?

<20 ☐ 1
20–39 ☐ 2
40–59 ☐ 3
60+ ☐ 4

Figure 3.2 A grouped metric scale.

use the data. If the researcher wishes to use the data to be able to calculate a product moment correlation coefficient (Pearson's r – to be explained in Chapter 6) with another metric variable, for example income, then he or she will need the actual age for each respondent. Such variables can always be grouped later if the researcher wants to cross-tabulate them with non-metric variables. The downside of asking for actual age (or for income for that matter) is that people may be reluctant to reveal this information, so broad categories may be better provided the researcher is not likely to need the full metric scale.

Some questions, however, allow respondents to pick more than one category, as illustrated in Figure 3.3. In such multiple-response questions the total number of responses will usually be greater than the total number of respondents. This means that it is possible either to report the proportion of respondents who tick a particular response, or the proportion of total responses accounted for by each category. Such questions may pose problems at the analysis stage because some computer programs (like spreadsheets and some statistical packages like Minitab) cannot handle multiple response questions. Each response category has to be treated as a separate binary variable – ticked/not ticked.

One of the mistakes frequently made in questionnaire design is not to make it clear to the respondent whether the question allows for more than one response category. It is usually a good idea to add an appropriate instruction like, 'Tick one box only' or, 'Tick as many responses as apply in your case'. Fixed-choice questions, whether single-response or multiple-response, are

In which of the following countries have
you been on holiday in the last five years?
(Please tick as many as apply to you)

UK ☐ 1
France ☐ 2
Spain ☐ 3
Greece ☐ 4
Turkey ☐ 5
Italy ☐ 6
Other ☐ 7

Figure 3.3 A multiple-response question.

relatively easy to analyse since all that is required is a simple frequency count of each answer category. However, they do tend to force respondents into answering in ways that may not correspond with their true feelings, or respondents may be tempted to just pick responses without a great deal of (or any!) thought.

Open-ended questions leave respondents free to formulate replies in their own words. The interviewer (or the respondent in a self-completed question-naire) writes in the answer, usually word-for-word. Normally there will be one or more blank lines for this purpose. Open-ended questions tend to be used in the following situations:

■ The researcher is unsure about what the responses might be, for example, 'Why did you decide to select brand X?'
■ The possible responses are too many to list, for example, 'How old are you?' or, 'What is the name of the shop where you last purchased tooth-paste?'
■ The researcher wants to introduce a topic by getting the respondents to formulate their thoughts in their own words, or to focus the respondent's attention on the subject.
■ The researcher wants to avoid pre-judging responses with set-choice answers.
■ The researcher wants to 'mop up' any views that may not have been elicited from fixed-choice questions.
■ The researcher wants to be able to enliven the final report with quotes from respondents.

Some questions may be a combination of fixed and open elements, for example giving respondents a list of responses including 'Other (please spe-cify)' with a space or line to treat as open-ended. Some questions may be grouped together into tables, grids or checklists where the response cate-gories are the same for each question, as in Figure 2.5.

Most questionnaires will contain some open-ended questions, although relatively few will consist entirely of such questions. The particular combina-tion of open-ended and fixed-choice questions in a questionnaire is often referred to as its degree of 'structuring'. Highly structured questionnaires consist largely of fixed-choice questions; unstructured questionnaires are mostly composed of open-ended questions, while semi-structured question-naires contain more of a balance between the two. Except for those questions eliciting a factual response, open-ended questions can often be difficult and time-consuming to analyse. They produce qualitative data that need to be interpreted, evaluated, or content-analysed (Chapter 6 will review the analysis of qualitative data). In consequence, the number of open-ended questions is normally kept to a minimum. Even factual open-ended questions still require that the responses be classified and numbered later on back in the office (a process called 'post-coding') so that the frequency of types of response can be counted up.

Question wording

Designing an effective series of questions is never easy. Three conditions need to be satisfied to maximize the possibility of obtaining valid responses:

- respondents must *understand* the questions, (and understand them in the same way as other respondents),
- respondents must be *able* to provide the answers,
- respondents must be *willing* to provide the information.

The first of these is largely a function of question wording, the second a function of routing, and the third has more to do with sequencing and overall length.

For respondents to understand a question, it must be clear, specific, brief, unambiguous and cover a single issue. In general, this means avoiding:

- long words that people may not be familiar with,
- leading questions,
- complex sentences,
- ambiguous questions,
- vague questions.

Using words like 'unilateral', 'devolution', or 'proximity', or jargon like 'marital status' or 'retail outlets' will cause misunderstanding of questions. Never present the respondent with just one of the answer categories – that amounts to a leading question, for example, 'Do you agree that dogs should be banned from public parks?' Always present both or all the alternative responses equally, so instead of, 'Do you like brand X?' ask, 'Do you like brand X or brand Y?' or 'Do you agree or disagree that . . . ?'

Complex sentences often arise because the researcher wishes to qualify statements or define terms. Where such qualifications or definitions *are* necessary, then it is better that they are part of a separate sentence, for example, 'Do you have full central heating in this house? By "full" I mean outlets in living rooms and most bedrooms.' Beware of the double question like 'Do you know or are you known personally by the shop assistants?'

Avoiding ambiguity is notoriously difficult. A question like, 'How many children are there in your family?' may refer to brothers and sisters for somebody who is unmarried, and to offspring for those married with their own children. 'Where did you buy this packet of soap?' may mean 'In what shop?' or 'In what geographical location?' Words like 'frequent', 'good' or 'recently' may be interpreted in various ways.

Vagueness and ambiguity tend to go together, but, as a general rule, be as specific as possible, for example, by defining timings and frequencies of purchases. Thus, 'Have you personally bought shampoo in the last seven days?' is better than, 'Have you personally bought shampoo recently?'

Hypothetical questions, for example, 'What would you do if . . .', or questions that relate to future behaviour, need to be avoided as far as possible. However, they sometimes are required to establish purchase intentions, for example, 'Would you buy this product for your personal use?'

Bear in mind that people, on the whole, like to be helpful and co-operative. This often means that they will try to give you the answers they think you want. Most questionnaires, it has been discovered, generate more 'yes' answers than 'no' answers.

Eliciting motivations or reasons for doing or not doing things can be particularly difficult. This may be approached by asking the respondents what they do and then asking, 'Why do you do that?' It is tempting for the researcher to try to list most of the possible responses in advance and then get the interviewer to tick the appropriate categories. This can only be done, however, if there has been considerable pre-testing or exploratory research in advance. If this has not been done, then it is probably better to leave the question open-ended and to classify answers at the analysis stage.

In 1951 Payne published a book that was devoted entirely to the wording of questions in formal questionnaires. In it he emphasizes that responses people give are extremely sensitive to the words or phrases used, and that experiments with questions where perhaps a single word was changed, for example from 'ought' to 'might', show very different results. He gives a 'rogues gallery' of problem words like 'all' and 'you', and concludes with a checklist of 100 'considerations' that need to be kept in mind when phrasing questions. While there are more recent works on survey questions, such as by Sudman and Bradburn (1982), Converse and Presser (1986), and Belson (1986), Payne's book stands as a 'classic' of its kind and is still worth a careful reading today.

Routing

For respondents to be able to provide information it is essential that they are asked only those questions that they are likely to be able to answer with some accuracy. This may mean establishing that the respondent has some experience of the situation or products that they are to be asked about, and not asking them to perform unreasonable feats of memory about past events. It is usually necessary to use 'filter' questions which sort respondents into categories so that follow-up questions can be asked only where appropriate. If the respondent does not fit in with that category (e.g. does not smoke), then the next few questions that relate to people who do, need to be skipped. This is usually described as 'routing' the respondent through the questionnaire. Sometimes there is a special 'Skip to' column that indicates the next relevant question for response categories for which the following question is *not* the relevant one. Some responses may have 'Go to Q . . . ' written against them. Examples of routing can be seen in Figure 3.4.

Sequencing

As a general rule the questionnaire should begin with simple questions that relate clearly to the topic the respondent has been led to believe the survey is about. Topics need to flow logically, rather than jump about, although this may be difficult in omnibus surveys (which are explained in Chapter 7) where respondents can be asked about anything from dog food to airline travel in the same questionnaire. If this happens, it is useful to indicate that a change of topic is taking place, for example, 'I would now like to turn to the topic of holidays' or 'May I now ask you a few questions about motoring?' It is usually better to put general questions before more specific ones. This may mean, for example, introducing the topic of leisure activities, then clothing used, then type of footwear, and finally use of a particular brand of trackshoe. This procedure is often referred to as 'funnelling'.

Demographic questions are usually asked at the end of any questionnaire as 'rounding-off' questions – they may be a little too personal to begin with. However, any demographics that are used for quota controls need to be asked at the outset. An example of a demographic section of a questionnaire is

SHOPPING AND TRAVEL

Would you help us by spending a few minutes answering the questions below. Please put a tick in the box that corresponds to your answer

Q1 About how often do you buy groceries for regular major shopping?

Every day	☐	1
4–5 days a week	☐	2
2–3 days a week	☐	3
once a week	☐	4
Less often	☐	5
Never	☐	6 Go to Q5

Q2 Are there any particular days you buy most of your regular major shopping?

Yes	☐	1
No	☐	2 Go to Q4

Q3 Which days are they?
PLEASE SELECT NO MORE
THAN TWO DAYS

Monday	☐	1
Tuesday	☐	2
Wednesday	☐	3
Thursday	☐	4
Friday	☐	5
Saturday	☐	6
Sunday	☐	7

Q4 When you make your regualr major grocery purchases, what form of transport do you usually use?

Car	☐	1
Bus	☐	2
Train	☐	3
Bicycle	☐	4
Motorcycle	☐	5
Walk	☐	6

Q5 During a normal week, how many hours would you spend travelling using each form of transport, for whatever purpose, not just travelling.
PLEASE TICK THE APPROPRIATE BOX IN EACH COLUMN

	Car	Bus	Train	Bicycle	Walk
None	☐ 1	☐ 1	☐ 1	☐ 1	☐ 1
< 1 hour	☐ 2	☐ 2	☐ 2	☐ 2	☐ 2
1–2 hours	☐ 3	☐ 3	☐ 3	☐ 3	☐ 3
3–4 hours	☐ 4	☐ 4	☐ 4	☐ 4	☐ 4
5–8 hours	☐ 5	☐ 5	☐ 5	☐ 5	☐ 5
8 hours or more	☐ 6	☐ 6	☐ 6	☐ 6	☐ 6

Figure 3.4 An example of questionnaire layout.

illustrated in Figure 3.6. Notice that the information required in the right-hand column is for identification rather than classification purposes, that is, it identifies one particular interview. It will be completed by the interviewer once the interview is finished. The information is required in case any check-back is needed, either to ensure that the interview took place, or if questions are missed out or completed incorrectly. The respondent may need to be reassured that his or her name and address are required only in case queries arise concerning any of the answers.

Questionnaire length

When drafting questionnaires there is always a tendency to put in all questions that might seem relevant or just interesting. This often happens when the objectives of the research have not been clearly defined and questions are added 'just in case'. The result can be very long questionnaires that may have an impact on the respondent's willingness to finish. Interviews carried out in the street may need to be very short, perhaps taking no more than 10 minutes or so. To keep the questionnaire within reasonable limits:

■ make sure every question is actually needed to fulfil the objectives of the research,
■ restrict the number of demographic questions to what is needed for sample validation and analysis. A page of classification questions can take 10 minutes to fill in, perhaps more when detailed occupational data are required,
■ use checklists or grids wherever possible to condense the material, for example, Question 5 in Figure 3.4.

Self-completed and interviewer-completed questionnaires

Questionnaires may either be completed by the respondent without an interviewer being present, or they may be filled in by an interviewer who asks the questions and completes the questionnaire on behalf of the respondent. Self-completed questionnaires may be sent and returned through the post, they may be personally delivered, to be returned by post or to be personally collected at a later date. The main implications for questionnaire design for self-completed questionnaires arise from the fact that:

■ there is no interviewer,
■ the respondent can see all the response categories before putting in a response,
■ the respondent can read through the questionnaire before answering.

The absence of an interviewer means that it must be clear to the respondent how replies are to be indicated. This will usually mean ticking boxes, putting circles around appropriate code numbers, or deleting responses as appropriate (but do not mix all three in a questionnaire – stick to one format).

The fact that the respondent can see all the response categories before replying means that it is not usually sensible to guess appropriate categories. If these have not been pre-tested and shown to be appropriate to the kind of respondent concerned, then it may be better to leave the question as open-ended. The use of the 'funnelling' technique is also inappropriate other the respondent may spot the 'correct' answer by looking at later questions.

Many of the characteristics special to interviewer-completed questionnaires arise from the fact that respondents cannot see the questionnaire. While, on the one hand, this makes it possible to use the funnelling technique because the respondents cannot see questions yet to come, on the other, it means that if the researcher is looking for choices from pre-set categories then, because the respondent cannot see the responses, it is necessary to do one of three things:

■ incorporate all the possible responses into the question, for example, 'Do you personally eat baked beans less than once a week, between one and three times a week, or four times or more?',
■ get the interviewers to read out the categories to the respondent,
■ list the categories on a separate card that can be shown to the respondent.

The interviewer will need an instruction as to whether he or she is to read out

Q12 How much would you say you knew about computer languages before you watched last night's programme?
READ OUT

A lot ☐ 1
A little ☐ 2
Not very much ☐ 3
Nothing at all ☐ 4

Q13 Which of the following phrases on this card best describes how you feel about this product?
SHOW CARD C

CARD C

I certainly would try this product ☐ 1
I might try this product ☐ 2
I'm not sure that I shall try it ☐ 3
I don't think I shall try it ☐ 4
I certainly will not try it ☐ 5

Figure 3.5 Examples of instructions to interviewers.

the responses or show a card, as illustrated in Figure 3.5. Where a large number of cards are needed they should ideally be clipped or bound together in order of use to help the interviewer. Incorporating responses into the question is, clearly, possible only when there are no more than three or four categories. Open-ended questions may instruct the interviewer to 'probe' (for example by asking, 'Why did you say that?' or, 'Is there anything else?').

Questionnaire layout

Space is at a premium in a questionnaire, but if it is too cramped it will be difficult to read and to write down answers. If space is wasted the questionnaire will look very long, it will be cumbersome to handle, and it will be expensive to print. It is helpful to remember that the questionnaire may need to be used in places where the lighting is not very good, so the print needs to be clear and probably at least a 12–point font size.

There will usually be a place – either at the beginning or at the end – for recording the name and address of the respondent (although this may already be known for some types of sampling – see Chapter 5), the date of the interview, the name of the interviewer, and perhaps the area code. The name and address may be omitted if this is seen to compromise confidentiality.

It is nearly always preferable for response categories to be listed one underneath the other rather than across the page. This is easier for both the person completing the questionnaire and for the researcher who can glance down the answer code column for data entry purposes. This, in turn, often implies that the page as a whole is better in two-column format to avoid wasting a lot of space, for example Figure 3.6. Boxes for ticking may be placed to the left or to the right of the response categories; to the right is usually preferable. It is a good idea if the boxes are numbered, since this facilitates data entry. It is usually helpful to number all the questions. This is useful for routing purposes, for example, 'If yes, skip to Q12'. Sometimes questions are grouped into topics or related issues, for example Q6a, Q6b Q6c, Q7a, Q7b and so on.

Instructions for completing the questionnaire need to be distinguishable from the questions themselves and from the pre-coded answers. The convention – by no means universally followed – is to use capitals underlined for

Q1 Sex of respondent   Male ☐ 1
    Female ☐ 2

Q2 In which of these   15–24 ☐ 1
age categories are you?   25–34 ☐ 2
SHOW CARD 1   35–44 ☐ 3
    45–54 ☐ 4
    55–64 ☐ 5
    65+ ☐ 6

Q3 How many adults (aged 16 or more) live here including yourself?

WRITE IN NUMBER _____

Q4 How many children aged 15 or less live here?

WRITE IN NUMBER _____

Q5 What is the occupation of the head of household or chief wage earner?

JOB TITLE _____
WHAT HE/SHE DOES _____

TYPE OF BUSINESS _____
_____

Q6 INDICATE SOCIAL CLASS   A ☐ 1
    B ☐ 2
    C1 ☐ 3
    C2 ☐ 4
    D ☐ 5
    E ☐ 6

Q7 SAMPLING POINT NUMBER

☐☐☐☐☐☐☐☐☐

Q8 INFORMANT'S NAME AND ADDRESS. PLEASE USE BLOCK CAPITALS

NAME _____
ADDRESS _____
_____
_____
POSTCODE _____

Q9 DATE OF INTERVIEW

_____

Q10 LENGTH OF INTERVIEW

Up to 15 minutes ☐ 1
15–29 ☐ 2
30–45 ☐ 3
Over 45 minutes ☐ 4

I certify that this interview has been personally carried out by me with the respondent at his/her address. He/she is not a friend or relative.

SIGNATURE _____
DATE _____
NAME _____
_____

Figure 3.6 Example of a demographic page.

instructions, capitals for the responses, and lower case for the questions themselves.

There will normally be an introduction to the questionnaire which is critical in winning the co-operation and interest of the respondent. For self-completed questionnaires there may be a separate covering letter, such as the one illustrated in Box 4.1, or it may be an introduction printed at the top of the first page. For interviewer-completed questionnaires the interviewer makes the introduction, but he or she will need to be told what to say. It is probably best for it to be written out at the top of each questionnaire. The introduction does a number of things. It:

■ explains which company or organization is undertaking the survey,
■ describes briefly what the survey is about,
■ checks that the respondent fits any criteria used for screening or for quota controls,
■ provides assurances that the survey is for market research only and that replies will be confidential,
■ asks the respondent for help by answering a few questions,
■ indicates how long it is likely to take.

Overall presentation is very important for a good response rate particularly for self-completed questionnaires. Getting them printed properly is an advantage if the expense can be met, otherwise word-processing packages, desk-top publishing and some survey analysis packages such as Marquis or Pinpoint can be used to produce presentable questionnaires. Pinpoint was used to produce Figures 3.4, 3.5 and 3.6 and is explained in Appendix 4. For interviewer completed questionnaires, layout and presentation may not be so vital, but, particularly where many part-time interviewers are to be employed, clear layout is still required.

Figure 3.4 illustrates some of these principles of layout. Notice that all the questions are clearly numbered. All the response categories are also numbered 1 . . . n. All the respondent has to do is tick boxes. Instructions are in capitals. There is a short introduction at the top. Question 5 is really five questions each with identical response categories. This tabular form saves a lot of space.

The process of questionnaire design

Designing questionnaires is always difficult. It is a skill that cannot be learned from books, but has to be acquired through experience (although reading guides to questionnaire design like the one above can, to some degree, make these experiences more productive). The first draft of a questionnaire is invariably a far cry from what is needed. It will help to keep the following steps in mind.

1   Review the research objectives. These should spell out what the research is designed to explore, measure or explain. If these objectives are unclear then think about them again before proceeding with designing the questionnaire – there is little point in doing so if you are not clear what it is meant to achieve. Review the discussion in Chapter 1 on research objectives. If the research is exploratory, the questions are more likely to be open-ended. If the research is descriptive, investigative or hypothesis-testing, then the key variables will need to be carefully measured and issues of scaling become important. The issues of measurement must be clarified before you proceed to designing questionnaires. It may well be, furthermore, that using questionnaires is only part of the overall research programme – keeping the role and purpose of these other aspects in mind will also be important.

2   Generate a list of topics to be covered by the questionnaire and think about the order in which they could or should be approached. Review the section above on sequencing.

3   Decide whether the questionnaire is to be self-completed or interviewer completed. This will influence a number of aspects of questionnaire design. Review the section above on self-completed and interviewer-completed questionnaires. Think about the questionnaire from the point of view of the likely respondents. What is their level of knowledge and interest likely to be? Think about the likely interviewers if the questionnaire is interviewer-completed. Will they be experienced and well trained? These considerations may influence your view on the kind of wording and instructions that may be needed. If you were thinking of interviewing children as respondents, think again! The process of interviewing children is highly specialized and includes many more pitfalls.

4   Think about how the data will be processed. If you are using a survey

analysis package like SPSS you will need to be clear which variables you intend or wish to be metric and which ones non-metric. If the technique of analysis that you intend to use presupposes metric data (e.g. factor analysis) then you will need to design your questionnaire in ways that will generate such data. That means, for example, asking people for their actual ages and not in broad groups. It means that, if you are using scaling techniques, you need to design your categories so that as far as possible they can be assumed to have equal intervals between the categories. If you wish to use a package like Pinpoint, which allows you to design and print the questionnaire, then you need to be aware of the design possibilities and limitations of the package.

5   Now you are ready to have a go at drafting the questionnaire itself. Do not expect this to be easy. Review the sections on question wording and routing. You may need several drafts which you can do either on paper or directly into a package like Pinpoint. The advantage of the latter is that you can change things and edit as you go along, and you can always print off the latest draft at any point.

6   When your draft is complete, it is time for some testing. First, try it out on some of your friends or colleagues and perhaps also on a 'pilot' group of respondents similar to those who will be used in the main study. The questionnaire is likely to go through further drafts before reaching its final form. There will inevitably be questions that:

- do not mean what the researcher intended,
- have been missed out completely,
- people do not understand or find too difficult,
- everybody gives the same answer to, that is, do not discriminate,
- give response categories that do not allow some respondents to answer in ways that are relevant to them,
- do not provide sets of categories that are exhaustive, mutually exclusive, and refer to a single dimension (key requirements for nominal scales),
- have routings that leave the respondent 'stranded' in the middle of the questionnaire or lead them into inappropriate sections of the questionnaire.

The piloting of questionnaires is frequently short-changed by market researchers and by students undertaking research in marketing. It is, however, critical for successful research. Once the questionnaire has been taken forward into the main data collection phase it is too late to make any changes. There are three main kinds of pilot study:

- qualitative research among the target population to check language and the range of likely opinions,
- pre-testing the questionnaire to see how it works,
- a small-scale pilot survey to obtain approximate results.

Pre-testing is essential for a successful survey. It is often surprising how many errors of design are uncovered at this stage, particularly if it has not been preceded by qualitative research or based on questionnaires that have already been tried. Small-scale pilot surveys are often regarded as a luxury except for large projects.

Diaries

While questionnaire design is a topic that is treated at great length in all texts on marketing research and on social research generally, diary design is rarely mentioned. It is possible to treat diaries as just another form of questionnaire, but they are sufficiently distinct to benefit from separate treatment. Diaries are distinguished by the fact that they are designed to record consumer behaviour on or between specific dates, perhaps even at specified times during the day. Furthermore, they require the respondent to complete an entry every time that behaviour occurs over the time period to which the diary refers – often a week, but perhaps two weeks or longer. Diaries thus record behaviour which is normally repeated at fairly frequent intervals, and which it would be difficult for a respondent to recall all at the one time in a questionnaire. Normally, attitudes are not measured in a diary, since such an activity may well influence the consumer behaviour being recorded. Thus if a respondent indicates certain negative views concerning a brand, then he or she may well be tempted to swap brands at the next purchase in order to be more 'consistent'.

Diaries are often used in continuous research either for panels or in regular interval surveys (see Chapter 5), but may also be employed in ad hoc survey research, experimental research of various kinds, and perhaps even to record observations made by the researcher. Normally, however, diaries will be self-completed; some may be placed personally by the interviewer, or sent by post, and may be collected personally or returned by post. Diaries may relate to individual consumers or to household activity. In the latter case, one person (usually the housewife) is made responsible for diary completion for the whole family.

There are three rather distinct kinds of diary:

- product diaries,
- media use diaries,
- contact diaries.

Product diaries record consumer purchasing and in some cases product use behaviour. They normally arrange entries on a product-by-product basis, usually covering a whole week's purchases. An example of a page from such a diary is illustrated in Figure 3.7. Such an arrangement makes it easier to obtain the specific details required for different brands, for example, to determine the flavour of yoghurt, or the kind of toothpaste dispenser. A diary also acts as a 'reminder' to the respondents, and this improves the completeness of reporting. Depending on the size of the product field, the level of detail required, and the frequency of purchasing, the diary format may be either structured, that is, all the answers are pre-coded, or semi-structured where respondents write in the brand, brand variant, shop, price, type of offer and so on. Many are a mixture of the two. Pre-coded diaries are better from the data entry and data analysis point of view, but may require very long code lists, and may need to be changed frequently as new brands are added or existing ones withdrawn. Semi-structured diaries, on the other hand, require less space, but need to be supported by sophisticated data entry systems that can allocate the appropriate codes at the data entry stage. Some product diaries are more time-based, for example, asking people to

Coffee Ground instant, freeze-dried	Brand name	Type (please tick one)				(please tick)		Weight or size on pack	No. of packs bought	Price paid per pack		Shop name	Offer on pack
		Instant		Ground		Decaffeinated				£	p		
		Powder	Freeze	Fine	Med	Yes	No						

Figure 3.7 Sample page from a product diary.

record what they ate by 'meal occasion' – breakfast, lunch, evening meal and snacks between meals.

Diaries recording the use of broadcast media tend to arrange entries by time segment on a daily basis. Radio listening diaries, for example, typically give 15-minute or 30-minute periods down the left-hand side of the page, and particular radio stations across the top, as illustrated in Figure 3.8. The respondent may be asked to tick every box against any station listened to for each time segment, or to draw vertical lines through all the time segments where listening took place.

Contact diaries ask respondents to list, check or tick each contact made with another member of a communication network. Communication networks consist of individuals who are interconnected by patterned flows of information and who create and share information with one another in order to reach mutual understanding (Rogers and Kincaid, 1981). Communication network analysis is a series of techniques for identifying the communication structures in a system and is based on the techniques of the much earlier idea of sociometry. The contacts made may be face-to-face, postal or telephone and the diary may well record contacts made on a daily basis as in Figure 3.9. The results may be fed into a communication network analysis program that measures, for example, the degree to which individuals have networks that overlap, the number of links in the shortest path joining two individuals, or the extent to which participants have like patterns of links and non-links.

Diary design

A key problem with the design of all diaries is the need to keep them up to date. Thus for structured product diaries new brands or brand variants may need to be added and others deleted where a manufacturer has dropped them from their range. Even semi-structured product diaries need to take into account the introduction of new product categories. For media diaries, the stations that radio listeners or television watchers can receive need to be continually updated, while programme diaries are notoriously difficult since last-minute changes may be made to the published programmes. Furthermore, there may need to be several versions of such diaries to take account of the

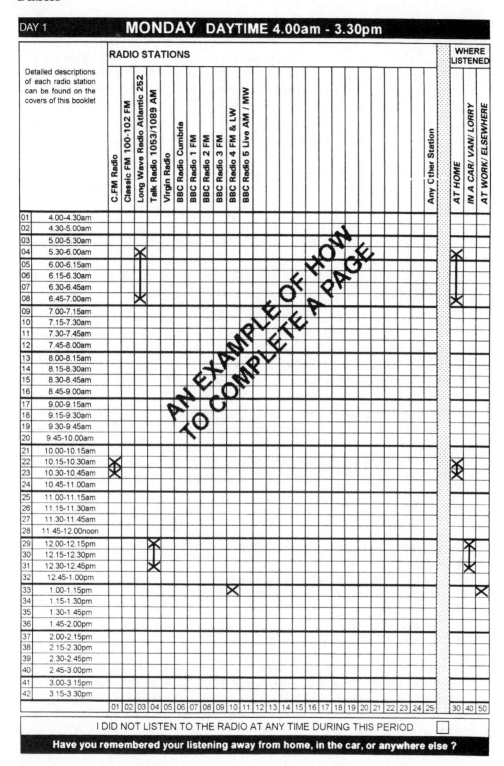

Figure 3.8 Sample page from a radio diary.

Monday

Name	Organisation	Contacts made by you										Contacts received by you									

Figure 3.9 Example of a contact diary.

different ranges of programme that may be received in different parts of the country.

In considering the overall layout and design of diaries it is necessary to bear in mind the potential sources of error in diary-keeping:

- The diary-keeper forgets to enter purchases, listening, viewing or contacts in the diary. This will often be because instead of making entries as they go along, many respondents will try to remember after a couple of days or even at the end of the week before sending the diary off.
- The record-keeper makes an entry, but makes a mistake on the details through faulty memory or erroneous recording.
- The diary is deliberately falsified either by omission of purchases, media use or contacts, or by the inclusion of imaginary purchases, uses or contacts.
- The diary-keeper is unaware of purchases or contacts made by other members of the household, or of their listening or viewing of broadcasts.

All of these sources of error may be affected by a number of factors, for example:

- the type of product or programme,
- the frequency of the activity,
- the position of the page in the diary,
- the position and prominence of the entry on the page,
- the complexity of the entry,
- the overall length and workload involved,
- the method of contact between researcher and respondent.

Thus grocery items are more likely to be remembered by housewives than personal care products, which are more often purchased by other household members. The more frequent the activity, the more likely it is to be remembered. Items at the beginning of the diary and on the tops of pages are more likely to be remembered than those in the middle and at the end if the diary, and those lower down the page. Some users of diaries, for example for radio audience measurement, rotate the order of the radio stations listed in the diary for different samples of respondents. Deliberate falsification in likely to increase with the complexity of the entry and with the overall length and workload involved.

In designing the layout of a diary, those products which are most likely to be forgotten should be put at the beginning or at the tops of pages. The effects of small diary changes can be measured by introducing changes in only a sub-sample of the total and noting differences in response. From the results of experiments in the USA, Sudman and Ferber (1979) report that adding or deleting a check box or changing the wording does not measurably affect the level of recording, but changing product headings, moving the position of a product listing in the diary, and putting in special reminders may alter, temporarily or more permanently, the level of product recording. In short, diaries are probably more sensitive than questionnaires to overall presentation and layout, but less sensitive to wording.

While it has been reported (for example, by Sudman and Ferber, 1979) that for consumer purchasing there is some evidence to suggest that survey recall data from questionnaires tend to overstate purchases compared with diaries and that the difference is greatest for well-known brands and for perishables, for media use it has been found that diaries produce more listening or watching than questionnaire recall methods (Menneer, 1989).

Recording devices

Questionnaires and diaries are mechanisms for capturing data that have been elicited by addressing listed questions to individuals. However, where a researcher observes products on a shelf or how consumers behave, observes some event taking place, like the purchase of a product or the watching of a television programme, or where a discussion without listed questions is being pursued, then some form of device, manual or electronic, needs to be employed to capture such data.

Manual recording devices are legion in business. Invoices, credit notes, stock lists, delivery notes, receipts, ledgers and accounts are often filled in by hand. The market researcher may, for example, use invoices to check how many customers, what they purchased, how frequently, what they paid and where they come from. Delivery notes may be used for retail panel operations as an input to making an estimate of sales once changes in stock levels have been checked.

When engaging in primary data collection, the researcher may use manual record sheets of various kinds to record observations. Thus interviewers from a market research company conducting a shop audit may use a manual audit form for writing in quantities of branded products observed on the shelves, on the counter and in the stockroom, and for recording the deliveries made after inspecting delivery notes. Structured observation may entail the researcher as observer noting on a record sheet the number of times a particular piece of behaviour occurs, and the amount of time taken to do or perform it. The difference between a manual record sheet and an unstructured questionnaire is that the latter depends on addressing questions to people and writing in their answers, while record sheets are used mainly to record observations made personally.

Electronic recording devices are becoming increasingly popular, particularly among the large market research organizations, who can afford the cost of the capital equipment involved. Electronic data capture may be put into four main groupings of technology:

- electronic point of sale data capture using scanning technology,
- electronic questionnaires and diaries,
- television set-meters and 'people' meters,
- audio and video-recording devices.

One innovation that is changing the focus of instruments of data capture away from paper questionnaires and paper diaries more than any other is the introduction of bar-coding on products and the utilization of laser scanners at the point of sale (sometimes called 'electronic point of sale' or EPOS technology) to capture the details of each purchase made. Bar codes give unique identification of products down to country of origin, manufacturer, brand, size, flavour and offer. In Europe a 13–digit code is used. The first two identify the country of origin, the next five are allocated by the Article Numbering Association to identify the manufacturer, the next five are allocated by the manufacturer to identify products and the last is a check digit allocated by a computer. When a laser is run over the bar code the price and other details are looked up from a central file held on a computer in the store, and are then printed out at the checkout cash desk.

Retailers have used such technology to improve the efficiency of stock control and the speed of checkout operations. Each time a sale is made the stock inventory is automatically amended, while details of products at the checkout are entered much faster. The customer also receives a detailed receipt giving a printout of each item, right down to the flavour of a brand of cat food.

Customer-based information can now be linked with each purchase by using 'smart' cards. These are similar to credit cards, and are presented at the checkout. Details of household demographics derived from the card application form and perhaps from the geodemographic characteristics of the postcode address are linked through the identification number to the purchases made on any shopping trip. Such systems do, however, require not only co-operation from the customer, but for manufacturers to benefit from such information the retailer has to pass it on, either directly or to a market research agency. It also requires that a substantial number of retailers have scanning equipment. Purchase data from such electronic recording devices can be linked with in-store customer behaviour and in-store pricing, layout and ranges of products to test the effectiveness of 'below-the-line' activity.

Scanning technology is now also being used in the home. The two largest consumer panels in the UK are equipped with electronic scanners able to read bar codes. This means that details of purchases can be recorded by the panellist simply by running the scanner over every item as the shopping is unpacked. Computer terminals may be used to enable panellists to key in prices and the names of the shops where the goods were bought. All this information is then transferred to a central computer, enabling rapid analyses of purchasing patterns to be produced.

Electronic questionnaires are increasingly used in two main contexts: computer-assisted telephone interviewing (CATI) and computer-assisted personal interviewing (CAPI).

With CATI the questionnaire is programmed into a central computer before interviewing begins. It is then displayed question by question on a number of visual display units in a central location. An interviewer sits in front of each screen and telephones the selected number. The replies are immediately entered via the keyboard. The advantages of this system are:

- no paper questionnaires are required,
- last-minute changes can be made to the questionnaire,
- routing is automatic, with the interviewer being passed straight to the next relevant question,
- results can be assessed at any time during the survey,
- tables can be run as soon as interviewing is completed,
- range checks and logical checks can be automatically applied.

With CAPI the interviewer has a market research terminal which is in effect a small portable computer with a screen which displays the questions as for CATI. Either the interviewer can key in the answers, or, in some cases, the respondent is handed the terminal to key in his or her own. The data can then be sent down the telephone at the press of a button (using portable telephone technology). Using CAPI has slashed the time it takes to produce comprehensive research results, but, of course, it is very much more expensive.

A more recent development still is interviewing over the Internet, or Computer Assisted Web Interviewing (CAWI). It is easy to attach a questionnaire to a World Wide Web site, but it is difficult to control who responds to it. Those who do may be very unrepresentative of the population of interest.

Meters have been used for measuring the use of television since the 1940s in the USA. Early meters simply recorded the total time the television was tuned on, and were used as a check against gross error in diary completion among a representative sample of panel households. More recent 'set-meters' recorded the channel to which the set was tuned on a continuous basis, but were still used in conjunction with diaries to record who was watching. Diaries could be abandoned only with the introduction in 1984 of AGB's 'peoplemeter'. This uses a remote control hand-set associated with each television for members of the panel household to indicate their presence in the room where a television is switched on by pressing a button with a number to which they have been allocated. They press the number again when they leave the room. Such 'push-button' or 'active' meter systems have had to become more sophisticated to cope with the use of VCRs to time-shift viewing, viewing on pre-recorded video tapes, viewing and recording at the same time, multi-set households, the use of television for teletext, home computers, and the introduction of cable and satellite television. At present, the peoplemeter system can cope with guest viewing by allocating button numbers to additional guests, but viewing of household members outside the home is a problem.

Every television set owned or rented by a panel of households is equipped with a 'slave' meter or remote detector unit. It sits on top of the television and has its own display screen for giving messages to or seeking responses from the people in the room. Each feeds to a master meter via the domestic wiring system. The master meter is in turn linked to the domestic telephone line and the day's electronic data are passed every night to a central computer which dials up each household to retrieve the viewing data. The figures are processed the following morning. The record is on a second-by-second basis, although viewing is aggregated to the nearest minute or some multiple of that. How these data are used to produce television ratings is explained in Chapter 8.

Audio and video-recording devices may be used for marketing research in a number of different ways. Traditionally, the tape-recorder has been employed for qualitative research, particularly for depth interviews, but increasingly group discussions are tape-recorded. The tape-recorder has the advantage of cheapness and portability. It also captures everything the respondent says and so cannot be accused of selectivity. Normally, the respondents' answers are transcribed before being used for analysis. Since the interviewer's questions are also recorded, the tape can be used to check that the interview was conducted in a proper manner. Tape recorders can, of course, also be used by the researcher for recording in words what he or she is observing, plus any thoughts that come to mind.

Video recorders, by comparison, are relatively recent, but the development of the 'camcorder' has facilitated the recording of consumer behaviour on a continuous basis and in most lighting conditions. Video recording may be in an organized data collection context, for example, for group discussions, or it may be in place of personal observation, for example, using the video to record the movement of people in and out of shops.

Further developments may well take the form of linking some of the various technologies together. Thus technically it is possible to link the purchases made by homes that have scanning equipment or 'smart' cards with those that have television meters installed. This means that television viewing may be directly linked with purchasing behaviour and with below-the-line activity in the shop. The direct effect of television advertising can thus be monitored on a continuous basis. As yet in the UK, television audience measurement panels are not linked up in this way, but the technology is there to make it possible.

While the introduction of such systems may be somewhat futuristic, their development would create a major leap in the quantities of data captured. Whether our ability to analyse them will be outstripped could turn out to be a major issue.

Summary

Data may be captured using one or more of three key instruments: questionnaires, diaries or recording devices, which may be manual or electronic. Questionnaires may be structured to varying degrees and may be self-completed or interviewer-completed. Formal, structured questionnaires tend to have a predominance of set-choice, pre-coded questions which may be used to collect demographic, behavioural or perceptual data. Questionnaire wording needs to ensure, as far as possible, that respondents understand the questions, have the information to enable them to provide answers, and are willing to provide the answers. Questionnaire layout and presentation are particularly important for self-completed questionnaires, but must not be overlooked where part-time paid interviewers are used. Layout needs to bear in mind not only the respondent's convenience, but also the needs of the interviewer and the data analyst. Questionnaires that are not pre-tested in some way are unlikely to meet the needs of the researcher and his or her client.

Diaries may be distinguished from questionnaires on the basis that they are time-based, and refer exclusively to repeated behaviour rather than to attitudes or possessions. Product diaries tend to be laid out on a product-by-product basis while media diaries are likely to utilize time segments. Diary design needs to bear in mind the potential sources of error in diary-keeping and the various factors that affect them. The issue of whether diaries or questionnaire recall methods result in the recording of higher or lower levels of activity is one on which the evidence so far is, at best, inconclusive.

Recording devices may be manual or electronic, but it is the latter that have seen the major development in recent times. These devices include point-of-sale scanning equipment, electronic questionnaires and diaries, television meters, and audio and video-recording equipment. Further developments in technology are likely to see these devices being used in conjunction with one another to provide quantities of data which, on present data analysis expertise and facilities, may be difficult to handle. While the use of electronic equipment often obviates the need for sampling and making estimates, they tend to be expensive and, in their more sophisticated versions, the preserve of the larger market research organizations.

Key concepts

questionnaire	pre-coding
fixed-choice question	routing
open-ended question	filter questions
single-response question	self-competed questionnaires
multiple response questions	interviewer-completed questionnaires
structured questionnaires	pilot study
unstructured questionnaires	diary
product diaries	
media use diaries	
contact diaries	
computer-assisted telephone interviewing (CATI)	
computer-assisted personal interviewing (CAPI)	
computer-assisted Web interviewing (CAWI)	

Further reading

■ Hague, P (1993) *Questionnaire Design*, London: Kogan Page.
■ Evans, N (1995) *Using Questionnaires and Surveys to Boost Your Business*, London: Pitman.

Questions for further discussion

1   A manufacturer of hair-dryers wants to find out:
    ■ what proportion of households in the UK own a hair-dryer,
    ■ what proportions and types of individual in households with hair-dryers use it on every occasion after hair-washing,

■ the major product features respondents are looking for.
Design a questionnaire for use in face-to-face interviews that will obtain this information from a sample of households.

2   Specify the changes that will be needed if the questionnaire in the previous exercise is to be used as a postal questionnaire.

3   British Telecom wants to discover the age profile and telephone use behaviour of different age groups. Discuss the strengths and weaknesses of using a diary compared with a questionnaire to capture such data.

4

Data collection methods

The instruments of data capture that were considered in Chapter 3 – questionnaires, diaries and recording devices – may be used in a variety of different data collection methods. Each may be utilized not only in survey research, but also in personal observation, qualitative research, a range of different experimental and quasi-experimental situations and in continuous research. All these methods create 'primary' data, but if such data are subsequently used for another purpose, they become 'secondary' data. It is, of course, nearly always sensible to begin any project by seeking out whatever data may already exist that are relevant to the purposes of the research, but it should not be forgotten that such data were originally collected using primary techniques. It is to these that we now turn.

Personal observation

Personal observation, as opposed to observations taken by mechanical means, can be used whenever it is possible to collect data by watching what consumers do in the process of purchasing goods or services, by checking the quality of services provided by retail and service outlets, or by noting the availability, quantity and prices of branded goods on shelves in shops or in the home./Observation may be the only realistic option available where to ask people questions may result in misleading information and where there are no mechanical or electronic means of taking systematic records.

Consumer behaviour can be watched either in its natural or in an artificial setting. In a natural setting an observer may, for example, note the length of queues at checkouts in a supermarket at specified intervals during the day, the length of time motorists spend in a filling station, or whether or not they are wearing seat-belts while driving. In pubs and bars at least one market research agency positions 'monitors' to watch how people go about ordering drinks. Observation in a natural context is usually disguised, that is, the people being observed are unaware of the fact. This is usually seen to be perfectly acceptable if the behaviour is in a public place where it can be watched by anybody. Disguised observation has the added advantage that the behaviour being recorded will not be affected by the process of observation. Undisguised observation in a natural setting is exemplified by what is often called 'accompanied shopping'. An observer from a market research agency accompanies a housewife as she goes round a supermarket, noting how she goes about making selection of brands, whether prices are checked and so on. The interview will usually begin in the respondent's own home with a discussion about his or her state of mind concerning the purchase and the influences that may affect the decision. Both respondent and researcher then go to the shop where the respondent will be encouraged to ignore the researcher and carry on looking, choosing and buying as normal. The researcher will observe and record the respondent's progress. The last part of the interview will involve a full discussion of what has taken place, how this matched expectations of the visit and how this differed from recalled behaviour. However, there is always the danger that if people are aware of being observed, they may try to act more 'rationally' than they would normally do.

In an artificial context, group discussions (to be explained later) may be tape-recorded or videoed in a systematic manner, or consumers may be invited to purchase goods in an artificial 'store' where their choice behaviour is monitored using in-store cameras.

One method for checking the quality of services provided by retail and other service outlets is mystery shopping or mystery customer research. This involves visits by specially trained assessors to shops, restaurants, banks or other businesses in which quality of provision is to be evaluated (Morrison *et al.*, 1997). The assessors pose as ordinary customers and check the attainment of pre-defined service standards that have been drawn up in consultation with the client. Thus, for a bank, was the assessor attended to within two minutes? Was she greeted with a smile? Was the transaction completed efficiently? Was she asked if she wanted any further services? From the results it is possible to compare branches of the bank and see what proportions reach given standards. These performances can then be compared with the performances of competitors. Any failings can be identified and incorporated into a training or retraining programme for staff.

Mystery shopping is ideal when the client has certain standards of actual service performance that he or she wants evaluated by a trained customer. There may be some aspects of service that the company deems to be important, so the mystery shopper is trained to look for these things that the ordinary consumer may not notice. One development of mystery shopping is competitor mystery shopping. Instead of getting assessors to pose as shoppers for the organization's own outlets, it does this to competitors. There are ethical issues here, particularly in relation to potentially wasting the time of assistants in competitor outlets.

Mystery customer research, although not without its critics (like Brown, 1990), is an industry currently worth an estimated £10 million annually in the UK (Miles, 1993) and is growing rapidly. A survey of commercial companies carried out by Dawson and Hillier (1995) found that more than two-thirds had commissioned mystery consumer research in their own companies, on competitor companies or both. Some companies, however, avoid using mystery shopping because of worries about potential problems that might arise in the absence of stringent guidelines to ensure accuracy of evaluations. Despite codes of conduct that have been introduced by the Market Research Society and ESOMAR, some aspects of the technique are open to interpretation and manipulation. Morrison *et al.* (1997) comment on potential threats to the reliability and validity of the data collected by such means. Various factors associated with the encoding, storage and retrieval of information by mystery consumer assessors are likely to influence the accuracy of the results. Thus memory may be affected by a range of factors like lighting, physical conditions, time of day, attitudes, social pressures or mood. Furthermore, individual differences between assessors should also be taken into account in designing such research, although such differences may be deliberately planned in to see, for example, if banks or insurance companies treat female or black customers in the same way as male or white.

To note the availability, quantity and prices of branded goods on shelves in shops or in the home, a number of market research agencies, particularly those which offer retail panel services, send observers into selected shops to record systematically, for a specified range of branded goods, whether these products are available on the shelves, in display areas or in the stockroom. The length of facings occupied by a brand may be measured, its price noted and perhaps quantities counted. In a full retail audit such data may be used in combination with records of deliveries to calculate sales. Some agencies restrict themselves to 'distribution checks' or offer 'shelf-observation' services. It is also possible, of course, to observe what products and what brands people have on the shelves, in cupboards, or in the fridge at home.

Except where observation is being used for exploratory research in order to get the 'feel' for some situation, it is usually structured. This means that observations are recorded into pre-determined categories so that the frequency of behavioural occurrences, or durations, or lengths of shelf space can be noted. The result is quantitative data that may be metric or non-metric. The key advantage of observation over asking people questions is that no reliance is placed on people's memories, guesses, or honesty. There is little point in asking people if they always wear a seat-belt when driving; they will always say 'yes'. It is better to observe how many in fact do.

Observation, clearly, has its limitations and drawbacks. Often it is just not possible or feasible. It is also labour-intensive – one person can observe the occurrence of only a limited number of phenomena. Observation can be only of behaviour; it is not possible to observe attitudes, opinion, or what people think. Observation is undoubtedly under-utilized as a data-capture technique in market research, but it is probably best used not on its own, but in combination with other techniques.

Qualitative research

Qualitative research in marketing is characterized by two main features:

- it is based on open-ended interview methods,
- it collects data that are largely qualitative and in the form of narrative rather than isolated statements.

Not all qualitative research is based on interview methods: in sociology, for example, participant observation is a key method. However, participating in and observing social groupings or communities in their own natural environment is not so appropriate in marketing. The open-ended nature of the interviews used in marketing means that the process of questioning is flexible and responsive to what individuals or groups of individuals say. It is not predetermined as in a formal survey. This maximizes the opportunities to obtain from the respondents what they, uniquely, have to offer by way of information, experiences, feelings, images, attitudes, ideas and so on.

The narrative offered by respondents will usually be captured using either a tape recorder or video camera. The problems and features peculiar to analysing and interpreting such data are considered later, once we have looked at the main types of qualitative research and their applications.

Other features common to qualitative research, but not defining characteristics of it, include:

■ the use of small samples of respondents who are not necessarily representative of a larger population,
■ the direct involvement of the research executive in a number of stages of the research, including the planning and design of the research, conducting the interviews, analysing the results, and presenting them to clients,
■ it is concerned with understanding consumer perceptions and consumer behaviour rather than measuring the extent of their occurrence.

Until the 1970s, qualitative research was very much the Cinderella of market research, often dismissed as not serious, lacking in scientific rigour, non-replicable, non-generalizable and subjective. However, in the last decade, the amount of qualitative research undertaken has undergone an explosive growth. By 1990 the value of qualitative market research undertaken by members of AMSO was just over £26 million, some 10 per cent of all commissioned research. This undoubtedly underestimates the proportion of qualitative market research carried out by non-AMSO agencies or conducted in-house. In 1981 the Association of Qualitative Research Practitioners (AQRP) was established, and it now has over 500 members who variously work in research agencies, advertising and in major client organizations. The Association Directory, first published in 1992, lists over 100 agencies offering qualitative research. Of the 500 agencies listed in the *Market Research Society Handbook* for 1994, over 80 per cent claimed to offer qualitative market research among their data collection methods. Many agencies were established to specialize in such activity; the larger ones set up separate divisions to handle qualitative research or bought out a subsidiary company to whom such work could be passed on.

The main reasons for this growth include:

■ a greater understanding and appreciation of the role of qualitative market research,
■ its relative cheapness and speed,
■ its proven effectiveness in a growing range of applications.

The main types of qualitative research

In the market research industry, practitioners talk about 'groups' and 'depths' in the context of qualitative research. The terms distinguish the two main types of qualitative research in marketing: group discussions (called 'focus groups' in the USA) and depth interviews. It is tempting to suggest that the key difference between them is that depth interviews are on a one-to-one basis between researcher and respondent, and that groups involve several respondents together with the researcher in the same room at the same time. However, some depth interviews may take place with married couples, families, or even two or three friends together; some group discussions may be in groups as small as five or six respondents. A more crucial difference is that in depth interviews the main lines of communication are between interviewer and respondent; in group discussions, it is the verbal interactions between respondents that assume a major role.

Group discussions

Most of the qualitative research conducted in the UK is by way of group discussions; so much so that qualitative research is regarded by some buyers and clients as synonymous with such methods. Clients, furthermore, often see group discussions as being little more than a convenient (and relatively cheap) way of gathering the views of more than one person at a time. However, as indicated above, it is the interactions between respondents that are important. Groups take on a life of their own, varying from group to group, and are influenced by a large number of factors including the size of the group, its composition, the personalities of those present, the tasks they are asked to perform, the physical conditions of the meeting place, and the 'chemistry' between interviewer and respondents. The group itself has an influence back on the individual, and what is said relates to the total experience of being in the group. The results achieved by group discussions are more than, or at least different from, the sum of what would be obtained by interviewing respondents individually.

Clearly, different views may be taken about the optimum size of group, but the norm that has developed in the UK is that 'standard' groups have seven to nine respondents, with eight being the favoured number since it facilitates different combinations in terms of the composition of the groups. A standard group discussion will not normally be longer than an hour and a half. Where it is felt that a longer time is needed, for example to perform more complex tasks, then such groups will be referred to as 'extended' groups.

When planning group discussions, the main considerations in terms of setting up and running the groups include:

- the type of group,
- group composition,
- the number of groups,
- recruitment,
- topics to be discussed,
- method of running the group,
- the places, venues and timings.

Apart from the standard groups already referred to, the main variations in types of group include those outlined in Table 4.1. Most groups, however, are standard. The variations may be used where standard groups have not produced fresh information or the kind of information required.

Group composition is a difficult decision. There are two main issues.

- Who does the researcher want to talk to?
- Should the groups be homogeneous or heterogeneous in terms of key characteristics?

The first issue means defining the population to be studied and from which the sample of respondents will be chosen. For branded products, a key choice is in terms of product usage. Should the groups consist of:

- brand users only,

Group types	Characteristics
Table 4.1 Characteristics of the main variations from standard discussion groups	
Mini-groups	For 5–6 people. Used for interviewing children, for sensitive, intimate or personal topics, when there is a need to explore individual behaviour, or for brief, quick-reaction groups.
Extended groups	Standard size, but last 3–4 hours. Use more complex tasks, a lot of stimulus material or projective techniques. For more in-depth explorations of psychological issues or for studying complex or fragmented markets
Reconvened groups	Meet on or than one occasion, e.g. two sessions separated by a week. Normally used for trying out a product between meetings
Sensitivity panels	The same respondents are used on a number of occasions, attending weekly or two-weekly sessions. Respondents are trained using a variety of different techniques. Best for exploration, invention and diagnosis, not evaluation
Creativity groups	Uses brainstorming or synectics for problem-solving in an innovative manner

■ product class users only,
■ users and non-users of the product?

It also needs to be decided whether the usage categories should include both sexes, all ages, all social classes or just some of these.

In terms of the second issue, the choices range from making each group homogeneous in terms of key characteristics to deliberately ensuring a cross-section in each group. Key variables will commonly be product usage, sex and age. If, for example, it has been decided to use four groups with product usage and age as the key variables, the creation of relatively homogeneous group might be as illustrated in Table 4.2. This facilitates analysis since, apart from perhaps mini-groups, it is not usually possible to identify which individuals have made which comments. However, if a particular comment comes only from groups I and IV, these are users; if it comes from II and IV, it is the older groups. The drawback is that discussions between users and non-users is eliminated; so is discussion between younger and older people. If the four groups are all mixed, there is maximum potential for divergent opinions, but relating these opinions to product usage or demographic characteristics will be difficult.

Using more categories, for example, four age groups and three usage categories – heavy, medium and light – or more variables, for example, sex and region, makes too many combinations for the number of groups required. One possibility is to use other experimental designs like Latin squares (explained later on pp. 105) in which not every combination is applied.

Qualitative research is small-scale research, and it would not be normal to run more than about 12 groups. Diminishing marginal returns rapidly set in

Group	Usage	Age
Table 4.2 An example of homogeneous grouping		
I	Users	20–35
II	Non-users	36–50
III	Non-users	20–35
IV	Users	36–50

thereafter and interviewers will find themselves anticipating most responses and learning little new from additional groups. In the 1980s a common design was to have four groups, two north, two south, two ABC1 and two C2DE. Further multiples of four facilitate other permutations. Goodyear (1990) suggests that for strategic projects or for exploratory research more groups, perhaps up to 30, may be required; tactical projects on the other hand may require only two to eight groups. Gordon and Langmaid (1988), however, suggest that unless the research is working in a highly segmented market, for example, financial services, it becomes unwieldy to conduct a large number of group discussions.

In terms of recruitment, there are two main aspects: sampling and persuading those selected to attend the group discussion. Sampling is usually disproportionate quota sampling. Part-time recruiters, who either work for the agency conducting the research or who operate freelance and who live in the area selected for one or more groups, are asked to recruit the required number of people who meet the quota requirements. Recruiters will receive both telephone and written instructions on the project.

Usually there will be a short recruitment questionnaire that screens out those not part of the population to be studied. For those remaining, the recruiter will ascertain the information required for quota controls and, where appropriate, for allocation to a particular group. The quotas will normally be in terms of sex, age, social class and product usage, but not necessarily proportionate to their numbers in the population. Thus the recruiter may be asked to obtain eight users and eight non-users of Brand A, even though, say, only 10 per cent of the defined population use Brand A. More recently, life cycle, lifestyle and attitudes may be used as quotas, but this complicates considerably the recruitment questionnaire.

How individuals who meet the quota requirements are located is usually up to the individual recruiter. Normally it will be by door-to-door interviewing, but if, for example, the recruiter is asked to obtain mothers with young children, she may stand outside a number of school gates or health clinics. Care is usually taken to avoid recruiting friends or relatives to the same groups, and to avoid people who have frequently or recently been interviewed for market research purposes.

Some difficult-to-find respondents may be obtained through social networks using snowball sampling, that is, using contacts to suggest others who may be in the same category, then using these contacts to suggest further contacts, and so on.

Qualitative research agencies each have their own ways of operating. Some use field managers or supervisors; others may employ direct researcher-to-recruiter contact. There is often a problem of over-researched areas where recruiters happen to live. There has also been talk of 'professional groupies' – those who seem to make a habit of appearing in group discussions.

Unlike other areas of market research, respondents in group discussions are usually paid an 'incentive' to cover travel expenses, time and inconvenience. Few people, however, attend just for the money. Curiosity is a powerful motivator, but it is usually the skill of the recruiter in establishing rapport on the doorstep that is the deciding factor. Good recruiters plan where and how to recruit, setting daily targets, and try to find the most difficult categories of people first. Sometimes, former respondents are recontacted after a statutory 'fallow' period, or members of the respondent's family are co-opted by telephone.

The topics to be discussed in the groups will be those agreed between the client and the agency at the briefing meeting, and may even be formalized in a written research proposal. The interviewers will normally be given guidelines on how the topics are to be introduced and in what order, but it will be up to the interviewer to decide when to move on to the next topic. This may be because time is pressing, because he or she has decided that the topic has been sufficiently aired or senses that respondents are beginning to dry up or tire of the topic.

It is in the method of running groups that there is probably most variation. The three key dimensions here are the role of the group interviewer, the use of stimulus material and the use of projective techniques. The group interviewer is usually referred to as a 'moderator'. He or she will usually be a research executive from the agency that specializes in qualitative market research and who will have been involved with the initial discussions and briefing with clients and who will write up the results and possibly present them. Where the number of groups is small, the same person will probably do them all, otherwise a small team may be required. Sometimes agencies will sub-contract to professional moderators operating on a freelance basis.

The main tasks of the moderator are to:

■ ensure that the conditions of the discussion are correctly set up,
■ get the discussion going,
■ introduce new topics as appropriate,
■ wind up the discussion in a satisfactory manner.

If the venue is a private house, then the moderator will need to check the seating arrangements. As far as possible, this should be in a circle with all the chairs the same height. This is often difficult with a mixture of sofas, armchairs, stools and dining chairs. Normally, the discussion will be tape recorded, so it is necessary to check that this is correctly placed and in working order. If stimulus materials are to be used, they, too, will need to be checked.

There is no agreed pattern or routine for getting the discussion going. Sometimes respondents are shown into the room where the moderator is as they arrive. The moderator will need to engage them in small talk until all are present, but it does mean that some rapport is set up in advance. Sometimes the respondents gather elsewhere in the house and are shown into the room together. When beginning, the moderator will introduce himself or herself, say on behalf of what agency the research is being conducted, and indicate the topics that are to be covered. Usually there will be reassurances that all responses are confidential, that it is not a 'test', so there are no 'correct' answers, that the tape recorder is only to help make a note of what people say. Some moderators believe in warm-up or ice-breaking strategies, for example, getting respondents to introduce themselves and say what they do. There is a danger here of establishing a 'turn-taking' routine with each communication being directed to the moderator. The moderator needs above all to encourage the respondents to interact and to communicate with each other.

Once a discussion begins, the moderator can follow one of three main roles: take a 'back seat' and just observe what is happening with little intervention (although the 'fly-on-the-wall' model is no longer accepted); become one of the group; continue to be the focus of attention. Each of these has its strengths and drawbacks. In the end it is probably best for the moderator to play the role that he or she feels most comfortable with or feels is appropriate for that particular group.

There are few general rules or guides as to how the moderator should proceed as he or she introduces the appropriate topics. The sequencing of topics and tasks will have been agreed with the client before the discussions begin. For example, should respondents be shown the new packaging for the product before they discuss the existing brand, or afterwards? The moderator will have a topic guide or perhaps even a full interview guide which explains how respondents are to be asked to take part in all stages of the interview. The moderator will need to understand the processes of group dynamics to ensure a successful outcome. Thus it has been suggested (for example by Tuckman, 1986) that all groups go through four key stages: forming, storming, norming and performing. In the forming stage there is a lot of superficial chat. The moderator needs to give respondents easy tasks to do and encourage them to develop a group spirit. As participants begin to size each other up, competitiveness creeps in, and there may be rivalries for attention and control. This is the storming stage, and the moderator will need to help the group to get to the next stage, norming, before it can work together effectively. Acceptable ways of doing things become established and people settle down to the task at hand. In the last stage, performing, the group should be ready to tackle more demanding tasks.

Winding up the discussion in a satisfactory manner is all too frequently neglected. A group that has been operating well together needs a few moments to wind down. Signals that the discussion is nearly over need to be given, for example: 'The last thing I'd like you to do is . . . '. If the moderator brings the discussion to an abrupt end, people my feel that they have been used and then just dropped, and a sense of dissatisfaction may develop.

In running groups, not only does the moderator have to be aware of group dynamics, he or she needs to use non-verbal communication – body language such as posture, tone of voice, eye contact, facial expression – to keep the social interaction proceeding smoothly. At the end of the day it is the moderator's responsibility to:

- direct the flow of the discussion over areas that are important to the research,
- recognize important points and encourage groups to explore them and elaborate on them,
- observe all the non-verbal communication between respondents and between respondents and moderator,
- create an atmosphere that allows respondents to relax and lower some of their defences,
- synthesize the understanding gained with the problems and objectives of the research,
- test out hypotheses generated by the information gained as the discussion proceeds.

All this requires training and it takes practice. Gordon and Langmaid (1988) suggest that, in their experience, two years is an absolute minimum from setting out as a novice to attaining a thorough grounding in both group and individual interviewing skills.

The role of the moderator, then, is crucial for how group discussions are run. There are, however, two other key factors that come into play: the use of stimulus materials and the use of projective techniques. Stimulus materials may be shown to respondents to communicate the idea of a new product, pack or advertising, and may be realistic or rough. Real materials include actual products, advertising or promotional materials. Wherever possible, real materials are to be preferred. If the topic for discussion is a particular existing brand of snack or drink then it can become part of the discussion. However, if the products are not yet fully developed, the rough materials might include:

■ concept boards,
■ storyboards,
■ animatics,
■ narrative tapes,
■ physical mock-ups.

Concept boards are single posters in which the product, pack or advertising for the product is described in words or expressed as drawings. It would be usual to use a set of concept boards for comparative purposes rather than one on its own. Storyboards illustrate key frames from a commercial, drawn consecutively like a comic strip. They may be accompanied by a script written below or by a tape recorder with sound effects. Sometimes the frames are revealed one by one using flip-over boards to stop respondents reading ahead. Animatics are a bit like crude cartoons with a sequence of frames videoed to represent live action and accompanied by a sound track. Variations are photomatics – using photographs to show the story more realistically – or admatics, which use computer-generated images to improve on animatics. Narrative tapes are audio tapes on which the product, the dialogue, the scene and characters are explained. The tapes may be accompanied by key visuals. Physical mock-ups may be of the product itself or of the packaging. The idea is to make the product as 'real' as possible.

The problem with such rough materials is that they are usually viewed as 'real' by respondents, who do not 'see' the concept board, but a real advertisement. In consequence, many researchers use more indirect means where the stimulus materials are ambiguous. Such 'projective' techniques, as they are called, have their roots in psychoanalysis and are based on theories that suggest that as children develop, they deal with those aspects of their behaviour and personality that are unwanted by projecting them out onto the environment, or by repressing them, that is, denying their existence. As a consequence, there are aspects of adult personality, feelings and emotions that people are not aware of at a cognitive level. Projective techniques tap these repressed or projected elements by asking individuals to respond to ambiguous stimuli. The result, so advocates of these techniques argue, is that respondents reveal layers of their personality, emotions and feelings that would otherwise remain hidden.

Practitioners tend to have their own preferred techniques, but the most common are procedures for:

- association,
- completion,
- transformation,
- construction.

Association procedures include word association (e.g. 'What do you associate with the word . . . ?'), collage building (from a wide variety of materials cut out from magazines), or psycho-drawing. Completion procedures include sentence completion, story completion or bubble cartoons (asking respondents to fill in thought bubbles of people drawn in simple cartoon style). Transformation procedures involve inviting respondents to imagine transforming brands into people (e.g. 'If this brand came to life as a person, what would he or she be like?') or into animals, or to transform themselves into a brand. Construction procedures ask respondents construct a role (e.g. acting out a buying situation) or to construct an obituary for a brand, saying what it would be remembered for and so on.

Interpreting responses to these procedures clearly requires skill and imagination. It also requires sensitivity to judge when is the most appropriate moment to introduce them. In addition, there is the danger of using such techniques casually and only as a form of substitute stimulus material.

The remaining issues concerning the setting up and running of group discussions concern the place, the venue and the timing. It is unreasonable to expect respondents to travel long distances to attend group discussions. In consequence, in the UK, there has been a tendency for groups to be held in the home of the recruiter to which both the moderator from the agency and the respondents come. Respondents are more likely to feel comfortable in a private house, particularly if the discussion is held in the evening. However, there are problems. People's living rooms will vary in many ways and are not always suitable in terms of seating arrangements or space to display a large concept board.

In the USA and in many other countries it is more usual to have specially equipped consumer laboratories or viewing rooms to which respondents are invited. Clients may view one or more of the discussions from behind a one-way mirror to get a feel for how they are conducted and the kinds of things that get said about their products. Viewing facilities in London are now becoming more commonplace, but in the regions they are rare. If a client wishes to see groups in operation he or she will need to join the group in person. However, if clients wish groups to be videoed, then recruiters' sitting rooms may not be suitable. It is frequently argued, however, that central viewing facilities tend to inhibit relaxed discussion and are more likely to induce groups to perform their tasks like committees.

Depth interviews

It has already been suggested that the crucial difference between depth interviews and group discussions is that in the former the main lines of communication are between interviewer and respondent (or respondents), rather than between respondents themselves. To distinguish depth interviews from the kind of standard questionnaire administered face-to-face interviews, it is helpful to remember that qualitative research is based on open-ended interview methods. This means that the interviewer is not constrained by pre-coded questions or even by a fixed sequence of questions. It is more along the lines of a conversation on an agreed topic, and the data are captured in the form of narrative rather than isolated statements.

When planning depth interviews, the main design considerations are:

- who to talk to,
- the type of interview,
- the degree of 'depth' required,
- the degree of structuring,
- the use of stimulus material,
- the location and method of data capture.

There are three key sub-issues relating to the first design consideration, who to talk to. First, what kind of person, second, how many people and third how they are to be selected. 'Executive' interviews will be with managers in organizations whether business or non-profit-making, and will concern either the role, actions or perceptions of that individual in the organization, or information about the way in which the organization (or parts of it) does things. Consumer interviews will be outside the organizational or work context and will treat individuals as private consumers. Since depth interviews are usually one-to-one, they take a considerable amount of time, so 10–15 interviews may be all that is needed to get a feel for the kinds of views being expressed. The selection of potential respondents to approach will, for executive interviews, be based on the position of the individual in the company; the selection of companies or organizations themselves will often be based on business directories or directories of other types of organization. The selection and recruitment of consumers will usually be on the same basis as for group discussions, that is, they are 'pre-recruited'. This means that they have already agreed to the interview at the recruitment stage.

Who to talk to overlaps with the consideration of the type of interview because, for example, executive and consumer interviews are different types of interview based on the kind of person. Interview type may also be based on the role the interviewee is expected to play, and on the number of people involved in the same interview. Interviewees may act as either (or both) informants or as respondents. As informants they give information which is not about themselves, but about the organization in which they work or are members. Many executive interviews are of this kind where the manager is being asked by the researcher for information about the organization and the way it operates. However, consumer interviews may be about information on other members of the family, for example, how much television they watch. As respondents, people give personal information – either their role in an organization or their role as consumers. The researcher may, of course, ask the interviewee to act in both these roles.

Not all depth interviews are one-to-one. Some are paired, triangular or family interviews. Executive interviewing will sometimes be with more than one executive together, for example, the marketing manager and the public relations officer. Consumer interviews may be with married couples or the whole family at home. Young children can often be more successfully interviewed in a family context than in a peer group environment. Willis (1990: 256) suggests that triangular interviews, consisting of three participants who often know one another are very useful among teenagers, particularly in sensitive product areas. Such interviews encourage interaction and can even be set up to encourage debate, for example, by deliberately recruiting a user, a non-user and a lapsed user to discuss a product. At this point the depth interview is barely distinguishable from a mini-group discussion, except perhaps in terms of the number of participants. Family interviews may be necessary where it is important to understand the influences of individual family members on the purchase of shared products.

The term 'depth' interview can be something of a misnomer for some of the interviews that are included in this category. Depth is a matter of degree, and some may be quite superficial. Some interviews may be journalistic in nature. They accept what people say at face value, they are descriptive and seek basic information from respondents. Genuine depth interviews go beyond the face value, looking for patterns and frameworks, and interpreting the meanings and implications of what was said. Projective techniques may be used to tap 'hidden' emotions. 'Mini-depth' interviews may be conducted over a short 15–30 minute period, for example, to test a specific piece of communication (such as a pack design), or to explore specific research objectives. A 'standard' consumer depth interview will last 45 minutes to an hour. 'Extended' depths may last for up to two and a half hours and will be used in circumstances similar to extended group discussions.

The degree of structuring may be anything from completely open-ended to a semi-structured interview in which there is a detailed interview guide to the topics to be covered. The various kinds of stimulus material and the use of projective techniques have already been explained in the context of group discussions, but the choice and design of the stimuli must be appropriate to the one-to-one nature of most interviews. It can be more complex than for group discussions since the respondent is not distracted by the interaction of the group environment.

The location of depth interviews is, in the UK, normally in respondents' own homes, but may be in the recruiters' homes, in a central location with a viewing room, or in a hotel. Factors affecting the decision will include the sensitivity of the topic matter, the status, availability and location of the interviewees, the nature and amount of stimulus material to be used, and the need for the interview to be observed by others. Executive interviews will usually be in the office of the executive or occasionally in one of the company meeting rooms.

Normally, the interview will be tape-recorded. In a central location viewing room there will usually be facilities for videoing the interview as well as to observe it while remaining unseen. This, however, may be unsettling for the individuals concerned, perhaps more so than for groups, when the feeling of being watched or videoed together may not be so threatening as when being individually 'exposed' or 'watched'.

The choice of method

Most qualitative research is undertaken using group discussions and it is felt by some writers (e.g. Gordon and Langmaid, 1988) that depth interviews are seriously underrated and often misused or misunderstood by buyers of qualitative research. In deciding which of the two methods to use, it is helpful to bear in mind the advantages and limitations of each.

The key advantages of group discussions are:

■ the group environment with 'everybody in the same boat' can be less intimidating than individual depth interviews,

■ what respondents say in a group often sparks experiences or ideas on the part of others,

■ differences between consumers are highlighted, making it possible to understand a range of attitudes in a short space of time,

■ it is easier to observe groups,

■ social and cultural influences are highlighted,

■ groups provide a social context that is a 'hot-housed' reflection of the real world,

■ groups tend to be dynamic and often, though not necessarily, more creative,

■ groups are relatively cheaper and faster than depth interviews.

The main disadvantages of groups are:

■ group processes may inhibit some people from making a full contribution and may encourage others to play to the audience,

■ group processes may stall beyond retrieval by the moderator,

■ some groups take on a life of their own, and what is said may have validity only in that context,

■ it is not usually possible to identify which group members said what unless it has been videoed.

Turning now to depth interviews, their key strengths are where the group discussion is weak, for example:

■ longitudinal information, for example, on decision-making processes, can be gathered one respondent at a time,

■ it is possible to identify exactly who said what,

■ both majority and minority opinions can be captured irrespective of personalities and group processes,

■ intimate and personal material can be more easily discussed,

■ respondents are less likely to simply express socially acceptable attitudes and behaviour,

■ problems of recruitment to a group are avoided.

The main disadvantages of depth interviews are:

■ they are time-consuming both to conduct and to analyse; a maximum of three to four a day is often all that is possible and travelling time between interviews can be considerable,

■ they are relatively more costly,

■ there is a temptation to begin treating depth interviews as if they were a questionnaire survey, thinking in terms of 'how many' rather than 'how', 'why' or 'what',

■ there is less opportunity for creativity arising from group dynamics.

Which of these advantages and limitations are important depends, clearly, on the objectives of the research, but also, crucially, on four other key factors:

■ the problems of recruitment,

- the geographical scatter of the sample,
- the nature of the product being researched,
- the amount of information required,
- the constraints of budget and time.

With difficult-to-recruit consumers or with busy executives the only practical solution is to interview individually, irrespective of other advantages and limitations. If the people to be interviewed are widely scattered or very heterogeneous it may be extremely difficult and costly to bring them together for group discussions. Where the subject matter relates to a personal or intimate topic, like sanitary protection, then, again, depth interviews may be called for, as will be the case where the information required means connecting comments with particular individuals, for example, on the history of the ownership of consumer durables. Perhaps the main reason, however, for the popularity of group discussions relates to time and budget constraints. This is not the best of reasons for choosing group discussions, but the alternative may be no research at all if time and money *are* limited.

The applications of qualitative research

These may be grouped into four main categories, although they will tend to overlap or be combined in any one particular piece of research:

- exploratory research,
- diagnostic research,
- evaluative research,
- creative development research.

Traditionally, qualitative research has been seen as a 'preliminary' to a larger scale quantitative study and in this sense is being used for exploratory purposes, usually in areas where little research has been done. Qualitative research will tend to be used for exploratory purposes where:

- the researcher does not know enough about a country or a market or some aspect of consumer behaviour to be able to design a piece of research, submit a worthwhile research proposal, or decide on the priorities and objectives of the research,
- the researcher wants to generate hypotheses or possible explanations before embarking on the main study,
- the researcher needs to design questionnaires in which the consumer perspective on or images of products and brands need to be tested and are not known in advance, or where the words, phrases or categorizations of markets or products need to be checked before proceeding to quantitative research.

Very often companies are aware that they have a marketing problem, but are unsure whether this is a symptom of a deeper-seated problem or the cause of other problems; they may be unclear how it is related to other problems, whether it is urgent or serious, and what factors may be affecting the problem. Qualitative research may be used to diagnose in detail company or organizational problems. It may be used for diagnostic purpose for consumers as well; for example, the researcher wants to unravel complex decision making processes, define consumer perceptions of competitive sets and brand sub-stitutes, or the dimensions that differentiate between brands.

In evaluative research, qualitative methods may be used to assess whether or not a particular marketing proposition or marketing mix will satisfy company objectives. Qualitative research, particularly group discussion, is frequently used to evaluate an advertising or promotional proposition. The procedure can be useful, but only if the criteria for evaluation – the bench-marks of success or failure – are clear. Thus an advertisement can be tested for understanding, link with the brand, memorability, enjoyability and so on. Some commentators (e.g. Sargent, 1989) are sceptical about the use of qualitative research for evaluative purposes. If the objective of the research is, for example, to pick a 'winner' from a range of ideas or executions, it is, argues Sargent, more sensible to rely on quantitative assessment techniques. Such techniques for the pre-testing of advertising are considered in detail in Chapter 7.

One of the major strengths of qualitative research, whether group discus-sion or depth interview, is its potential for creativity and it is frequently used to generate ideas for new products, ideas for modifying products, to identify gaps in the marketplace, or to generate advertising themes or ideas for promotional activity. Special techniques like brainstorming, synectics and a range of projective techniques are often used to help in this process.

It is important for a research executive in an agency to recognize what type of application a client is looking for because that will affect the approach to sampling, interviewing, analysis and reporting. Two or more applications may, of course, need to be combined into the same research.

The analysis and interpretation of data from qualitative research

As was explained in Chapter 2, there are two kinds of qualitative data:

■ single, isolated statements in words such as will be derived from open-ended questions in a questionnaire survey or from seeking reactions to specific questions in an experimental design,
■ narrative text such as is derived from tape-recording, videoing or making close notes in depth interviews or group discussions.

The analysis of the first type of qualitative data will be considered in Chapter 6 on data analysis. This section will look only at approaches to the analysis of narrative text. What, for example, do you do with a set of audio or videotape recordings? There are no standard or 'correct' ways of proceeding, unlike quantitative research where there are generally accepted routines for the analysis and interpretation of the results. The researcher needs to deliberate on all that was said, to structure it in a meaningful and relevant way, and to identify the key areas of usefulness for the client.

Qualitative researchers each have their own styles of analysis, but whatever the style it may be broken down into three key stages:

■ transcription,
■ mechanical analysis,
■ interpretive analysis.

Most tape-recordings are transcribed into written or printed text as a first stage. However, some researchers insist on doing this themselves, or, at least, claim a preference for doing so. The argument is that the person who has to report the results needs to pick up the cues on not just *what* was said, but *how* it was said. If it is a video-recording, then other cues are picked up from who said it and the accompanying body language. However, some qualitative researchers do not have the time or the inclination for what, after all, is a tedious activity and will hand the tapes over to secretaries to transcribe. Transcription may, of course, be literal, including all the 'ums' and 'ers' and false starts; others may be a paraphrase into grammatically correct English, or may even be just notes and summaries of what was said. For depth interviews the transcript will be on a respondent-by-respondent basis; for group discussions on a group-by-group basis.

Mechanical analysis has the aim of sorting and classifying what people said into categories with a view to bringing together comments that are on the same topic. This may mean generating, modifying, developing and refining a framework of categories as the analysis proceeds. Several attempts or 'passes' at the transcripts may be needed before a set of categories is satisfactory. As far as possible the categories should be exhaustive and mutually exclusive, and they should not be too many in number. More than six or so will make the next stage – interpretation – all the more difficult. The search is then on for patterns. Is there a tendency for the replies of users and non-users of the brand to be systematically different on particular topics? Is there a difference between the men and the women; the older and the younger age groups; the ABC1s and the C2DEs?

There are two main approaches to mechanical analysis. First, the 'large-sheet-of-paper' approach, which is basically a cross-tabulation of major dependent variables by independent variables, and the cells contain quotes, observations, summaries or interpretations. Essentially, it is a topic-by-topic analysis. Second, there is the 'annotating-the-transcripts' approach. The annotations may highlight differences between sample segments, contradictions, majority and minority viewpoints or interesting quotes. The process may involve underlining, parenthesizing, highlighting, commenting in the margin or cross-referencing, using coloured pens and so on. The process is done transcript-by-transcript, taking a holistic approach to each one.

Interpretive analysis involves trying to work out the meaning of what was said, and then considering the implications of this for the objectives of the research. It means going beyond what people say; not taking their comments at face value. It means attending to what some writers on qualitative research have referred to as 'the space between the lines', or to the 'Eureka' moments. Those writers who have tried to describe *how* they do this talk about ideas 'swimming around in the head' or 'mulling them over'. The brain is a kind of 'black box' that, over time, in an invisible process, sorts things out, comes up with structures and frameworks, with patterns, solutions and, hopefully, answers – in short, with 'insight' or a 'way forward', which may involve a 'leap of faith'.

All this sounds very unscientific and lacking in objectivity – which worries some clients, but unless it is a process to which the qualitative researcher is prepared to devote time and energy then the analysis of the data will remain at the journalistic level. Researchers will simply report back to clients what respondents have said. Emphasis will be on the coding of responses and treating the research as if it were a quantitative survey. Responses will be simply summarized and assumed to provide the answer to the problems outlined by the client. For some qualitative research this may, indeed, be all that the client wants; for others the client may be getting poor value for his or her money. A proper analysis is slow, labour-intensive and highly energy-absorbing; but to neglect the analysis and interpretation stage may undermine the value of unstructured interviewing – the yield in terms of information, insight and creativity is short-changed and the analysis and interpretation is more superficial then it should be.

The role of analysis and interpretation does, however, vary according to the type of application. Where the research is for largely exploratory purposes then the focus may well be on establishing patterns and generating conceptual frameworks. Diagnostic research calls for lateral thinking and insight rather than the mechanical sorting of ideas. For evaluative research the analysis may be quite straightforward – the responses of consumers have to be compared with intended or desired responses. For creative development, the researcher needs to 'absorb' what the respondents are saying in their own terms and in their own language.

Some writers (e.g. Gordon and Langmaid, 1988) have emphasized that analysis is not a stage that takes place after the fieldwork is completed, but carries on continuously, right from the initial contact with the client. The client's problem and the research objectives are stored at the back of the researcher's mind as the research proceeds, demanding conscious and unconscious attention, while tentative hypotheses are developed and continually tested.

The presentation of results

Once the analysis has been completed the researcher involved in the project will usually present the findings to the client in a face-to-face session at the client's own premises, giving managers the opportunity to ask questions about the research. It takes time and skill to convert the findings into a well-structured oral presentation. When planning what format the presentation should take, the researcher will need to bear in mind:

■ the original problems presented in the brief,
■ who will be at the presentation,
■ what time is available,
■ whether visual aids should be used,
■ the order of the topics,
■ how informal or formal the occasion is likely to be.

Jargon and technical terms need to be kept to a minimum. As far as possible the presentation should be enjoyable and entertaining, involving all those who are attending. Commentary on the background and methodology should be very brief; busy executives are usually more interested in the results, conclusions and recommendations.

Not all projects require a detailed written report. Creative development work for advertising may need only a quick summary to act as 'evidence' of the findings. In an exploratory study for market entry, by contrast, a detailed report will probably be very important. There is likely to be too much information to be commented on in a single presentation. A close study of the written report will be needed as a basis for decision-making. The overall structure of management reports is explained in Chapter 7.

The validity of qualitative research

As is clear from the section above on the analysis and interpretation of results, such results are reached not by a scientific, rigorous and objective process, but by a mysterious, subjective and often subconscious 'black box' activity in the brain. This has implications for the validity of the results obtained. There is no single 'truth' buried in the tape recordings that can be excavated and 'discovered' by the researcher. Interpretations depend on the individual and on the broader context of knowledge and data that already exist. No two researchers will come to exactly the same conclusions; achieving validity through replication is thus not usually possible.

According to Sykes (1990), in qualitative research 'validity' may refer to:

■ the 'goodness' of the data – the kind, accuracy, relevance, richness, colourfulness of the data derived from individual sample units, be they single individuals or groups,
■ the 'status' of the qualitative findings – their hardness, generalizability, truth, or the extent to which they are 'scientific'.

Which of these is appropriate depends on the research objectives. If the purpose is to generate ideas for new products, then the number and quality of ideas is important; the question of 'truth' in any absolute sense is certainly not. It is in this sense of validity that qualitative research has a particular advantage over other types of research. Topics and ideas can be pursued from a variety of angles and perspectives; it is the flexible and responsive interaction that sparks ideas and gets respondents to think creatively.

If the purpose of the research is for evaluation, or to pick the 'best' idea for an advertising theme, then the status or truth of the data is crucial. It is this question that concerns the confidence with which inferences can be made from the data. Some researchers have argued simply that *no* inferences can be made; samples are too small and purposively selected and the inductive approach does not allow hypothesis-testing. The smallness of the samples has been shown by some studies not to be a great impediment to the kinds of conclusions arrived at, and that qualitative samples can and do satisfy the theoretical requirements for making generalizations, a point argued by Griggs (1987). It has been suggested, furthermore, that quantitative research, too, uses inductive as well as deductive processes and that hypothesis-testing in the sense of relating ideas to data (not tests of statistical significance against the null hypothesis) lies at the very heart of qualitative research.

Inferential validity in qualitative research can be established in a number of ways:

■ face validity is said to exist when the research produces the kind of information wanted or expected,
■ internal validity refers to the internal coherence of the findings and means checking out responses for consistency, and ruling out ambiguity and contradiction,

- criterion validity is said to exist when the interpretations from qualitative research match the conclusions drawn from alternative procedures.

Face validity, it can be argued, is a necessary but not sufficient condition for establishing validity. Internal validity means examining the text as a whole and seeking support for a particular interpretation from the textual evidence. However, although a high degree of internal validity is usually possible in qualitative research because of the opportunities for responsive cross-checking and amplification of ideas as they emerge from the data, the process is not open to scrutiny and the data may be consistent or be made to look consistent with a number of different interpretations.

Conclusion

Qualitative research provides data rich in ideas, insights, hypotheses, explanations and suggestions. It answers such questions as, 'What?', 'Why?' or, 'How?', but not, 'How many?'. The focus is always on understanding consumers or other kinds of respondents from their own perspective; it is never a key role to measure the extent to which these views, feelings or behaviour are held.

The cost of qualitative research can, at first sight, seem high, but it is cheaper, on the whole, than ad hoc survey research. Cost is generally based on the number of interviews rather than on researcher time. Typically, a group discussion will cost £1000 or more per group (including analysis and report). The cost of depth interviews varies enormously. Executive interviews tend to be the most expensive. For the agency, there will be many variables that affect the cost, and hence profitability, of the research undertaken. These variables include:

- how full and formal a written report is required,
- the number of briefing meetings needed,
- the difficulty of recruiting the sample,
- the size of the groups and how long they are to last,
- the type of venue.

Buyers are often looking only at the cost per group and not at variations in the levels of service provided by the agency. The chairman of the AQRP has argued that costings should be on a professional fee for time plus direct costs basis. The former would make provision for briefing meetings, setting up the project, carrying out the fieldwork, analysing and interpreting the data, presenting the results and writing the report. Direct costs would vary according to the number of groups and would include the fees paid to recruiters, costs of finding and hiring rooms, the financial incentives paid to respondents, refreshments that may be given during the interviews, and the travelling and subsistence of the moderator.

Survey research

A survey is the collection of data based on addressing questions to respondents in a formal manner and taking a systematic record of their responses. The record will normally be a questionnaire, but may be a diary or direct data capture using electronic means. Survey research may be used in either ad hoc

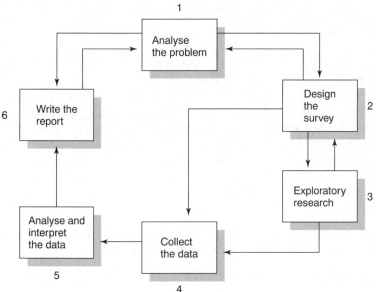

Figure 4.1 The stages of ad hoc survey research.

or continuous research. Continuous research is described in a later section. This section addresses itself to the design and conduct of ad hoc surveys, which are one-off pieces of research, and are usually custom-designed for a particular purpose or client. They also tend to be cross-sectional, that is, they treat the period over which the research is conducted as one unit of time.

Ad hoc surveys tend to go through a number of stages such as those outlined in Figure 4.1. The researcher begins by analysing the problem or problems that the research is to address before designing the most appropriate kind of survey to conduct. However, before data are collected it may be wise, if not essential, to undertake some exploratory research, as a consequence of which some redesign of the survey may be necessary – hence the 'double arrow' in Figure 4.1. This time it may be possible to proceed directly to data collection without further exploratory research. Once the data have been collected they need to be analysed and interpreted, and a report written of the results. The report should, in turn, address the original analysis of the problem to complete the 'loop' in the survey research process. Reflection on this problem may prompt the researcher to revise the report before submission. Between stages five and six there may be a face-to-face presentation of the preliminary results to the client.

In looking at the various types of ad hoc survey, we can make distinctions along a number of dimensions, for example:

■ by topic,
■ by type of researcher,
■ by method of questionnaire administration.

A basic distinction in terms of topic is between consumer surveys, which study individuals or private households as final consumers of products and services, and business surveys, which address questions to individuals in business organizations concerning those organizations, not their private purchasing behaviour.

Surveys distinguished by type of researcher include the following.

- In-house surveys, which are carried out by the company itself using its own market research department.
- Market research agency surveys, which are commissioned by a client organization. These may be custom-designed for a particular client, or syndicated in some way, for example companies may share either the organization of a survey or the data that emerge.
- Academic surveys, which may be done on a consultancy basis, or for the purposes of scholarly research.
- Governmental surveys such as those carried out by the Office of National Statistics.

Methods of questionnaire administration fall into three main categories: *interview surveys*, *telephone surveys* and *postal surveys*.

Interview surveys

Most survey work in the UK is conducted through face-to-face interviews, for the most part by full-time or part-time employees of a market research agency or by individuals offering their services on a freelance, self-employed basis. Occasionally they are conducted by research executives or by academic researchers. The prevalence of this method of questionnaire administration is explained largely by the key advantages of this form of social encounter:

- the interviewer can check and ensure respondent eligibility before the interview is started,
- personally administered questionnaires ensure that all questions are asked in the required order, and that all applicable questions are asked,
- the interviewer can encourage respondents to answer as fully as possible and check, as appropriate, that the question is correctly understood,
- materials that need to be shown to the respondents can be properly presented,
- response rates are consistently higher than for other methods of questionnaire administration,
- where quotas are applied, the interviewer can ensure that the target number of interviews is achieved,
- interviewers can usually persuade respondents to complete the interview.

These advantages together mean that the quality of the data derived from interview surveys is generally superior to that obtained by other methods.

Interview surveys can be grouped into five styles according to the type of location in which they occur:

- the street,
- the home,
- a hall,
- a shop,
- a business organization.

Street surveys are usually conducted in busy town centres, particularly in shopping malls or precincts. In the USA they call them 'mall intercept' interviews. The interviewer tends to stay in one position, approaching potential respondents as soon as a previous interview is completed. This eliminates travel time between interviews and makes recruitment fairly speedy. However, street interviews need to be brief, since respondents are unlikely to stop for more than about 10 minutes, while the use of materials to show also needs to be controlled. Furthermore, enclosed shopping malls are considered to be private property and the permission of the centre manager will be required to carry out the interviewing. Some centres have a no-interviewing policy; others may charge for the facility on a pre-booked basis.

In-home interviews are conducted in those surveys where recruitment is door-to-door. 'Doorstep' interviews, however, may be a more accurate description of the typical location. Interviewers may be given lists of names and addresses or they may be limited to a prescribed number of streets, or to an area (a sampling point). In addition, they may have instructions about how to proceed, for example, calling at every nth house, or missing out a certain number of houses after every successful interview. Whereas street interviews are always 'cold', in-home interviews may be pre-recruited by telephone. Door-to-door recruitment can be time-consuming and it relies on people being at home. Although longer interviews are usually possible, interruptions are always a hazard whether it is from other members of the household (including pets) or from the television or the telephone.

Interviews carried out in a pre-booked location are usually referred to as 'hall tests', even though it may not be in a hall, but in a public room in a hotel. Furthermore, it may not be a 'test' in the sense of the kind of hall tests conducted and described later as experimental research. Recruitment is usually from a street nearby and respondents are invited to 'answer a few questions' about a particular product or whatever is the topic of the survey. Respondents can be given refreshments while being interviewed and this facilitates completion of more complex tasks. Interviews conducted indoors, furthermore, can use a much greater array of materials, including videos or elaborate displays. A team of interviewers may work from the same hall where they can be supervised and monitored.

In-store surveys may take place in a shop or just outside. The researcher or the market research agency will, clearly, need to obtain permission from the store, and in many cases also the co-operation of the store personnel. Recruitment may be on the basis of people entering or leaving the store – which is appropriate will be determined by the subject matter or objectives of the research. Thus a study of shopping intentions will require the former. As with interviews taking place in halls being called 'hall tests', so interviews taking place either outside or inside the shop are usually called 'store tests', even though they are not, strictly speaking, tests using any form of experimental design.

Business interviews will normally take place in the interviewee's office or in one of the company meeting rooms and will probably have been pre-arranged. There is always the danger, however, that some 'crisis' has occurred and the interview is cancelled, postponed or truncated.

How many interviews the interviewer is able to conduct in a day or in a week depends on:

- the location,
- the recruitment time,
- the interviewing time,
- the travel time.

It may be possible to conduct 20–30 interviews a day using street quotas; an interviewer will be lucky to do 10 in-home, or perhaps two business interviews.

Wherever the interview is carried out, the interviewer has a number of key tasks. These include:

- preparation,
- locating the respondents,
- obtaining the agreement to conduct the interview,
- asking the questions and noting down answers,
- completing records of interview assignments and returning completed questionnaires.

Interviewers' jobs begin when their packages of work arrive. The interviewers will need to go through the pack carefully, making sure that all the materials and information needed have been provided. If there are any problems, he or she will need to contact the supervisor or the office. The interviewer may need to prepare a strategy for recruitment, since there may be considerable freedom as to when the interviews are carried out and where recruitment takes place. Strategies may, in fact, be similar to those adopted for recruitment to group discussions. Finally, the interviewer must be thoroughly familiar with the questionnaire. He or she is then ready to face the public.

With random sampling techniques, interviewers are given lists of names and addresses taken either from the Electoral Registers or the Postcode Address File. Having found the address, the interviewer needs to locate the named person drawn as part of the sample. If the person concerned is not at home, there is usually an instruction to make at least three call-backs at different times of the day. No substitutes are allowed. In random location and random route sampling, the interviewer will have instructions about the selection of houses and the streets in which such selections are to be made. With quota sampling, there may be no instruction about how, within a specified sampling point, the interviewer obtains her quotas, but whether the interviews are to take place in-home or in the street *is* usually specified.

Interviewers are normally trained on the best ways of obtaining the agreement of the named or selected person to participate. The response rate for experienced interviewers is generally consistently higher than for novices. The interviewer will have an identity card which shows that the person named on the card is registered as a bona fide interviewer. This is usually presented while the interviewer explains that he/she is conducting market research on a given topic (usually the agency will be identified, but not the client), and would like to ask a few questions seeking their opinion. Assurances of confidentiality and that personal details will not be used for selling purposes are usually given.

When asking the questions, apart from conversational pleasantries, the interviewer is normally instructed to follow exactly the wording in the questionnaire. Some questions may have 'probe' written against them, indicating that the interviewer has discretion over whether to pursue a more detailed answer than the one the respondent has just offered. When recording the answers, for set-choice questions, the interviewer just has to tick boxes or put circles round numbered responses. For open-ended questions the interviewer may be instructed to write down exactly what the respondent says, or to paraphrase.

An interviewer will normally be given an assignment of perhaps 15–20 interviews to do in a week if in-home, or rather more if based on street interview. A record of all contacts and non-contacts will be kept and this will be returned to the agency at the end of the week along with the completed questionnaires. In some cases, interviewers have hand-held market research terminals. The terminal will have a screen that displays each question in turn and the responses. The selected response is entered as the respondent gives it. The terminal then prompts with the next relevant question, which may depend on which response has been entered. The data are stored on a disc which is then returned to the agency where the data are read directly into the computer.

Interviewing is a skilled activity. The interview itself is a process of social interaction which is highly artificial and its outcome, including answers to questions, will often depend on the sex, age, social class, dress, accent and personality of both interviewer and respondent. It is quite easy to obtain systematic differences between interviewers that need, as far as possible, to be controlled. The interviewer is, on the one hand, trying to be 'standard' in all his or her approaches to respondents, but, on the other hand, may need to react to individual circumstances for the successful completion of the interview – in short, the interviewer needs to act like a robot with all the appearance of a human being.

Interviewer bias may present a problem and may occur in one or more of several ways. At the recruitment stage an interviewer given an assignment with quotas may, consciously or unconsciously, select (or avoid) people of a particular type. The way the interviewer handles the initial approach will affect the response rates and probably differentially by type of respondent; the way she or he asks the questions may affect the responses given, so might the way he or she reacts verbally or non-verbally. Probing or prompting may be approached in different ways. Market research companies recognize these problems and try to minimize their impact in a number of ways. These include:

- training,
- briefing,
- quality control,
- fieldwork management,
- industry guidelines.

All interviewers are put through some kind of training programme, which should have two components: teaching the interviewer the skills he or she will need to carry out good interviews, and integrating interviewers into the industry. The skills required include the techniques for approaching respondents, persuading them to take part, and sustaining their level of interest. Interviewers frequently need to be able to classify respondents very quickly into the A, B, C1, C2, D, E social class categories and, for example, to be able to define the head of the household. Being made aware of the potential sources of bias is the first step in their minimization. Interviewer integration into the industry means that the interviewer needs to be able to understand what marketing and marketing research are about, and that the rules that have to be applied can be understood and appreciated. Training programmes usually involve an in-house session (of, typically, one to three days) entailing lectures, exercises and simulations. Normally, there will be a manual for the interviewer to study and for future reference. In-field training will usually be under the supervision of a field supervisor. As each new topic of work is assigned the interviewer may be accompanied by a senior interviewer or the supervisor.

Before each new assignment, there will be briefing sessions. These may be formal personal briefings where area fieldstaff are gathered together and the researcher explains all the aspects of the survey. Supervisors may be briefed first and they, in turn, brief the interviewers. Some briefings may be over the telephone. There will usually also be detailed written instructions, sometimes standing on their own, sometimes supporting other briefing methods. Any of these methods may, of course, be combined together.

The methods used for quality control are various. The accuracy of the data collected and the legitimacy of respondent recruitment may be subjected to 'backchecks'. Supervisors recall on respondents and re-administer part of the questionnaire. Some 5–10 per cent of respondents may be recontacted in this way. It may be done over the telephone, by post or by personal visit. Some agencies have a policy of accompanying interviewers in the field on a regular basis. Any bad habits can then be picked up and rectified. Central monitoring may be used to identify interviewers who regularly make mistakes or submit incomplete work; feedback from field supervisors on how well the questionnaire is performing may be used to alert other supervisors of potential difficulties.

The overall management of the field force is an important factor in maintaining standards of interviewing. There will typically be a head office team led by a senior manager. There will be a number of regional supervisors working from home, controlling local teams of interviewers. These people may be salaried or they may work freelance. They all try to assure a high standard of selection and training in their area and they will attempt to get each interviewer to work across the entire range of types of respondent so that any biases will be equally distributed.

In the UK, industry guidelines are given by the Market Research Society, which provides a Code of Conduct for research, parts of which apply directly to interviewers. This Code will feature in any training programmes. The MRS and the Association of Market Survey Organizations (AMSO) endorse an Interviewer Quality Control Scheme (IQCS), which is a voluntary programme set up for monitoring data collection procedures, and which ensures that all member companies operate the same minimum standards of fieldwork in terms of interviewer selection, training, supervision and quality control. The MRS has introduced a uniform interviewer identity card which seeks to reassure the public as to the legitimacy of the interview, and to stop the practice of 'sugging' – selling under the guise of doing market research.

The skills of professional interviewers have allowed data collection methodologies to become more complex and sophisticated; but they are costly and time-consuming, particularly where geographically dispersed sampling is required, or where quota requirements make respondents hard to find. While interview surveys are still the dominant mode of data collection, that dominance is being challenged, particularly with the growth in telephone research, to which we now turn.

Telephone surveys

In the 1970s, telephone interviewing became well-established in the UK as a method used by industrial or business market researchers to obtain information and opinions from managers and professional people. Business premises were usually on the telephone and managers were accustomed to using them. Only more recently, however, have telephone interviews with the general public become possible. By 1980 some 75 per cent of households in the UK had a telephone, and by 1990 it was approaching 90 per cent. The number of agencies offering telephone research has grown rapidly in the last decade.

Employing interviewers and supervisors to telephone from their own homes was, however, not practicable and most agencies offering telephone interviewing services now have central location telephoning. This concentrated interviewing in a small number of closely supervised locations. In addition, most of these centres have taken advantage of computer-assisted telephone interviewing (CATI), which has greatly increased the advantages of central location interviewing. The questionnaire is programmed into the computer prior to the commencement of the interviewing, and is displayed question-by-question on a visual display unit in front of each interviewer. The reply is immediately input into the computer via the keyboard. Telephone interviewing has two main advantages over face-to-face interviewing:

- it produces faster results,
- it is not necessary to cluster the interviewing in sampling points thereby reducing sampling error.

Telephone interviewing is faster because there is no travelling time or wasteful callbacks. Sampling for telephone surveys is rather different from that required for interview surveys. In the first place, there is a standard, accessible and comprehensive sampling frame – the telephone directories. Sampling from them can be on a systematic or random basis. Some 10 per cent of numbers, however, are ex-directory in the UK, but by adding one digit to every number selected, the correct proportion of such numbers will be sampled. Telephone ownership, however, is not universal, and non-telephone households are likely to be ones with particular characteristics – the elderly, the poor, students and so on.

Three main approaches to the exclusion of non-owners are possible:

- redefine the population as all telephone-owning households,
- impose quotas on the recruitment of respondents so that groups who would otherwise be under-represented are correctly represented,
- weight the data afterwards to correct for over and under representations.

If the research is concerned with luxury consumer durables, then redefining the population may be acceptable and appropriate. For measuring trends, reweighting the data may give accurate results of changes taking place. However, if absolute estimates of market quantities are required, then reweighting may not be adequate since the procedure assumes that the telephone-owning section of the population who are in the under-represented groups are themselves representative of those who do not own telephones. The imposition of quotas faces the same difficulty.

For business research, there are many ready-made lists and directories of companies and organizations. British Telecom offers its Business and Residential UK Telecom User Sampling (BRUTUS) service, which provides samples specifically for market research. The database consists of all BT's business customers' installations, plus a 5 per cent sample of residential users.

In spite of all the advantages of telephone surveys, there are a number of drawbacks:

- they are limited to verbal exchanges – it is not possible to show people lists, cards or other visual materials (unless they are posted in advance),
- there are no observational data; in particular, it is not possible to watch the facial expression and body language of respondents,
- telephone interviews have to be very short and factual, which does limit their use,
- the rise of telesales – selling over the telephone – has made many people suspicious of calls from strangers,
- answerphones and call-screening equipment has made telephone interviewing more difficult.

Postal surveys

While postal research accounts for only about 5 per cent of turnover of commissioned research, some 25 per cent of all interviews are conducted using this method. Postal surveys are, in fact, extremely cost-effective, requiring neither interviewers not telephone systems. They are perhaps one third of the cost of telephone surveys and one eighth of interview surveys. The growth of direct marketing has in recent years, furthermore, given an impetus to postal surveys since recipients of postal questionnaires are likely to be customers of the company and therefore more likely to respond. Other advantages of postal surveys are:

- central control of the survey is facilitated,
- unclustered sampling is possible without cost penalties,
- more time can be devoted to the completion of questionnaires by respondents,
- respondents can fill them in when it is convenient to them,
- respondents can confer with other members of the household before filling in answers,
- there is no interviewer bias.

It is often argued that the main disadvantage of postal questionnaires is the low response rate. While response rates for some postal questionnaires are, indeed, very low, if they are used in appropriate situations and properly executed with good covering letters, reminders, incentives and so on, the response rates can be equal to that of telephone surveys and may, on occasions, approach that of interview surveys. There are, however, a number of other disadvantages:

- there is no assistance or encouragement from an interviewer,

- respondents can read all the questionnaire in advance, so 'unfolding' or 'funnelling' techniques cannot be used,
- there are usually delays in getting completed questionnaires back,
- the person filling in the questionnaire may not be the one selected in the sample,
- answers have to be accepted as they are written without further probing.

Evidence suggests that a good covering letter is crucial to the response rate, other things being equal. The letter must 'sell' the value of the survey to the respondent and encourage him or her to respond. The letter should, at a minimum, explain:

- who is carrying out the research,
- what is the purpose of the research,
- how the respondent was selected,
- that responses will be confidential,
- how to complete and return the questionnaire.

It may, in addition, help to emphasize why it is important for people to participate, how the survey will help others in the future, and that they will receive a mystery gift or token of appreciation if they return the questionnaire by a certain date. Enclosing the incentive (for example, a pen) with the original letter is, so it is sometimes argued, more effective. An example of a covering letter is given in Box 4.1. It is normal to include a stamped, addressed envelope. If it is intended to send reminders after two to three weeks, questionnaires will need to be numbered to identify those who have not responded. The letter may need to explain that the number will be used only for this purpose.

Interview, telephone and postal surveys may, of course, be used in combination. For example, pre-recruiting by telephone can avoid a lot of wasted legwork. After an initial personal interview, a self-completed questionnaire can be left with the respondent to complete in order to collect additional information, perhaps from other members of the household. If the survey requires an interview and follow-up, the call-back may be conducted by telephone, or a postal questionnaire may be sent. Using combinations of techniques in this way can increase the flexibility of research design.

Experimental research

Instead of relying on answers to questions addressed to individuals in a survey, in an experiment the market researcher tries out some marketing action on a small scale, carefully observing and measuring the results and controlling, as far as possible, for the effects of factors other than the marketing action being taken. Experiments have three main characteristics:

- the manipulation of one or more independent variables that the researcher wishes to test the effects of,
- a comparison of at least two measures of a dependent variable,
- the control of extraneous factors that may affect the results.

Groups or geographical areas to be subjected to a test are usually matched in

ABC Research
11 Eastgate
London

Dear Mr Brown

I am writing to a carefully selected sample of people throughout the UK. Your name has been selected as someone who could answer a few questions on gardening, and I would greatly appreciate your help. It will only take a few minutes of your time.

The survey is designed to provide information on the way in which gardeners use the products and services that are available from garden centres. The results will be used to improve the range of products that such centres can offer to people like yourself.

Your reply is very important to us and it will be treated as totally confidential. It will be analysed along with other responses and none of your views will be tied to your name. Please take my personal assurance that you will not be pestered by salesmen as a result of helping me.

All you need to do is read through the questions and put a tick in the box which corresponds to your answer. Please remember that there are no 'correct' answers - it is your opinion that I am interested in.

When you have finished, please send the questionnaire back to me in the stamped, addressed envelope that I have provided. It would be very helpful if you could do this by the end of the month.

To show my appreciation of your effotrts I will send you a mystery gift when I have received your reply.

I look forward to hearing from you.

Yours sincerely

James Auld
Marketing Manager
ABC Research

Box 4.1   An example of a covering letter

such a way as to control for selected demographic characteristics that may affect the outcome of the research, for example, sex, age, social class, marital status or neighbourhood type of those participating. In some cases, recruitment to tests may be restricted to certain kinds of people, for example users of

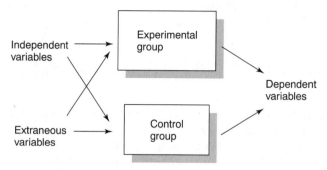

Figure 4.2 The components of an experimental design.

a particular brand. Other factors that are *not* subject to control may, of course, also affect the results of the experiment. These might include unanticipated events during the course of the experiment, maturation or fatigue of those taking part, measurement inadequacies or errors, bias in the selection of respondents, or loss of participants during the experiment. The main components of an experiment are summarized in Figure 4.2.

The key advantage of experimentation is that the researcher chooses which factors or variables he or she is going to try out. This in turn facilitates the drawing of conclusions in respect of causal relationships between variables. Indeed, some textbooks on market research, having made the distinction between exploratory, descriptive and causal research, proceed to equate causal research with experimental procedures. This is not totally justified, since it is possible to draw causal inferences from other types of research, although the analysis is 'ex post facto', that is, after the event. In other words the investigation of relationships between variables and of the robustness of those relationships when other variables are controlled, is done *after* the data have been collected. Controls are established by performing analyses on sub-groups of the sample instead of assigning categories of people to experimental situations.

Experiments tend to get used where new or revised elements or combinations of marketing mix variables would be difficult or expensive to try out on the entire market; hence the emphasis on 'small-scale' tests in the definition of experimentation. Changing marketing mix variables for the total market is, in any case, not really 'experimentation', but taking the decision itself.

Experimental design

Experiments may be designed in many different ways. There are, however, two main dimensions along which most can be identified:

- whether or not there is an attempt to make observations or take measurements *before* as well as after the test has taken place,
- whether or not there are control groups of people who are similar in terms of the control variables to the test group, but are not subjected to the test condition.

Table 4.3 combines these two factors in a cross-classification, giving four different types of experimental design.

Table 4.3

Types of experimental design

Measurement	After test	Before and after test
Control		
No control	After only	Before and after
Control group	Aftrer only with control	Before and after with control

'After only' designs are not truly experimental, and amount only to a 'try-it-and-see' approach on a small scale. Thus attitudes towards a product may be measured only after an advertising campaign. The problem is that there may be no measurement of what those attitudes were before the campaign began, so the amount of change is unknown. Furthermore, there is no control over extraneous variables that could have affected the results. Such designs cannot justifiably be used to test hypotheses, but can be useful where a 'quick-and-dirty' analysis is adequate for the kinds of decisions to be taken.

After only with control designs add a control group to the after only design in order to take account of extraneous sources of bias. Participants are normally randomly assigned to the treatment and control groups, and in addition may be matched on a set of demographic variables. The difference between the experimental group and the control group is taken to be a result of the test conditions. However, there is no guarantee that both the control and experimental groups were not affected by extraneous factors and may have changed since before the test was conducted.

Before and after designs allow for some calculation to be made of the amount of change in a dependent variable before and after the test. There is, however, the danger that the process of making observations or taking measurements before the test may itself affect the behaviour or attitudes of those participating. In some cases, of course, measurements of, say, sales, already exist before the test and may readily be compared with sales after it.

Before and after with control designs add a control group to the before and after design. The difference between the control group and experimental group before the test is compared with the difference between them after the test has been applied to only one group. The aim is to discount both extraneous variables and the impact of the first measurement on the second.

In practice, control groups are often not used in marketing experiments. More often there will be two or more matched experimental groups each given a different product formulation, pack design, or advertisements to try out or react to. A large number of experimental groups may be set up in different parts of the country to detect any regional differences. This may be done systematically by, in effect, 'stratifying' by region using a 'randomised block' design. Suppose there are three product formulations, A, B and C, to test and the market is limited to England, which is divided into three regions, North, Midlands and South. Within each region the three formulations could be tried separately in each of three branches of a retailer that has agreed to

Table 4.4

A randomized block design

Region	Product formulation		
North	A	B	C
Midlands	A	B	C
South	A	B	C

Region	Type of outlet		
North	A	B	C
Midlands	C	A	B
South	B	C	A

Table 4.5
A Latin square design

Sugar content	Salt content		
1	1A	1B	1C
2	2A	2B	2C
3	3A	3B	3C

Table 4.6
A factorial design

have the experiment staged in some of its branches. The design would look like Table 4.4. The assignment of the product formulations (and the selection of branch) could be by random processes. Analysis of variance (see Chapter 6) may be used to test the statistical significance of differences between product formulations, and to isolate this from between region sources of error.

Sometimes a factor like region may be only one of two or three crucial factors. To take every combination, for example, every product formulation in every region in every type of outlet would produce a very large number. A more economical design is the 'Latin square'. This could, for example, take every product formulation A, B and C and test it is each type of outlet (multiple, co-operative or independent) and in each region, but not in each type of outlet in each region. The design might look like that in Table 4.5. Here, there are two extraneous variables, region and outlet type. These form the rows and the columns of the table. Product formulations A, B and C are then assigned randomly to cells in the table, but subject to the restriction that each appears only once in each row and once in each column. A randomized block design with every combination would have required $3 \times 3 \times 3$ or 27 test sites. The Latin square reduces this to nine sites, but it is still possible to estimate error due to the two sources of error, again using analysis of variance. There is the assumption, however, that there is no relationship between type of region and type of outlet.

If it *is* necessary to take account of the interaction effects between variables, a 'factorial design' may be more appropriate. This design is frequently used for product testing. Suppose a new biscuit can have different levels of salt content (high, medium and low), and different levels of sweetness (high, medium and low). Each combination may then be tested. These combinations are shown in Table 4.6. This would require nine matched groups of testers. This may well be feasible, but if there were, for example, also a crucial decision about making the biscuit with either butter or margarine, then 18 matched groups may be too many. Again, some kind of Latin square may be designed so that the butter and margarine biscuits are tested separately at each level of sugar content and at each level of salt content, but not in each combination.

Types of experiment

Experiments in marketing are of two main kinds: *laboratory experiments* and *field experiments*.

Laboratory experiments

These take place in an artificial environment in which the experimenter has direct control over most, if not all, the crucial factors that might affect the experimental outcome. They are often used for product testing, package testing, and in advertising effectiveness studies. Sometimes their purpose is to optimize the marketing mix *before* a product or service is exposed to the open market; such tests may be referred to as 'pre-tests'. However, laboratory experiments may also be used on existing or previously launched products and may be referred to as 'post-tests'. For either type of experiment, a key dilemma is that while elements of the marketing mix such as formulation, packaging, pricing and so on are likely to be the subject of separate experiments to help assess the contribution made by each to the overall performance, perceptions of overall performance will be influenced by the interaction and impact of all these elements together. Ideally, some attempt to assess the interaction effects needs to be included in the design of experiments.

There are three main research environments in which laboratory type experiments may be conducted: *hall* tests, *van* tests and *test centres*. In hall tests, people are recruited off the street or shopping precinct in the vicinity of the hall that has been hired by the research agency. The purpose is to show products, packages or advertisements to people selected by quota sampling in order to measure their reaction. Selection is often restricted to users of the product being tested. Where hall tests are used for product testing, the products are generally new or modified, and the aim is to obtain a measure of acceptance, preference, or attitude. The tests are often blind and comparative. Not all products, of course, are suitable for hall tests. Thus toiletries would be more suited to home placements tests. However, hall tests are popular for food and drink. Samples tend to be quite large (maybe 500 or so) and spread over several venues and probably in different parts of the country. They may be subject to various forms of experimental design like randomized block or Latin square.

Van tests are similar to hall tests, but recruitment is to a mobile van that can be taken to many different venues. Van tests have the advantage that all the equipment needed for testing does not need to be set-up in every location. However, space may be too restricted for some types of test.

Test centres may be used in preference to vans or halls where the product for testing is too large, expensive or complicated to be taken to the consumer. An example is the car clinic, which is a product test on vehicles held in a test centre. Respondents are invited to evaluate one or more individual aspects of car design such as exterior styling, roominess, or interior layout. For a description of the procedures used in such clinics, see Wimbush (1990).

What actually takes place in a hall, van or test centre is often really only a survey in which respondents are asked questions and their responses noted. Although they are usually called 'hall tests' or 'van tests' they are experiments only if there are before and after measures and, ideally, if there are control groups. This is frequently not the case.

Field experiments

These are conducted in a realistic research environment in which the products are exposed to the open marketplace and tested in situations where they will be bought, used or consumed in circumstances similar to those where these activities will normally happen. The degree of control exercised by the researcher is considerably less than for a laboratory experiment, but, being less artificial, may be a better guide to future behaviour. Field experiments are used mainly for trying out products or marketing mix variables in the market-place either in the home or factory, or in a selected test area. Inevitably this makes them more expensive than laboratory experiments since the products need to be made, packaged, priced, possibly even promoted, in their final form. Exposure, furthermore, means that competitors become aware of what the company is about, and may copy the idea and perhaps even launch it first.

Many factors make field experiments more difficult to control than labora-tory experiments, for example, uncharacteristic competitor activity during the course of the test. At the same time, however, there are important elements in the marketing mix that do not lend themselves to laboratory tests, for example, experiments relating to distribution, trade incentives or mer-chandizing. Relying on the results of experiments in an artificial laboratory may be an unsound basis on which to make serious estimates of what will happen in a national launch of a new product.

The principles of experimental design explained above apply as much to field experiments as to those in the laboratory, so decisions have to be made about the use of data or taking observations before as well as after the test and whether or not there will be control groups or control areas.

Three main types of field experiment may be distinguished: *in-home place-ment* tests, *store* tests and *test marketing*, In-home placement tests give selected consumers the product to try at home and to report back. Several large companies make regular use of products placed with panels of consu-mers, and are sometimes referred to as product testing panels. Demographic and product-use characteristics of panel members are recorded. and experi-mental and control groups with the required characteristics for the particular tests are then selected. Test products are distributed by hand or through the post to panel members who complete questionnaires on the reactions to the products received. There is the danger, of course, that panel members learn from their testing experience and cease to be typical consumers. However, if the panel is sufficiently large it is possible to avoid over-exposure of panel members to a particular type of product. On the other hand, if panel members receive products too infrequently, their level of interest tends to drop and the questionnaire response rate drops.

Some of the elements of the marketing mix such as packaging and point of sale promotions lend themselves to store tests, although some manufacturers are tempted to try out new products or price adjustments in selected stores. The design of some experiments amounts to no more than 'let's try it in a few shops and see if it sells' strategy. However, the more thoughtful designs of store test will take account of:

■ the need to include a cross-section of types of retail outlet,
■ the need to allow for regional differences,
■ the need for 'control' stores matched against those trying the test product,
■ the completeness, accuracy and validity of the data that will be used to measure the results of the test.

Obtaining the co-operation of stores to participate in the tests is often a problem. Such co-operation, furthermore, needs to extend to allowing the researchers to control the conduct, layout or positioning of the test product. For most in-store tests the effect of the test is measured by changes in sales, but for consumer promotions may in addition be measured in interviews with matched groups of consumers.

Test marketing is a controlled experiment carried out in one or more limited, but carefully selected, parts of a market area. Test marketing uses a range of experimental designs to predict and explore the consequences of one or more marketing actions for new or modified product introductions, or to estimate the payoffs and costs of changes in the marketing mix for existing products.

The 'consequences' (the dependent variables) that test marketing seeks to predict might include:

- sales by volume and by value,
- market shares,
- profitability and return on investment,
- consumer behaviour, e.g. trial and repeat purchase, and attitudes concerning products,
- the reactions of retailers and distributors to the product,
- the effects of different marketing strategies in different test areas.

The conduct of test marketing includes a number of key stages:

- planning,
- pre-tests,
- main test,
- post-test,
- evaluation.

Planning includes defining clearly the problem or problems to which the test marketing is addressed and the measures that will be used to evaluate the outcome. It also means deciding where the test is to be conducted. In selecting test areas it will be necessary to pay attention to:

- the demographic structure of the area, which should be representative of the total market,
- the industrial and occupational structure,
- the structure of retailing and distribution,
- the availability and use of media, especially local newspapers that could be used for advertising.

Once the test areas have been selected it is necessary to pre-test measurements of the variables to be used to evaluate outcomes. It is changes in these as a result of the test that will be recorded. Sometimes sufficient base data may be already available; sometimes it may be necessary to conduct primary research. More often, manufacturers will purchase into retail panels so that they can monitor the effects of the test over a period of time. Pre-tests may also be carried out in areas that are to be used as 'controls', that is, not subject to the experimental stimulus.

The main test might involve the launch of a new or modified product along with associated marketing communications, or the change in the marketing mix itself, for example a new pricing policy. The duration of the test has to be long enough to allow the situation to stabilize after the new experimental conditions have been imposed.

In the post-test, measurements are repeated of the key dependent variables and compared with measures derived in the pre-test.

In the last stage of evaluation, account needs to be taken of the factors that may have influenced the results, and some prediction made of what is likely to happen in a national launch. This is not a simple matter of extrapolation of the results in the test area to the whole country – that would be dangerous. It means taking account of any special circumstances in the test area, including actions of competitors, that may not hold for the country as a whole.

Test marketing has not been so fashionable in recent years, largely because there are a number of problems with it. Thus test marketing may not be the best way of predicting sales or market shares when:

- surprise is vital to the success of the product,
- lead times are too short to protect the advantage of being first into the market,
- competitors can easily sabotage the tests, for example, by running a competitive advertising campaign in the test area,
- competitors are already doing tests that you can capitalize upon,
- the costs and risks of launch are low,
- the product is subject to rapidly changing fashion,
- the product life cycle is very short.

Quite apart form the circumstances in which test marketing is inappropriate, it can also be very expensive. Thus the direct costs include:

- equipment or plant needed to make the new or modified product,
- the advertising and employment of advertising agencies to support the test product,
- the research data needed for the pre-test and the post-test; this may mean purchasing syndicated data from consumer panels or retail panels,
- sales promotions at the point of sale,
- dealer discounts and incentives for participating in the test.

In addition, there will be indirect costs that include:

- the opportunity cost of what the company could be doing instead of the test market,
- the management time taken up with the tests,
- the diversion of salesforce activity on the new product,
- the impact of the test product on the sales of other products in the range,
- the cost of letting the competition know what you are up to.

Perhaps the key problem of test marketing, however, is that of projecting the results in the test area to the total market. Test results may be unrealistic because:

- there is experimenter effect, for example, salesmen have been trying harder to make the new product a success,
- special inducements may have been used, for example, to get traders to accept the product,
- competitors may deliberately (or unwittingly) confound your results,

- many retail chains will not allow companies to sell products in only part of the country.

Attempts have been made by market research agencies to minimize the effects of some of these drawbacks by developing:

- mini-test marketing,
- simulated test market modelling.

Mini-test marketing is designed to simulate test marketing conditions without exposing the products to the open market and without incurring the costs of a full test market. Its purpose is to estimate or predict potential sales volume or market share for new products. Research International ran a Mini Test Market for over twenty years. This consisted of a panel of 1000 households who were visited weekly by a mobile grocery van fitted out like a supermarket, but was operated by the company itself. All products in the van were bar-coded, and the panel member had a shopping card with an identification number. The actual purchases made by panel members, including quantity, brand, size, price and any special offers were recorded electronically at the checkout using EPOS equipment. Panellists were given a magazine that contained high quality advertisements for selected products including the one being tested. The procedure enabled measures to be taken of the cumulative market penetration achieved by the new product, the repeat purchases made, and the average purchase quantity.

There are a number of advantages of using mini-test markets:

- they avoid exposing the test product in the open market until its repeat purchase potential is known,
- they require only small quantities of the test product,
- they need advertising only in embryo form,
- they obtain results more quickly than in the open market because awareness of the test product is rapidly obtained through the magazine,
- new products are tested in a real-life market situation alongside competing products, and may be supported by advertising, promotions and merchandising,
- the agency can control the range of competitive products on sale and the competitive pricing, promotion and so on,
- different versions of the product can be tried out in different parts of the country.

Research International finally had to abandon its Mini-Test Market, however, because of mounting overheads. Furthermore, since it was a real shop on wheels, it had to be run every day, whether or not there was a client, while competition from the superstores meant that people could not be bothered with the van, and it still took 16–20 weeks to complete a study.

Simulated test market modelling uses sophisticated modelling techniques to estimate trial and repeat purchase for new, modified or relaunched products. Trial and repeat purchase are, in turn, used to make predictions of sales volume and brand shares that will be achieved. These models are described in detail in Chapter 7. They are not really 'field' experiments since most are based on some kind of hall test in which a product or product concept test takes place.

Conclusion

The distinction between laboratory and field experiments sometimes gets a little blurred. Thus Research International's Mini Test Market was really part van test and part test marketing. Furthermore, different procedures may be used in combination. Thus participants in a hall test, say for a new brand of whisky, may be given a bottle to take home and try. They are then subsequently telephoned or sent questionnaires to record their reaction.

It must be remembered that, since experiments are, by definition, small scale and based on samples, they are subject to sampling error. This means that, although compared with surveys there are many more controls over extraneous variables, there will be random sampling fluctuations so that discovered differences between treatments may not, in fact, represent real differences in the population from which the sample was drawn. Alternatively, the failure to discover differences may also be a result of random errors.

Continuous research

In Chapter 1 continuous research was distinguished from ad hoc research. The latter is 'one-off' research, usually geared to specific issues or problems and custom designed for a particular company. As a 'piece' of research, it has a beginning point and comes to a conclusion, going through a number of stages from an initial brief or analysis of the problem to be investigated to data collection, data analysis and the presentation of a final report. Continuous research, by contrast, takes measurements on a regular basis in order to monitor changes that are taking place, often in the consumer market, but may be in the business market or even within the client organization itself. There is no envisaged end to the research process, and it is not normally custom designed for a specific client. Because of the expense of setting up and maintaining a system for the continuous or regular collection and production of data, continuous research is typically syndicated, that is, the research process or the data or both are shared between a number of clients. Usually this means that a large market research organization collects the data and sells them to a number of clients, or that several clients buy into a survey conducted by the agency.

Some continuous research really *is* continuous in the sense that interviews are conducted every day of the year, even though aggregation of the results may take place weekly, two-weekly or four-weekly. Other research, which some purists might argue is, strictly speaking, not continuous, is conducted at regular intervals with a gap between periods of data collection. The continuity of data collection, whether periodic or not, may be achieved in one of two ways:

- obtaining data from the *same* individuals, households or organizations on a continuous or regular basis,
- picking a *fresh* sample of respondents every day or every measurement period.

Panel research uses the first procedure and regular interval surveys the second.

Panel research

In panel research the same data are collected at regular intervals from a representative sample of a defined survey population. A panel is a representative sample of individuals, households or organizations that have agreed to record, or permit the recording of, their activities or opinions in respect of an agreed range of products or services on a continuous or regular basis. Panels are used mostly either to provide quantified estimates of market characteristics (market measurement panels) or of the use of the media (media panels). For the most part they measure behaviour rather than attitudes, since there are problems in asking respondents for their attitudes towards products on a repeated basis. However, for the purpose of evaluating audience reaction to television or radio programmes, television opinion panels or listeners' panels may be asked their opinions of the programmes they have watched or heard.

Market measurement panels are themselves of two main kinds: *consumer* panels and *retail* panels.

Consumer panels

Consumer panels are representative samples of individuals or households whose purchase and use of a defined group of products is recorded either continuously or at regular intervals, usually over a considerable period of time. The first commercial panel in the UK was launched in 1948. Since then the number of panel services available has grown steadily, and the defined groups of products concerned have extended from panels concerned with groceries and fresh foods to panels recording the acquisition of consumer durables and electrical goods, motorists' panels, household (non-food) panels, and panels recording the purchase of toiletries and cosmetics, or baby products.

Unlike regular interval surveys whose respondents are approached for information only on one occasion (or twice if there is some kind of follow-up), panellists are asked to provide information or to perform data collection tasks on a regular basis, often without any specified time limit. Consequently, besides the problem of making the initial selection of panellists in such a way that they are representative of the population being studied, there is the additional problem of maintaining the representativeness of the panel over time. Furthermore, panels can provide consistent trend data over time only if, once they have been set up, there are no changes in panel methodology. Consequently, the initial design needs to be as accurate as possible, and capable of being sustained at a consistent quality over time.

Recruitment to panels tends to be a little more difficult than for ad hoc surveys, since respondents are being asked to do rather more. Some recruitment may be on the back of another large-scale survey operation that the market research agency or one of its subsidiaries or sister companies is already conducting. Respondents to an omnibus survey, for example, who have the required demographic characteristics may be screened for willingness to participate in the panel at the time of the interview. Recruiters may then subsequently approach such respondents to explain the tasks involved, the incentives offered, and to give any training needed.

Once the panel has been recruited it needs to be maintained at a consistent quality of representativeness; furthermore, its members need to be encouraged to report regularly for as long as is desirable. Each year the panel is, of course, getting a year older and would, if no other changes took place in membership, rapidly become unrepresentative. It is, therefore, necessary to recruit younger members and to retire some of the older ones just to keep the age profile correctly balanced. However, for a variety of reasons, people leave the panel, or their circumstances change, for example, they get married, set up separate households, have children and so on. In consequence there is the constant need to 'balance' or 'control' the panel by replacing those who leave with respondents whose demographic characteristics are under-represented. It must be remembered, furthermore, that the population that the panel is meant to represent is itself changing all the time, and panel composition must reflect these changes.

To locate individuals or households required for panel balancing it is normal to use a database of screened respondents from a regular interval survey that the agency undertakes anyway. To keep panellists reporting, there is usually a system of newsletters, prizes, competitions, mystery gifts or points accumulated for catalogue gifts; it is not normal to pay them directly. The newsletter can be important for making the panellist feel a member of a team and to keep him/her informed of developments or reminders to complete certain tasks. If panellists repeatedly fail to report or to perform the agreed tasks then they may be dropped.

The capture of data from panellists is undertaken using one of the three main instruments of data capture: diaries, questionnaires or electronic recording devices. Until recently, diaries have been the most common. Diary design was considered in detail in Chapter 3. Diaries are designed either for the individual or for the household; in the latter case details will normally be entered by the housewife. The details collected will normally include:

- brand name,
- size of pack,
- flavour, colour, type of dispenser, or other brand variant,
- price paid,
- quantity bought,
- any special offers,
- name of shop,
- type of shop.

Questionnaires have been used to a lesser extent, largely in an interviewer-based home audit procedure. Interviewers visit panel members on a regular weekly basis, they carry out a visual inspection of stocks of groceries and other household items by checking cupboards, pantries, fridges and so on, and enter on a questionnaire all items purchased since the previous week. Items consumed during the week are recorded from packaging or labels that are retained. The costs of undertaking home audits are, clearly, very high, and the main example of such a procedure in Europe, if not in the world, namely the Television Consumer Audit run by AGB (now Taylor Nelson AGB) has been replaced by an electronic panel.

New technology has transformed consumer panel data collection techniques, and Taylor Nelson AGB's electronic panel, Superpanel, is described in detail in Chapter 8. Essentially, it involves equipping each panel household with computer terminals and laser scanners for reading the barcodes on packs following each shopping trip.

Panels provide a wealth of data that, if not translated into succinct information that can be absorbed and acted upon, can readily become indigestible. Most panel operators offer both standard and special analyses. Standard trend analyses are produced usually at monthly or four-weekly intervals, and they show the progress of the market and its major brands since the previous period. Clients usually subscribe on an annual basis to receive these reports over the year. The reports are tables of figures that give results by product field grossed up to the Great Britain population (Ulster is usually treated separately), or to a particular region. Such tables typically show for the current month, the previous month and the same month in the previous year:

- sales volume for the total market, for each brand and each brand variant,
- consumer expenditure at current retail prices for the total market, for each brand and each brand variant,
- market shares for each brand,
- market penetration,
- special offers,
- average prices.

Special analyses tend to be fairly standard 'optional extras'. Thus a 'source of purchase' analysis will show volume, value and prices paid by type of outlet, including breakdowns by key accounts like Tesco, Sainsbury or Asda. A 'cumulative penetration' analysis will measure the rate of increase in the number of new buyers over time, and can be used to show the effect of promotional support. A 'frequency of purchase' analysis shows the percentage of buyers purchasing each brand at least once, twice, three times and so on. This will show the extent to which a brand is dependent on a small number of regular buyers rather than a larger number of infrequent buyers. There will, in addition, be a variety of demographic analyses, describing the buyer profile of the market and its major brands in terms of age of purchaser, social class, household size, ACORN classification, presence of children and so on. Because panel data are longitudinal and can track individuals through time, it is possible to look at inter-purchasing between brands, brand loyalty, repeat buying, and gains from and losses to competitors. These, in turn, can be used as inputs to making volume and brand share predictions (see Chapter 8).

Because panels are samples they are subject to the kinds of sampling and non-sampling error described in the next chapter. Although panels are balanced to keep them representative as far as possible, this is not always, if ever, totally achieved. In consequence, the results from panels are weighted to make finer adjustments for over- and under-representation of sub-groups. In addition, they suffer from problems of coverage and pickup. Lack of coverage means that consumer panels often produce lower estimates of total sales than are reflected in either ex-factory shipments or trade estimates. Consumer purchase panels measure only purchases made by private households, not purchases by offices, forces bases, old people's homes, student accommodation, exports, purchase by other organizations or items lost, damaged or pilfered in transit. Some market research agencies may apply 'field weights' to their data to make adjustments for lack of coverage so that market estimates eventually reflect actual total market volumes and values.

Pickup errors result from tendencies of panellists to overlook some of their purchases, or not to know about the purchases made by other members of the household. Occasionally, deliberate falsification may be provoked by the complexity of the tasks respondents have to perform, or they may be suffering from lack of motivation and commitment to the panel. The level of pickup tends to vary from product to product, and may be anything from 50 per cent to 200 per cent of independent market estimates. However, provided this level is fairly constant then 'product field' or 'market size' weights may be applied before estimates are grossed up to the population.

Retail panels

Retail panels are representative samples (or, in some cases, the complete universe) of retail outlets whose acquisition, pricing, stocking and display of a defined group of products are recorded either continuously or at regular intervals. Such panels were first set up by the A. C. Nielsen Company in the USA in the 1930s. Nielsen began retail tracking operations in the UK in 1939. In the 1950s and 1960s demand tended to exceed supply and the key problem for any manufacturer to solve was efficient distribution to ensure product availability. In this situation, information on distribution was crucial. Nielsen rapidly expanded its operations and a number of companies set up competing retail panel services. The current Nielsen Retail Index system is described in detail in Chapter 8.

Retail panels are used largely to provide estimates of over-the-counter sales of products, brand-by-brand and brand variant. This information is sometimes available directly from the use of electronic data capture techniques using bar-scanning equipment. It is otherwise necessary to undertake a retail audit. This involves physically counting the stocks in the panel shops at the beginning and at the end of the audit period (usually four weeks or a month). By subtracting stocks for each brand and brand variant at the end of the audit period from deliveries and those stocks held at the beginning, sales can be deduced. Even where electronic data are available, it may still be necessary to undertake retail audits in order to determine the prices charged, the shelf-space allocated to brands, the quantities held in the 'reserve' areas, and any in-store promotions. Auditors from the market research agency offering panel services visit the panel shops on a regular basis. They may spend two or three days in the shop, counting stocks and entering their observations into a portable data entry terminal. These may then be placed in a modem for transmission of the data to a central computer via the telephone.

Where universe data are not available, it is necessary to take a sample of shops from which to make estimates. The key problem with sampling retail outlets is that stores vary enormously in terms of turnover. Over- or under-representing stores of different sizes will seriously affect the estimates made. Consequently, it is necessary to stratify the selection of shops by turnover range as well as by type of shop (e.g. multiple, co-operative or independent) and by region. Unfortunately, in order to do this it is necessary to know:

- how many shops of a given type fall into a particular turnover range in that area,
- the annual turnover of the sampled shops,
- annual turnover of the universe.

Acquiring this information is a large undertaking. For most of the major multiples and for the co-operatives this information may be provided by the multiple chain, or by the Co-operative Wholesale Society in the case of co-operatives. For independents and smaller multiples Nielsen, for example, carries out an extensive enumeration followed by a survey of a sample of enumerated shops.

Once shops have been selected and have agreed to co-operate, data collection is likely to be some combination of:

- visual inspection of products on shelves and their location in the store,
- checking delivery notes,
- getting retailers to complete questionnaires or other records specially for the agency,
- obtaining data that have been captured electronically or that have been entered on a computerized database.

All operators of retail panels produce tables that give distribution and price data along with estimates of sales volumes and values on a brand by brand and brand variant basis. Since the major multiples normally supply data on deliveries to their outlets and allow access to their barcoded data only on the understanding that the tables do not identify particular named groups, the tables aggregate data for these groups. It is not possible, therefore, for example, to compare what is happening in Tesco with Sainsbury or Asda. The kinds of tables and charts produced by Nielsen are described in Chapter 8.

Consumer panels and retail panels compared

Both consumer panels and retail panels generate estimates of sales volumes, values and market shares on a brand-by-brand and brand variant basis every four weeks or every month. Such information helps companies to:

- evaluate company strengths and weaknesses in the marketplace,
- diagnose market opportunities and competitor threats,
- set realistic long-term objectives,
- develop plans to achieve them,
- monitor the impact of trends in the market.

Beyond this, consumer panels and retail panels are suited to different purposes. Consumer panels are able to track consumer behaviour, for example, in terms of purchase frequency and brand loyalty; retail panels can track what happens in the distribution system up to the point where the consumer makes a purchase. The manufacturer can, for example, tell how many shops who usually handle his stock were out of stock in the last period, what competitor brands are set alongside his own brands and in what kinds of shops, what price differentials are, what levels of stock are held where in the shop, and how these have changed since the last measurement period.

Operators of both types of panel will make claims to the superior accuracy of their service for the data produced in common. Consumer panel operators will point out that by asking consumers about where they purchased their products, *all* the outlets selling the particular brand will be covered. Retail panels cover only those outlets included in the particular sample of shops. Because their data are derived from consumers, consumer panels are able to produce named group data, that is, data broken down by named account. Retail panels are restricted by their agreement with the major multiples, as explained above, *not* to produce such data. Retail panel operators will claim, on the other hand, that retail panels do not rely on the memories of consumers, but systematically record actual sales in the sample shops. Some of the data, furthermore, are not estimates based on samples, but universe data. They will argue, too, that in highly fragmented markets, consumer panels will pick up only small quantities of a particular brand. Retail panels, by contrast, will record all the sales of every brand in the sample shops.

Since the services are, in many ways, complementary, the trend has been for the larger agencies to offer both types of panel. Thus Taylor Nelson AGB purchased the National Market Research Association (NMRA) from the Mars Group so that it could do its own retail panel operations. By the same token, Nielsen has set up its own Homescan service to provide consumer panel data. This means that clients can have access to both types of data from the same market research organization.

Other types of panel

Media panels are used mostly for television audience measurement and for estimating audience appreciation of television and radio programmes. These panels are described in detail in Chapter 8. Some panels are 'single source', that is, they collect data both on product purchasing and on media usage. Thus Taylor Nelson AGB's 'Adlab' is based on a sample of 1000 housewives in the Central Television area. Panel members complete two separate weekly diaries. One records purchasing of groceries, toiletries and household items, and the other is in a daily format to record housewife television viewing, radio listening and her readership of newspapers and magazines. By collecting both types of data from the same source, it is possible to more directly look at the effect of media exposure on purchasing behaviour.

Regular interval surveys

These are surveys of respondents carried out at regular intervals using independent samples for each measurement period. Like panels, they are used for market measurement and for media usage, but, in addition, they are used by the Office for National Statistics and other government bodies for collecting various forms of government statistics.

Market measurement regular interval surveys include *omnibus* surveys and *market tracking* surveys.

Omnibus surveys

These are surveys that market research agencies undertake to run with a stated frequency and with a pre-determined method. Clients buy space in the questionnaire by adding and paying for questions of their own according to number and type of question. The agency draws a fresh sample of respondents each time, administers the questionnaire, processes the data and reports the results. This means that the costs of setting up the survey, administration, collection of demographic data and analysis are shared between several clients. Over the past decade omnibus research has become more popular, varied and competitive, giving clients the opportunity to buy inexpensive research as and when required. More than 30 companies in the UK now run such surveys; other companies 'offer' the service on a consultancy basis, buying their fieldwork from those organizations actually running an omnibus.

Omnimas, the largest, is described in detail in Chapter 8. There are, however, different types of omnibus depending on:

■ the general or specific nature of the population being sampled,
■ the type of sampling method,
■ the method of questionnaire administration.

General consumer omnibuses sample a general cross-section of the adult population, while special omnibuses are dedicated to specific groups in the population, for example, motorists, mothers with babies, doctors, business-men, architects, travel agents or farmers. Random omnibuses use random sampling techniques to select respondents, while quota omnibuses use random location or straight quota samples. The next chapter explains these forms of sampling. Random omnibuses tend to be a little more expensive, but the accuracy of the sampling is, on the whole, superior. They are worthwhile if good estimates are required of population values. Some omnibuses are personal, using face-to-face interviewing, while others use telephone research. The latter are quicker, but may work out a little more expensive; furthermore, no visual material can be shown to respondents. They tend to use a random selection methodology for selecting the telephone numbers, and then to impose quotas on age, sex and social class.

Consumer omnibuses tend to be run on a weekly basis while the more specialized ones may be monthly. Sample sizes vary from 1000 up to 3000. Telephone omnibuses are mostly 1000; face-to-face consumer omnibuses are typically between 1500 and 2000.

Most agencies have a master questionnaire with a classification section containing the demographic questions that are asked each time. These are usually completed at the end of the interview. The main part of the questionnaire is often divided into two sections: continuous and ad hoc. The continuous section includes questions that are inserted for clients on every survey. They will usually be in the same order and in the same place every time to avoid the effect on answers of changing positions. This will also mean that the questionnaire always begins in the same way, which helps the interviewers to begin their interviewing. The ad hoc questions are usually inserted in a first-come-first-serve basis, but the agency will try to put them together in a sensible way. Question sets for competing fields cannot be allowed in the same survey.

Agencies tend to place few restrictions on the topics covered. However, questions on security, for example, 'Do you have a burglar alarm in your home?' may not be allowed. Some agencies place restrictions on the number of questions that may be included from any one client (or on the amount of time they take) plus an overall limitation on the size of the survey. The average number of questions per client is 6–10 – omnibus surveys cease to be cost effective if many questions are to be included.

The questions themselves may be pre-coded or open-ended. Some agencies place restrictions on the number of code positions allowed, or may charge extra. Open-ended questions may cost up to double the cost of pre-coded ones. Sensitive probing of answers is not usually feasible – interviewers already have a tough time handling a questionnaire that is really a series of questionnaires going from topic to topic.

Some clients will submit their questions already worded in the way they want them; others require the help of the market research agency in framing them. Such help is normally included in the price of the question. Most companies will do split runs, that is, testing two or three versions of a question or question-set among different respondents. However, these can seriously complicate the organization of the survey. The use of show cards is fairly common; these might give definitions, lists of products or brands, photographs, copies of advertisements, telepics or pack fronts. Sometimes these may all be made into a specially produced booklet.

All suppliers of omnibus services make a charge per question, currently ranging from £200 per question to over £500. However, it would be misleading to buy into an omnibus on that basis alone. The analyses and services that are included as part of the price vary considerably. Some agencies charge extra for questions with many pre-codes, for prompt cards, show cards or other materials, and for open-ended questions. Some give discounts for more than a certain number of questions or for inserting them on a regular basis. Some give discounts when only part of the sample is being used. Some charge a joining fee that may vary from £100 to £500 or more. Sometimes this fee is waived when more than a certain amount of business is commissioned. Agencies have different approaches to deciding what counts as one question. A question with four sub-sections may be treated as one or as four questions.

Basic analyses of the pre-coded questions are usually available within a few days of fieldwork completion. Open-ended questions are usually post-coded (in co-operation with the client) and these will take a little longer. Results may be accumulated over a period of time to produce monthly, quarterly or even annual reports. Most agencies include standard breakdowns by key demographic questions within the price of the question. Optional extras include the production of charts, writing mini-reports, market or brand mapping, cluster analysis or analysis by one of the geodemographic systems like ACORN. The tables themselves will normally refer to volumes, frequencies or Sterling values that have been grossed up to the population, usually after weighting.

Omnibus surveys may be used for continuous or for ad hoc purposes – or some mixture of the two. The range of uses to which clients put omnibuses includes:

- market measurement, for example, the volume and value of sales, brand shares, frequency of purchase, brand loyalty, brand switching,
- assessing the effectiveness of an advertising campaign, for example, by tracking brand or advertising awareness,
- media measurement, for example, the readership of certain magazines,
- tracking the impact of or forecasting sales of new product launches,
- tracking brand image or corporate image,
- new product concept tests and product tests,
- test market assessment,
- product usage and attitude,
- testing questions using split-run techniques,
- building up samples of minority groups.

The main advantages of omnibus surveys are:

- the questions are custom-designed and the results are confidential to the client,

- they are quick and relatively inexpensive where the information can be gathered with a few questions,
- they are there when needed and can be used at short notice,
- they are, on the whole, well-conducted and well-respected in the industry,
- they can obtain samples of a reasonable size for minority groups over a period of time,
- they can be used for recruitment purposes for other surveys.

Omnibuses are unsuitable, however, for detailed probing or where lengthy question-sets are required. Telephone omnibuses have the additional disadvantage that they cannot be supported by showcards or other visual materials. Sample designs are fixed by the market research organization and cannot be modified to suit client needs. Clients can, of course, shop around for an omnibus that is more suitable in terms of sample design.

Market tracking surveys

These surveys are carried out at regular intervals, but the agency designs the whole questionnaire, and the data collected are sold to as many clients as possible. They tend to get used instead of panels where pickup would be a considerable problem. Examples are Taylor Nelson AGB's Recall survey, which provides market measurement and consumer profiles of slower moving personal toiletries, cosmetics and fragrances, over-the-counter medicines and photographic software. Public Attitude Surveys (PAS) operates a drinks market survey, while the British Market Research Bureau (BMRB) offers its Target Group Index as the only single-source regular interval survey combining product usage with media exposure. The TGI is explained in detail in Chapter 8.

Market tracking surveys use wide range of sampling techniques, although few go to the expense of random probability sampling. A key advantage of market tracking surveys is that it is possible to base analyses on large numbers of individuals, offering the ability to do lots of breakdowns. Clients can buy from the agency just those data that they require for their purposes. However, the results are not confidential and data are available to groups of competing manufacturers.

Panels and regular interval surveys compared

The main advantages of panels over regular interval surveys include:

- sampling errors tend to be less since there is statistical association between successive measurements,
- memory errors will tend to be less because regular interval surveys depend on recall of purchases while panels either record purchases in a diary or they are recorded electronically,
- it is possible to follow through an individual's purchasing behaviour over time, making it possible to analyse brand switching, brand loyalty, and repeat purchasing behaviour.

The main advantages of regular interval surveys over panels include:

- over a period of time large numbers of respondents are interviewed, making it possible to build up samples of minority groups,

- it is possible to include attitude questions because there are no fears about respondent conditioning over time,
- they are cheaper to operate, largely because there is no panel maintenance to be undertaken,
- the real response rate tends to be higher because individuals are being asked to do less,
- they will pick up a higher proportion of purchases for products that are bought infrequently or only by minority groups,
- they are more flexible, for example, it is easier to change the questions being asked without upsetting other clients,
- they can be used for questionnaires that take longer to complete.

These advantages and limitations need to be kept in mind when considering what kind of research is appropriate for resolving or analysing the problems faced by a particular company.

Desk research

Many data, once collected, processed and stored, will be used later on for further, secondary, analyses. Some of these data may be published and will be available either free or at very little cost. Some may be purchasable from agencies that have collected them. Some data will be confidential to the client, but the client company can, of course, re-use its own data. What is called 'desk research' entails the pro-active seeking-out of data, qualitative or quantitative, that already exist and which may be useful in the analysis, planning or control of marketing activity. Sometimes the original 'micro' data are available, that is, data that relate to individual cases. In this situation it is possible to reanalyse the data for example by correlating or cross-tabulating them with other variables. Many published statistics, however, are 'macro' data, that is, the original cases are no longer identifiable and tables consist of summaries, groupings, averages and so on. Here, further analyses are limited because variables in the tables cannot be related to variables in other tables on a case-by-case basis.

Typically, desk research is used in an exploratory phase of research, but, on occasions, it may be discovered that sufficient data are available to avoid the need to collect data specially for the research at hand. Activities that may be included in desk research are making library searches, searching in-house company records and information systems, making on-line database searches, buying data and reports from commercial sources or using the Internet.

Data to which a desk researcher may have access will have been collected for purposes other than those being currently pursued, and accordingly may not be in a form that is ideal. Nevertheless, it is often unwise to begin a project before seeking out what has already been written or data that have already been collected on the topic. For academic, scholarly research this is an essential part of any dissertation, thesis, article for publication in an academic journal, or for a research monograph. For textbooks such as this one, however, it would probably be distracting to have a review of the entire literature on every topic or subject mentioned, so only those sources that might be of interest to the reader are referred to.

In commissioned research there is frequently no desk research phase and in many studies, particularly of the consumer market, desk research may be less relevant since secondary data are, by definition, largely historical, whereas what is required are data on consumer behaviour or consumer attitudes now or very recently. Clients, furthermore, would not be interested in reading literature reviews, for example, on the origin and design of tracking studies, before getting to the results of the tracking of their own products. However, the use of accumulated databases that go back several years for the analysis of trends or for the purpose of parametizing market models may be thought of as desk research which is used as inputs to secondary analysis, that is, the re-analysis of existing data. There are, however, a lot of data on organizational, business and industrial markets, and market research on these (often referred to as 'business-to-business' research) is more likely to have a specific desk research phase.

Sources for desk research

A lot of data that may be usable for marketing purposes are often already available within the organization that is the focus of the research. Three main sources may be distinguished:

- operating data and company accounts,
- previous research,
- data contained in information systems.

Operating data might include information on the performance of individual products that the firm makes, for example, on sales, profits and costs; on the various sections, divisions, factory sites or subsidiaries of the company; on the functions it performs – manufacturing, distribution, marketing, purchasing or research and development. Company accounts will supply information on the overall performance of the organization – turnover, costs, revenue, profits, a balance sheet and profit and loss statement. Invoices or records of purchases may be able to supply information on customer addresses, types of purchases, dates and frequencies of purchase, discounts, credits, delivery and so on.

Previous research may have been carried out both on the company and on the market to which it sells. Reading the reports of such activities may enable researchers to familiarize themselves with the background of the current situation, and perhaps use them as a guide or input to the design of the research to be undertaken. It may even be possible to utilise such research as a bench-mark for measuring change from an earlier period. It makes sense to classify and store such reports in a library and in such a way that they may be easily retrieved on future occasions. Unfortunately, it is still common practice for copies of reports to be kept on the shelves of the managers who commissioned them.

Management or marketing information systems combine various data inputs, store them on a computerized database, and usually have the ability to produce integrated reports on a regular basis using an agreed system. They may operate at various levels of sophistication. At a basic level they are simply data storage and retrieval systems that make existing data more readily accessible and presentable. Standard database packages do this very well and they provide the mechanisms for abstracting and indexing information and retrieving it in particular formats. More sophisticated are systems for monitoring and control that check progress and alert management to variations, departures or variances from plans, criteria or budgets. Analytical information systems use statistical models to answer, 'Why?' questions, to make forecasts or recommendations, or to answer, 'What if . . . ?' questions using simulation techniques. While such systems can thus produce large amounts of data and endless reports, the ability of management to absorb and react to such information may be limited.

Data from sources external to the organization may be derived from:

- environmental scanning,
- official and unofficial published statistics,
- buying data or reports from business publishing houses, market research agencies or advertising agencies.

Environmental scanning refers to the process of compiling and evaluating qualitative and quantitative information on what is happening generally in the marketplace, particularly the activities of competitors, and in the wider social, political, economic and technological environment. The result is usually referred to as 'market intelligence', which is a collection of pieces of information, often incomplete and subjective, but which allows the researcher to keep abreast of events as they unfold. These sources include:

- reading business and financial newspapers like the *Financial Times* or *the Wall Street Journal*, general business magazines like *Business Week* or *The Economist*, trade and technical journals like *Computer Weekly*, and academic periodicals like the *Harvard Business Review* or the *Journal of Management Studies*,
- personal contacts in other organizations,
- feedback from the salesforce,
- watching competitors,
- going to conferences, exhibitions, courses, or meetings.

In many market research agencies, executives are assigned to particular groups of clients and are expected to familiarize themselves with their markets. Most environmental scanning, however, is probably undertaken in-house by company managers. The process of environmental scanning may be very informal with no specific purpose in mind, it may be conditioned to a particular type of information, it may be a pro-active but unsystematic search, or there may be formal procedures for finding, storing and retrieving the information. Whatever form the scanning takes, the resulting market intelligence should enable the firm to adapt more easily to a changing environment, it may act as a source of inspiration for innovation, or it may alert management to opportunities or threats (see Piercy and Evans, 1983, ch. 4, for a detailed exposition of marketing intelligence).

A problem with market intelligence data lies in the procedures used for their collection. Unless these are systematic the data will be unrepresentative and may be misleading. Managers and salespeople need a straightforward reporting system organized in a way that minimizes the work involved. Perhaps more importantly, however, there needs to be a feeling that such reports are of real value to the organization and that they do actually feed into the decision-making process.

Official statistics may be subdivided into governmental and non-governmental sources. The collection and dissemination of government statistics is organized by the Office of National Statistics. This was a body created in 1996 from the merger of the former Central Statistical Office (CSO) and the Office of Population Censuses and Surveys (OPCS). The ONS produces a number of different types of series including:

- continuous, multi-purpose datasets like the *Family Expenditure Survey*, the *General Household Survey* and the *National Food Survey*,
- multi-source publications like the *Annual Abstract of Statistics*, the *Abstract of Regional Statistics*, the *Monthly Digest of Statistics*, *Economic Trends, Social Trends* and *Population Trends*,
- censuses like the *Census of Population* (every 10 years) and the *Census of Production* (every five years).

One particularly important source for marketers is *Business Monitors* which provide detailed information about most of the important industries in the UK. In a unique development, Taylor Nelson AGB and the CSO (now the ONS) announced in 1994 a joint venture to produce a new series called *UK Markets*. Nearly 100 annual and over 30 quarterly reports are produced by Taylor Nelson AGB from data collected by the ONS from 28,500 manufacturers covering 90 per cent on the UK manufacturers' sales and 4800 types of product.

Non-governmental statistics are produced by bodies like the European Union and the United Nations. There are nearly 100 publicly available databases of European statistics including *Europe in Figures*, *Facts through Figures*, *Eurostat Yearbook* and *Basic Statistics of the Community*. Non-official sources of data in the UK are published by trade associations, banks, the press, television networks, Chambers of Commerce and so on. These sources are usually free or available at very little cost. In addition there is a range of commercial subscription sources that includes BMRB's *Target Group Index*, *Mintel Market Intelligence Reports*, *Keynote Publications*, *Market Research GB*, *Market Research Europe*, and *Retail Business*.

Financial analysis reports, business news services or computer access to on-line databases may be purchased from some agencies. Subscribing to continuous market measurement services such as consumer panels or retail panels is another possibility. A year's subscription will pay for 12 four-weekly reports on the products or brands you choose, detailing sales by volume and by value on a brand by brand basis, broken down by a whole series of geographical, demographic and behavioural characteristics.

There are a number of guides to sources of secondary data. Keynote Publications produces its *The Source Book*; Euromonitor offers a *Compendium of Marketing Information Sources*; Industrial Aids Ltd has *Published Data of European Markets*. There is also the government's own *Guide to Official Statistics* (HMSO). Apart from such guides there is a range of indexing services, for example, the *British Humanities Index*, the *Social Sciences Citation Index*, the *Research Index* and the *Financial Times Index*. There are a number of compendiums giving all sorts of useful marketing data, for example, the *Marketing Pocket Book*, published by the Advertising Association.

The uses of desk research

There are two key uses of desk research: providing background materials for primary research and providing an alternative to doing primary research.

In the former application, desk research is one of a number of stages in the conduct of a marketing research project. Usually, it will be an early stage and may need to be completed before the primary research can be designed, or it may be necessary to check that a similar study has not already been carried out, or that the data required are not already available. However, desk research may also continue while the primary research is in progress, deepening the understanding of the market research executive, keeping him or her abreast of current developments in the marketplace. The results of desk research may be used in the final report to provide an overview of the general economic environment, the size and structure of and trends in the market, and the main competitors before looking at the performance of the client's brand derived from the primary research.

In the second application, desk research may reveal that no further research is required, for example, because it has shown that the potential market is just not large enough to support a new product under consideration. Many an annual marketing plan is preceded by a desk research review of the market with no further research input. Sometimes the re-analysis of existing data provides a sufficient basis for making a marketing decision or pursuing some marketing activity.

Strategies and tactics of desk research

Desk research cannot be fully structured – it is more like a treasure hunt or piece of detection work. What will emerge is often unknown beforehand. It requires skills of methodicalness, persistence and ingenuity. It means knowing where best to begin and how to proceed thereafter. For the research executive in a market research agency, the first step will be to determine from the client what data are accessible in the company itself. There will certainly be accounting and operating data, but there may also be a customer database, and the client may well be subscribing to one or more syndicated sources that provide data on products, brand by brand, and on markets and consumers on a continuous basis. The client may have a library containing past reports or a management information system that can be accessed. The executive may next check what statistical series are kept by the agency itself. These are likely to include *Business Monitor*, *Market Research GB*, *Retail Business*, *Marketing Week*, *Business Week*, and so on. Next, the executive may contact the appropriate trade associations to see what data they hold (usually generated from their own members).

To obtain information on companies, the most accessible source is usually one or more of the excellent company directories. One of the best on the UK industry is *Kompass*. It lists over 30,000 companies, grouped by county and town, together with their addresses, directors, number of employees, main activities and brief financial data. Comparable information may be found in *Kelly's Directory*, *Manufacturers and Merchants* volumes, and in two directories published by Dunn and Bradstreet, The *National Business Directory* and *The Key British Enterprises*. Some agencies, like Extel Statistical Services, gather this information together and will provide company profiles.

Increasing quantities of data are now available on electronic databases and going 'on-line' can save considerable time. Most are available commercially and the client can subscribe to a particular supplier or using the Internet. Key word searches are particularly beneficial; it can take just a few minutes to find every mention of a word, phrase or product in the database being used. Thus Finsbury Data Services offers its Profile database which gives full text retrieval of media articles in British newspapers, magazines and selected commercial outputs, for example, from Euromonitor and Mintel. Reuters's Textline offers an international database of media sources; ABI Inform covers academic periodicals in the business area.

Limitations of secondary sources

Because secondary data normally appear in printed or even published form, it is often forgotten that they were originally collected as primary data, albeit for some other purpose, using the data capture instruments described in the previous chapter and the primary data collection methods explained above. Very often the data are estimates based on samples, so it is necessary to bear in mind also all the potential sources of error outlined in the next chapter.

Not all secondary data are of the same quality in terms of validity and reliability, and it may be necessary to ask a number of questions about them, including:

■ Who produced the data?
■ Why were the data collected in the first place?
■ How were they collected?
■ When were they collected?
■ What definitions were used?

It is a good idea to bear in mind the agents who were responsible for the original collection, analysis and presentation of the data. We saw in Chapter 2 that data are created, not discovered. They are a product of human activity and are manufactured within a structure of competing interests. Irvine *et al.* (1979) argue that statistical practice is not a purely technical matter of utilising the 'correct' sampling techniques, statistical analyses, probability theory and so on. Data are social products that have been created by individuals, groups or governments with their own economic and social agendas. Data are never totally neutral; they are a selection of the data that could have been collected. There may well be a convenient lack of information on sensitive topics like the real levels of poverty or unemployment, and the data that would have been useful to the researcher are not collected. So, in asking who produced the data, it is as well to recognize that, for example, trade associations exist to further the interests of their members and may well hesitate to publish data that are inimical to those interests.

Answering the question concerning why the data were collected in the first place may well give insights into the value of that information. Thus the original purpose of the Family Expenditure Survey, begun in 1957, was to provide information on spending patterns for the Retail Prices Index, not to measure the levels of poverty.

Some secondary data may have been originally collected by using methods that are prone to error or bias, for example, using quota samples to select respondents, or random samples with a poor response rate. Some published data may well have been collected some time before their publication. This is particularly true of government statistics.

Finally, definitions of the original case – whether 'household', 'housewife', 'establishment' – or of the original variables and the scales of values used, may not be the ones the researcher would have chosen. The result is that the data are published in a format that is not particularly useful to him or to her, or that, because of changes in definitions, the analysis of trends becomes dubious.

Summary

The instruments of data capture – questionnaires, diaries and recording devices – may be used for personal observation, in qualitative research, survey research, experimental research or continuous research. Each comes in a number of sub-varieties and each has its own particular strengths and limitations. These need to be kept in mind in designing research to solve particular problems or to use as a basis for making a particular decision. Unless these problems and decisions are clearly analysed, the basis for choosing or justifying one type of research over another remains obscure. Primary data collected using these techniques may subsequently be used for secondary analysis, and any research project should ideally begin by seeking out what data may already have been collected and may be available in published or purchasable form.

Key concepts

primary data
secondary data
personal observation
disguised/undisguised observation
accompanied shopping
mystery shopping
qualitative research
group discussions
depth interviews
survey research
interview surveys
telephone surveys
postal surveys
experimental research
laboratory experiments
field experiments

continuous research
panel research
market measurement panels
consumer panels
retail panels
media panels
regular interval surveys
omnibus surveys
market tracking surveys
desk research

Further reading

■ Gendall, P, Hoek, J and Esslemont, D (1995) ' The effect of appeal, complexity and tone in a mail survey covering letter', *Journal of the Market Research Society*, Vol 37, No 3, pp 251–68.

■ Gordon, W and Langmaid, R (1988) *Qualitative Market Research. A Practitioner's and Buyer's Guide*, London: Gower Press.

■ Griggs, S (1987), 'Analysing qualitative data', *Journal of the Market Research Society*, Vol 29, No 12, pp 15–34.

- Irvine, J, Miles, I and Evans, J (eds) (1979) *Demystifying Social Statistics*, London: Pluto Press.
- Klose, A and Ball, A (1995), 'Using optical mark read surveys: an analysis of response rate and quality', *Journal of the Market Research Society*, Vol 37, No 3, pp 269-86.
- Morrison, L, Colman, M and Preston, C (1997) 'Mystery customer research: cognitive processes affecting accuracy', *Journal of the Market Research Society*, Vol 39, No 2, April, pp 394-61.
- Taylor, H (1997) ' The very different methods used to conduct telephone surveys of the public', *Journal of the Market Research Society*, Vol 39, No 3, pp 421-32.

Questions for further discussion

1   A major manufacturer of men's underwear wants to discover the main criteria that purchasers use in selecting the brand and style of underwear. The manufacturer wants a series of group discussions. Advise the company on the kind of groups and group composition that would be appropriate.
2   A manufacturer of office furniture wants to find out the key characteristics of desk users and on the sizes and uses of desks. The managing director has asked for a survey of medium to large companies in the UK. Would you recommend an interview, a telephone or a postal survey? Give your reasons.
3   A large producer of confectionery wants to find the best combination of levels of raisins, nuts and honey in a chocolate bar. Each may be high, medium or low in content. Explain to the manufacturer the various ways of designing an experiment to find this out. Which would you recommend?
4   To what extent are retail panels and consumer panels in direct competition for the continuous monitoring of consumer markets?
5   Design six to 10 questions for inclusion in an omnibus survey that would enable a travel company to analyse the relationship between type, destination and duration of holidays taken in 1997 by UK nationals.

Useful Web sites

http: //www.emap.co.uk

5

Sampling cases

Chapter 2 explained that data arise from the process of keeping systematic records on one or more cases – the individuals, households, families, products, events or organizations that are the focus of the researcher's interest. Sometimes the number of such cases is large and it may be necessary to take a sample rather than to try to study them all. This chapter considers when it is necessary or advisable to take samples; it then turns to sample design and the kinds of error that arise in the process.

When we need to take samples

In some kinds of research it is not necessary to take, or even to consider taking, a sample. If a company asks a market research agency or a management consultant to investigate a particular problem which is totally internal to the company, then there is only one case – the company – whose characteristics are being measured.

Sometimes, the set of cases that are the focus of the researcher's attention, the 'population', is sufficiently limited in number for him or her to study them all, that is, to take a 'census'. This often happens in a study of organizations in a particular industry or sector of the market. There may only be 20 or 30 firms that manufacture a particular product, and the researcher will almost certainly try to contact each one. In other situations, the electronic recording of data enables data to be captured for the total set even of a large number of cases. Thus where retail outlets all have laser-scanning equipment, it is possible to measure the sales of every product, brand and brand variant in every store without having to take a sample of stores from which to make estimates.

It makes sense to take a census of all the cases in which the researcher is interested whenever this is feasible. However, the population of cases may be very large, consisting of many thousands, perhaps millions. Thus a study of all households in the UK will involve some 20 million such cases. To study them all would take a very long time, and would be very expensive (although it *is* done every ten years in the official Census carried out by the Office for National Statistics). Market researchers, however, have limited funds and results are usually required quickly. In such circumstances it is usually necessary to take a sample – a subset of cases selected and then studied by the researcher for the purpose of being able to draw conclusions about the entire population of cases. Such a procedure may even be deemed preferable where contacting or observing every case would be feasible, but nevertheless difficult, slow or too expensive. Attempts to contact every case may, in any event, not be totally successful, and the researcher may end up with an incomplete census. This may be less representative than a carefully drawn sample.

Researching a small sample carefully may, in fact, result in greater accuracy than either a very large sample or a complete census, since the problems associated with handling a large number of interviewers and a large number of questionnaires may create errors of a greater magnitude than those arising from the sampling process.

Sample design

Sample design is an integral part of the overall research design (which is considered in detail in Chapter 7). The quality of the sample has a significant impact on the overall quality of the research, but designing an appropriate sample is seldom easy, partly because many factors need to be taken into account and partly because, particularly for national samples, the design may need to be both complex and sophisticated.

There are various bases on which the researcher may make his or her selection, but a key distinction is between *purposive* samples and *representative* samples. Purposive samples are generated when the selection of cases is made by the researcher using his or her own judgement. The selection may be made on the basis of contacting those cases that are easiest to access, those that are deemed to be the most important, those that reflect a variety or extremes, or those that are typical. A researcher may, for example, select those organizations in which he or she already has contacts, or those that are within travelling distance. If the study is of retailers and electronic data are not available, then a sample of retailers may need to be taken; but some have much higher turnovers than others. So, the researcher may deliberately choose all the major multiples, and then make a purposive selection of the remainder based on turnover, type of shop and location. The researcher may choose cases on the basis that each one is an example of every type of situation that the researcher wishes to cover. Sometimes the researcher may pick extreme cases, for example all the most marketing-oriented companies may be selected in order to look at the extent to which or the manner in which they use marketing planning procedures. Finally, cases may be chosen because they are 'typical'. Thus particular towns, cities or areas may be chosen because they have typical or average populations, or industrial, institutional and social structures.

Purposive samples are used, quite legitimately, for exploratory research, for qualitative research and for a lot of experimental research where the focus is on understanding situations, generating ideas or evaluating products, ideas for products, advertising or ideas for advertising. These research methods were described in detail in Chapter 4. Purposive sampling is also sometimes used in quantitative research. Thus Nielsen's selection of shops for its retail index system includes purposive elements (see Chapter 8).

Representative samples, by contrast, are chosen in such a way that they reproduce the structure and features of the population of cases from which the sample was drawn; in short, so that they are a microcosm of the entire set of cases. They are used primarily for quantitative analysis, either to make estimates of the size or frequency of a population characteristic, or to measure and test the extent to which the characteristics of cases are related together in the population. Ideally, the results obtained from the sample should be broadly the same as those that would have been obtained had the whole population of cases been studied. The selection of cases is made using one of three main techniques:

■ randomized,
■ systematic,
■ interviewer selection.

Randomized selection is the selection by chance, using a technique that is independent of human judgement, from a complete list of the population of cases which is to be sampled (the 'sampling frame'). Sampling techniques entail using some form of lottery, like taking names out of a hat, using tables of random numbers to select numbered units, or relying on computerised random procedures.

Systematic selection creates a rule that determines the selection of the units, thereby removing, or largely removing, human judgement. This may mean taking every nth name from a list at N/n intervals where N is the population size and n is the sample size, or taking every nth house along a street and following some rule about the selection of streets.

Interviewer selection clearly involves human judgement, but this judgement will, normally, be limited in a number of ways, often in combination, by restricting:

■ the numbers of types of people to be chosen, that is, interviewers are given quotas, for example, of so many men and women, so many of different age groups,
■ the time of day at which interviews may take place, for example, allowing no interviews of males before 5 pm to get a cross-section of men in employment, or observing customers in pubs and bars at specific times of the day,
■ the area in which the interviewer may make his or her selection, for example to particular streets or other locations.

Types of sample

Most textbooks on marketing research make a basic distinction between random (or probability) samples and non-random (or non-probability) samples. The former use techniques of selection that are independent of human judgement producing a known and non-zero probability of any one particular case in the population of cases being included in the sample. Consequently, it is possible to apply the laws of chance (probability theory) to undertake a statistical evaluation of sampling error, enabling the researcher to assess how likely the sample is to be unrepresentative and by how much. Types of random sample will typically include simple random samples, stratified samples, cluster samples, multi-stage samples and multi-phase samples. Non-random samples arise where human judgement is involved in the selection process making it impossible to apply any systematic scientific model that could be used to assess the degree of sampling error. Such samples typically include quota samples, convenience samples and judgemental samples.

The problem with this 'shopping list' type of approach is that most samples are, in practice, a mixture of different elements, and it is seldom possible to classify any particular sample uniquely into one of the categories. Further-more, there are varying degrees of 'independence' from human judgement, so the distinction is not always as clear-cut as the theory suggests. Moreover, neither practitioners nor theorists agree among themselves as to which parti-cular sample selection procedures count as 'random'.

What statisticians do tend to agree, if not insist, upon is that the 'theory' of statistical inference, which is explained in Chapter 6, is based on the assump-tion that the kind of sample drawn is a simple random one. Such samples use either randomized or systematic selection techniques (and some purists would argue that systematic procedures are not strictly 'random', but only an approximation) from a complete list of the population of cases, giving all cases to be sampled an *equal* chance of being selected. Thus if we select a sample of 300 names from a list of 3000 students at a university, then each student has a one in ten chance of being selected.

However, in practice, simple random samples are seldom used because:

- they require a sampling frame for the total population of cases to be sampled – this could mean taking random selections from lists containing maybe 40 million people, perhaps on a regular basis,
- if face-to-face interviewing is to be carried out (or even questionnaires or diaries left personally for respondent completion) the interviews would be scattered throughout the length and breadth of the geographical area to be sampled, and interviewers would have a considerable amount of travelling to do,
- the resulting samples may still not accurately reflect the structure of the population of cases in respect of a number of variables whose incidence or size is already known – in other words, simple random samples do not utilize data that are already available on the population structure.

Departures from simple random sampling are a result of the application of one or more of three main procedures:

- stratification,
- clustering,
- imposing quotas.

Stratification is a procedure that utilises information already contained in sampling frames to construct a sample that is guaranteed to be representative in respect of that information. Thus if a list of individuals contains information on the sex of each person, then the proportion of males to females is known. Suppose it is a list of members of a golf club, and 60 per cent are male. We can then ensure that 60 per cent of our sample is male. Thus if we wanted a sample of 100 members, we could select 60 men at random and 40 women at random (using either randomized or systematic techniques). If the list also contained data on age, and we knew that 30 per cent of members are aged 16–30, we could select 30 individuals from this age group (again at random) and the appropriate numbers from other age groups. If we stratified by sex *and* age together, then our 30 individuals aged 16–30 could be selected on the basis of 60 per cent (that is 18) men and 40 per cent (12) women. Provided the proportions in the sample are the same as the proportions in the population (usually called 'proportional stratification') then the resulting sample is likely to be *more* accurate and representative than the simple random sample because some of the sources of variation have been eliminated. However, it does require an accurate sampling frame and one that contains information on the factors we want to use for stratification.

Sometimes the stratification is disproportionate. Suppose our golf club contained only 10 per cent women and we wanted to be able to compare the views of the women with those of the men on the facilities provided to members. A proportionately stratified sample of 100 would give only 10 women – not enough on which to base an analysis of responses to a questionnaire, so we might select 50 women and 50 men, that is, deliberately oversample the women. This would enable us to make our comparisons, but if we wanted to estimate the extent of certain views or characteristics overall, then the answers of the men would have to be upweighted and the answers of the women downweighted to their original proportions. This type of weighting is described in some detail in Chapter 6.

Where interviewing is to be face-to-face it makes sense for each interviewers' respondents or potential respondents to be geographically concentrated in order to minimize travel time. Accordingly, it is normal to cluster interviewing in limited geographical areas. Market research agencies do this by selecting (usually at random) a fixed number of 'sampling points' and allocating one interviewer to each. These will usually be parliamentary constituencies, electoral wards, polling districts or postcode districts or sectors. The sampling points are usually carefully chosen in such a way that they are a representative cross-section of types of area. Normally the selection will be stratified by a number of variables. This is possible because, while there may be no lists if individual respondents that contain data on variables that can be used for stratification, there *will* be lists of polling districts or whatever area is to be used as a sampling point, and there will usually be plenty of information about each.

The key stratification factor used by most market research agencies is region. Thus if the selection of sampling points is 'stratified by region', then the selection is done within each region such that the number of sampling points in each reflects its population size. This keeps the sample in line with the regional distribution of the population. Further stratification may be by degree of 'rurality' so that appropriate proportions of urban, rural and mixed sampling points are selected.

Because equal numbers of interviews are given to each interviewer at each sampling point, the selection of the points within the region will usually be made with 'probability proportionate to size'. This means that sampling points with more people in them are given a higher probability of selection, thereby offsetting the lower probability of households or individuals in the larger sampling points being selected.

The selection of sampling points will often be carried out in two or more stages. Thus the first stage may be to sample parliamentary constituencies from the population of 635 constituencies (there are a further 17 in Northern Ireland). The selection will probably be stratified by type of constituency, typically the proportion of Conservative or Labour vote in order to get a balance of political complexion. Those selected may constitute a 'master sample' of first stage units that are used for all future survey work. Thus an agency's fieldwork may be concentrated in 200 constituencies and all samples are drawn from these as required.

In the second stage, within the constituencies selected, polling districts may be sub-sampled, usually with probability proportionate to size and stratified by region, so that the number of polling districts reflects the regional population size. The polling districts may then be used as sampling points and the interviewer is given a list of names and addresses in that district if it is a random sample, or may be given quotas to fill if it is a quota sample.

While, as explained earlier, the effect of stratification is to reduce the random sampling error, the effect of clustering is to increase it. How much it will do so depends on how 'tight' clustering is. For small-area clusters the error will be greater than for larger areas. In practice, the reduction in error due to stratification is very limited since it is usually only the selection of sampling points that is stratified, not the selection of individuals or households within them. Accordingly, the departure from simple random sampling brought about by the stratified selection of clusters has the effect, overall, of increasing the sampling error. This *may* be taken into account in the calculation of estimates and tests against the null hypotheses by applying a design factor. These factors are explained in Chapter 6.

The imposition of quotas can take a number of forms. In some situations, cases are selected from a list at random, but interviewers are then asked to fill quotas from these lists. Such a procedure might be called 'random sampling with quotas', but the imposition of quotas will increase the sampling error since substitutes are, in effect, being allowed. The main context, however, in which quotas are imposed is for quota samples in which the interviewer decides who to approach in the street.

Quota sampling is generally regarded by statisticians and the textbooks on market research as 'non-probability' or 'non-random' sampling. This is mainly because the final selection of respondents is made by the interviewer, so human judgement enters into the selection process. The interviewer, instead of being issued with a pre-selected list of names and addresses, is given an assignment in the form of a quota. This might, for example, require the interviewer to find, usually at a fixed sampling point, 20 adults aged 16 and over:

- 10 of them female,
- 10 aged 45 or over and 10 aged 16–45,
- 8 in social class ABC1,
- 12 in social class C2DE.

In this case, sex, age and social class would be described as the 'quota controls'. These controls may be interlaced (or 'interlocked') as in Figure 5.1. While this ensures that, for example, not all 10 under 45s are in social class ABC1, the interlacing can get quite complicated, and independent quotas are often applied. The selection of which variables to use as quota controls depends on which variables the researcher thinks are most strongly associated with the variables being estimated or tested. The usual quotas are on sex, age and social class, because these are associated with many other characteristics, behaviours and attitudes. However, for some products, like double-glazing, type of property or tenancy may be more relevant.

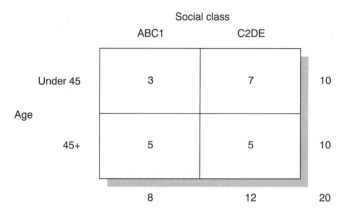

Figure 5.1 Interlaced quota controls.

Sampling in practice

The kind of sampling used in practice will depend, in the first instance, on whether respondents are to be approached via the telephone, through the post or face-to-face. For telephone interviews, since there is by definition a complete sampling frame available – the telephone directories – and clustering is not required, there seems little point in using other than systematic random sampling from the listed names. The only decision is whether there should be prior stratification, for example by region and whether there should be any imposition of quotas as the telephoning proceeds. This would amount to random sampling with quotas. For postal surveys the telephone directories will leave out non-telephone households, so the Post Office Postcode Address File would be a more appropriate sampling frame. These sampling frames are described below. Again, clustering is not required and the imposition of quotas is not possible since this requires information on the quota variables at the point of initial contact.

It is for face-to-face interviewing that a market research agency needs to make a real choice between random sampling and quota sampling. In both cases there is likely to be clustering into sampling points to minimize interviewer travelling time. Random sampling in practice means that interviewers are given lists of names and addresses and they have to make systematic efforts to obtain interviews with the individuals listed and to take no substitutes. The main advantage of random sampling is its accuracy. Compared with sampling techniques that are not strictly random, random samples:

■ minimize bias in the selection procedure,
■ minimize the variability between samples,
■ will, with a measurable degree of error, reproduce *all* the characteristics of the population from which the sample was drawn, not just those selected as quota controls,
■ will, where samples are drawn at regular intervals, reflect any changes that are taking place in the population,
■ allow probability theory to be applied to calculate the chances that the sample result was not a random sampling fluctuation.

There are, however, disadvantages to random samples:

■   they are slower and more expensive than non-random techniques,
■   they need a sampling frame,
■   the sample achieved will almost certainly be smaller than the sample drawn.

Surveys using quota samples can often complete fieldwork in two to three days: for random samples it is likely to be two to three weeks. This can be important when quick result are needed. Random samples are, furthermore, an expensive process in terms of administration and interviewer costs. The sample drawing procedures can be quite complex, while interviewers may be instructed to make at least three callbacks in the evenings or at weekends before recording a 'non-contact'. This all adds to the cost. Random samples can in fact easily be twice the cost of quota samples of the same size. However, some statisticians argue that, because such samples are more accurate, it is more cost-effective (in terms of accuracy per £1 spent on fieldwork) to design a smaller, high quality random sample than a larger quota sample (Wolfe, 1984).

Random samples need a sampling frame, that is, a complete list of the population which is to be sampled (normally within selected sampling points). Ideally, such lists should:

■   be adequate, that is, cover exactly the population which is to be surveyed,
■   be complete, that is, have no units missing,
■   not duplicate any entries,
■   be up-to-date.

Sometimes such lists do exist, for example, a list of all branches of a major multiple retailer from which a sample is to be drawn. To obtain names and addresses of consumers within sampling points there are two main sources in the UK:

■   the Registers of Electors,
■   the Post Office Postcode Address File.

The Registers of Electors have been the standard sampling frame for decades, but there are problems with them. They are completed every October and published the following February, so are already four months out of date. They contain the names and addresses of all British subjects aged 18 and over who are entitled to vote and are registered. No information about age and sex of the person is available (other than first names). Many of the market research agencies take 'adults' to mean 16 and over, so 16–18 year olds will be missing from the frame. Special procedures are often used to obtain a sample of that age group. Also, many of the 18 year olds will be missing from the lists; so will people who are not entitled to vote (e.g. non British subjects), or who are not registered. While the Registers are readily accessible, their validity is constantly affected by deaths and removals. Up to 12 per cent of electors are no longer at their registered address by the time the Registers come up for renewal. Non registrations almost certainly became higher while the Poll Tax was in operation.

The Postcode Address File covers some 22 million addresses in 1.5 million postcodes within 8900 sectors within 2700 districts within 120 postcode areas. The file tends to be more complete and more up-to-date than the

Registers of Electors, and is good for sampling households in a multi-stage process. However, for sampling individuals it is necessary to have some procedure for selecting individuals within a household. The postcodes are often used in association with CACI's ACORN classification of residential neighbourhoods, that is, each postcode is assigned to one of the 38 neighbourhood types that have been derived from a multi-variate treatment of Census data.

Other kinds of sampling frame include:

- membership lists of clubs, associations, societies or other kinds of organization,
- registers of various kinds, for example the Kompass Directory,
- frames that have been constructed from market intelligence or from surveys that have been carried out on a regular basis.

One 'solution' to an inadequate sampling frame is to redefine the population of cases being studied. Thus it is known that certain kinds of people are missing from the Registers of Electors. If the problem is ignored, then the survey population is being redefined as only those addresses appearing in the Registers. A sample that uses the telephone directories can define its population as all telephone subscribers. It is common for market research agencies to exclude outlying areas and sparsely populated parts of the country, for example in the North of Scotland. Again, the survey population is being redefined.

Perhaps the most serious drawback of random samples, however, arises from the fact that there is always a degree of non-response. There will always *be* non-response whatever method of selection is used, and at least the response rate is known for random samples. However, it does mean that the sample which is drawn (the target sample) is seldom the sample which is achieved. For ad hoc surveys the response rate will be typically 60–70 per cent of the sample drawn. Provided those not responding are not significantly different in key respects from those who do, the size of the achieved sample may simply have to be lived with, and the response rate reported as part of the results.

For continuous market measurement purposes, however, this procedure may not be adequate because results are to be used for making estimates of purchases, sales, and so on, not only for the population as a whole, but for a wide range of sub-groups within it. Consequently, all these sub-groups must be represented in appropriate numbers so that estimates can be made for that sub-group. Furthermore, response rates where people are asked to join a panel will tend to be considerably lower than for independent surveys.

The problem may be approached in one of two main ways.

1 *Oversample* so that the achieved sample size is the one originally desired. A variation on this is to continue drawing samples and obtaining interviews until the required sample size is reached. This is fine as long as those not responding are not significantly different from those who are, because this procedure will emphasize their significance.

2 *Apply quotas*: interviewers may be given lists of names and addresses drawn at random, but are asked to fill quotas by sex, age and social class. While this does mean that, in respect of the quotas, the sample is of the desired composition (and overall size), if interviewers are given long lists

from which to select a few respondents, and particularly if no callbacks are made, then this procedure is no better than some of the quota sampling techniques described earlier.

The key feature of quota sampling in practice is that it is the interviewer who makes the final selection in the street or in the shopping centre. Unlike stratified samples where a random selection is made in advance of the data collection process according to defined proportions within strata, in quota sampling the characteristics to be used for quotas are not known in advance and the interviewer needs to establish these. A typical approach will be to address a person who looks likely to meet quota requirements as follows: 'Good morning, my name is [name of interviewer] from [name of market research agency]. We are looking for men aged 30–49 who have a driving licence to answer a few questions about motoring. Do you fit into that category?'

The key advantages of quota samples are that they:

■ are quicker, cheaper and relatively simple to administer than random samples,
■ they do not require a sampling frame,
■ the sample size and sample composition in terms of the quota controls is always achieved.

The speed of quota sampling is derived from two sources. First, if in-home quotas are used, no callbacks are required, and if street quotas, there is no travelling time between interviews. Second, the procedures for drawing the samples are very simple and there is no need to give interviewers lists of names and addresses. In terms of cost per interview, quota samples thus work out a lot cheaper. Furthermore, no sampling frame is required. However, data on the structure of the population being sampled are needed in order to be able to set the size of the quotas. Since each interviewer continues until his or her quotas of sexes, ages and social classes are filled, the exact size and basic structure of the sample can be determined in advance.

There are, however, a number of disadvantages:

■ there is considerable potential for bias,
■ there is more variability between samples,
■ the application of probability theory to such samples is questionable,
■ they impose a structure on the sample.

Bias arises from two main sources: the interviewer and the high (and generally unrecorded) level of non-response. It is normally left to the interviewer how he or she goes about finding respondents who meet quota requirements in the sampling point. This leaves open the possibility of the interviewer avoiding certain types of locations or types of people, and for there to be systematic differences between one interviewer and another. Thus one interviewer may consciously or unconsciously avoid approaching people in groups, while another may avoid people who look like they are in a hurry.

It is, furthermore, often forgotten that there is considerable non-response when either street or in-home quotas are used. On the surface, there is no problem of non-response since all quotas are filled, or mostly filled. However, this is only because the non-response is undeclared and, effectively, substitution is being allowed. People who cannot be contacted or who refuse at the first attempt are excluded. The effective response rate in quota sampling is unknown, but certainly huge. The average random sample survey achieves a response rate of only about 25 per cent at first calls. This is boosted by subsequent callbacks to 60–80 per cent. So quota samples, at best, probably have an effective response rate of 25–30 per cent.

Work on actual surveys suggests that even good quality quota samples produce at least twice as much variability from one sample to another as do random samples. The implication, according to some researchers, is that calculations made of the extent of variability based on simple random samples need to be multiplied by a factor (called a design factor) of not less than 2.5. Others will argue that, because quota sampling is non-random, then the application of probability theory to such samples is not legitimate, since the probability of inclusion in the sample for any one case is unknown. In practice, agencies tend to treat quota samples as an approximation of random samples and will apply probability theory, sometimes with and sometimes without a design factor.

The structure imposed on the sample by the quotas will have been derived from data that reflect the population of cases as a whole. This, in turn, means that these quotas will not reflect the different composition of the sampling points, nor any changes that have taken place since the original data were collected. Thus social classes A and B may be over-represented in a sampling point in a depressed mining village, and under-represented in expensive, fashionable areas. It can even be difficult to fill some quotas in some of the sampling points.

Some agencies have attempted to get around some of these limitations of quota samples without the considerable additional expense of probability random samples by using 'random location', or 'random route' sampling. Geographical areas are selected as sampling points in such a way that they are representative of the universe. Within each area some form of systematic sampling is imposed. This removes from the interviewer discretion over who to interview, and should make the sample selected representative of the area in which the sampling takes place rather than being in accordance with arbitrary quota controls.

In random location sampling the interviewer may be instructed to call at every nth house in pre-defined streets. In random route sampling, the interviewer will be given a random starting point and then told in which directions to turn at road junctions, but again taking every nth house. In neither case are quotas imposed on social class, and usually not on age either, although there may be quotas for sex and working status since the latter reflect the probability of selection rather than the survey variables. Thus women and individuals not in paid employment are more likely to be at home (or in a shopping centre). The method does have its limitations, however, because if the interviewer works over a wide area, the stratifying power of the initial selection begins to break down; if the work is highly concentrated, there may be severe clustering effects.

Sample size

Determining the size of sample that is needed for a particular piece of research is a complex issue that needs to take into account a large number of factors.

Textbooks tend to take a statistical approach which calculates the size of sample needed in order to achieve a specified degree of sampling error and a minimum level of accuracy. The problem with such calculations is that they assume that the researcher is able to specify an acceptable level of sampling error in advance of undertaking the research. This is usually impossible, particularly since errors will vary from one variable to the next. Such calculations also fail to take into account very practical issues such as that larger samples will cost more and will take more time to complete. There may well be a limit to the size of sample that can be afforded or is practicable. Furthermore, how large a sample is needed also depends on the variability of the population characteristics and on the purpose of the research. The more variable the characteristics the larger the sample will need to be. Furthermore, if the purpose of the research is accurate assessment of quantitative variables then larger samples will again be required. If the purpose is to generate ideas for new products then a small sample of product category users may well be sufficient.

For any kind of quantitative analysis a minimum sample size of 100 is needed even to be able to calculate simple percentages for each variable. If, as is so often the case, analyses need to be performed on sub-groups, then the smallest sub-group must contain sufficient cases for reliable estimates to be achieved. If the variables are to be cross-tabulated then much larger samples will be required – 300 or so at a minimum. Most market research agencies will need to do a series of breakdowns for clients and will tend to take samples of at least 1000. Few samples for ad hoc research will be much above 3000, but where the research is continuous and based on separate samples it may be possible to accumulate samples of 30,000 or more over the course of a year.

Sampling errors

Whatever kind of sample is taken and whatever the sample size there will always be error arising from the sampling process. The extent of such error may be defined as the difference between a sample result, and the result that would have been achieved by undertaking a complete census. Such errors arise because particular types of cases are under-represented or over-represented in the sample compared with the population as a whole. If, for example, the cases are individual consumers, then the under- or over-representation of the sexes, ages or social classes will affect the measurements (and, more importantly, the estimates made from them) of a large number of variables. Lack of representation in the appropriate quantities may be a product of two factors: *systematic* error (or bias) and *random* error (or variance).

Systematic error

Bias arises when the sampling procedures used bring about over- or under-representation of types of cases in the sample which is mostly in the same direction. This may happen because:

■ the selection procedures are not random,

- the selection is made from a list that does not cover the population, or uses a procedure that excludes certain groups,
- non-respondents are not a cross-section of the population.

If the selection procedures are not random then it means that human judgement has entered into the selection process. For example, interviewers may be asked to choose respondents at some geographical location or to select households in specified streets. The result is likely to be that certain kinds of people or households or organizations are excluded from the sample. Thus choosing respondents in a shopping centre will miss out people who seldom or never go shopping; the selection of households by an interviewer may result in the omission of flats at the tops of stairs.

If the Electoral Register is used to select adults aged 16 or over, then, as indicated earlier, 16 and 17 year-olds and many of the 18 year-olds will be missing from the list and will be under-represented in the final sample. The use of telephone directories will under represent certain social groups less likely to be in the telephone book (or those who are ex-directory). Duplication in lists, for example in the Yellow Pages, may result in some over-representation. If we try to estimate sales of soap from a sample of private households, then all users in institutions of various kinds will be excluded.

Non-response is a problem for both censuses and samples. For censuses it means that the enumeration will be incomplete. If large numbers are missing, it would be inappropriate to treat those successfully contacted as a representative 'sample'. For samples, it means that estimates made from the sample will be biased if non-respondents are not themselves representative of the population. If they are representative, then non-response is not so much of a problem; but it may still mean that analyses are made on the basis of too small a sample.

Whatever the reason for the systematic error, the effect will be that all samples that could be drawn from a population will tend to result in the same direction of over- or under-representation. The average of all these samples will then not be the same as the real population average or proportion. Thus if we took lots of samples using a procedure that tended to omit working mothers with young children, then all the samples will manifest such under-representation rather than some over-representing them and some under-representing them so that the average of all samples was very close to the real population proportion.

Systematic errors cannot be reduced simply by increasing the sample size. If certain kinds of people are not being selected, cannot be contacted or are not responding, it will not be 'solved' by taking a bigger sample. Indeed, some kinds of errors will increase with more interviewers, more questionnaires and greater data-processing requirements. All the researcher can do is minimize the likelihood of bias by using appropriate sample designs. Biases for some variables can be checked, for example against Census data or data from other sources. Sometimes attempts are made to discover the characteristics of non-responders, for example by sending out interviewers to non-respondents to a postal survey, taking 'late' responders as typical of non-responders, or gaining demographic data from the results of another survey that the non-responders *have* taken part in.

Random error

If we took a number of random, unbiased samples from the same population there will almost certainly be a degree of fluctuation from one sample to another. Over a large number of samples such errors will tend to cancel out, so that the average of such samples will be close to the real population value. However, we usually take only one sample, and even a sample that has used unbiased selection procedures will seldom be exactly representative of the population from which it was drawn. Each sample will, in short, exhibit a degree of error. Such error is often called 'sampling error', but it would be clearer to think of it as 'random sampling error' to distinguish it from bias (which some statisticians and some textbooks, confusingly, categorize as 'non-sampling' error).

Unlike bias, which affects the general sample composition and relates to each variable being measured in unknown ways, random sampling error will differ from variable to variable. The reason for this is that the extent of such error will depend on two factors:

■ *the size of the sample* – the bigger the sample, the less the random sampling error (but by a declining amount),
■ *the variability in the population for that particular variable* – a sample used to estimate a variable that varies widely in the population will show more random sampling error than for a variable that does not.

These two factors are used as a basis for calculating the likely degree of variability in a sample of a given size for a particular variable. This, in turn, is used as an input for establishing with a specified probability the range of accuracy of sample estimates, or that sample findings are only random sampling fluctuations from a population of cases in which the findings are untrue. These calculations are explained in Chapter 6.

Non-sampling errors

Not all errors in a piece of research are a result of the sampling process. Certain kinds of error may arise even if a complete census is taken. There are four main categories of such error:

■ response errors,
■ interviewer errors,
■ non-response errors,
■ processing errors.

Where research is based on asking people questions then response errors may arise where, for one reason or another, respondents give 'wrong' answers. This may be through dishonesty, forgetfulness, faulty memories, unwillingness or misunderstanding of the questions being asked. Many of these errors arise as a result of poor or inadequate questionnaire design: putting it the other way round, the potential for such errors to arise can be minimized by careful design of question-wording, question formulation and questionnaire layout. This topic was considered in detail in Chapter 3.

In interview surveys, whether face-to-face or by telephone, interviewers may themselves misunderstand questions or the instructions for filling them in, they may be dishonest, inaccurate, make mistakes or ask questions in a non-standard fashion. Interviewer training, along with field supervision and control can, to a large extent, remove the likelihood of such errors, but they will never be entirely eliminated, and there is always the potential for systematic differences between the results obtained by different interviewers. The process of interviewing was considered in detail in Chapter 4.

In nearly all research there will be missing cases, but in survey research there will always be a degree of non-response because some people will refuse to be interviewed or to complete a questionnaire, some will be ineligible because they turn out not to be part of the survey population, some will terminate the interview or refuse to answer some of the questions, and some will be non-contactable, for example, because they have moved away, died, or are on holiday at the time of the survey. Even where a census is attempted, it will often remain incomplete. The extent of non-response will vary considerably according to the type of research, the topic of the research, and, where based on face-to-face interviews, on the experience and training of the interviewers. Calculating the amount of non-response can be confusing since some researchers will, for example, take the proportion of refusals in the sample drawn, others will take refusals and non-contacts as a proportion of those found eligible, and so on.

Processing errors can arise back at the office, particularly at the stage of entering answers to questions onto a computerized database via a keyboard and screen. Agencies sometimes validate these entries by, in effect, entering them twice, and the computer checks to see if the two entries are identical. Alternatively, some agencies check samples of the entries. It is possible, in addition, to apply range checks and logical checks.

There are, then, a number of sources of non-sampling error, and it is important to bear these in mind when interpreting survey results, whether based on a sample or not. The crucial point is that such errors can arise even if a census is taken.

Total survey error

Any research that is based on addressing questions to people and recording their answers risks error resulting from the respondents themselves and from interviewers where these are used in addition to those kinds of error that arise in any research from data handling, and from inadequacies of sampling. Total survey error is the addition of all these sources of error, both sampling and non-sampling. It is difficult to estimate what the total survey error is in any one survey, and it will tend to vary from question to question. What is certainly true is that the error that results from random sampling fluctuations – which is the only kind of error that is taken into account when confidence intervals are calculated or tests are made against the null hypothesis – accounts for only a very small proportion of the total survey error. Assael and Keon (1982) for example, estimate that it is perhaps only about 5 per cent. For a full discussion see Kish (1965, ch. 13), or Churchill (1995, ch. 12).

Errors of various kinds can always be reduced by spending more money, for example, on more interviewer training and supervision, on random sampling techniques, on pilot testing or on getting a higher response rate. However, the reduction in error has to be traded off against the extra cost involved. Further-more, errors are often interrelated so that attempts to reduce one kind of error may actually increase another, for example, minimizing the non-response errors by persuading more reluctant respondents may well increase response error. Non-sampling errors tend to be pervasive, not well-behaved and do not decrease – indeed may increase – with the size of the sample. It is sometimes even difficult to see whether they cause under- or over-estimation of population characteristics. There is, in addition, the paradox that the more efficient the sample design is in controlling random sampling fluctuations, the more impor-tant in proportion become bias and non-sampling errors.

Controlling error

In practice, market research agencies make all reasonable attempts, within the limits imposed by cost and time constraints, to minimize or at least measure the impact or make some estimate of non-sampling errors and of bias in the sampling procedure. Thus, as far as response errors are concerned, agencies may:

- pilot-test questionnaires in order to check for misunderstandings of questions,
- analyse tendencies to overclaim or underclaim for certain kinds of con-sumer behaviour, for example, the tendency to underclaim the consump-tion of alcohol, or to overclaim television watching,
- use 'aided-recall' techniques (prompted lists) to help respondents remem-ber products that they may have purchased and forgotten about, or radio programmes that they forgot they had listened to,
- use questioning techniques that minimize the effort respondents need to make.

To minimize interviewer error, agencies will often:

- set rigorous training standards for interviewers,
- monitor the process of interviewing by doing 'backchecks' – calling or telephoning respondents who have already been interviewed to check that the interview was carried out properly, or sending supervisors to accompany interviewers on a regular sample basis,
- computer analyses may be made of questionnaire errors to identify inter-viewers who may need retraining or reminding of particular points.

To minimize errors resulting from non-response, agencies do one or more of several things:

- for interview surveys interviewers may be asked to make a specified number of callbacks if the respondent was not at home on the first call. Three or four such callbacks may be made, ideally at different times and days of the week,
- interviewers may make an appointment by telephone with the respondent,
- self-completed questionnaires may be left where no contact has been made,

- monetary incentives or gifts may sometimes help to improve the response rate,
- interviewers may get a 'foot-in-the-door' by having respondents comply with some small request before presenting them with the larger survey,
- non-respondents to a postal survey may be sent interviewers to persuade respondents to complete the questionnaire, or they may be sent further reminders.

Processing errors will be minimized by careful editing and checking of the questionnaires in addition to the use of data entry validation procedures.

Market research agencies will try to minimize bias by using carefully constructed sample designs that use random procedures wherever possible, or by imposing restrictions on interviewer choices where it is not. These sample designs were described earlier. Biases will still remain, however, and sometimes these are known. Thus it may be known that there are too many women in the sample, or too few men aged 20–24, compared with known population proportions. Many agencies will make corrections to the data to adjust for these biases by 'weighting' them.

In the real world of market research agencies and their clients it is unfortunately true that many clients do not understand or lack interest in the basics of sampling. In consequence many clients do not ask for estimates of bias or calculations of random sampling error. At the same time the agencies feel that to produce calculations, for example of confidence intervals (these are explained in Chapter 6) for a large number of variables will only add confusion and perhaps distrust of the data. In consequence, sampling errors are often quietly ignored, and the estimates given are taken to be the 'truth'. Agencies will instead try to assure their clients that the occurrence and impact of non-sampling errors have been minimized by:

- demonstrating that the procedures for the collection, analysis and reporting of the results are 'respectable', meticulous and thorough,
- showing that the research design features are such as to minimize sources of error within the parameters set by time and cost,
- emphasizing the extent of quality control checks that will uncover, correct and minimize the occurrence of 'mistakes',
- making corrections to the resulting data so that known biases are adjusted for.

Beyond these assurances, clients are sometimes given some indication of the extent of random sampling error that remains. Clients may be given 'read-off' tables for groups of products or types of variable, based on the 'average' variability for that group or type, given a particular sample size.

Summary

Where it is not feasible, economic or practical to study every case for the purpose of undertaking any particular piece of research, a selection of cases will have to be made. This may be done on a purposive or on a representative basis. Purposive samples are selections made by the researcher and are used mainly for exploratory or for qualitative research; representative samples are chosen by randomized or systematic techniques, or by an interviewer follow-ing certain rules, and are used for quantitative research where the objective is either to estimate the size or frequency of characteristics or the relationships between them in the population of cases from which the sample was drawn.

In designing samples, the researcher will almost certainly want to make use of procedures for stratification, clustering or imposing quotas. Clustering is needed only where face-to-face interviews are to be conducted. The selection of clusters to use as sampling points is nearly always on a random basis, but is usually combined with stratification. The final selection of cases may be random or quota, and both procedures have their strengths and limitations. For telephone and postal surveys no clustering is required and there is no need to use interviewer selection, but where the sampling frame used to get telephone numbers or postal addresses is felt to be inadequate, quotas may be imposed, even if the selection from the list was random. Whether this procedure counts as a 'random' sample is an issue that will either be hotly debated – or send people to sleep!

The errors that arise when taking samples are a combination of those errors that might happen irrespective of the procedures used for selecting cases and will occur even when census studies are made, and those errors that arise from the over or under representation of types of case when sample selections are made. Sampling errors include both bias (systematic error) and variance (random error). Statistical measures based on probability theory that are used to estimate 'sampling error' in fact refer only to variance, and, strictly speak-ing, only to those samples where random selection of the final cases is made. Variance, furthermore, accounts for only a very small proportion of total survey error.

In the final analysis, market research agencies go to considerable lengths to minimize and control both non-sampling and sampling errors. The attention paid by statisticians and textbooks on measuring the incidence of sampling variance is probably misplaced.

Key concepts

sample	random samples
population	quota samples
census	sampling frame
purposive samples	sampling point
representative samples	sampling error
simple random samples	systematic error (bias)
stratification	random error (variance)
clustering	non-sampling errors
quotas	total survey error

Further reading

- Henry, GT (1990) *Practical Sampling*, London: Sage.
- Kish, L (1965) *Survey Sampling*, New York: John Wiley.
- Sudman, S (1976) *Applied Sampling*, San Francisco: Academic Press.

Questions for further discussion

1 Use the table of random numbers (Table 5.1) to select a sample of $n = 15$ without replacement from a population of $N = 73$

2 ABC Products has 200 workers whose output in units per week is measured and recorded on a card (Table 5.2). The cards are numbered 001 to 200. Use Table 5.1 to draw 20 numbers at random between 001 and 200. Use the outputs of these employees to calculate the average output of that sample.

3 Carefully define the relevant population for the following projects. Decide whether sampling is necessary and if so suggest an appropriate sample design:

■ A manufacturer of domestic lawnmowers in Scotland wants to know the proportion of households that own various types of lawnmower.

■ A hospital administrator wants to find out if the single parents working in the hospital have a higher rate of absenteeism than parents who are not single.

■ A company is about to launch a new product which is a vibrating massage cushion for use by motorists. The manufacturer wants to know what kinds of motorist are likely to consider purchasing the product.

85967	73152	14511	85285	36009	95892	36962	67835	63314	50162	**Table 5.1**
07483	51453	11649	86348	76431	81594	95848	36738	25014	15460	Random numbers
96283	01898	61414	83525	04231	13604	75339	11730	85423	60698	
49174	12074	98551	37895	93547	24769	09404	76548	05393	96770	
97366	39941	21225	93629	19574	71565	33413	56087	40875	13351	
90474	41469	16812	81542	81652	45554	27931	93994	22375	00953	
28599	64109	09497	76235	41383	31555	12639	00619	22909	29563	
25254	16210	89717	65997	82667	74624	36348	44018	64732	93589	
28785	02760	24359	99410	77319	73408	58993	61098	04393	48245	
84725	86576	86944	93296	10081	82454	76810	52975	10324	15457	
41059	66456	47679	66810	15941	84602	14493	65515	19251	41642	
67434	41045	82830	47617	36932	46728	71183	36345	41404	81110	
72766	68816	37643	19959	57550	49620	98480	25640	67257	18671	
92079	46784	66125	94932	64451	29275	57669	66658	30818	58353	
29187	40350	62533	73603	34075	16451	42885	03448	37390	96328	
74220	17612	65522	80607	19184	64164	66962	82310	18163	63495	
03766	02407	06098	92917	40434	60602	82175	04470	78754	90775	
75085	55558	15520	27038	25471	76107	90832	10819	56797	33751	
09161	33015	19155	11715	00551	24909	31894	37774	37953	78837	
75707	48992	64998	87080	39333	00767	45637	12538	67439	94914	
21333	48660	31288	00086	79889	75532	28704	62844	92337	99695	
65626	50061	42539	14812	48895	11196	34335	60492	70650	51108	
84380	07389	87891	76255	89604	41372	10837	66992	93183	56920	
46479	32072	80083	63868	70930	89654	05359	47196	12452	38234	
59847	97197	55147	76639	76971	55928	36441	95141	42333	67483	

Table 5.2

Employee output for ABC
Products

Employee	Output	Employee	Output	Employee	Output	Employee	Output	Employee	Output
001.	30	041.	59	081.	65	121.	47	161.	62
002.	38	042.	56	082.	42	122.	64	162.	29
003.	33	043.	65	083.	73	123.	55	163.	37
004.	49	044.	50	084.	44	124.	50	164.	27
005.	33	045.	54	085.	54	125.	65	165.	36
006.	43	046.	61	086.	67	126.	53	166.	43
007.	60	047.	57	087.	49	127.	32	167.	30
008.	31	048.	55	088.	38	128.	44	168.	41
009.	34	049.	26	089.	59	129.	38	169.	59
010.	61	050.	41	090.	42	130.	37	170.	63
011.	49	051.	64	091.	46	131.	53	171.	55
012.	64	052.	25	092.	30	132.	44	172.	32
013.	62	053.	28	093.	64	133.	27	173.	32
014.	37	054.	49	094.	28	134.	40	174.	31
015.	25	055.	53	095.	64	135.	43	175.	35
016.	38	056.	25	096.	46	136.	45	176.	33
017.	65	057.	33	097.	59	137.	33	177.	58
018.	56	058.	28	098.	60	138.	60	178.	31
019.	55	059.	25	099.	46	139.	62	179.	38
020.	43	060.	60	100.	27	140.	30	180.	29
021.	58	061.	34	101.	59	141.	51	181.	43
022.	38	062.	25	102.	43	142.	49	182.	56
023.	71	063.	61	103.	50	143.	31	183.	53
024.	47	064.	42	104.	51	144.	29	184.	64
025.	65	065.	48	105.	39	145.	36	185.	38
026.	54	066.	57	106.	59	146.	50	186.	36
027.	74	067.	26	107.	33	147.	54	187.	59
028.	36	068.	55	108.	60	148.	38	188.	68
029.	62	069.	36	109.	26	149.	60	189.	26
030.	31	070.	33	110.	72	150.	65	190.	72
031.	48	071.	63	111.	25	151.	36	191.	29
032.	35	072.	48	112.	44	152.	25	192.	32
033.	26	073.	37	113.	58	153.	28	193.	73
034.	62	074.	49	114.	49	154.	56	194.	63
035.	51	075.	46	115.	31	155.	51	195.	69
036.	67	076.	31	116.	56	156.	53	196.	57
037.	30	077.	26	117.	37	157.	40	197.	38
038.	57	078.	28	118.	66	158.	33	198.	50
039.	50	079.	63	119.	55	159.	26	199.	60
040.	62	080.	37	120.	66	160.	42	200.	28

6

Data analysis

The different types of qualitative and quantitative data were explained in detail in Chapter 2. The section in Chapter 4 on qualitative research explained the various approaches to handling qualitative data when they manifest themselves as narrative or text. This chapter looks at the analysis of qualitative data that arise as isolated statements or words from open-ended questions in a questionnaire survey or from seeking verbal reactions to specific situations in experimental research. It then turns to what is involved in analysing quantitative data.

Whatever the type of data to be analysed, the process consists of three distinct activities:

■   data display,
■   data reduction,
■   statistical inference.

Data display takes the 'raw' data and presents them in tables and charts so that it is possible for readers to 'eyeball' the total distribution and draw out some meaning, interpretation or significance from them (e.g. Figure 6.1). Data reduction uses statistical methods like calculating averages or measures of association to reduce the data to a few key summary measures. Statistical inference is appropriate when the data relate to a representative sample and the researcher wishes to make estimates or to test hypotheses about the population based on evidence from the sample that was drawn.

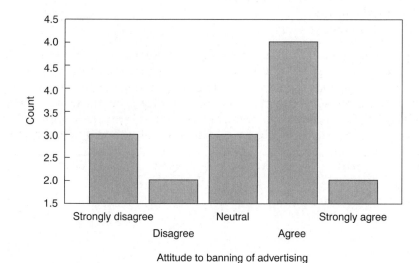

Figure 6.1   A simple bar chart.

Analysing qualitative data

Data display for qualitative data may take several forms, for example:

- quoting extracts from the text,
- producing checklists or tables,
- rearranging or reordering lists.

   Where respondents have used words, phrases or sentences that are particularly revealing or apposite to the research, then a verbatim quote may nicely illustrate, for example: 'As one marketing manager put it . . . '. This may perform a role somewhat similar to drawing a graph for quantitative data and may, furthermore, liven up the reports of research. However, such quotes should be use sparingly and with caution. There is little point in verbatim reports unless what is said or written down is distinctive or particularly appropriate. Putting in lengthy quotations or sticking extracts of text end to end is pointless. It must be remembered, furthermore, that such extracts are only illustrations; they are highly selective and not necessarily representative of the views or thoughts of other respondents.

   It is sometimes helpful to draw up a table or checklist of what individuals or kinds or categories of individual mentioned which particular points, as illustrated in Table 6.1. Such tables enable the researcher to view the data at a glance, to make comparisons, to see where further analysis may be called for, and they may be directly transferred to the report of the findings.

   Sometimes reordering or rearranging lists may reveal patterns, or at least make them more accessible. Thus rearranging individuals A–F in Table 6.1 in terms of salary or position in the company may reveal patterns of responses more clearly.

   Data reduction for qualitative data may involve one or more of the following activities:

- paraphrasing and summarising what people have said,
- classifying responses into categories,
- using quasi-statistics,
- undertaking content analysis.

   If respondents or interviewers have written comments in a questionnaire in response to an open-ended question, or if verbal reactions to new product ideas or advertising copy are recorded, then paraphrasing or summarizing may take the form of restating comments in another, clearer, condensed form, or picking out key words, phrases or statements. A more systematic approach is to classify all responses into categories which, ideally, should be exhaustive

Table 6.1

A checklist for analysing qualitative data

Individual	Safety	Economy	Speed	Reliability
A	✓			
B			✓	
C	✓	✓	✓	
D				✓
E		✓		
F		✓		✓

and mutually exclusive, not too many in number, and should refer to a single dimension that is important to the objectives of the research. Developing such sets of categories may mean making several 'passes' over the data, modifying or refining the categories until all responses can be classified.

An attempt may be made to summarize further by giving some indication of the numbers or rough proportions of respondents replying in particular ways, using words or phrases like 'a few', 'a large minority', 'most', or 'nearly all'. Such 'quasi-statistics' are helpful when the number of cases does not permit sensible use of percentages. Content analysis converts qualitative data into quantitative data by systematically counting up the number of times a word, phrase, idea or theme is used in a group or sub-group of respondents. Thus younger respondents may well use different words or phrases in response to a new product concept.

While statistical inference is not possible on qualitative data, some market researchers will argue that, while a key role of qualitative research is generally acknowledged to be to generate hypotheses, it is nevertheless often possible to match ideas against the data and in this sense to 'test' them as well. In the 'interpretive' phase in the analysis of narrative text, it was suggested earlier that 'insight' or the 'Eureka moments' were the result of some mysterious 'black box' activity in the brain. This may be appropriate where the text needs to be treated as a whole – as an entity that may not be accessible to systematic procedures. However, for the analysis and interpretation of isolated statements, it can be argued that inferences, while not statistical, may be derived from:

■ noting sequences,
■ looking for patterns or relationships,
■ noting attributions of causality.

The order in which people do things, or at least how they perceive the sequences of events may give some guide to possible causal relationships. Although the fact that one event always follows another does not establish cause, temporal order is a necessary, although not sufficient, condition for causality to exist. Unless there *is* a regular sequence (cause first, effect later) then causality can be ruled out. Noting any patterns in the way events, behaviours, characteristics or expressed opinions happen together can also be suggestive of causal connections. Unless there *is* some pattern, causality can, again, be ruled out. Final proof, of course, is never possible; but neither is it for quantitative data. Qualitative data in fact may be better than quantitative where it is possible to ask people for their explanations of events or attributions of causality. Where there is a degree of consensus on these explanations, it may be worth the researcher's time pursuing further evidence, perhaps by conducting further research.

Griggs (1987) argues that the process of analysing qualitative data should be a public process, not a private, 'magical' experience. The researchers should be able to demonstrate how conclusions were arrived at, and in such a way that others could, if necessary, dispute them. Sometimes, continues Griggs, it is possible to replicate a study – doing it again to see if the same conclusions are reached. This may not be feasible in market research, but seeing if similar conclusions may be drawn across all groups of individuals in a study may lend weight to those conclusions.

Analysing quantitative data

Most textbooks on statistics make a basic distinction between 'descriptive statistics' – data display and data reduction, and 'inferential statistics' – drawing conclusions about a population of cases from the data when the data represent only a sample of them. However, there are other features of quantitative data analysis that are at least as important. One is the crucial distinction that was made in Chapter 2 between non-metric and metric data. Thus what we can actually do by way of data display, data reduction and statistical inference depends on the kind of data we have. The analysis of variables, furthermore, may be treated one at a time, two at a time or more than two at a time. Thus univariate analysis takes each variable on its own and displays, reduces or infers from the results independently of other variables in the dataset. Bivariate analysis studies the patterns of relationships between two variables, while multivariate analysis takes three or more variables into consideration at the same time.

The presentation of data analysis in this chapter begins by looking at non-metric data, considering what can be done by way of univariate, bivariate and multivariate analysis. Initially, the focus will be on descriptive statistics – data display and data reduction. The same arrangement is then followed for metric data. Only then are inferential statistics approached, but still distinguishing between procedures for non-metric data and for metric data.

Data display and data reduction for non-metric data

Univariate analysis

Non-metric data, as will be recalled from Chapter 2, may be binary, nominal, ordinal or ranked. A first stage in analysing these data is to display them in the form of tables or charts. In the first instance, this display will be univariate – treating variables one at a time.

A table is any layout of two or more pieces of information in rows, in columns, or in rows and columns combined. For non-metric data, we can display the frequencies or relative frequencies (percentages) of the various categories. Tables for univariate analysis are often called 'one-way' or single-variable frequency tables, as illustrated in Table 6.2, which displays the frequencies for an ordinal variable, social class. Clearly, for binary variables there will be only two categories giving, for example, the number of people saying 'yes' and the number saying 'no' to a question in a survey. Furthermore, it is really only necessary to state one of the two percentages (or proportions). If 64 per cent said 'yes' to a question then, by definition, 36 per cent said 'no', since they must total 100. In this situation it may not be necessary to tabulate the result at all.

For nominal data there will be three or more categories. Precisely because the scale is nominal it does not matter in what order the categories are placed. However, if the number of categories is large it may make sense to list or group them in a particular way. For ordinal data the categories should be in the intended order of magnitude, usually with the highest, largest, fastest, etc. at the top.

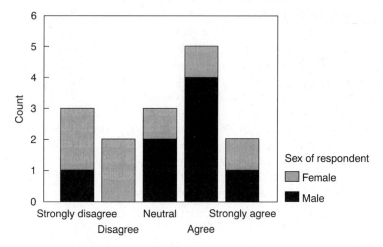

Figure 6.2 A component bar chart.

Table 6.2 illustrates a number of points about table layout:

- the categories and the frequencies are usually in columns,
- both are labelled at the top so that we know to what variable the categories refer and whether the figures represent frequencies, percentages or proportions,
- totals are given at the bottom of the columns
- there is a table number and a title, which is usually at the top of the table,
- only horizontal lines are used to indicate the top and the bottom of the table and to separate the headings from the body of the table,
- there may be a source of the data at the bottom of the table if these data were derived from other than the results of the research being reported.

This format of table layout is fairly standard in most published research. Some tables may contain two or more adjacent univariate distributions, as in Table 6.3. Such multi-variable tables do not relate or interlace the variables. Thus we do not know from Table 6.3 which males are in which social classes or in which age groups.

'Chart' and 'graph' are terms that are often used interchangeably to refer to any form of graphical display. Charts for non-metric data are limited largely to bar charts and pie charts. In bar charts each category is depicted by a bar, the length of which represents the frequency or percentage of observations falling into each category. All bars should have the same width and a scale of

Social class	Frequency	%
AB	30	15
C1	50	25
C2	70	35
DE	50	25
Total	200	100

Table 6.2 A single-variable frequency table: respondents by social class

Table 6.3 A multi-variable frequency table: purchasers of brand X

		Frequency	%
Sex	M	104	52
	F	96	48
Social class	AB	30	15
	C1	50	25
	C2	70	35
	DE	50	25
Age	20–29	10	5
	30–39	30	15
	40–49	64	32
	50–59	56	28
	60+	40	20

frequencies or percentages should be provided. What each bar represents should be clearly labelled or given a legend. A simple bar chart produced by SPSS is illustrated in Figure 6.1. If you want to know how to produce such charts, refer to Appendix 3.

Notice that while for tables the title is, as we have seen, usually at the top, for figures it is normally at the bottom. The bars will often be constructed horizontally rather than vertically for non-metric data and the actual figures for each bar may be written at the end of the bar. It is possible to represent a second non-metric variable in one chart using a component, or 'stacked', bar chart, as in Figure 6.2, but there should not be more than three or four categories in the second variable. Component bar charts are sometimes a little difficult to interpret particularly when the variable being used as a component has very variable proportions within each bar. An alternative way of presenting two variables in a bar chart is in a 'clustered' bar chart, as illustrated in Figure 6.3.

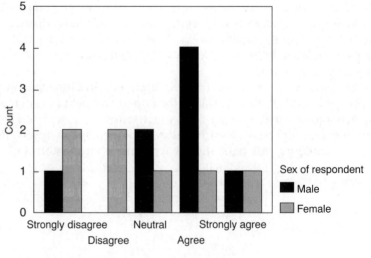

Figure 6.3 A clustered bar chart.

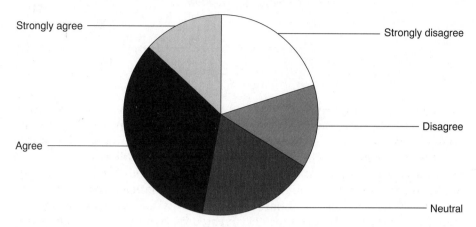

Figure 6.4 A pie chart.

In a pie chart the relative frequencies are represented in proportion to the size of each category by a slice of the circle, as in Figure 6.4. The total for all categories must be 100 per cent. The bar chart is normally preferred to the pie chart because the human eye can more accurately judge length comparisons against a fixed scale than angular measures. However, pie charts are nicer to look at and they clearly show that the total for all slices adds up to 100 per cent.

Neither bar charts nor pie charts, however, are particularly useful for binary data. For nominal data they can certainly help to display the data where there are between about four and 12 or so categories. Bar charts in particular can preserve the order of the categories for ordinal data, but the ordering may be lost in pie charts.

Tables and charts may be used, then, to considerable effect for nominal and ordinal data, but are less useful for binary and ranked data. Data reduction in the form of calculating a single summary measure like an average is not feasible for non-metric data; you cannot have an 'average' category. However, it does sometimes make sense to reduce the number of categories by grouping them and adding together their frequencies. Thus if there are data on the number of offices in different parts of the UK, these could be grouped into English, Scottish and Welsh offices, and offices in Northern Ireland. If the data are ordinal it may make sense to group the highest and the lowest categories. Thus a five–point Likert scale may be reduced to a three-point scale by adding together the frequencies for 'strongly agree' and 'agree', and then doing the same for 'strongly disagree' and 'disagree'. If the number of cases used in the research is small – less than 100 or so – then this process may be necessary anyway before any further analysis is possible otherwise there will be too few observations in most of the categories to come to sensible conclusions.

Bivariate analysis

To display the relationship between two non-metric variables a bivariate cross-tabulation is required. These are sometimes referred to as 'contingency' or 'two-way' tables. A cross-tabulation is a particular kind of table in which the

Table 6.4

A cross-tabulation of age by sex

Sex	Age 20–39	40–49	Total
Male	60	40	100
Female	20	50	70
Total	80	90	170

frequencies or proportions of cases that combine a value on one categorical variable with a value on another are laid out in combinations of rows and columns. In other words a cross-tabulation presents the frequencies of two variables the values of which are interlaced. Thus in Table 6.4 there are 60 individuals who combine the characteristics of being both male and aged 20–39, 50 individuals who combine the characteristics of being both female and aged 40–59, and so on. The combination of a row and a columns creates a 'cell'. In Table 6.4 there are four cells created by two variables, each having two categories, so it is often called a 'two-by-two' (2 × 2) table. The totals at the end of each row (100 and 70 in this table) are called 'row marginals', and the totals at the bottom are 'column marginals'.

Cross-tabulations may be of any size in terms of rows and columns. Thus Table 6.5 is a '3 × 6', having 18 cells. As tables get larger they become increasingly difficult to interpret and they require many more cases to avoid having very small numbers in most of the cells. Thus if the 170 cases in Table 6.4 were put into Table 6.5 with 18 cells, there would be an average of 170/18 or fewer than 10 per cell. The only solutions are either to increase the number of cases or to reduce the size of the table. Thus we could add together the 15–24 and the 25–34 age groupings to give 15–34, and do the same for 35–54, and 55+. This will reduce the age categories to three, giving a 3 × 3 table with nine cells.

Cross-tabulations display the way categories of two variables interlace. They cannot be displayed graphically. However, data reduction is possible in the sense that a single statistic may be calculated that represents the degree of association between the two variables. By drawing up a cross-tabulation we have recorded the frequency with which values on two variables occur together. If there is a tendency for some combinations of values to be very frequent and for others to be relatively infrequent, it can be said that there is some tendency for certain combinations to go together, for example in a survey the men say they like Guinness and the women say they do not. Formally, we can say that an association exists when the proportion of values in one category or a variable differs between categories in another.

Look back at Table 6.4. If we were to calculate the proportions of men and

Table 6.5

A cross-tabulation of vodka usage by age

Age	Heavy users '000	Medium users '000	Light users '000	All users '000
15–24	656	1341	1348	3345
25–34	360	796	1247	2583
35–44	267	556	1027	1852
45–54	164	330	685	1170
55–64	94	275	497	865
65+	74	199	307	580

Sex	Age 20–39 %	40–49 %	Total n
Male	75	44.4	100
Female	25	55.6	70
Total	100	100	170

Table 6.6
Table 6.4 converted into column percentages

women in each age group, we would generate Table 6.6. This shows that 75 per cent of the younger age group are men compared with 44.4 per cent of the older group. This means that there is an association between the two variables. The proportions of men in the two age groups differ. If we calculate the percentage difference (75 − 44.4 per cent, or 55.6 − 25 per cent) we arrive at 30.6 per cent. The percentage difference ranges from zero per cent when the proportions are the same, to 100 per cent when there is complete association. It thus makes a feasible measure of association, but it only works for a 2 × 2 table – otherwise there are lots of differences!

The percentage difference is an *asymmetric* measure of association; it depends on which variable we select as our measure of association. If we had percentaged across instead of down, we would have generated Table 6.7. Here, 60 per cent of the younger group is male and 28.6 per cent female, a percentage difference of 31.4 per cent – a different answer from Table 6.6.

The percentage difference is of limited value, however. Since it can be used only on 2 × 2 tables, unless all the tables in a piece of research happen to be of this size, it cannot be applied to each one. When we come to look at other criteria for evaluating measures of association, we will see that for other reasons in addition it does not stack up very well. There are, however, alternatives that are much better.

Statisticians have developed a bewildering array of measures of association for cross-tabulated variables. Each statistic, however, will give a different answer. Each will have its own strengths and weaknesses, and there will be circumstances in which its calculation is misleading or inadvisable. Many of these measures are just not considered in standard textbooks on statistics. Many textbooks consider none of them; some mention just a selection, but will take a different view as to their strengths and weaknesses. The student looking for a comprehensive guide will be disappointed. Such a guide, if developed, would necessarily be long and complex. The solution adopted here is to take the most commonly used survey analysis package – SPSS – and explain in some detail the collection of statistics proposed in its *Crosstabs* procedure. The version of SPSS used for illustrative purpose will be SPSS for Windows, although the description of the statistics will apply to all versions. Although the manual covering this programme does, of course, refer to the

Sex	Age 20–39	40–49	Total (%)
Male (%)	60	40	100
Female (%)	28.6	71.4	100
Total *n*	80	90	170

Table 6.7
Table 6.4 converted into row percentages

statistics selected, the description is very brief, and there is no evaluation and comparison.

All the measures of association explained below have been developed on one of three rather distinct bases:

- departure from independence,
- proportional reduction in error,
- pair-by-pair comparisons.

Departure from independence involves imagining what the data would look like if there were no association, and then saying that association is present to the extent that the observed data depart from this. Thus if 120 respondents consisted of 60 males and 60 females responding 'yes' or 'no' to a question, and equal numbers of each said 'yes' and 'no', the marginals would look like Table 6.8: 60 out of 120 are male, that is, half. Therefore if there were no association, we would expect half of the 60 'yeses' to be male, that is 30. The expected frequency for any cell can always be found by multiplying the row and column marginal for that cell, and dividing by n, the number of cases. In this example:

$$\frac{(60)(60)}{120} = 30$$

The expected frequencies for each cell are illustrated in Table 6.9. This shows that just as many men as women are likely to say 'yes' (or 'no'). Suppose, however, that all the men said 'yes' and all the women said 'no'. The result is shown in Table 6.10. The difference between the observed and expected frequencies for each cell is now either +30 or −30 (the maximum difference that is possible in this table). Simply adding these up will, of course, produce zero. If, however, we square the difference and take that as a proportion of our expectations for each cell, then we take account of whether the absolute difference is based on a large or small expectation. We can now add these up for each cell.

Table 6.8
Responses by sex

Sex / Answer	Male	Female	Total
Yes	–	–	60
No	–	–	60
Total	60	60	120

Table 6.9
Reponses by sex: expected frequencies

Sex / Answer	Male	Female	Total
Yes	30	30	60
No	30	30	60
Total	60	60	120

Sex Answer	Male	Female	Total
Yes	60	–	60
No	–	60	60
Total	60	60	120

Table 6.10 Responses by sex: actual frequencies

If *fo* = observed frequency and *fe* = expected frequency, then:

fo	*fe*	*(fo − fe)*	$\dfrac{(fo - fe)^2}{fe}$
60	30	+30	30
0	30	−30	30
0	30	−30	30
60	30	+30	30
			120

120 is the maximum value that the sum of the squared differences as a proportion of expected values can take. This is a statistic called *Chi-square*, usually symbolized as χ^2. Chi-square will be zero if there are no differences between observed and expected frequencies. The maximum value it can take depends on the number of cases and the number of cells. For a 2 × 2 table the maximum value for Chi-square is always the number of cases, *n*. While it is difficult to use Chi-square itself as a measure of association, various adjustments to it have been proposed that result in more acceptable measures. These measures make no assumptions about the order in which the categories are placed – in fact, their calculation is unaffected if we list them in different ways. Accordingly, they are particularly appropriate for tables where both variables are scaled at the nominal level. They are all based on calculating Chi-square in the first instance and are described below. One feature of this basis for measuring association is that it does not require us to select one variable as dependent, hence all measures based on Chi-square are symmetric measures.

Proportional reduction in error involves arguing that if two variables are associated then it should be possible to use knowledge of the values of one variable to predict the values of the other for each case. Thus if, in a survey, all the men say 'yes' they would purchase brand X and all the women say 'no', then, for each person, if we know their sex, we can perfectly predict their answer to the question. In practice, of course, prediction is seldom perfect, but what we can do is to measure the extent to which knowledge of the value on one variable reduces the number of errors in predicting the other.

To generate a measure of association we imagine that we are called upon to predict, for each case, which value of a dependent variable each is likely to exhibit. We do this first without any knowledge of the value of an independent variable for each case, and then see whether such knowledge enables us to improve our predictions. The proportion of errors that we can eliminate in this process is called the proportionate reduction in error (PRE). There are many statistics that use this notion, and they may be referred to as 'PRE' statistics. Like those measures based on departure from independence, these measures are unaffected by the order of the categories and hence are also described in the section below on coefficients appropriate to two nominal scales. Unlike departure from independence, however, all PRE measures require that we select one of the variables as dependent; choosing the other, as we saw from the percentage difference, will produce a different result. In other words all PRE measures are asymmetric.

Making pair-by-pair comparisons relies on assessing the tendency for all possible combinations of pairs of cases to show similar orderings on both variables. Recall that the essential property of ordinal measurement is the ability to determine which of two observations is the larger. We can then consider a pair of cases and note whether or not the case that is larger on variable A is also larger on variable B. If there is a general tendency for this to happen, then there is a positive association. Relatively high values on one variable are associated with relatively high values on the other. Negative association means a tendency for relatively high values on one variable to be associated with relatively low values on the other.

Look at Table 6.11. The case in cell 'a' is higher than case 'd' on both variables (a 'concordant' pair). If there is a predominance of pairs of this type in a table then there is a positive association. If there are predominantly more pairs like 'b' and 'c' (a 'discordant' pair) there will be negative association. Various measures of association have been developed that assess the relative predominance of concordance over discordance or vice versa.

The idea of pair-by-pair comparisons can be generalised to tables of any size. Measures of association based on these comparisons differ largely in the way they treat the pairs that show no association. However, these statistics all depend on the way in which the categories are ordered and changing the order will alter the statistic. They are therefore appropriate for cross-tabulations where both scales are ordinal and cannot sensibly be used where both or one of them is nominal. They are considered below in a section on coefficients appropriate for two ordinal variables. Pair-by-pair comparisons do not depend on selecting one of the variables as dependent, so they are therefore symmetric measures, but, given that there is a sense of order in the categories, these measures do introduce the notion of negative association, that is, high values on one variable being associated with low values on the other.

Whatever measure of association is used it needs, ideally, to meet certain criteria to be useful for the purpose of making reliable analyses of the data. The basic criteria are:

- it must be applicable to all sizes of table,
- it must vary between zero to represent no association and unity or minus one to represent perfect association,
- it must be possible to interpret the results where values between zero and unity are obtained,
- it must be robust.

Table 6.11

Pair-by-pair comparisons

Variable A Variable B	High	Low
High	a	b
Low	c	d

Some measures of association are restricted to 2×2 tables, or to tables where either rows or columns have only two categories. Measures that apply to only certain sizes of table are of limited value since the researcher is likely to have a variety of tables of different sizes. It is, of course, possible to reduce all the tables to the appropriate size, but information may well be lost in the process and there may not be a sensible way of collapsing categories together. Since different statistics produce different results, the researcher cannot simply apply different statistics according to table size. If, however, the sample (or the population) is very small, it may be necessary to reduce the size of the table anyway. Either way, the same statistic *must* be used if the degree of association between tables is to be compared.

Measures of association are usually designed so that they vary either between zero and plus one, or between minus one and plus one. The results of calculating such measures are usually described as *coefficients*. Some coefficients, however, may take values greater than one, or have maximum values less than one. The problem here is that if, say, the maximum value a statistic can take is 0.707, then what does a coefficient of 0.51 mean? If the two scales are nominal, the statistic should vary between zero and plus one – the notion of 'negative' association is nonsensical unless there is some kind of order between categories. If the two scales are ordinal, then the statistic should be negative if higher order values on one variable are associated with lower order values on the other. It is not that applying a statistic that cannot take negative values to two ordinal scales is necessarily 'wrong', it is just that the statistic will not reveal whether the association is positive or negative. This may be no big deal, however, since this is usually obvious just by looking at the table.

Proportional reduction in error (PRE) measures are probably best for allowing the researcher to interpret the numerical result. Thus if the result is, say, 0.52, then it is possible to interpret this as showing that 52 per cent of the errors in predicting the dependent variable have been eliminated by using knowledge of the dependent variable. Measures based on pair-by-pair comparisons can be given a 'PRE' interpretation, but it is a little stretched. Thus we could say that if any pair of cases is drawn at random from a cross-tabulation and we try to predict whether the same or reverse order occurs, our chances of being correct depend on the relative preponderance of either concordant or discordant pairs. However, a result of, say, +0.8 can really only be interpreted as saying that, of all the pairs considered, 80 per cent are concordant. Chi-square based measures are probably the most difficult to interpret, because the result is only a measure of a general tendency for the table to depart from what would be expected of there were no association.

As far as possible, statistics should be robust, that is, they can be applied in a wide range of circumstances and do not produce nonsensical results if particular conditions hold. Some statistics, for example, are overly sensitive to marginal distributions that are highly skewed and may, for example, revert to zero even if there is clearly some association in the table. Some statistics revert to unity if any of the cells in the table are empty, even if the association is clearly not perfect. Such statistics will have a tendency to 'flatter', that is, enhance the degree of association if the frequencies in some of the cells is very low. A surprising number of statistics are affected if the tables are non-square, i.e. do not have the same number of rows and columns. Ideally, measures of association should not be affected by the marginal distributions, by empty or low frequency cells, or by the table being rectangular.

It is important to bear in mind, however, that if the researcher constructs large tables with many cells when the number of cases is small – 100 or less – then there will be many empty cells or very small numbers in the cells. In these circumstances *all* statistics loose their cool! If you have a small sample it is wiser to collapse the tables to 2×2 or 2×3 before calculating your measures of association. Also, bear in mind that few measures meet all the criteria for a good statistic, so what counts as the 'best' statistic to use in any particular situation is not always evident.

Coefficients appropriate for two nominal variables

The coefficients offered by SPSS for Windows are shown in Figure 6.5. (The procedures for using the Crosstabs command are described in Appendix 3.) Notice that they are conveniently grouped into measures appropriate for nominal data, measures appropriate for ordinal data, and for nominal by interval (metric) combinations. The value of Chi-square may be obtained separately by clicking the appropriate box. The contingency coefficient, Phi and Cramer's *V* are all measures of association based on Chi-square and require the calculation of this statistic first. They are thus measures based on the notion of departure from independence, and they are symmetric. Phi is, as we shall see, identical to Cramer's *V* for 2×2 tables, and for tables where either rows or columns are binary (having two categories). This is why they

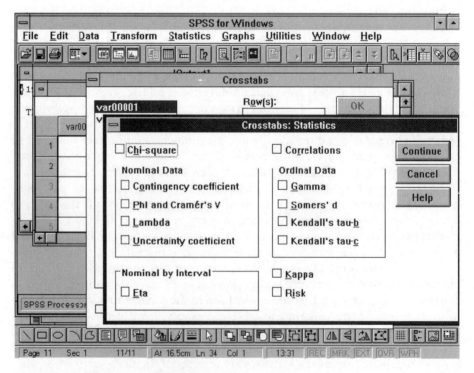

Figure 6.5 The SPSS Crosstabs window.

are put together. The statistics Lambda and the uncertainty coefficient are both based on the proportional reduction in error in measuring association.

The contingency coefficient

The problem with Chi-square itself is that while it reflects the extent to which the observed values in a table depart from what would be expected if there were no association, it does not vary between zero and one. Certainly the minimum value is zero, but the maximum value depends on the number of cases. For a 2 × 2 table this maximum value is the number of cases itself, as we saw earlier. For larger tables the maximum value can exceed the number of cases. Various measures have been proposed that adjust for sample (or population) size. One of the earliest measures was proposed by Pearson. This divides Chi-square by the number of cases added to the value of Chi-square itself and takes the square root. The formula is:

$$C = \sqrt{\frac{\chi^2}{\chi^2 + N}}$$

To calculate the statistic, follow the two steps below.

1 Calculate the statistic Chi-square using the formula:

$$\chi^2 = \sum \frac{(fo - fe)^2}{fe}$$

where fo is the observed frequency for any given cell and fe is the expected frequency. Calculate fe by multiplying the column and row totals for that cell and dividing by N,

2 Enter Chi-square in the formula for C above.

Table 6.12 records whether or not 85 women and 120 men in a survey accurately recalled the price of brand X. The expected frequency for women with accurate recall is (115)(85)/205 = 47.7. If 85 out of 205 respondents are women, we would expect 85/205 of the 115 who have accurate recall to be women, i.e. 85/205 (115) = 47.7. In other words, if sex and price recall are independent then the expected frequency, fo, is 47.7. In fact there are 75 women who have accurate recall. The remaining expected frequencies can either be calculated in the same way or subtracted from the marginals. The full calculation is set out in Table 6.13.

The key features of the statistic are that C becomes zero when the variables are independent, that is, for each cell there is no difference between what would be expected if there were no association and what is, in fact, observed. The upper limit of C, however, depends on the number of rows and columns.

Sex Price recall	Women	Men	Total
Accurate recall	75	40	115
Inaccurate recall	10	80	90
Total	85	120	205

Table 6.12
Price recall by sex of respondent

Table 6.13
The calculation of Chi-square for Table 6.12

	fo	fe	$(fo - fe)$	$\dfrac{(fo - fe)^2}{fe}$
a	75	47.7	+27.3	15.6
b	40	67.3	−27.3	11.1
c	10	37.3	−27.3	20.0
d	80	52.7	+27.3	14.1
				60.8

$$C = \sqrt{\frac{60.8}{60.8 + 205}} = 0.48$$

For a 2 × 2 table, for example, it is 0.707. Although this upper limit increases as the number of rows and columns increases, this limit is always less than one. For this reason, C is more difficult to interpret than other measures. Thus it is not easy to interpret a result of 0.48 when the maximum value is 0.707. A further complication is that two contingency coefficients are not comparable unless they are derived from tables of the same size.

The contingency coefficient may legitimately be used on a table of any size when both variables are scaled at the nominal level and where no distinction is being made between the dependent and the independent variable. However, given the very serious nature of its limitations, there are few contexts in which it is preferable to other statistics which do not suffer from the same drawbacks. C is the oldest of the contingency measures and therefore has been used quite widely, but better measures are available.

Phi and Cramer's V
It has already been noted that Chi-square is directly proportional to N for a given size of table. If we simply divide Chi-square by N we obtain a measure called Phi-square, usually symbolized as $Ø^2$. Phi-square has a minimum value of zero when the two variables are independent. For 2 × 2 tables and for tables where either rows or columns = 2, it also has an upper maximum of unity when the relationship between the two variables is perfect. For tables of this size, then, Phi-square is a good measure. However, for larger tables, Phi-square can attain a value considerably larger than unity. An adjustment to the formula was suggested by Cramer, and is known as Cramer's V. This divides Chi-square by N multiplied by a value which is either rows minus 1 or columns minus 1, whichever is the minimum. The usual formula is:

$$V^2 = \frac{\chi^2}{NMin(r - 1)(c - 1)}$$

Notice that the value of $NMin(r - 1)(c - 1)$ for a 2 × 2 or 2 by m table is one, so is identical to Phi-square. Whether we choose to call the resulting measure Phi or V is perhaps not important.

To calculate the statistics, follow the two steps below:

1 Calculate Chi-square,
2 Enter the value in the formula for V^2.

Phi^2 and V^2 for Table 6.12 is 60.8/205 = 0.3. On the face of it this is a very different answer from the contingency coefficient above, namely 0.48, except that if we took C^2 it becomes 0.23.

Cramer's V varies between zero and unity for all sizes of table and is a symmetrical measure. It can be used for two nominal scales that have been cross-tabulated. Like all measures based on Chi-square, however, its interpretation is not clear. They all tend to give greater weight to those columns or rows having the smallest marginals rather than to those with the largest marginals. They are therefore sensitive to marginal distributions. Notice, too, that sometimes Phi and V appear as squared, sometimes not. It can be shown that, for a 2 × 2 table only, Phi-square is identical to the coefficient of determination based on Pearson's r, namely r^2. It seems sensible, therefore to treat Phi-squared and V^2 as the appropriate measure of the strength of association, as with r^2. The unsquared version of the statistic probably tends to flatter the degree of association.

For all situations where a symmetrical measure is required, where there is a variety of table sizes and where the scales are at the nominal level, then V^2 is the preferred statistic. However, where one variable clearly *is* dependent on the other, it seems sensible to use a statistic that takes this into account. The remaining two statistics in the Nominal Data box, Lambda and the Uncertainty Coefficient, are based on the proportional reduction in error in determining the degree of association. It is to these statistics that we now turn.

Lambda

If two variables are associated, then, as explained earlier, it is possible to use knowledge of the value of one variable to predict the value of the other for each case. Thus if all men say 'yes' and all women say 'no', then for each person, if we know their sex, we can safely predict the answer to the question. In practice, prediction is seldom perfect, so what we can do is measure the extent to which knowledge of the value on one variable reduces the number of errors in predicting the other.

Take the case where nearly all men say 'yes' and most of the women say 'no', as in Table 6.14. To generate our measure of association, we need to calculate how many errors predicting the answer to the question we would make *not* knowing a person's sex. If we know the marginal totals of 'yeses' and 'nos', but not each individual case, then the 'best' guess we could make for each person is to predict that all answers are 'yes' (since there are more of these), and be wrong for 90 out of the 200 cases.

Suppose, now, we know a person's sex, then knowing that a person is male and that 90 out of 100 males say 'yes', then, clearly, it is sensible to predict 'yes' for all males and make only 10 errors. If, on the other hand, we predict 'no' for all 100 women, we make only 20 errors. That totals 10 + 20 = 30 errors in all. This may be compared with the original 90 errors. This is a 66 per cent

Sex Answer	Male	Female	Total	Table 6.14
				Responses by sex
Yes	90	20	110	
No	10	80	90	
Total	100	100	200	

reduction, or 0.66. Clearly, if we eliminate all errors, we will end up with a measure of unity. If we eliminate none, we will end up with a value of zero.

It is difficult to generate a formula for Lambda that you can use just to plug in selected values. Most formulae that have been generated are rather complex. It is probably best to be clear that Lambda is based on the following calculation:

$$\frac{\text{number of errors eliminated}}{\text{number of original errors}}$$

In the above example, this is:

$$= \frac{90 - 30}{90}$$
$$= 0.66.$$

SPSS calculates an asymmetric Lambda for each of the variables. In addition, a kind of average of the two is calculated, giving a symmetrical version that makes no assumption about which variable is independent; it measures the overall improvement when the prediction is done in both directions.

The main features of Lambda are:

- it varies between zero and unity; it cannot be negative,
- it can be used on *any* size of table. The errors remaining after taking the 'best guess', not knowing, then knowing the value of the other variable, need to be added up,
- it is an asymmetric measure, that is, the prediction is one-way. It makes sense to predict the dependent variable from the independent variable. If the independent variable is at the top, then it is the categories forming the rows that should be predicted. If the prediction is made in the other direction, then a different value for Lambda will be derived.

Lambda has an advantage over Chi-square based measures in that its interpretation is much clearer. Thus a result of 0.66 means that 66 per cent of errors can be eliminated by using knowledge of categories of the independent variable to predict categories on the dependent variable.

The main drawback of Lambda is that it will take on a numerical value of zero in instances where all the other measures will not be zero and where we would not wish to refer to the variables as being statistically independent. This may occur where one of the row marginals is much larger than the rest, so no matter what the category of the independent variable, the prediction of the dependent variable category will be the same. In large tables, even if a single marginal total does not dominate, it is likely that some of the less numerous categories will not enter into the computation of Lambda at all.

Where an asymmetric measure for two nominal variables is required, Lambda is to be preferred over Cramer's *V*, partly because it takes account of which variable is independent, and partly because its interpretation is much clearer. However, where the marginals of the dependent variable are very unevenly distributed the statistic will revert to zero and another measure may be required.

The uncertainty coefficient
This measures the proportion by which uncertainty in the dependent variable

is reduced by knowledge of the independent variable. The concept of uncertainty comes from information theory and has to do with the ambiguity of data distributions. Whereas Lambda takes the modal category as the 'best guess' for a set of categories, the concept of uncertainty recognizes the probability that any one particular case may be in one of the non-modal categories. Hence the entire distribution, not just the mode, is considered. It uses a logarithmic function to calculate the average uncertainty in the marginal distribution of the dependent variable, and then calculates what proportion of uncertainty may be eliminated by looking at the categories in the independent variable.

The maximum value for the uncertainty coefficient is 1.0, which denotes the complete elimination of uncertainty. The minimum value is zero when no improvement occurs. As with Lambda, SPSS calculates both asymmetric versions and a combined symmetrical version.

While this measure clearly eliminates one of the main failings of Lambda by taking into account the distribution in the marginals of the dependent variable, its calculation is a 'black box' to all but a fully-fledged mathematician. The statistic is so unknown that the only reference to it is in the manual for the mainframe version of SPSS. It was, apparently, originally developed by Theil (1967).

Coefficients appropriate for two ordinal variables

SPSS lists four statistics as appropriate for ordinal data, but, fortunately, they all are based in the principle of pair-by-pair comparisons that was explained earlier. The key difference between them is in the way they treat 'tied' pairs.

Gamma

This statistic was developed by Goodman and Kruskal. It calculates the number of pairs in a cross-tabulation having the *same* rank order of inequality on both variables (concordant pairs) and compares this with the number of pairs having the *reverse* rank order of inequality on both variables (discordant pairs). Gamma is the simplest of the pair by pair measures because it ignores all other combinations in the table. Gamma takes the difference between concordance and discordance and divides this by the total number of both concordant and discordant pairs. Its formula is:

$$G = \frac{C - D}{C + D}$$

The calculation of the statistic is demonstrated in Table 6.15 which is a 3×2 cross-tabulation of product usage by product satisfaction. To obtain the number of concordant pairs, take each cell and multiply its frequency by the sum of the frequencies of all the cells below and to the right. Add together the results for each cell. Begin in the top left-hand cell. Only two cells are below and to the right. The next cell along has only one cell below and to the right. No other cells have others both below and to the right, so the calculation is:

$$C = 10(8 + 10) + 8(10)$$
$$= 180 + 80 = 260$$

To calculate the number of discordant pairs the procedure is the same, except that we take cells below and to the left. So, begin in the top *right*-hand cell. The calculation is:

$$D = 4(4 + 8) + 8(4)$$
$$= 48 + 32 = 80$$
$$G = \frac{C - D}{C + D} = \frac{260 - 80}{260 + 80} = \frac{180}{340} = 0.52$$

Gamma varies between minus one and plus one. Zero indicates no association; the number of concordant pairs equals the number of discordant pairs. A result of 0.52 indicates a 52 per cent predominance of concordance over discordance, so there is a moderate degree of association between the two variables. Remember that *G* is a symmetric statistic; we do not need to distinguish between dependent and independent variable. Notice also that it is 'margin-free'; its value does not depend on the row or column marginals. Gamma can be applied to any size of table, but the variables must be in categories that can be ordered. It has the drawback, however, that it is overly sensitive to empty cells. This is because no matter how many cases in a cell, if multiplied by zero in an empty cell, the result will be zero.

For 2 × 2 tables Gamma is identical to a statistic that is commonly used on such tables, namely Yule's *Q*. This is calculated from the formula:

$$Q = \frac{ad - bc}{ad + bc}$$

a–d refer to the cells as labelled in Table 6.11. Notice that *ad* = *C*, the number of concordant pairs and *bc* = *D*, the number of discordant pairs.

Gamma can be used on any size of table provided both scales are ordinal. It is simple to calculate and easy to understand. However, it is insensitive to other than concordance and discordance. This is why the other measures calculated by SPSS may be more appropriate.

Somers' d

This statistic is similar to Gamma except that it takes account of those pairs that are tied on one variable but not on the other. Accordingly, it is an asymmetric measure since there will be two results depending on which variable is taken. The numerator of the equation is the same as Gamma, but the denominator adds a value, *T*, which measures the number of ties on variable *A*, but not on variable *B*, or vice versa for the other result. The general formula is:

$$d = \frac{C - D}{C + D + T}$$

To calculate *T* take each cell in turn, beginning in the upper left hand cell, multiply the frequency in that cell by all the cases falling to the right of the cell in the same row. The calculation for Table 6.15 is:

$$T = 10(8 + 4) + 8(4) + 4(8 + 10) + 8(10)$$
$$= 120 + 32 + 72 + 80$$
$$= 304$$
$$\text{So } d = \frac{260 - 80}{260 + 80 + 304}$$
$$= 0.28$$

The alternative d will perform the same operation, but on the columns. d will always give a result substantially below G, since in all cases we are dividing by a value to which T has been added.

Kendall's tau-b
This is a still more stringent measure of association. It includes ties in both directions, so it is similar to Somer's d, but includes both versions of T, Tx and Ty. The formula is:

$$\tau_\beta = \frac{C - D}{\sqrt{(C + D + Tx)(C + D + Ty)}}$$

This is now a symmetrical measure. However, it varies between minus one and plus one only when the table is square, that is, the number of rows equals the number of columns. It is appropriate where the researcher is concerned with the strict ordering of the variables.

Kendall's tau-c
Tau-*b* above can be used only when the number of rows and columns in a table is the same. Otherwise it is better to use Tau-*c*. This uses the following formula:

$$\tau_c = \frac{2m(C - D)}{N^2(m - 1)}$$

m is the smaller of rows or columns. For Table 6.15 this is calculated as follows:

$$\tau_c = \frac{(2)(2)(260 - 80)}{44^2}$$
$$= \frac{720}{1936}$$
$$= 0.37$$

In the case of square tables where $R = C$, tau-*c* will generally be smaller than tau-*b*, though it may be greater than tau-*b* in rectangular tables.

In summary, Gamma is a somewhat loose interpretation of association that looks only at the general tendency for either concordance or discordance to predominate. It is always larger than tau-*b*, tau-*c* or Somers' *d*. This is not necessarily a disadvantage if Gamma is being used to compare degrees of association in a number of tables. Tau-*b*, tau-*c* and Somers' *d* probably give a better assessment of the actual degree of association since they take into account tied pairs. Tau-*b* is best for square tables, tau-*c* for rectangular tables

Product usage Satisfaction	High	Medium	Low
High	10	8	4
Low	4	8	10

Table 6.15
Customer satisfaction by product usage

and Somers' *d* where the researcher wishes an asymmetric measure. Different textbooks give different advice on the advisability of various statistics. At the end of the day it is up to the researcher to make up his or her own mind.

Coefficients appropriate for two ranked variables

There is only one statistic on SPSS appropriate for two ranked variables: Spearman's rho. Recall that in a ranked scale each observation is assigned a number from 1-*n* to reflect its standing relative to other observations. There are as many ranks as cases to be ranked. Consider five types of ground coffee ranked 1-5 in terms of taste and aroma by five people as in Table 6.16. Spearman's coefficient is calculated from the formula:

$$\text{rho } (r_s) = 1 - \frac{6 \sum d^2}{n(n^2 - 1)}$$

where *n* is the number of pared observations and *d* is the difference between ranks for each pair of observations. Where the ranks are identical then $d = 0$ and $r_s = 1$. The calculation for Table 6.16 is set out in Table 6.17. Rho varies between +1 and −1. Zero indicates no association. To use Rho on metric data it is necessary to convert the metric values into ranks. It has the advantage that, by doing so, it is unaffected by extreme values.

Coefficients appropriate for mixed variables

SPSS for Windows suggests only one statistic for situations where the independent variable is nominal and the dependent variable is metric (or interval), namely Eta. Eta-squared is sometimes known as the *correlation ratio* and can be interpreted as the proportion of the total variability in the dependent variable that can be accounted for by knowing the categories of the independent variable. The statistic takes the variance (the square root of the standard deviation) of the dependent variable as an index of error in using the mean of the variable to make a prediction for each case. This is then compared with the variance in each sub-group of the independent variable. If the variables are associated, the variance within each sub-group will be less than the overall variance. The correlation ratio is then:

$$n^2 = \frac{\text{original variance} - \text{within-group variance}}{\text{original variance}}$$

The correlation ratio (Eta-squared) is always positive and ranges from zero to one. It is an asymmetric measure and is an index of the degree to which scores on an interval scale can be predicted from categories on a nominal scale. To use in SPSS the nominal variable must be coded numerically.

Respondent	Taste	Aroma
A	5	3
B	3	4
C	1	1
D	2	2
E	4	5

Table 6.16
Coffee ranked by taste and aroma

Respondent	Taste	Aroma	d	d²	
A	5	3	2	4	
B	3	4	1	1	
C	1	1	0	0	
D	2	2	0	0	
E	4	5	1	1	
			Total	6	

Table 6.17
Calculation of Rho

$$\text{Rho} = 1 - \frac{6(6)}{5(25-1)} = 0.7$$

For other combinations of scales there are other statistics. Thus for one nominal and one ordinal scale there is a measure called the coefficient of differentiation developed by Wilcoxon and is an extension of Wilcoxon's signed-ranks test. For describing association between one ordinal and one interval scale there is Jaspen's coefficient of multiserial correlation. Neither of these statistics is calculated by SPSS for Windows and will not be covered here. For further details see Freeman (1965). If you do have these combinations of scales, it would be more usual to treat the higher-order scale as at a lower level of measurement. So, for an ordinal by nominal combination, treat them as two nominal scales. For an ordinal by metric combination, treat them as two ordinal scales. Treating an interval by nominal combination as two nominal scales will mean throwing away a lot of information with a much less sensitive measure, but for this situation, SPSS does give us Eta, which we can square to give us the correlation ratio.

The remaining boxes on the Crosstabs window relate to Kappa and Risk. *Kappa* measures the extent of agreement between two identical scales, for example two customers rating a product on a three-point scale. A simple measure of such agreement would be the proportion of cases for which the raters agree. However, this figure should be corrected for the amount of agreement that would be expected by chance. Cohen's Kappa takes the difference between the observed proportion of cases in which raters agree and that expected by chance, and normalizes it by dividing by the maximum difference possible for the marginal totals.

Risk refers to the relative risk ratio. It is estimated as the ratio of two incidence rates. Since the ratio does not vary between zero and one, but can take values considerably greater than one or minus one, it is difficult to interpret. It is of limited value.

Selecting the appropriate statistic
In deciding which statistics are appropriate for your cross-tabulations, it is first essential to be clear about the scales used for measurement purposes. This will enable you to use the appropriate grouping of statistics – Nominal Data, Ordinal Data or Nominal by Interval. If either or both variables are nominal, choose between the contingency coefficient, Phi-square, Cramers' V or the uncertainty coefficient. If there is no clear distinction being drawn between dependent and independent variables, select C, Phi-square or V^2. V^2 is preferable to C in all circumstances, so choose this statistic. For 2×2 and $2 \times m$

tables it will be identical to Phi-square anyway. If one of the variables clearly *is* dependent, choose Lambda unless the marginals are very unevenly distributed, in which case use the uncertainty coefficient. You could, of course, arbitrarily pick one of the variables as 'dependent', but the results may be misleading.

If both variables are ordinal, choose from Gamma, Somers' *d*, Kendall's tau-*b* or tau-*c*. Gamma is the simplest of these measures. Choose this if you wish to compare a number of ordinal by ordinal tables or if you want a 'quick-and-dirty' indication of the degree of association. If one of the variables is clearly dependent, select Somers' *d*. If not and you want a tightly controlled measure of association, pick tau-*b* if the table is square and tau-*c* if it is not.

All this suggests that the decision needs to be taken for each table on the basis of the level of measurement and whether a symmetrical or asymmetrical measure is required. However, researchers are usually comparing *many* tables in any particular piece of research. It is not essential that the same statistic is used for all tables, but where the degree of association is to be compared, the same statistic *must* be used. Pick one that suits each grouping of tables.

Remember that for the asymmetric measures, SPSS for Windows will produce three statistics, one for each variable taken as 'dependent', and one that combines the two, so you will need to pick the appropriate coefficient carefully – SPSS will not do it for you. If your research, for example, is looking at a range of factors that may be associated with a particular dependent variable, then always use an asymmetric measure, selecting this as the dependent variable for the appropriate statistic. If you are looking largely for patterns of relationships or interconnections between variables then choose a symmetrical measure.

Do not forget that establishing a high degree of association between two variables does not establish anything about causality or even influence. That requires further investigation into temporal sequences and lack of spuriousness. Remember, too, that measures of association are *descriptive* statistics; they report on the cases that are in the table. If your cases are, in fact, a sample, you may wish to use *inferential* statistics (in addition to descriptive ones) to make or to test statements about the population of cases from which the sample was drawn. For bivariate and multivariate cross-tabulation it is usual to use the Chi-square statistic. This statistic, along with other inferential statistics, is explained later.

Large tables with many rows and many columns are difficult to interpret. Large cross-tabulations are a result of using a lot of categories for each variable. Thus two variables cross-tabulated, one with six categories and the other with five will result in a table with 6×5 or 30 cells. Unless the total number of cases on which the table is based is considerable, the frequencies in the cells will be very small. For example, with 30 cells a sample of 100 respondents will average out at just over three per cell! There are bound to be many cells that are empty. This not only makes the interpretation very difficult, it also means that *any* measures of association we calculate will be unreliable.

The usual solution is to condense larger tables into smaller ones. Very often this involves creating two dichotomies and producing a 2×2 table with four cells. Suppose a table is cross-tabulating price awareness against brand loyalty, as in Table 6.18. This table – a 3×3 table – has nine cells. That may still be too many if the sample is small. However, if those who buy only one brand are

Price recall	Buys only one brand	Buys two brands	Buys many brands
Accurate price recall	64	9	11
Overestimate	8	24	18
Underestimate	12	13	31

Table 6.18
Price awareness by brand loyalty

Price recall	One brand only	More than one brand
Accurate racall	64	20
No accurate recall	20	86

Table 6.19
Table 6.18 reduced to a 2 × 2 table

contrasted with the rest, and those who recall price accurately are contrasted with the rest, then we can create a 2 × 2 table, as in Table 6.19. In effect, both variables are being recoded and in most survey analysis packages it will be necessary to carry out this recoding before the condensed cross-tabulation can be produced. From the collapsed table it is now easier to see that accurate recall is associated with brand loyalty.

Multivariate analysis

Bivariate analysis is limited to looking at the relationships between variables two at a time; multivariate analysis techniques allow the analysis of three or more variables simultaneously. It has a number of advantages over univariate and bivariate procedures, namely:

- it permits conclusions to be drawn about the nature of causal connections between variables (see pp 209–211),
- it facilitates the grouping together of variables that are interrelated, or cases that are similar in terms of their characteristics,
- it provides the ability to predict dependent variables from two or more independent variables and hence improve on predictions made on the basis of only one variable.

Where all the variables are non-metric, it is possible to conduct a series of three-way analyses. Four-way, five-way up to *n*-way analyses *are* possible, but they become exceedingly complex and require very large sample sizes as the number of sample splits grows. An example of a three-way cross tabulation is illustrated in Table 6.20. This shows the relationship between income and product purchase 'controlled' by age. The original two-way table is shown in Table 6.21. This indicates that there is a relationship between buying product A and income (63 per cent of those with high income purchased product A compared with 36 per cent of those with low income). However, when age is controlled, then within similar age groups, there is little difference between

Age Income	35–50 High		35–30 Low		16–34 High		16–34 Low	
	n	%	n	%	n	%	n	%
Purchased product A	85	85	48	80	10	20	27	18
No purchase	15	15	12	20	40	80	123	82
Total	100	100	60	100	50	100	150	100

Table 6.20
Purchase behaviour by income and age

Table 6.21
Purchase behaviour by income

Income	High		Low	
Purchase behaviour	n	%	n	%
Purchased product A	95	63	75	36
Not purchased	55	37	135	64
Total	150	100	210	100

income and purchase of product A; it is just that older people tend both to have higher incomes and to buy product A. Thus whereas the original percentage difference in Table 6.21 is $63 - 36 = 27$ per cent. For Table 6.20, for the older group the percentage difference is $85 - 80 = 5$ per cent, and for the younger group is $20 - 18 = 2$ per cent.

The original and the three-way cross-tabulations can be compared using any of the appropriate measures of association in the Crosstabs/statistics window of SPSS. Since purchasing is a binary variable, the Nominal Data statistics are appropriate. Thus the Lambda for Table 6.21 is:

$$\frac{170 - (55 + 75)}{170} = 0.23$$

For Table 6.20 both Lambda for the younger and the older groups are zero. The association has 'disappeared'.

Data display and data reduction for metric data

Univariate analysis

Metric data, you will recall from Chapter 2, are derived from scales that possess a metric with which it is possible to specify scale values in terms of numerical quantities. Metric scales were subdivided into continuous and discrete. To display metric data, tables and charts are again appropriate. Again, in the first instance, these are likely to be univariate. It will be useful at this stage, however, to make a distinction between tables containing metric values and frequency tables. An example of the former will be a table giving sales by volume in tons or by value in £ sterling, or aggregations or summaries of such measurements, for example, average consumption of beer per head in pints per week. Such figures appear in columns, rows or in the cells of tables. Such tables may themselves be variable listings or breakdowns.

A variable listing shows individual metric values, one for each of a number of metric variables, that relate to one case, as in Table 6.22 or to a set of cases. Variable breakdowns contain the metric values of a single variable in each of two or more sub-categories, or ranges of values. There is always a minimum of two variables involved: one is a metric scale whose values are recorded *in* the table, and one or more is a non-metric, discrete metric or grouped continuous metric scale. The latter break down the original values into sub-categories. Thus in Table 6.23 consumer sales and stocks are broken down by brand. Variable breakdowns *must* be distinguished from cross-tabulations, which contain frequencies, and for which measures of statistical association

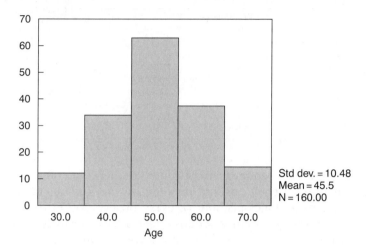

Figure 6.6 Histogram for Table 6.24.

may be calculated. It is not meaningful to attempt such calculations on metric tables.

Frequency tables report the frequency with which scale values occur. Since for metric scales there is likely to be a large number of such scale values, it is usually necessary to group them into class intervals, as in Table 6.24. There should be between about five and 12 intervals that are non-overlapping. Such tables give some idea of the distribution of the data, although a better display is achieved if we produce a histogram, as in Figure 6.6. Histograms may be thought of as vertical bar charts in which the rectangular bars are constructed at the boundaries of each class. The variable of interest is plotted along the horizontal axis and the vertical axis shows the number, proportion or percentage of observations per class interval.

In terms of data reduction, metric data may be described in terms of three major properties:

- central tendency,
- dispersion,
- shape.

Many metric variables show a distinct tendency to group or cluster about a certain central point, in which case it becomes possible to select some typical value or average to describe the entire distribution. The *arithmetic mean* is

	Profits	Revenue	Employees	
Company XYZ	£3.2m	£2.61m	310	**Table 6.22** A variable listing

Consumer sales	(£000s)	(tons)	Stocks (tons)	
Product class Z	4,116	1,714	92	**Table 6.23** A variable breakdown
Brand A	1,475	576	28	
Brand B	687	269	17	

Table 6.24

A frequency distribution of age

Age	Frequency	%
20–29	12	7.5
30–39	34	21.3
40–49	63	39.4
50–59	36	22.5
60–69	15	9.3
Total	160	100.0

the most commonly used measure of central tendency and it is calculated by summing all the observations and dividing by the number of observations involved. The mean takes account of every observation in the distribution. While this is normally seen as an advantage it may result in being unduly affected by extreme values. An alternative is the *median*, which is the middle value in an ordered sequence of observations. It is the value above which and below which half of the observations lie when arranged in ascending or descending order and will be unaffected by extreme values. It can be more representative than the mean if the distribution is highly skewed. A third type of average is the *mode* – the value in a distribution that occurs most frequently. This will usually be the class interval with the highest frequency – the modal class – but the value of the mode will depend on the choice of class interval. Unless the data are grouped, however, then, certainly for continuous data, each observation will have a frequency of one and there can be no mode. The mode is a very rough and ready measure that ignores the bulk of the data. Some distributions, furthermore, may be bimodal, that is having two relatively large frequencies. It is, of course, possible to have a modal category for nonmetric data, but this is not a particularly insightful observation. Categories can hardly 'cluster' about a central point if they may be put in any order.

Dispersion in a set of observations concerns the amount of variation or spread in the data. The mean, for example, gives no indication of the extent to which the set of values are all close to or are widely scattered about the mean. The mean for 21,22,23,24,25 is 23; it is also 23 for 11,17,23,29,35. We could compare the *range* in the two sets of observations – in the first it is 4 (25–21) and in the second it is 24 (35–11). The range, however, takes no account of how the data are 'bunched' – the values could nearly all be near the upper or lower end of the range.

A more sophisticated measure of dispersion takes the average of the distances between the mean score and all the other values in the set. The generally accepted statistic is the *standard deviation*, which adds up the squared distances, divides by the total number of values in the set, and then takes the square root. For the first set of five numbers above this involves subtracting 23 (the mean) from each value, squaring the result and adding up the totals. This gives the sum of the squared deviations of 10 [i.e.$(21 - 23)^2 + (22 - 23)^2 + (23 - 23)^2 + (24 - 23)^2 + (25 - 23)^2$]. The standard deviation is then $\sqrt{10/5} = 1.41$

For the second set of five numbers, the standard deviation is 8.5, clearly indicating the wider spread.

A third important property of a set of observations is the shape of the distribution. Some distributions are symmetrical, that is, the shape below

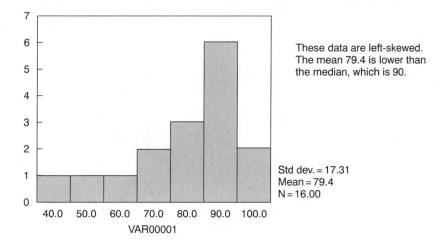

These data are left-skewed.
The mean 79.4 is lower than
the median, which is 90.

Std dev. = 17.31
Mean = 79.4
N = 16.00

Figure 6.7 Data skewed to the left.

the mean is a mirror-reflection of that above the mean. Other distributions may be skewed, either to the right or to the left. These shapes are illustrated in Figures 6.7 and 6.8. If a distribution is symmetrical, the mean and the median will be equal. If the mean exceeds the median the data may be described as positively or right-skewed. If the mean is smaller than the median the data are negatively or left-skewed.

Bivariate analysis

We have seen earlier that to display the relationship between two non-metric variables we cross-tabulate them. If we have two metric variables, we can plot the relationship on a scatter diagram (or scattergram). Suppose four students (cases A,B,C and D) take two tests that are scored out of 10. The results are shown in Table 6.25. You can see that there is a tendency for those who

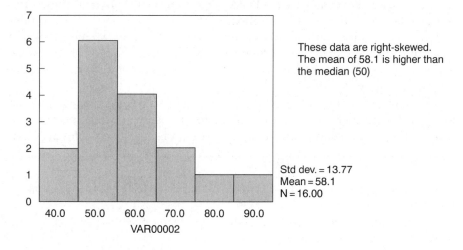

These data are right-skewed.
The mean of 58.1 is higher than
the median (50)

Std dev. = 13.77
Mean = 58.1
N = 16.00

Figure 6.8 Data skewed to the right.

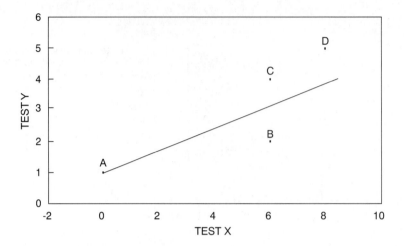

Figure 6.9 Scattergram of X on Y.

perform well in test X also perform well on test Y. In a scattergram the horizontal axis of a graph is used to represent values of one of the variables and the vertical axis to represent the values of the other. Figure 6.9 shows the scattergram for Table 6.25. From this you can see the tendency for high values on Y to be associated with high values on X – and vice versa. If one of the variables is considered to be the independent variable, its values are placed on the horizontal axis and it is called variable X. The dependent variable is scaled along the Y-axis. (This is the same as putting the independent variable at the top of a cross-tabulation.) Each bivariate observation (of which there are four in Table 6.25) is represented as a dot on the graph, placed at the intersection of the X and Y values. There will be as many dots on a scattergram as there are cases.

Data reduction involves calculating a measure of association similar to those we calculated for cross-tabulations. The good news is that there is only one measure that is universally used – Pearson's r, otherwise known as the correlation coefficient or the product-moment correlation coefficient. The bad news is that it is a bit more difficult to explain than the measures we have looked at so far. If you have access to SPSS then it can be calculated for you at the click of a mouse button. However, the point is to understand the statistic and what it is telling you. So, here goes.

If the two variables are correlated, then high values on one variable are associated with high values on the other for a positive correlation and with low values for a negative one. The problem is that the two scales will have

Table 6.25
Scores of A–D on two tests

Individual	Test X	Test Y
A	0	1
B	6	2
C	6	4
D	8	5
Total	20	12

different means and are likely to be in different units (e.g. one in years old and the other in £ sterling). However, if we say by how much an observation for a particular case is above the mean of Y for variable Y and above the mean of X for variable X, then if we multiply the result we will get a large positive product. The same will happen if both are large negative figures. If we add all these products for all cases together, we will get a large sum. If, on the other hand, high values on one variable are associated with low values on the other, we will get a large negative sum. If there is little correlation, then positive and negative values will tend to offset one another. So, the sum we are calculating – the covariation in technical parlance – is an indication of the extent to which the two variables are correlated. The formula is:

$$\sum (X - \bar{X})(Y - \bar{Y})$$

If we divide this covariation by the number of cases, n, we get an average covariation called the covariance, which takes account of the fact that the mean of X and the mean of Y may be different. To take account of the differences in units, the covariance is divided by the standard deviation of X multiplied by the standard deviation of Y. This standardizes the covariance. If we divide both the numerator and the denominator by n, the formula for r becomes:

$$r = \frac{\sum (X - \bar{X})(Y - \bar{Y})}{\sqrt{[\sum (X - \bar{X})^2][\sum (Y - \bar{Y})^2]}}$$

The calculation of r for Table 6.25 is shown in Box 6.1.

The correlation coefficient, r, measures the amount of spread about a linear equation – in other words, how close to a 'best-fitting' line (a regression line) the actual observations are. The maximum value for r is 1.00, indicating a perfect correlation. A value of $r = 0.84$, for example, would indicate that most observations are close to the line. A coefficient of $r = 0$ or nearly zero would mean that the line is no help in predicting X from Y or vice versa. Pearson's r can be negative and the regression line will have a negative slope. Pearson's r itself is a little difficult to interpret, but if we square the result to produce r^2 then we have what is often called the *coefficient of determination* which

	X	Y	$(X - \bar{X})$	$(Y - \bar{Y})$	$(X - \bar{X})(Y - \bar{Y})$	$(X - \bar{X})^2$	$(Y - \bar{Y})^2$
A	0	1	−5	−2	+10	25	4
B	6	2	+1	−1	−1	1	1
C	6	4	+1	+1	+1	1	1
D	8	5	+3	+2	+6	9	4
Total	20	12			16	36	10

$\bar{X} = 20/4 = 5$
$\bar{Y} = 12/4 = 3$

$r = \dfrac{16}{\sqrt{36(10)}} = 0.84$

Box 6.1 Calculating Pearson's r

gives the proportion of the variance on the Y observations that is accounted for or 'explained' by variations in X. Thus if $r = 0.84$ then r^2 is 0.71. This means that 71 per cent of the variance in Y is accounted for by the variance in X.

If the value calculated for r^2 is very low or zero, do not assume, however, that there is no relationship between X and Y – it might be that the relationship is not linear but curvilinear. The best way to check is to draw or get SPSS to draw the scattergram.

Multivariate analysis

Where the data are metric, a number of sophisticated multivariate techniques become possible. There are two approaches, however. One is to look at the relationships between variables among the set of cases; the other is to take each case in turn and to analyse the pattern of responses, case by case. Three of the most widely used techniques using the first of these two approaches, or 'macro' analysis, include:

- multiple regression,
- factor analysis,
- cluster analysis.

Multiple regression attempts to predict a single dependent variable from two or more independent variables and is an extension of bivariate regression. As we saw earlier, a linear regression line may be used to make predictions of a dependent variable from a single independent variable. The statistic r^2 indicates how 'good' that line is in making such predictions. In reality, not one but several variables are likely to affect the dependent variable. Thus the level of sales is affected not only by price but by, for example, advertising expenditure, interest rates, and personal disposable income. The formula describing any regression line is:

$$Y = a + bX$$

Multiple regression extends this to:

$$Y = a + +b_1X_1 +b_2X_2 +b_3X_3 \ldots +b_nX_n$$

where $X_1, X_2, X_3 \ldots .. X_n$ are the independent variables. The values b_1, b_2, b_3, b_n indicate the rates of change in Y consequent upon a unit change in $X_1, X_2, X_3, \ldots X_n$. The calculation for each value of b is made with the degree of correlation between Y and the other variables held constant. As with the bivariate procedure, the value for r^2 indicates the percentage of variation in Y associated with the variation in the independent variables.

While multiple regression is one of a number of 'dependence' methods that attempt to explain one or more dependent variables on the basis of two or more independent variables, factor analysis is an 'interdependence' method. These methods review the interdependence between variables or between cases in order to generate an understanding of the underlying structure, and to create new variables or new groupings. Factor analysis recognizes that when many variables are being measured (usually, but not always, by asking people questions in a survey), some of them may be measuring different aspects of the same phenomenon and hence will be interrelated. It systematically reviews the correlation between each variable forming part of the analysis and all the

Variable	1	2	3	4	5
1	1.00	0.61	0.47	−0.02	−0.10
2		1.00	0.33	0.19	0.32
3			1.00	−0.83	−0.77
4				1.00	0.93
5					1.00

Table 6.26
A correlation matrix

other variables, and groups together those that are highly intercorrelated with one another, and not correlated with variables in another group. The groups identify 'factors' that are in effect 'higher order' variables. This helps to eliminate redundancy where, for example, two or more variables may be measuring the same construct. The factors themselves are not directly observable, but each variable has a 'factor loading' which is the correlation between the variable and the factor with which it is most closely associated. The effect, and advantage, of factor analysis, is to reduce a large number of variables to a more manageable set of factors that themselves are not correlated.

Factor analysis begins by calculating a correlation matrix – a table of the value of Pearson's r for each variable with each other variable. If there are, for example, just five variables, then the correlation matrix might look like that in Table 6.26. From visual inspection it is clear that variables 4 and 5 are highly correlated and both are negatively correlated with variable 3. Variables 1 and 2 are also correlated, but neither is correlated with variables 4 or 5. A factor analysis might produce a 'solution' like Table 6.27. Variables 3, 4 and 5 combine to define the first factor and the second factor is most highly correlated with variables 1 and 2.

There are problems associated with factor analysis. First, it is possible to generate several solutions from a set of variables. Second, a subjective decision needs to be made as to how many factors to accept. Third, the grouping has to make intuitive sense. Thus if variables 1–5 above were consumer reactions to a new product, then variables 4 and 5 might be two questions that tap the 'value-for-money' factor, and variables 1–3 are different aspects of 'benefits-derived-from-use'. Factor analysis will always produce a solution; whether it is a good or helpful one is another matter. There may not, in fact, *be* any factors underlying the variables.

All scientific fields have a need to group or cluster objects. Historians group events; botanists group plants. Marketing managers often need to group customers, for example, on the basis of the benefits they seek from buying a particular product or brand, or on the basis of their lifestyles. Any procedure for deriving such groupings is clearly crucial for market segmentation. Cluster analysis is a range of techniques for grouping cases (usually respondents to a

Variable	Factor 1	Factor 2
1	−0.25	0.72
2	0.06	0.87
3	−0.94	0.33
4	0.94	0.21
5	0.95	0.26

Table 6.27
Factor loading on two factors

survey) who have characteristics in common. Cases are placed into different clusters such that members of any cluster are more similar to each other in some way than they are to members in other clusters.

Two very different approaches are possible, however. One is based on taking individual cases and combining them on the basis of some measure of similarity, such as the degree of correlation between the cases on a number of variables. Each case is correlated with each other case in a correlation matrix. The pair of cases with the highest index of similarity is placed into a cluster. The pair with the next highest is formed into another cluster and so on. Each cluster is then averaged in terms of the index being used and combined again on the basis of the average similarities. The process continues until, eventually, all the cases are in one cluster.

The other approach is to begin with the total set of cases and divide them into sub-groups on a basis specified by the researcher. Thus the researcher may want a four-cluster solution of 1200 respondents on 10 variables. An iterative partitioning computer program might begin by setting up four equal-sized groups at random. The centre of each cluster on the 10 variables is then calculated and the distances between each of the 1200 respondents and the centres of the four groups is measured. On the basis of these distances, respondents are reassigned to the group with the nearest cluster centre. The new cluster centres are recalculated and the distances again measured, with a further reassignment taking place. This process is repeated until no further reassignments are needed.

Unfortunately, the different methods of cluster analysis can produce quite different solutions. Furthermore, cluster analysis, like factor analysis, *always* produces clusters, even when there are, in fact, no natural groupings in the data. The various techniques work by *imposing* a cluster structure on the data rather than allowing the structure to emerge from the analysis.

Regression analysis, factor analysis and cluster analysis are all examples of 'macro' analysis. Even cluster analysis, which groups cases, is based on the degree of correlation between cases based on the analysis of variables. The identity of the case is lost as soon as analysis begins. An alternative approach is to analyse the data case by case; in other words the analysis is based on the patterns of responses given by a particular respondent. Once the analysis has been carried out, the results may then be summarized or aggregated in some way. Currently, there are three main techniques of micro analysis:

- conjoint analysis,
- multi-dimensional scaling,
- micromodelling.

Conjoint (or 'trade-off') analysis looks at the ways in which respondents trade off combinations of product characteristics when attempting to max-imize their overall satisfaction, and calculates the degree of importance or 'utility' that respondents place on each characteristic. The results are normally input into product design so that customer satisfaction can be maximized.

Suppose a biscuit manufacturer wishes to find the best combination of saltiness, sweetness and butter content for a new kind of biscuit. If there are two levels of saltiness (high and low), three levels of sweetness (high, medium and low) and butter versus vegetable fat, then there are $2 \times 3 \times 2 = 12$ product combinations. In some cases the desired features are fairly clear, but it is a zero-sum operation in which it is not possible to have all the features. Thus everybody wants a car that is fast, cheap, economical, reliable and with high specification. However, it is not possible to combine all these, so to what extent is the customer prepared to trade off petrol economy in order to get more acceleration? Or cheapness to get reliability?

The input data for conjoint analysis are the preferences for each combination of characteristic. Respondents may be asked to rank *all* combinations, or to take just two at a time. A computer algorithm then produces utilities for each level of each attribute for each individual case. When these are summed for each product combination, the rank order of the total utility scores should match the respondent's rank ordering of preference. The process is an iterative one in which the utilities assigned are continually modified until they can reproduce the rankings for product characteristics that the respondent has given. Each respondent will have his or her own set of utilities and the analysis is conducted one case at a time. An average respondent, however, can be created by averaging the input judgements into 'pooled' utilities.

Conjoint analysis is not without its problems. The task of ranking a large number of product combinations can be quite daunting, and, if treated two at a time, may be unrealistic. However, since the input data are only rankings, conjoint analysis is a technique that can be used for non-metric data, provided they are rank ordered. One particularly ingenious solution to the task of establishing preferences has been developed by Research International for its customer satisfaction research package called SMART (Salient Multi-attribute Research Technique). This technique is described in detail in Chapter 8.

Multi-dimensional scaling (MDS) is used most often in marketing to identify the relative position of competing brands or shops as perceived by customers, and to uncover key dimensions underlying customers' evaluations. While, like conjoint analysis, it is based on micro analysis, unlike conjoint analysis it is an interdependence technique rather than a dependence one. It seeks to infer underlying dimensions from a series of similarity or preference judgements provided by customers about objects within a given set. In a sense it does the reverse of cluster analysis: while the latter groups objects according to similarities on prespecified dimensions, MDS infers underlying evaluative dimensions from similarities or preferences indicated by customers. These data can be in the form of ranks (i.e. non-metric, so the technique is sometimes referred to as non-metric MDS), or in the form of numerical ratings.

Suppose a customer is given a set of six multiple chain stores (like Asda, Tesco, Sainsbury) and asked to say how similar each store is to the others. The customer is asked to compare pairs of stores, and then rank the pairs from most similar to least similar. With six stores there are $n(n-1)/2$ or 15 pairs. The ranks given by just one customer might look like those in Table 6.28. MDS,

Multiple	A	B	C	D	E	F
A		12	11	1	7	3
B			5	15	4	10
C				13	6	14
D					9	2
E						8

Table 6.28
Similarity rankings of six multiples

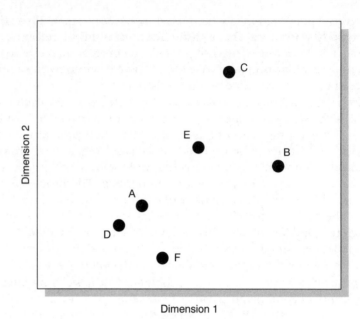

Figure 6.10   A multi-dimensional map based on ranking in Table 6.28.

like cluster analysis, is an iterative process that can be carried out using one of several available computer programs. Such a program would generate a geometric configuration of stores so that the distances between pairs of stores are as consistent as possible with customer's similarity rankings, so that the pair of stores ranked 15th are furthest apart, the pair of stores ranked 14th next furthest, while the pair AD is the closest together. The objects are presented usually in two-dimensional space, as in Figure 6.10, which shows a two-dimensional configuration of the six stores in which the interstore distances are consistent with the rankings in Table 6.28.

It is necessary to know, however, what the two dimensions represent. Labelling them is a subjective process and involves inspecting the relative position of the objects along each dimension and inferring what the dimension is most likely to represent on the basis of prior knowledge about the objects themselves. Looking at the first dimension, we might notice that the stores D and A offer the lowest prices, and C and B the highest. So dimension one could be price. Looking at dimension two vertically, we may observe that store C has a large product range and store F a limited product range, with the others in between. So, dimension two could be product variety. It is possible, of course, that somebody else looking at the same diagram may see other dimensions. However, it is possible to infer that this customer implicitly used price and product variety as the key criteria for comparing the six stores. Other customers may, of course, have other perceptions, resulting in a totally different multi-dimensional map. Where the maps from customer to customer differ greatly, making global inferences may be difficult. In such a situation the researcher may attempt to identify segments of customers with fairly similar multi-dimensional maps, perhaps using appropriate cluster analysis techniques.

Micromodelling so far has had little development. However, Research

International's Microtest is based on micromodelling techniques that try to analyse the pattern of responses in a single individual in order to make a prediction for that individual of his or her likelihood of trying a new product and subsequent repurchase. The predictions of a sample of individuals are then aggregated so that forecasts can be made of future sales. Research International's Microtest is explained in more detail in Chapter 8.

Statistical inference for non-metric data

Estimation

We have seen how we can describe each variable for a set of cases in terms of a variety of tables, charts and summary measures depending on the type of scale used. We can also analyse the strength of any relationships between the variables. Thus, we may be able to conclude that 63 per cent of respondents to a survey bought a magazine in the last week, their average age is 48.2 and the association between the amount of radio listening and response to magazine return coupons is $V = 0.54$. However, we also saw in Chapter 5 that the set of cases may, in fact, be a sample from a population of cases and that a range of different kinds of error may arise in the process. One particular kind of error was random sampling error – random sampling fluctuations from one sample to another will occur even if all forms of bias and non-sampling error have been eliminated or can be ignored. Despite this error, we may still want to make various statements about the population from which the sample was drawn based on evidence from the sample. There are two rather different situations in which we may wish to do this. In one circumstance we may not have a very good idea of the summary measure for the population (often called a population 'parameter'), so we use the sample to make an estimate of it. In the other situation, we may think we know the value of the parameter and we use the sample statistics to test or confirm our hunch or hypothesis.

Any statement we make should have two properties: it should be relatively precise and it should be correct. If we took a random sample of adult consumers and found that 46 per cent purchased a chocolate bar in the last seven days, we could just say that the per cent in the population of adult consumers is just the same. This statement is very precise and is called a *point estimate*. Very often, this is all clients wanting various estimates are interested in. Accordingly, agencies will 'correct' their estimates in various ways, usually through weighting, and will then 'gross up' their estimate to give a figure for the population as a whole. Weighting and grossing up are explained later. Point estimates, however, are seldom likely to be correct. It would be very unusual for the value found in the sample to be exactly the same as the actual value in the population. As an alternative, we could say that the per cent who purchased a chocolate bar in the last seven days is between 0 and 100 per cent. This statement is undoubtedly correct, but not very precise. A statement of this kind is called an *interval estimate*. To be more precise we could say that the per cent who purchased a chocolate bar in the last seven days is between 42 per cent and 50 per cent (that is, 4 per cent either side of the sample result). There is still a risk, however, that this statement is wrong. To make it correct as well as relatively precise we need to calculate the

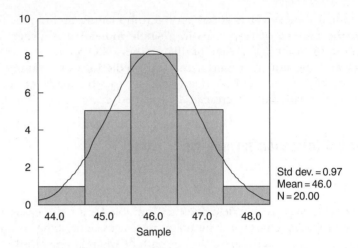

Figure 6.11   A sampling distribution of sample size *n*.

probability that the statement is correct. This is where statistical inference comes in. The same principles apply when we are testing an hypothesis about a parameter from evidence from a sample.

A concept basic to all statistical inference is the *sampling distribution*. Imagine that we take lots of samples of a given size and calculate a particular statistic for each sample, say a proportion. If the real proportion in the population is, for example, 46 per cent, we may take a sample and obtain a proportion of 47 per cent. Another may come out as 45 per cent. In fact, most sample results will cluster around 46 per cent with relatively few producing 'rogue' results of, say, 33 per cent. The tendency for this to happen will decline as the sample gets larger and increase as it gets smaller. If we plot the results as a distribution, we might obtain something like Figure 6.11. If we in fact took every conceivable sample of size *n* from a population and plotted the results we would obtain what is called a *normal* distribution like the one imposed on Figure 6.11. In practice we would not of course actually do this, but it can be achieved statistically by calculating a theoretical sampling distribution.

The normal distribution has a number of interesting characteristics. It is bell-shaped, it is symmetrical and its tails never quite touch the base. The last feature means that, in theory, the range is infinite, but in practice nearly all observations will lie within three standard deviations above and below the mean (that is, a range of six standard deviations). The standard deviation, you will recall from p. 176, is the average of deviations about the mean. The mean and the standard deviation together define the normal curve. Every time we specify a particular combination of mean and standard deviation a different distribution will be generated. Figure 6.12 shows three different distributions. Distributions A and B have the same mean but different standard deviations. Distributions A and C have the same standard deviation but different means. Distributions B and C depict two distributions that differ in respect of both.

Because the normal curve has a standard shape, it is possible to treat the area under the curve as representing total certainty that any observation will be encompassed by it. We can say, furthermore, that 50 per cent of the area is

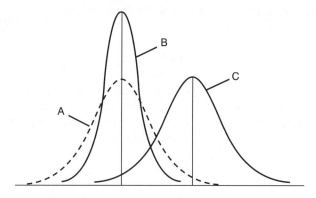

Figure 6.12 Three normal distributions with differing parameters.

above the mean for that variable, and 50 per cent below. In other words, there is a 50 per cent chance that any observation will be above (or below) the mean. This argument can be taken further so that we can calculate the area under the curve between the mean and one standard deviation. The area is, in fact, 34.1 per cent (see Figure 6.13). Thus just over two thirds or 68.2 per cent of the area is between plus one standard deviation and minus one standard deviation. Thus if the mean score of a set of cases is 20 with a standard deviation of 6, then just over two thirds of the area (and, by implication, of the observations) would be within 20 $\pm$ 6 or between 14 and 26. Figure 6.13 also shows that all but 4.6 per cent of the area lies between plus and minus two standard deviations. There are, in fact, tables of areas under the normal curve, so that if we wished to know how many standard deviations encompassed exactly 95 per cent of the area, we could look it up and discover that 1.96 standard deviations either side of the mean does so.

Each sampling distribution has its own standard deviation called the *standard error*. Since taking samples will result in less variation about the population parameter than picking one case, the standard error will be less than the standard deviation for the population. In fact we divide by the square root of the sample size, so that we halve error in a sample of four, it is one third in a sample of nine, one fifth in a sample of 25 and so on. For proportions, it can be

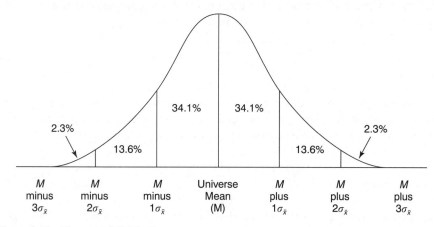

Figure 6.13 The normal distribution.

shown (using binomial theory, which we will not be considering here) that for samples over 30, the expression:

$$\sqrt{np(1 - p)}$$

where p is the proportion possessing a characteristic and n is the number of cases, gives the standard deviation of the population proportion. The standard deviation of the sampling distribution (the standard error of the proportion) is then given by:

$$\sqrt{\frac{p(1 - p)}{n}}$$

In constructing an interval estimate, the first thing we need to do is decide on the confidence level for our estimate, that is, we have to decide how often we want to be correct that our interval will in fact contain the population parameter in question. If, for example, we want to be 95 per cent sure that our interval contains the population parameter then we need to know how many standard errors enclose 95 per cent of the area in a normal distribution. We saw earlier that this will be 1.96 standard errors. (Do not forget that the standard error is the standard deviation for the sampling distribution.)

Thus if a sample of 300 found that 40 per cent had purchased brand A in the last week, then we can be 95 per cent confident that the real population proportion lies between:

$$0.4 \pm 1.96 \sqrt{\frac{(0.4)(0.6)}{300}}$$

$$= 0.4 \pm 1.96(0.028)$$
$$= 0.4 \pm 0.06$$

or between 0.34 and 0.46 (34 per cent and 46 per cent).

For a given sample size the larger the proportion that report a given characteristics (up to 50 per cent) the greater will be the sampling error. For example, if only 1 per cent of a random sample of 300 said they had purchased a particular brand, the error will be roughly plus or minus 1 per cent at the 95 per cent level of confidence, i.e:

$$1.96 \sqrt{\frac{(0.01)(0.99)}{300}} = 0.01$$

Thus we can be 95 per cent certain that the true result lies between zero per cent and 2 per cent. If 50 per cent said they had made such a purchase, the error will be plus or minus 5.7 per cent at the 95 per cent level, i.e:

$$1.96 \sqrt{\frac{(0.5)(0.5)}{300}} = 0.057$$

Thus we can be 95 per cent certain that the true result lies between 44.3 per cent and 55.7 per cent. A larger sample would mean that the standard error of

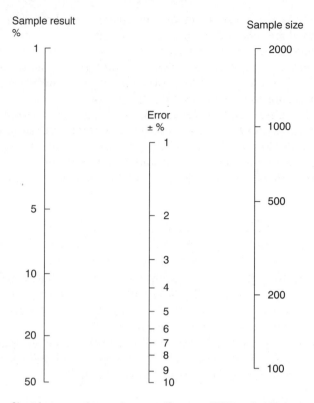

Figure 6.14 Chart for measuring random sampling error (95% probability).

both of these results would be lower. A fair estimate of the percentage error can be derived from a chart as illustrated in Figure 6.14. For example, if in a random sample of 500 adults, 20 per cent said they had been unemployed at some time in the last five years, then by laying a ruler between the 20 per cent sample result on the left and the 500 sample size on the right, the error will be approximately 3.5 per cent where the ruler cuts the middle line. Such a chart can be usefully used to determine the minimum size of sample required to achieve various levels of sampling error.

When constructing interval estimates, remember that you are assuming that the sample is a simple random sample, that there is no bias in the selection procedure, that there is no non-sampling error, and that the sample is 30 or more in size. When interpreting the confidence interval remember that the particular interval you have constructed is only one of many possible intervals based on different samples. So, if you *say* you are 95 per cent confident that the real population parameter lies between the intervals you have con-structed, appreciate that what you *really* mean is that 95 per cent of all possible intervals constructed in this way will include the parameter con-cerned (and thus the particular interval involved has a 95 per cent chance of being one of them).

Weighting and grossing up

While such calculations do give some idea as to whether estimates are likely to be tight or fairly loose, in practice, calculations of standard errors and confidence intervals are often not made, and many clients would not understand them if produced by the market research agency. A point estimate is, therefore, as indicated earlier, preferred. Point estimates can be improved through a process of weighting. A weight is a multiplying factor applied to some or all of the responses given in a survey in order to eliminate or reduce the impact of bias caused by types of case that are over or under represented in the sample. Thus if there are two few women aged 20–24 in a sample survey compared with the proportions in this age group known to exist in the set of cases such that only 50 out of a required 60 are in the achieved sample, the number who, for example, purchased brand X in a measurement period of, say, four weeks, will be multiplied by a weighting which is calculated by taking:

$$\frac{\text{target sample number}}{\text{actual sample number}} = \frac{60}{50} = 1.2$$

This means that if, for example, this group are heavy purchasers of brand X, then estimates of sales of brand X will not be underestimated because that group is under-represented in the sample from which the estimate is to be made. A worked example of weighting is given in Box 6.2.

There are, however, many different reasons why the actual sample may not reflect the population, and the effect of applying weights differs accordingly. Thus groups may be over or under-represented because:

- it is part of the sample design,
- there are problems of coverage,

A random sample of 100 adults produces 40 men and 60 women; but it is known that in the population from which the sample was drawn there are 48 per cent men and 52 per cent women. The weighting for the men would the 48/40 = 1.2 and for the women, 52/60 = 0.87. Table A below shows the unweighted results from the sample, who were asked if they had drunk beer in the last four weeks. From this it can be said that 30/40 or 0.75 of the men had done so, whereas this was true for only 25/60 or 0.42 of the women. A projection to the population based on the unweighed results will suggest that 55 per cent of the population (55 people out of the 100) had drunk beer in the last four weeks.

Table B Shows the weighted results after the responses of the men have been weighted by 1.2 and the responses of the women by 0.87. This shows that the proportions of men and women is now correct at 48 per cent and 52 per cent.

The new estimate will be based on the 57.7 per cent having drunk beer in the last four weeks.

Table A: Unweighted sample results

	Drank beer	Did not drink beer	Total
Male	30	10	40
Female	25	35	60
Total	55	45	100

Table B: Weighted sample results

	Drank beer	Did not drink beer	Total
Male	36.0	12.0	48
Female	21.7	30.3	52
Total	57.7	42.3	100

Box 6.2   A worked example of weighting

■   there are problems of pickup,
■   there are problems of unrepresentative non-response,
■   there are random sampling fluctuations,
■   the selection procedures are not random.

Sometimes minority groups in a population are deliberately over-sampled, otherwise there would be too few on which to base sensible analysis. Thus the BBC's Radio Listening Panel deliberately over-samples Radio 4 and Radio 3 listeners. This ensures that analyses of these programmes are based on adequate numbers. However, when the results from all radio listeners are aggregated, the responses of Radio 4 listeners are downweighted to their correct proportion in the population. Radio 3 listeners are so heavily over-represented that comments made by Radio 3 listeners on the output of other networks are not analysed at all!

Problems of coverage and pickup may be tackled by applying what some agencies call 'field' or 'market size' weights. Thus if it is known that a particular procedure for recording sales in shops misses out certain types of retail outlet that normally account for 25 per cent of total sales of brand X, then future estimates may be multiplied by 4/3 or 1.33. Similarly, where a procedure does not pick up a known proportion of sales or usage, for example, asking people to remember purchase of chocolate bars will fail to pick up all purchases, then weights may be applied. The problem of coverage may be created by an inadequate sampling frame, but if the proportions of specific sub-groups missing from the frame are known, then the responses of those in that sub-group who have responded can be upweighted to their correct proportion.

For random samples the effect of non-response is to reduce the achieved sample size, usually by different proportions in various sub-groups of cases. The result is bias, and the application of weightings is designed to alleviate the effects of that bias. Correcting for non-response, however, rests on the untested assumption that those people who did respond can adequately represent those members in the same sub-group who did not respond in respect of the variable being estimated. This means that sampling error is likely to be greater, and by an amount which is additional to that resulting from the reduction in sample size. The degree to which the effect of bias through non-response is reduced by applying weights depends on the extent to which the variables used for weighting are associated with those being estimated. Thus if we adjust for imbalances in the sex, age and social class composition of the achieved sample, then the effect of doing so will depend on the extent to which these variables are associated with, for example, the purchasing behaviour we are trying to measure. If the behaviour concerned is unaffected by, say, age then weighting by age will have no impact. Ideally, different sets of weightings should be used for each variable being estimated. In practice this would be very complex, so most agencies will select sex, age and social class (or employment status – working full-time, part-time, or unemployed) as characteristics that are associated in varying degrees with a large number of variables being estimated.

Even random samples that do not suffer from problems of coverage, pickup or non-response, will show fluctuations in which over and under-representations are a random phenomenon. Again, those variables used for weighting need to be carefully selected so that adjustments are made where under or over-representations are greatest, and for variables that are associated with those being estimated. By definition, these over and under-representations will vary in both extent and direction from sample to sample. Ideally, checks should be made against a large number of such variables – usually demographic, but may include such things as heavy, medium and light usage of a product. Thus individuals giving responses to a television programme may have their answers weighted according to whether the correct proportions of 'heavy', 'medium' and 'light' viewers have been selected in the sample.

Adjusting for random deviations of the sample profile from the known population characteristics is a process sometimes called 'post-stratification' weighting or even 'true' post-stratification to distinguish it from weightings applied in the correction of non-sampling errors or biases. The effect of applying such post-stratification weightings is to reduce sampling error, and hence to increase the efficiency of the sample for the purposes of estimation. By contrast, the use of weightings to correct for sample imbalances where the sampling is non-random is, some statisticians would argue, difficult to justify. This is because the weighting does not overcome the basic theoretical weakness of such samples, namely, that the selection method will introduce biases in respect of unanticipated demographic or other independent variables that associate or correlate with those being estimated. The imposition of quotas ensures that the sample is balanced in respect of the quota variables, but not in respect of those not subject to quota control. The degree of non-response in most quota samples is unknown, which makes the assumption that responders can adequately represent non-responders in respect of variables to which weights are being applied even more dubious than for random sampling. Furthermore, the variables used for weighting are often the same as those used for quota controls, so the weightings will be close to unity provided the quotas have been filled.

The use of weightings for *any* kind of sample, random or non-random, to correct for unrepresentativeness is believed by some researchers to be unethical window-dressing of the data. However, Sharot (1986) argues that the correct incorporation of weightings into the overall survey design can improve the cost/accuracy equation beyond what could be achieved by unweighted responses alone. Provided that the details of the weighting process are available and pointed out to users of the data it is, believes Sharot, difficult to see why this should be unethical.

Weightings are used largely to minimize the impact of sample imbalances and may be seen as a cheaper, and in many respects a cost-effective, alternative to minimizing the occurrences of those errors in the first place. Changing research designs so as to, for example, minimize non-response may be a more expensive process than applying weightings after the data have been collected. It also has to be said that attempts to minimize one kind of error, like non-response, may result in increased errors of other kinds, for example response errors may increase because more potential non-responders have been persuaded to co-operate in a survey.

When all the adjustments have been made to the data, the researcher may want estimation not so much of averages or proportions, but actual quantities, for example the national and regional amounts spent in £ sterling on a particular brand in the UK, the actual number of packets sold, or the total number of households that possess a particular characteristic. To do this requires a process of 'grossing up' to the population. In principle, this is a fairly simple operation of multiplying the sample quantities by a factor that represents the proportion a sample represents of the population, that is:

$$\frac{\text{population size}}{\text{sample size}} = \frac{N}{n}$$

Thus if a sample of 2000 households purchased 8000 tins of baked beans in a four-week period, and the population of households in Great Britain is 24 million, then it can be estimated that,

$$8000 \ (N/n) = \frac{8000 \ (24,000,000)}{2000}$$

or 96 million tins were sold in that period. This is only the same result that would be achieved by multiplying the sample proportion or average by the population figure (i.e. (4)(24) million). In practice, as ever, it is not quite so simple. Grossing up is usually done on a cell-by-cell basis so that if within region X there are 50,000 women aged 20–24 and a sample of 10 showed that they had purchased five packs of brand A, then it can be estimated that (5)50,000/10 or 25,000 packs were purchased by that age group of women in region X. These results will then be added to the other age group purchase estimates to give a regional figure. The regional estimates may then be aggregated into a Great Britain total. Alternatively, Great Britain estimates for particular age groups can be made. The estimates for brands can be aggregated into product class estimates, and so on. In short, by grossing up on a cell-by-cell basis, estimates can be aggregated in many different ways according to the breakdowns required by the client.

The design factor

Since sampling is seldom simple random sampling, then, strictly speaking, an adjustment needs to be made to the standard error to take this into account. This adjustment is in the form of a *design factor*, which is the ratio of the variance of the sample actually used to the variance of a corresponding-sized simple random sample. This ratio should, ideally, be specially worked out for each survey; in practice typical design factors are applied based on experience. Thus for stratified random samples (which usually include a degree of clustering) the design factor is usually about 1.25, so the standard error is multiplied by this factor. For clustered randomized samples (like random route with several call-backs) the design factor is about 1.5, or 2.0 if there are no call-backs. Heavily stratified fully interlocking quota samples often have a design factor of at least 2.0, while simple quota samples should be given a factor of not less than 2.5. Unfortunately, these adjustments are not always made and the standard error reported is the one calculated for simple random samples. Furthermore, to make matters worse, whether or not a design factor has been included is not always stated. Charts, like the one in Figure 6.14, or read-off tables, *may* be adjusted to include a design factor. It is, therefore, important to be clear about what adjustments have been made before interpreting the results from sampling.

Testing the null hypothesis

Estimation is only one aspect of drawing conclusions from univariate analysis. Another is to test statements or predictions made *before* the analysis begins against the results drawn from a sample in order to calculate, with a pre-determined probability, whether a sample result was likely or unlikely to have been derived from a population of cases in which the statement or prediction is true. We normally test one of three kinds of statement: univariate, bivariate or multivariate. The first is a statement about one variable, the second is a statement about the relationship between two variables and the third is a statement about the relationship between three or more variables.

Univariate statements

A researcher may have reason to believe – on the basis of a deduction from theory, on the basis of marketing principles or on the basis of past research or personal experience – that 70 per cent of a population of cases possess a particular characteristic (e.g. that 70 per cent of women in the UK object to advertising of highly personal products on television). If a sample of 100 cases found that 60 possessed this characteristic, could this proportion of responses in the sample easily have been obtained from a population in which the real proportion is in fact 70 per cent? The statement or prediction that is made about the population of cases in advance is usually called the 'null hypothesis'. 'Null' means empty of significance, void or containing nothing. For univariate statements the null hypothesis is not really null in this sense. It is rather a statement we are assuming is true of the population form which the sample was drawn.

As with estimation, a sampling distribution of the test statistic is used. However, unlike estimation, where we use the sample result to estimate the standard error, in testing the null hypothesis *we assume that the null hypothesis is true* and use the predicted proportion to estimate the standard error that would exist if the null hypothesis is true. In the example above, if the null hypothesis is true, then the standard error of the proportion is:

$$p = \sqrt{\frac{p(1-p)}{n}} = \sqrt{\frac{(0.7)(0.3)}{100}} = 0.046$$

This implies that 95 per cent of all samples of size 100 will produce results that vary between:

$$0.7 \pm 1.96(0.046) \text{ or between 61 per cent and 79 per cent}$$

Since the original sample result was 60 per cent, it lies outside this range and so is unlikely to have come from a population in which $p = 0.7$. In other words, random error is an unlikely explanation of the difference between the sample result of 60 per cent and the predicted 70 per cent. Note that we cannot conclude from the sample result that the real proportion is 60 per cent, but only that it probably did not come from a population in which the null hypothesis is true.

Why, it may be asked, did we not simply use the sample result for estimation purposes rather than going to the trouble of setting up a null hypothesis prior to the analysis? The answer is that if we have a theory, a principle or a wealth of experience that we think allows us to make a prediction, it is this prediction that we want to test. If we wanted, for example, to compare the results of two or more pieces of research, then it is their support or questioning of the theory or principle or experience that we want to compare. Calculating confidence intervals does not test the hypothesis because the results could be consistent with a large number of hypotheses or predictions.

For univariate non-metric data, besides tests for proportions there are also tests for goodness-of-fit for which the Chi-square statistic may be used. Suppose a company has two brands of a product and these are measured for preference in a survey of 100 respondents. The results suggest that 60 prefer brand A and 40 brand B. If we wished to test the null hypothesis that there is equal preference for the brands, then, in theory, we would expect 50 to prefer brand A and 50 brand B. The difference between the observed and expected frequencies is 10, so Chi-square is:

$$x^2 = \sum \frac{(fo - fe)^2}{fe}$$

$$= \frac{10^2}{50} + \frac{10^2}{50}$$

$$= 4$$

Like many other probability distributions, the x^2 distribution is not a single probability curve, but a family of curves. These vary according to the number of observations that can be varied without changing the constraints or assumptions associated with a numerical system. Thus if our sample is 100 then any number between 1 and 100 may prefer brand A. Once it is discovered that 60 prefer brand A then, by definition 40 $(100 - 60)$ prefer brand B. In short, there is only one 'degree of freedom' – only one figure is free to vary. The probability of obtaining Chi-square values of a given magnitude can be looked up in a table of critical values for Chi-square. A simplified table is illustrated in Table 6.29. This shows, for example, that the value of 3.841 will not be exceeded more the 5 per cent of the time in a random sample with one degree of freedom. With two degrees of freedom this value rises to 5.991 and so on. We can conclude that the sample result of Chi-square = 4 was unlikely to have occurred with a probability greater than $p = 0.05$. At the 5 per cent level we could reject the null hypothesis and conclude that the difference between the sample result and our expectation was unlikely to have been a result of random sampling fluctuations. However, if we had chosen the one per cent

Probability Degrees of freedom	0.05	0.01	0.001
1	3.841	6.635	10.827
2	5.991	9.210	13.815
3	7.815	11.341	16.268

Table 6.29
Critical values of Chi-square

level of confidence, then the null hypothesis would have been accepted since the critical value is 6.635.

An alternative goodness of fit test is the Kolmogorov–Smirnoff (K–S) test which is particularly useful for testing whether observed values may have come from a normally distributed population.

Bivariate statements

Statistical inference for bivariate non-metric data takes a rather different form. We do not usually use estimation for bivariate data. Technically, we could, for example, calculate the probability that some measure of association derived from a sample lies between certain limits. Thus we might be able to calculate that we can be 95 per cent sure that the population coefficient lies between 0.5 and 0.7 when the sample result was 0.6. This would entail constructing a sampling distribution for the coefficient concerned. However, the mathematics of doing so would be highly complex and the result would be less useful than for situations where we are interested in the estimation of quantities. It is more usual to test the null hypothesis that there is *no* association in the population from which the sample was drawn. If the null hypothesis can be rejected, then we can conclude that the sample result was unlikely to have come from a population in which the null hypothesis is true and that there is, indeed, some association.

If we are going to use the null hypothesis of no association then the obvious basis for such a calculation is departure from independence. The statistic Chi-square, you will recall, is based on the difference between observed frequencies and the frequencies that would be expected if there were independence between the two variables. This is the same notion as the null hypothesis of no association. Whatever measures of association may have been calculated, for example Cramer's *V*, Lambda or Gamma, it is usual for researchers nevertheless to use Chi-square as a test of statistical significance.

Turn back to Table 6.12. Recall that from this table we calculated Chi-square to be 60.8 (see Table 6.13). In a 2 × 2 table, once the value of one cell has been determined, the rest are all fixed – it has one degree of freedom. The critical values for one degree of freedom are shown in Table 6.29. Since 60.8 is larger than 3.841, the critical value of Chi-square at the 0.05 level of significance, we can reject the null hypothesis that the two variables are independent in the population of cases from which the sample was drawn. We can conclude that there *is* an association, but note that this does *not* tell us how strong the association is. For that we would need to calculate Cramer's *V* or some other appropriate measure of association. As we shall see later, for large samples – over 100 or so – even very small degrees of association can be statistically significant.

Beware that 'relationships' between nominal variables are sometimes described in textbooks on statistics as *differences* between groups or even as a 'two-sample' situation. Thus the use of Chi-square on cross-tabulated data may be referred to as the 'two sample Chi-square test' where the independent variable is binary and each category is seen as a different sample or sub-group, or as the 'k-sample Chi-square test' where the independent variable has three or more categories, i.e. is nominal. Thus a relationship between sex of respondent and purchase of brand X can be expressed alternatively as a difference in brand purchasing between the sexes. The statistical tests available may then be labelled 'two-sample' tests or described as 'making comparisons'. Relationships, according to this approach, arise only when we can talk about directionality – positive and negative relationships. This means that the data have to be at least ordinal. However, we will continue to think of cross-tabulations involving binary or nominal scales as illustrating the relationship between the variables concerned.

Multivariate statements

For non-metric data it is usual to restrict tests against the null hypothesis to univariate or bivariate statements. An overall test for three–way and n-way cross-tabulations does not exist.

Statistical inference for metric data

Estimation

The good news is that most of the concepts you require for statistical inference for metric data have already been explained in the context of non-metric data. The bad news is that we need a whole new battery of statistics that are called 'parametric' statistics that use the mean and the standard deviation as the key parameters for all variables. It was explained earlier that the sampling distribution for any statistic has its own standard deviation called the standard error. If we are concerned, for example, with estimating a population mean, then we need the standard error of the mean. This is the standard deviation of the sampling distribution we would derive by plotting the means for all possible samples of a given size. We can calculate the standard error of the mean by taking:

$$\frac{\sigma}{\sqrt{n}}$$

where σ is the standard deviation of the population and n is the sample size. Thus the standard error increases with an increase in the standard deviation for the population of cases, and decreases with an increase in sample size, but as the square root of the sample size. Where the standard deviation for the population of cases is unknown – which is usually the situation – the standard deviation found for the sample variable is taken as an estimate of the population standard deviation. In this case we need what is called an 'unbiased' estimate which divides the sample standard deviation by the square root not of n, but $n - 1$:

$$\frac{s}{\sqrt{n - 1}}$$

Thus if the mean score of a sample of 60 cases is 20 with a standard deviation of 6, then we can be 95 per cent certain that the real population mean lies between the achieved sample mean plus or minus 1.96 standard errors, that is:

$$20 \pm 1.96 \left(\frac{6}{\sqrt{60 - 1}} \right)$$

or between 18.5 and 21.5. Subtracting one only makes a meaningful difference if the sample is quite small. Some statisticians will argue that if the standard deviation of the population is unknown we should use not the normal distribution but what is called the t distribution. For samples over 30 or so, however, this makes very little difference.

Testing the null hypothesis

We can also use the standard error of the mean to test hypotheses about the mean. Suppose we hypothesize that the mean age of a population of members of an organization is 36 and we take a sample of 120 members that produces a mean of 37 and a standard deviation of 8.2 years. If the null hypothesis is true then 95 per cent of samples will produce means in the range:

$$36 + 1.96 \left(\frac{8.2}{\sqrt{120 - 1}} \right) = 36 + 1.47 \text{ or } 34.53 - 37.47$$

Since 37 is within this range we do not have enough evidence to reject the null hypothesis. Note that this does not prove that the null hypothesis is true. The result does not, for example, prove that the mean is 36, only that from the sample evidence we cannot say that it is not 36. Furthermore, there is still a 5 per cent probability that we might have accepted a null hypothesis that is in fact false. So, remember that if we say we 'accept' the null hypothesis – which appears to be the standard, accepted term – we actually mean that we cannot reject it. We have to behave as though the null hypothesis is true. If our sample result had produced a mean of, say, 38, then we could have rejected the null hypothesis.

Whenever we reject a null hypothesis, the conclusion we accept is usually called the 'alternative' or the 'research' hypothesis. Note that there may be different alternatives:

- the population of the mean is not 36,
- the population mean is > 36,
- the population mean is < 36.

In the first situation, we have little idea in rejecting the null hypothesis whether the real mean is above or below 36. The 5 per cent area of the normal distribution outside the hypothesized interval could be at either end of the distribution as in Figure 6.15. If we divide the two tails into 2.5 per cent each, then 2.5 per cent of the area is above 1.96 standard deviations and 2.5 per cent below minus 1.96 standard deviations. Suppose, however, that we were interested only in whether the mean is above 36. All the 5 per cent of the area needs to be in the right tail as in Figure 6.16. Here, 5 per cent of the area lies above 1.645 standard deviations, so we could have constructed our interval as:

$$36 + 1.645 \frac{8.2}{\sqrt{120 - 1}} = 37.24$$

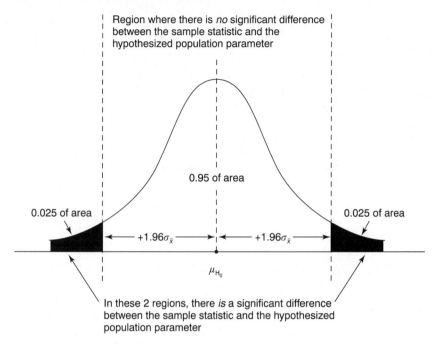

Figure 6.15 Critical regions.

Clearly, we would still reject the null hypothesis that the mean is 36 if the sample result has been 38, but by a slightly greater margin, but the alternative is no longer that the population mean is not 36, but that the mean is greater than 36. In the first situation we have constructed what is usually called a 'two-tailed' test and in the second situation a 'one-tailed' test.

An alternative way of undertaking tests of significance is to construct what is sometimes called a z-test. The result is exactly the same, but the procedure is a little different. Instead of constructing intervals under the assumption that the null hypothesis is true, we calculate differences between the sample statistic

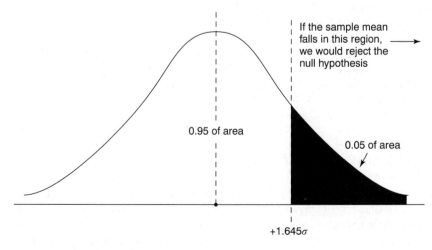

Figure 6.16 Critical region – one-tail.

and the hypothesized population parameter in terms of standardized units, that is, we take, in this example, the difference between the sample mean and the hypothesized mean and divide by the standard error:

$$z = \frac{X - \mu}{s/\sqrt{120 - 1}} = \frac{37 - 36}{8.2/\sqrt{120 - 1}} = 1.33$$

In a two-tailed test, the critical value of z at $p = < 0.05$ is 1.96 and for a one-tailed test is 1.645. Since 1.33 is less than either of these figures we cannot reject the null hypothesis. If the sample result had been 38:

$$z = \frac{38 - 36}{8.2/\sqrt{120 - 1}} = 2.67$$

Since this is larger than 1.96, we would reject the null hypothesis and accept the two-tailed alternative (that the sample probably did not come from a population in which the mean is 36).

The rhetoric of conventional statisticians insists that the critical values be established in advance of the test and that the null hypothesis is then subsequently accepted or rejected. To shift the critical value after the results have been seen is, apparently, not a legitimate practice. However, modern computer programes give not a decision, but the probability of obtaining a test statistic as extreme or more extreme than the one actually obtained by looking up the tables of the standard normal distribution. This probability is known as the p-value. The lower it is the stronger the evidence against the null hypothesis. Thus a probability of getting $z = 1.33$ or higher is 0.184 (two-tail) which means that there are over 18 chances in every 100 samples of getting a z-value of 1.33 or more. The probability of $z = 2.67$ is 0.0076 (two-tailed) – fewer than eight chances in every 1000 samples. The p-value provides more information on how far down in the significance region the result lies. The result of $z = 2.67$ might be written by researchers as $p = < 0.05$ (or even $p = < 0.01$) using the critical value approach with the conventional cut-off points; but giving the result as $p = 0.0076$ allows researchers to form their own judgement about the significance of the results. Different people may feel that different levels of significance are appropriate. However, it does mean that the rhetoric of setting up the test criteria in advance is compromised. Given that the conventional cut-offs of 0.05 and 0.01 are just that, conventions, there is little case in fact for preferring these over reporting the actual p-values. However, it *is* necessary to accompany p-value information indicating whether they relate to one or two-tailed tests.

The significance of significance tests

Most textbooks on statistics pay a great deal of attention to statistical inference and in particular to the process they usually refer to as 'hypotheses testing'. Remember that this does not amount to testing our ideas against the data we have generated from our research. How this is done will be considered below. For the moment, it is necessary to be clear about the role and value of significance tests in marketing research. Significance tests would be better described as 'tests against the null hypothesis'. They calculate the probability that the null hypothesis is true in a population from which a random probability sample has been drawn. These tests take into account only random sampling error, not bias or non-sampling error arising, for example, from non-response or interviewer mistakes. As we saw earlier in Chapter 5, random sampling error accounts for maybe 5 – 10 per cent of total survey error, so in rejecting the null hypothesis and accepting the alternative hypothesis, we are really saying, 'ignoring all other kinds of error except random sampling error, we can be 95 per cent sure that we are making the correct decision from evidence from our sample'.

Assuming that we have made the right decision, what have we accepted? We have accepted either:

- a non-directional hypothesis, for example, the mean age is not 32 years, or there is an association between two variables,
- a directional hypotheses, for example, the mean age is higher than 32 years, or there is a positive association between two variables.

Bear in mind, however, that 'positive' or 'negative' do not really apply when binary or nominal variables are involved. Instead, we need to specify what combination of categories tend to be found together. Where the null hypothesis is one of no association, then the distinction between one and two-tailed tests does not apply.

In accepting the alternative hypothesis we are not saying anything about the magnitudes involved. If we accept that the mean age is greater than 59 years, we cannot say by how much greater. If we accept that there *is* an association between two variables, we are saying nothing about the strength of that association. For a 2×2 table, for example with one degree of freedom, the critical value of Chi-square is 3.841, so any Chi-square value greater than this will lead us to reject the null hypothesis. However, as explained in Chapter 5, sample sizes need to be at least 100 even for a very simple quantitative analysis. Cramer's V (or Phi) will be $3.841/100 = 0.038$. That is a minuscule degree of association and will be of very little theoretical interest. (In fact a negative finding would be of more interest!) In short, with samples of 100 or more, *any* association in which we have the remotest interest will, by definition, always be statistically significant. For larger tables, the critical value for Chi-square is much higher. Thus a 5×4 table has $4 \times 3 = 12$ degrees of freedom. The critical value at $p = 0.05$ is 21. For a sample of 100 this will give a Cramer's V of 0.21. But, of course, with 20 cells a sample of 100 will be far too small. A sample of 500 would be more appropriate (giving marginals averaging 100), but then Cramer's V will be $21/500 = 0.042$ – again, minuscule. In short, a statistically significant result is not necessarily an important or interesting result. With samples of 100 or more, tests against the null hypothesis are quite probably a waste of time.

A further limitation of tests of significance is that because they depend on a selected critical value (and, more often than not, arbitrarily selected, or just accepting the traditional 0.05 level) it means that there is a non-zero probability of getting it wrong anyway. Now if we look at 100 tables and pick out five that are 'significant' at the 0.05 level, then we are probably just picking out the five accidents we would expect anyway. In effect, the hypotheses have just been tested on the same data that suggested them in the first place. This is why it is so important, if tests of significance are going to be used, that hypotheses are set up in advance. If we pick out tables from the data, then to test any hypotheses that arise, we really need to test them on another dataset from another survey.

The whole edifice of significance tests depends on random samples. But a lot of research is based on sampling procedures that are certainly not simple random samples and may well have non-random elements involved in the selection of cases. Some procedures, like judgemental sampling and quota sampling are distinctly not random and the potential for bias is considerable. Some practitioners will argue that the resulting sample is, nevertheless, representative; that it is an approximation of a random sample and that tests against the null hypothesis will nevertheless tell us something we would otherwise not know. Purists will argue that non-probability samples cannot be a correct basis for using probability theory. Does this mean that such tests should not be used on other than simple random samples? An answer (but one that most statisticians would find unpalatable) is that even in random samples there will always be some degree of non-response and quite possibly other failings in the sampling frame and data collection methods, so the presentation of 'significant' results as 'findings' is almost certainly misleading whether the sample was random or not.

Tests of significance may look 'scientific', giving clear conclusions, but the choice of critical value is a subjective one, as is the choice between alternative tests where these are available. Furthermore, the statements we can legitimately make from statistical inference are so circumscribed that they are of limited value anyway, and in consequence are liable to misinterpretation. Thus to say that we 'accept' the null hypothesis can be misleading unless we appreciate that all we can really say is that there is probably ($p = 0.05$) insufficient evidence in the sample to reject it since the result obtained could have been the product of random sampling fluctuations.

Criticism of statistical inference is certainly not new. Over 40 years ago Selvin (1957) argued that tests of statistical significance are generally inapplicable in non-experimental research where the influence of antecedent variables is not taken into account as it is in the design of an experiment. In survey research, 'significant' results are reported without reference to other conditions or possible influences. All too often, 'significant' results are seen as the final evidence instead of merely the beginning of a further analysis into results that need some kind of explanation.

Some researchers have even conducted tests of significance on total populations on the basis that such a population may still represent a sample of some wider, hypothetical and infinite universe. The issue, however, is not always clearcut. If the researcher selects all the employees in an organization, then this is a census and the researcher should have no reason for concern about sampling error. However, if a researcher interviews all residents in streets selected at random in a particular city, then is this a census of the streets concerned, is it a 'sample' of the population of the city, is it a sample of all people living in cities in a given area, or is it a sample of the entire population at large? Some researchers will argue that, since the streets were selected by probability methods, then randomness was involved and that tests of significance are appropriate. Technically, however, it is a random sample of streets, not of households or individuals, and to conduct a test of significance, for example on the relationship between household size and income, would be meaningless. The idea that we can study the operation of sampling error when there is no real sample is wishful thinking.

So, if statistical inference is of limited value in non-experimental research, what is the alternative? Certainly, the more informed use of bivariate and multivariate descriptive techniques would yield better analyses than relying on tests of significance in circumstances where they are dubious. More attention could be paid to the potential sources of bias in a dataset, and some attempt could be made to determine the effects of such bias. More careful and sophisticated measurement procedures would pay higher returns on the quality of research than assuming that we have a perfect random sample, and a focus on measuring the reliability and validity of measurement scales would be more informative than concluding that we can or cannot reject a null hypothesis.

As explained earlier, tests of significance do not, in fact, constitute a test of our theories against the data derived from the research. At best, in carefully selected samples, they enable us to take into account the possible effects of random sampling error. So how do we test our ideas against the data? The following section explains what hypotheses are and outlines the stages to be followed in testing research hypotheses.

Testing research hypotheses

Research hypotheses are statements, as yet untested, that researchers make about one or more variables that are the focus of the research. Once they have been tested, they become research findings, even if the data do not support the statements. Hypotheses may be set up in advance of undertaking the data collection process, or they may be generated by the data once they have been collected. Be clear that it is possible to test only those hypotheses that are stated before data are collected. Hypotheses generated by the data may be regarded as empirical generalizations, but they remain hypotheses – as yet untested. To do that requires further research and another dataset.

Hypotheses may be univariate, bivariate or multivariate. Univariate hypotheses make statements about one variable, or several variables that are unrelated, for example, 'the group is predominantly male, exclusively from social classes A,B and C1, with a mean age of 33'. There is no implied relationship between sex, social class and age. Bivariate hypotheses relate just two variables together. Some may not spell out the nature of the relationship involved, for example, 'variable A is related to (associated with, correlated with) variable B'. Others may specify or imply some degree of influence, causality or determination, for example, 'variable A is a major factor giving rise to variable B', or 'variable A is a cause (or the cause) of variable B'. Sometimes influence or causality is implied, but the direction of influence may operate both ways, for example 'variable A and variable B are mutually interdependent'. Multivariate hypotheses specify relationships between three or more variables. Again, these may or may not specify or imply the nature of those relationships.

Univariate, bivariate and multivariate research hypotheses may be used as a basis for setting up null hypotheses if the researcher wishes to conduct tests of significance where the data represent a random sample from a population. Where the research hypothesis makes reference to relationships between variables, then the null hypothesis is always that there is no association.

The setting up of hypotheses in advance of conducting the research tends to be associated with the positivist approach – but there is no reason why the marketing psychiatrist or the marketing physician should not also develop and test hypotheses. As indicated earlier, the topic of 'hypothesis testing' in most textbooks on marketing research or statistics usually refers to testing sample data against the null hypotheses, that is, conducting tests of statistical significance. Books on the philosophy of science, on the other hand, tend to look at the logic of empirical inquiry and whether hypotheses can ever be proven or disproven. In practice, researchers simply want to compare the data they have generated with the ideas with which they began. This involves a number of fairly general stages:

■ clarifying the research hypothesis,
■ operationalizing and measuring each variable,
■ collecting data,
■ creating and analysing a dataset,
■ checking for sampling error using statistical inference, if appropriate,
■ comparing the results with the original hypotheses.
■ analysing and explaining the relationships between variables.

Research hypotheses spell out in testable terms the statements that the proposed research is designed to investigate. These may be a 'refinement', 'clarification' or 'specification' of the hypotheses that have been deduced from the theory. Thus the theory may be that attitudes towards the advertising of products potentially harmful to consumers is affected by lifestyle. The research hypothesis might spell this out as: the degree of agreement with the statement that the advertising of cigarettes should be banned is associated with participation in sport, membership of a political party and the concern for 'green' issues.

Operationalization involves spelling out of the indicators that are to be used in the process of measurement and, if there are several, how they are to be combined. The processes of measurement and scaling were considered in some detail in Chapter 2.

Collecting data will entail designing a data capture instrument, for example, a questionnaire, a diary or an observation schedule, or some form of mechanical or electronic recording device. The researcher will need to decide on a method of data collection and define the population of cases to be studied and, where sampling is deemed to be necessary, the techniques for selecting cases to be used.

Creating a dataset will involve editing the questionnaires after completion and coding any open-ended questions. The data will then need to be entered into a survey analysis package such as SPSS or Minitab. We now turn to strategies for the creation and analysis of datasets in more detail.

Strategies for creating and analysing datasets

Creating a data matrix

The process of creating a data matrix from a dataset itself involves three key sub-stages:

- editing,
- coding,
- data entry.

Editing

As was explained earlier in Chapter 5, there are many different kinds of error that can arise in the processes of selecting cases and collecting data on them. A major purpose of research design, which is considered in Chapter 7, is to minimize the sources and impact of such errors. However, the end-point of the data collection process is that questionnaires (either respondent completed or interviewer completed) are returned to the researcher for every respondent successfully contacted, or the field department in a market research agency passes on data collected from telephone interviewing or from experimental research either in hard (paper) copy, or held electronically. Editing is the process of scrutinizing completed data collection forms and taking whatever corrective action is required to ensure that the data are of high quality. It is a kind of quality control check on the raw data to ensure that they are complete, accurate and consistent.

A preliminary or field edit is a quick examination of completed data collection forms, usually as they are received at the head office. Its purpose is twofold: to ensure that proper procedures are being followed in selecting respondents, interviewing them and recording their responses, and to remedy fieldwork deficiencies before they turn into a major problem. Speed is crucial and it needs to be done while the fieldwork is still in progress. Typical problems that are discovered in field edits include:

- inappropriate respondents,
- incomplete questionnaires,
- illegible or unclear responses.

When any of these arise, the errors will be traced back to the interviewers concerned who will be advised of the problems and, if necessary, undergo further training.

A second stage of editing, a final or office edit, is undertaken after all the field-edited questionnaires are received. It involves verifying response consistency and accuracy, making necessary corrections and deciding whether some or all parts of a questionnaire should be discarded. Some of these checks are undertaken by the computer at the data entry stage (see below), but will include:

- logical checks, for example, the 17 year-old claiming to have a PhD,
- range checks, for example, a code of '8' is entered when there are only six response categories for that question,

■ response set checks, for example, somebody has 'strongly agreed' with all the items on a Likert scale.

Where a question fails a logical check, then the pattern of responses in the rest of the questionnaire may be scrutinized to see what is the most likely explanation for the apparent inconsistency. Range check failures may be referred back to the original respondent. Response set checks may indicate that the respondent is simply being frivolous and the questionnaire may be discarded.

Coding

The tasks involved in transforming edited questionnaires into machine-readable form are generally referred to as coding. Most survey analysis packages will accept only responses or other data that are in numerical form. Metric data already have numerical scale values that can be entered directly, for example, a person's age as '59'. For non-metric data the scale values may be in words or symbols that the computer cannot accept. Hence all responses or other types of observation need to be classified and numbered. These numbers are the codes, and the process of coding is to ensure that all data that are to be analysed have a code.

Some, if not all, of the non-metric responses will be pre-coded, that is, they are numbered on the questionnaire. If not, they need to be coded afterwards in the office. Qualitative responses to open-ended questions may be classified into categories, and the categories numbered. 'Don't know' responses usually have their own category for each question. A more difficult issue arises when, for a particular question, there is no response at all. It may be that the respondent refused to answer, or that the interviewer forgot to ask it, or to record the answer. These questions for which answers *should* have been obtained, but were not for some reason, are regarded as 'missing values'. These are frequently given a standard code. Computer survey analysis packages will not usually allow empty cells. SPSS, for example, enters a period if a cell has been passed over. However, it is better to enter a code so that when analysis it taking place, the researcher can choose to exclude or include such missing values from the analysis.

For some survey analysis packages it is necessary to keep a separate record of what response categories each code refers to for each question. Such a record is normally referred to as a 'coding sheet'. More modern survey analysis packages, however, tend to keep labels, or labels in words can be added, both for the questions and for the responses, so coding sheets are not needed because the labels are printed out with the results. Dedicated surveys analysis packages like SPSS will tend to accept multi-response questions, that is, questions where the respondent is allowed more than one reply. Where statistical packages like Minitab have been used instead, only one value per question may be entered. In these cases, multi-response questions may need to be recoded so that each response category is treated as a separate question with two possibilities: selected or not selected.

Data entry

When editing and coding is complete, the data are ready to be keyed into an analysis package. Most survey packages will have inbuilt range checks so that invalid responses will not be accepted. However, this does not check that the correct numbers have been keyed in if they are within the range of acceptable values for that question. To overcome this, data may be subjected to double-entry data validation. In effect this means that the data are entered twice, usually by two different people, and any discrepancies in the two entries are flagged up by the computer and can be checked against the original questionnaire. Some market research agencies do this, but only on a sample basis so that, for example, only 10 per cent of the questionnaires may be subject to double-entry data validation.

The end-product of data entry is the creation of a data matrix, that is the record of a numerical score or code for each value for each case for each variable, arranged in rows and columns. This may not, of course, necessarily be a physical sheet of paper, but the electronic equivalent. As a spreadsheet or as a Minitab worksheet, the arrangement in rows and columns is visible on a computer screen. In other survey analysis packages, the data matrix will be invisible, but held on an electronic file in the background and used as a basis for creating whatever analyses are being requested by the user.

Analysing a data matrix

Once the data matrix has been created, the first stage in its analysis is to obtain a set of univariate tables which display the frequencies of each response, one variable at a time. On SPSS, use the *Frequencies* procedure, which is in the *Statistics/Summarize* drop-down menu. The procedure also contains a *Charts* facility for getting bar chart, pie-charts and so on. Univariate analysis may show, for example, that for some variables the responses are very unevenly distributed among the categories, or, indeed, that for some questions nearly everybody has given the same answer. Such variables will be of little use for analysis. Where the response categories are ordinal or grouped metric, it *may* make sense to regroup the categories by adding some of them together. Suppose respondents are given a satisfaction scale like that in Table 6.30. The numbers who indicated 'very satisfied' or 'very dissatisfied' are very low. It would make sense to combine these responses with the 'satisfied' and 'dissatisfied' categories respectively to produce three categories: satisfied, neither satisfied not dissatisfied, and dissatisfied. Most survey analysis packages will allow the researcher to recode the response categories into a reduced set in this way. Which categories it makes sense to add together can often be determined only from an inspection of the one-way tables. In SPSS the *Recode*

Please indicate your degree of satisfaction with the following aspects of our service

	Very satisfied	Satisfied	Neither	Dissatisfied	Very dissatisfied
Opening hours	10	84	90	60	3
Range of goods	3	106	131	6	1
Speed at till	8	98	124	15	2
Parking	4	134	92	12	5
Store layout	1	52	114	72	8

Table 6.30
Categories that may need to be regrouped

procedure is in the *Transform* menu. For more details on how to use SPSS for univariate and bivariate analysis, see Appendix 3.

Once univariate analysis of the dataset is complete the next stage is either to look for or to test for relationships between variables. Complete datasets may, however, be approached in different ways. To explain these approaches it is helpful to draw an analogy between the different activities of dredging, fishing and hunting.

Dredging in the normal sense means casting a net or other mechanical device to trawl whatever in on the sea bottom. In the context of data analysis it means trawling the dataset without specific hypotheses to test, or perhaps even without hunches or specific issues to pursue. The data are 'dredged' in every conceivable way to see what patterns emerge. Researchers may, for example, cross-tabulate every variable by every other variable in the dataset in order to see which ones produce the strongest associations. It is an inductive process that produces empirical generalizations from the ground up. Data dredging is often seen to be reprehensible: an admission that you do not know what you are looking for. However, some patterns *are* discovered by chance, and dredging may turn out to be a fruitful way of producing new insights. The researcher should beware, however, of testing sets of tables derived in this manner against the null hypothesis. As we saw earlier, this amounts to testing the hypothesis on the same data that suggested them in the first place.

At the other extreme to dredging is hunting for a specific quarry. Hypotheses deduced from theory are set up in advance and the hunt is on for data that will put these hypotheses to the test. If the expectations implied by the hypotheses are not fulfilled then they may be rejected; if such expectations materialize, then the hypotheses stand, at least for the time being, and the theory is substantiated. The marketing physicist is likely to pursue this hunting procedure.

In between dredging and hunting is the activity of fishing. This is an iterative process of moving backwards and forwards between expectation and reality; of trying out various locations with rather more general empirical aspirations in mind. These aspirations may, in turn, be modified in the light of events. In terms of data analysis, deduction and induction are used in alternation; hypotheses are reworked in the light of empirical findings.

Analysing and explaining relationships between variables

To the marketing 'physicist', when we say we have 'explained' something, it means that the researcher has engaged in the process of establishing causal connections, and the success of the undertaking is judged by the extent to which the analysis provides the ability to predict patterns. To the marketing 'psychiatrist', explanation provides understanding, and instead of causal analysis, makes reference to means and ends, motives and reasons, intentions and dispositions. Its success is judged by the extent to which the audience is satisfied with the level of understanding communicated. From this perspective, while the researcher *can* establish that variable A causes variable B, and that it is possible to make perfect predictions, this can be achieved without understanding *why*. *Why* does A cause B? That is a different question from, *Does* A cause B?

From the point of view of the marketing 'physician', an 'explanation' is to be found neither in establishing causes, nor in interpretive understanding, but in discovering a dialectic – a process of change that contains its own dynamic and which arises from a conflict between opposing forces or inherent contradictions. Causes are important, but only as a means to making the 'patient' well again. Causes *describe* what variables or factors in a system or a body influence or determine other variables or factors. Understanding the internal dynamics of an organization, a market system, a distribution channel or an entire mode of production is another matter.

The answer to the question, then, concerning, 'What is an "explanation?"' is that it depends on who you ask. The three approaches mentioned above are reviewed in more detail below. Remember, however, that the three certainly do not exhaust the list of different approaches to explanation, for example, when a statistician talks about 'explanation', he or she means that the statistical variance in a dependent variable is accounted for by the variance in one or more independent variables.

Causal analysis

It is difficult for social scientists to avoid the notion of causality, and this has certainly been the dominant mode of 'explanation'. It fits with our own experience of connections between events. But what is 'causality' and how do we establish it?

Causal analysis is concerned with the ways in which some events or circumstances can produce or bring about others. The presumed causes are the 'independent' variables and the effects are the 'dependent' ones. Evidence for such causality comes from three main sources:

- While the existence of a correlation or association is no proof of cause, it *is* a necessary precondition, and its absence would demonstrate that no causality is present.
- The independent variable must precede the dependent variable in time, that is, the causes must come first and the effects afterwards.
- The apparent relationship between the variables must not be spurious, that is, a result of their joint relationship with other prior variables.

Establishing each of these is, however, problematic. In a literal sense, to establish that variable A 'causes' variable B, it is necessary that there is a perfect association between the two variables – otherwise other factors are involved and we have to say that variable A is *a* cause (among others) of variable B. Measures of correlation or measures of association are, in practice, seldom perfect, that is, coefficients seldom approach unity. If we accept a 'high' correlation or association as evidence, we have to make a decision about what counts as 'high'. Statisticians often assume that a measure that is 'statistically significant' *does* exist. However, this really only means that, for random samples, it is unlikely to have come from a population of cases in which there is no association. If we calculate a coefficient of correlation between two variables that works out at, say, 0.23 and which, because it was based on a large sample, is 'statistically significant', does this mean we have fulfilled the first criterion for establishing causality? Probably not.

Establishing the temporal sequence between variables can be even more difficult. For some variables it is not easy to say at what point of time they 'happen'. They may be states or conditions that exist for periods of time. Exactly at what point of time a customer becomes 'brand loyal' may be difficult to determine. Much market research, furthermore, is cross-sectional, that is, measurements are taken at one moment of time, in which case it is impossible to say which variables preceded or followed others in time.

The testing of relationships for lack of spuriousness can be more complex still. There are at least three forms of spurious interpretation:

1   The association is a result of a joint relationship with an extraneous variable. Thus there may be a correlation between essay grades and examination performance. One is not the 'cause' of the other; rather they are both the outcome of some prior combination of ability and work effort.

2   The two variables apparently associated are in fact components of a wider system. Thus certain toilet-training techniques for babies and the use of public libraries may correlate. Again, one does not 'cause' the other, but both are components of a 'middle-class' style of life.

3   The relationship between two variables may not be totally spurious, but indirect or conditional. Thus other variables may intervene or one of the variables may be influenced by factors other than the variables with which it is being correlated.

The investigation of spurious relationships may to some extent be carried out in a statistical manner. If the variables concerned are non-metric then three-way cross-tabulation is appropriate. The method essentially involves looking at what happens to the association between two variables when another is introduced. Thus there may be a degree of association between variable A and variable B. If a 'control' variable, variable C, is introduced, then supposing variable C has two categories Ca and Cb, then the researcher examines what happens to the association between A and B when Ca is true and compares it with what happens when Cb is true. The procedures for doing this were explained on pp. 173–174. If the variables are metric then multiple regression may be used to control for these other factors.

Ideally, the researcher should undertake three-way analyses for every factor that could conceivably affect the relationship between the hypothesized variables. In practice this is often not done and researchers are often tempted to draw causal inferences from the occurrence of reasonably high measures of association.

Some philosophers argue that causal analysis is itself inadequate as a form of explanation. Some would argue that the notion of cause is itself an abstract concept – it is a 'black box', a mystical concept. Establishing association, temporal sequence and lack of spuriousness is evidence of causality – but not *proof*. That can never be established. Some philosophers have doubted that cause inheres in the nature of things. Scientists can always observe that variable A is always associated with variable B, but we cannot observe what binds them together.

Is there, then, such a thing as a 'causal explanation'? Is it not a contradiction in terms, an oxymoron? If we accept that explanation is the provision of understanding to an audience, then whatever an audience accepts as providing such understanding, counts as an 'explanation'. From this perspective, cause *is* explanatory, but only to those who accept a largely positivistic view of the world – the marketing physicists.

Interpretive understanding

Understanding is something whose function is to resolve puzzlement in an audience. This, however, *may* mean establishing a connection between beliefs, motives and actions, that is, we try to understand why somebody, or some group or organization, did something. Another form of understanding, which is usually referred to as 'teleological', involves explaining events in terms of purpose. In other words we say: 'The purpose of A is to produce B', or 'A exists in order to achieve B'. This may be focused at the group or social level – that certain social structures arise to meet the needs of society, or at the individual level – 'I did this in order to . . . .' People must think in teleological terms if they are to be held responsible for their actions. Such forms of 'explanation' can be psychologically satisfying, but are ultimately difficult to prove, test or justify. Max Weber, one of the founding fathers of sociology, tried to establish the method of constructing 'ideal-types' so that we could understand more easily the relationship between means and ends. 'Functional' analysis, which also uses teleological relationships, looks at the relationship of the parts of a system to the whole. The parts are there 'because' they perform some function for the system or the system's purpose. Other procedures that we can use to facilitate interpreting understanding include the use of analogy, extrapolation and metaphor.

Dialectical analysis

This may take many forms. The idea goes back a long way, probably to Plato, but its classic formulation was in the hands of Hegel. To him a dialectic is a process in which for every proposition – a thesis, there is an alternative – an antithesis. This ultimately, forms the basis of a new synthesis – hence the process of change. Karl Marx used the notion of dialectical materialism in which any form of economic development contains the seeds of its own destruction. Thus in capitalism there are inherent contradictions that, eventually, will result in the overthrow of the capitalist system. Dialectical analysis, however, is not necessarily a deterministic approach to knowledge. It is possible to intervene to change the course of history once the internal, underlying dynamics have been revealed and understood.

For Hegel and Marx a dialectic entailed a final point of arrival. For contemporary writers – who would certainly not think of themselves as 'Hegelians' or 'Marxists' – the approach signifies more a pathway, an underlying process in which things will progress, develop or change in particular ways if left to themselves. The product life-cycle thesis can be considered in this mode.

The problem with this form of explanation is that it is untestable in the way that causal analysis may be subjected to empirical validation, and, furthermore, it may not necessarily relate to demonstrable ways in which social actors perceive their own realities, as with interpretive understanding.

All three approaches to explanation are concerned with the notion of 'prediction'. For marketing physicists, however, it means predicting that certain hypotheses will be supported by the data that have yet to be collected. To the marketing physician it means producing predictable results from our actions. The marketing psychiatrist might be more interested in forecasting what *will* happen in the future.

The quality of data

However sophisticated, innovative or brilliant may be the techniques of statistical analysis applied to data, if the data are of poor quality in the first place, then the resulting analysis will be at best poor and at worst entirely misleading. 'Garbage in – garbage out' (or GIGO) is a well-known aphorism in the market research industry. But how can we detect 'garbage'? How can we judge the quality or our data? There are two main approaches to this question:

■ We can judge whether and to what extent the research methods used for measuring, collecting, editing and analysing he data followed established and theoretically sound procedures.
■ We can judge how well market research data mirror the realities they are intended to measure.

The first approach will almost certainly be the one adopted by our marketing physicist. The marketing physician may well be inclined to the second of these approaches, but will be reluctant to abandon the first. The consequence is a dilemma. Should market research data, for example, be adjusted to accord with independent estimates, and should data sources be integrated or fused to obtain the 'best' estimates of behaviour or attitudes? In some circles, data modelling and adjustment are topics only spoken about between consenting adults!

In some areas, such as consumer research into attitudes, beliefs and perceptions or in media research, there are no 'independent' estimates with which the data can be compared. With market measurement, however, the data provided by consumer panels, retail panels, market tracking surveys and omnibus surveys should match up with other sources of information, for example manufacturers' ex-factory shipments and other trade estimates. Where they do not, it is likely that there are sources of bias resulting in, for example, lack of coverage or pick-up. These biases tend to be consistent and so can be predicted. Market measurement estimates can then be calibrated or modelled to remove it. The dilemma is whether or not this practice is 'unscientific' or even unethical.

As we saw earlier in Chapter 2, the measurement of some variables is indirect, using indicators, or derived, combining indicators together in various ways. If the procedures used are unreasonable or inappropriate, the result may well be garbage. Far more attention needs to be paid to the issues of validity and reliability than has frequently been the case either for academic researchers or for suppliers of market research data.

The availability of computer packages like SPSS means that scores of tables and graphs can be produced at the click of a mouse button. Sophisticated statistical analyses can be readily applied to research data; but research reports can easily be clogged up with endless, even mindless, tables. Computers will do whatever analyses researchers ask of them. SPSS will have no trouble in calculating an average sex of 1.634 if males have been given a code of 1 and females a code of 2. The researcher must understand his or her data and what procedures and statistics it is appropriate to use on them. Researchers need to understand the kinds of assumptions that are made about their data, for example, in allocating scores 1–5 in a five–point rating scale and calculating an 'average' score or performing a factor analysis on several items, they need to realize that the 'distance' between the five points are assumed to be equal. That may not be a valid assumption.

Summary

Whatever type of data are to be analysed, data display and data reduction are involved. Analysing qualitative data can be approached in a systematic manner and in ways that, in many respects, parallel those used for the analysis of quantitative data. Quantitative data tend to be analysed in stages, proceeding from univariate to bivariate and then to multivariate techniques. However, whether the data are metric or non-metric determines in the first instance which particular procedures are appropriate.

Where the data represent a random sample drawn from a population of cases, then statistical inference may be appropriate if the sample is quite small and the sample selection method was random. Testing against the null hypothesis is, in fact, only a small step in testing hypotheses against research data. Establishing causal connections between variables can be accomplished only in part by statistical means and quite probably can never be conclusively proven. At the end of the day it is the quality of the data that is crucial to the production of useful and reliable information.

Key concepts

data display	central tendency
data reduction	dispersion
statistical inference	scattergram
quasi-statistics	estimation
content analysis	point estimate
univariate analysis	interval estimate
bivariate analysis	sampling distribution
multivariate analysis	standard error
frequency tables	weighting
charts	grossing up
pie charts	design factor
cross-tabulation	null hypothesis
departure from independence	editing
proportional reduction in error	coding
pair-by-pair comparisons	data entry
coefficient	data dredging
variable listing	causal analysis
variable breakdown	interpretive understanding
	dialectical analysis

Statistics

Chi-square	arithmetic mean
Contingency coefficient	median
Phi-square	mode
Cramer's V	standard deviation
Lambda	Pearson's r
Uncertainty coefficient	multiple regression
Yule's Q	factor analysis
Somers' d	cluster analysis
Kendall's tau-b	conjoint analysis
Kendall's tau-c	multi-dimensional scaling
Spearman's rho	standard error of the proportion
	standard error of the mean

Further reading

- Bowles, T and Blyth, B (1997) 'How do you like your data: raw, al dente or stewed?', *Journal of the Market Research Society*, Vol 39, No 1, pp 163–174.
- Bowers, D (1996), *Statistics from Scratch. An Introduction for Health Care Professionals*, Chichester: Wiley.
- Diamantopolous, A and Schlegelmilch, B (1997) *Taking the Fear out of Data Analysis*, London: The Dryden Press.
- Silvey, J (1975) *Deciphering Data. The analysis of social surveys*, London: Longman.

Questions and further discussion

1   A bank conducted a survey of 300 of its non-business customers selected at random. One question asked respondents whether they had been experiencing any problems with any aspect of the services in the last three months. One third answered 'yes', while the remainder answered 'no'. On the basis of respondents' transactions with it, the bank was able to classify respondents into 'high volume' and 'low volume' categories. Of the respondents who said they had experienced problems, ten were 'high volume' customers, while 130 of those not experiencing problems were 'high volume'. The bank wants to explore the question of whether customers experiencing difficulties were likely to do less business with it than those not experiencing problems.

   (i)   Construct a bivariate cross-tabulation of response versus transaction. volume.
   (ii) Calculate appropriate percentages.
   (iii) Calculate Phi-square and Lambda.
   (iv) Test the statistical significance of your results using the Chi-square test.
   (v)   Can you conclude from your calculations that customers experiencing problems *are* likely to do less business with the bank?

2   A random sample of 500 was used to estimate what proportion of households in a particular area owned a microwave oven.

(i) Calculate the standard error of the proportion for each of three results:
■   250
■   100
■   20

(ii) Calculate the confidence interval for the 95 per cent level of confidence for each of these results.

3   The brand manager for brand X, on the basis of past studies, hypothesizes that 10 per cent of the target market purchases his brand. A simple random sample of 1200 individuals recorded that 96 people had purchased brand X in the last four weeks. Test the manager's hypothesis at the 95 per cent level of confidence.

4   A simple random sample of 81 families in a city had a mean income of £13,000 per annum with a standard deviation of £4500. Construct the 95 per cent confidence interval.

5   From Table 6.25 (p. 178) rank order the four individuals A–D on Test X and Test Y and compute Spearman's rho. Compare your answer with Pearson's r.

7

Designing, selling and buying research

So far we have been examining the considerable range of tools that are available for the marketing researcher to use. It is now time to see how these tools are assembled in the design of research that is intended to address specific marketing problems and how the results of research are presented in a research report.

Designing research

Designing research is in many ways more difficult than understanding the various elements that go into a design. The first thing we need to do is to distinguish between commissioned research and scholarly research.

Most commissioned research, whether ad hoc or continuous, is designed for clients who are paying for the research and who wish to utilize the results to further organizational objectives. Research that is designed in-house by a business or non-profit organization will also be for similar purposes. Scholarly research, on the other hand, is designed to further academic objectives and will be carried out for career purposes by students and academics. Such research is not undertaken on behalf of any particular client (although it may be funded by one of a range of organizations that support research). Some scholarly research, however, may be undertaken by individuals in market research agencies. It is not specifically commissioned, but is intended for presentation at conferences and for publication. Sometimes the distinction between these two kinds of research is not very clearcut, for example, an academic who uses research that he or she has been commissioned to do, but feeds into research for publication. However, the objectives and design of the two kinds of research are very distinct, and the researcher wishing to use commissioned research for academic purposes will have to be very careful not to reveal confidential information about a client company.

Designing commissioned research

Research designed to achieve organizational objectives is not neutral. It is designed on behalf of the organization for which the research is being conducted. Its purpose is not restricted to scientific study of the ways in which marketing variables relate or function; the focus is rather on producing solutions to problems. It is predisposed towards making recommendations for action, and is likely to take the perspective of the marketing physician that was described in Chapter 1. This is interventionist and partisan. If the researcher is not part of the solution he or she is part of the problem; the point is not to study the world but to change it. The design of commissioned research will normally include the following elements:

- diagnosing organizational problems or issues,
- assessing organizational strengths and weaknesses,
- clarifying the decisions that need to be taken and defining action standards,
- specifying the information that will be required,
- formulating the objectives of the research,
- producing a research brief,
- drawing up and presenting a research proposal.

The researcher – whether in-house or in a market research agency – will often be involved only in the last stage of drawing up and presenting research proposals. The other stages are often undertaken by the client organization. However, clients increasingly look for help in understanding some or all of the design elements, so the researcher may become involved, for example, in helping the client to produce a research brief, or even right back to helping the client to diagnose company problems.

Diagnosing the problem

In Chapter 1 it was argued that marketing research will be a waste of time unless it is designed in the context of carefully defined problems that particular companies have or issues or decisions that they face. The first stage in any research design should, then, be a detailed analysis of these problems, issues and decisions. Problem diagnosis is, unfortunately, often given insufficient attention before research is designed. One reason for this is that it is often the most difficult (and in some cases, depressing) part of the process. Sometimes the person requesting the research has no clear idea about what the key problems of an organization *are* that the research can tackle, or what decisions depend on the results of the research. What particular individuals *see* as 'the problem' may well differ from one person to another. One person's 'problem' may be another's opportunity. Furthermore, what individuals may be describing are the symptoms rather than the underlying causes.

It may be helpful to think about a number of related issues when diagnosing problems:

- the nature of the discrepancies between actual and desired performance,
- the relationship between problems, and between problems and symptoms,
- the seriousness of the problems,
- the factors that affect or might be affecting the problem.

Problems arise where there is some discrepancy between the actual, current or anticipated future performance of the organization, and the desired performance or outcome. Discrepancies may be of various kinds:

- *Historical*, for example, the organization is not performing as well as it has in the past; profits are declining or sales stagnating.

- *Environmental*, for example, the organization is not performing as well as competitors or other similar organizations. What organizations are taken as standards and which measures of performance are used may, however, be crucial in making such comparisons.
- *Planned or budgeted*, for example, there may be variances between budgeted costs of materials and the actual costs, or between planned growth and actual growth.
- *Theoretical or analytical*, for example, the organization may be less marketing-oriented than the theory of marketing suggests should be the case, or its planning procedures do not match the principles of marketing planning.

It is helpful to understand what comparisons are being made when the nature of the marketing problems facing an organization are being considered. Making historical comparisons may lead management to view the problem rather differently than if comparisons are being made with selected competitors.

There is seldom just one problem facing an organization at any given point of time. Problems are often inter-related and form clusters of related issues, for example, problems in terms of sales, profits and market shares. There is frequently a hierarchy of problems and symptoms; each symptom is the result of a more basic problem. The 'problem' may be declining sales; but this may be a symptom of other aspects of an organization. Such deeper problems, like rising costs, may themselves be symptoms of still more fundamental issues, like work practices. Sometimes the relationship between problems is reciprocal rather than hierarchical. For example, advertising expenditure affects sales which, in turn, affect future expenditures on advertising. Sometimes several causes combine to produce a single effect; sometimes a single cause may produce several effects.

Whenever a problem is being described, it is often a good idea to ask, 'Why?' Why are sales declining? Why are costs rising? Why are work practices inefficient? There is no ultimate cause, but such probing may help us to dig deeper into the structure and processes of an organization.

Some problems are more serious than others. Some may be urgent, but not important, others may be important, but not urgent, and some may be both. The urgency with which the results are required and the degree of importance attached to the problems to which the research is addressed will clearly have an impact on the kind of research that may be appropriate. Such a diagnosis may be necessary for deciding in which order to tackle problems. Information may be needed to measure exactly *how* serious a problem is. Some of this information may be already available; some may require market research. In any event, it is helpful to spell out exactly what information *is* required for this purpose.

Factors that may affect the problem may be internal or external to the organization. Internal factors may relate to such things as payment or incentive systems, industrial relations, changing technology, depreciation of plant and equipment. External factors will include the immediate micro environment of trends in market size, changes in market structure or in buyer behaviour and attitudes, competitor activity, supplier power, and the role of intermediaries like retailers and wholesalers. The wider macro environment will include changes in demographics, the economy, technology, politics, the legal environment, and the social and cultural environment. We shall see in Chapter 8 the role marketing research plays in market measurement and market analysis and a lot of this activity assists in problem diagnosis.

Strengths and weaknesses of the company

Any marketing action will need to build upon company strengths or particular capabilities. What these are is not always obvious or easy to diagnose, and may require further analysis or research. It is likely that many of the weaknesses will have surfaced as 'problems' at the problem diagnosis stage. However, there may well be other weaknesses that are not connected or obviously related to the problems being diagnosed. Assessment of strengths and weaknesses is often undertaken as part of a 'SWOT' analysis that also looks at the opportunities and threats in the marketplace. Such analyses assume that information is readily available and that accurate assessments can be made of each element. Marketing research often has a key role to play in the more systematic marketing auditing process which is usually comprehensive, periodic and undertaken by a group that is independent of those being audited. The audit will normally have both an internal and an external element. The internal audit will seek to identify:

- those factors that give any company in a market sector or in an industry a strategic advantage,
- the capabilities and incompetences of the company,
- those capabilities that link with the strategic advantage factors.

Marketing research can help assess each of these elements. Where a capability matches a strategic advantage factor then it is a company strength; where it does not, it may be a weakness. The external audit will take a systematic look at the environment, particularly the immediate environment, and will, for example, seek to discover:

- who are the major competitors,
- what are their objectives and strategies,
- what are their strengths and weaknesses,
- what are their typical reaction patterns.

From this it should be possible to identify the extent of any threat from competitors, the power possessed by customers and suppliers, and the threat of substitute goods and services emerging. What is sometimes called 'environmental analysis' will probably involve gathering market intelligence. This might include:

- scanning reports, newspapers and journals,
- speaking to the salesforce, consultants or academics,
- attending meetings or conferences.

The marketing researcher may be involved in all, some or none of these activities.

Decisions and action standards

It is one thing to feel that you now fully understand the situation facing the company; it is another to be clear about the decision or decisions that need to be taken. It must be remembered that marketing research is not geared exclusively to the taking of marketing decisions. Decisions about pricing or levels of production may have a marketing input, but there will almost certainly also be inputs from accountants or production managers or engineers. Decisions about communications with customers may well be the preserve of the marketing manager, but communications for example with suppliers, intermediaries, competitors, shareholders and so on may well involve other kinds of manager. If the company decided, for example, to conduct a survey of opinion among its shareholders, this would probably still be regarded as 'market research', but decisions to issue additional shares or to merge with another company are unlikely to be for the marketing manager to make.

Unless the precise role the results from market research activity will play in the making of decisions of whatever kind is defined, the results are likely to be ignored. It is only too easy for managers to argue that marketing research is needed before any decision can be taken, but without first clarifying which decisions in fact depend on further information. The best way to specify the role of research is to define action standards. These are actions or decisions specified in advance of the research that will depend on particular outcomes. Thus a company may specify that it will launch a new product provided at least 40 per cent of respondents in a survey say they will either 'probably buy' or 'definitely buy' the new product. Furthermore, the 40 per cent should not be a 'finger-in-the-air' approach, but a result of careful diagnosis of the results of past research and how these related to the success or failure of products in that industry or in that company.

The information required

Once the decisions have been clarified, it is necessary to consider:

- exactly what information is required,
- the quality of information required,
- when it is required by.

Knowing what information is needed for making a particular decision is often a matter of experience or gut feeling. However, if the decisions to be taken have been clarified then, if, for example, one decision is what size of pack to use for a new product, then it should be clear that information is required on the sales of existing pack sizes both for the company and for competitors, on how consumers react to existing packs, and how they would react to new sizes or types of pack. In short, it should be possible to list the key concepts that need to be addressed, and perhaps begin to suggest the key variables that need to be measured.

Considerations about the quality of information will include accuracy, detail and comprehensiveness as well as sample quality. Thus random samples will produce higher quality data than quota samples. Bigger samples will be more reliable than smaller ones (but by a declining amount). At the same time, getting high quality data will be more costly, so a degree of trade-off may be required.

When information is required by, will of course, be governed largely by when the decision needs to be taken, but other considerations, like the time needed to analyse and digest the information, may need to be kept in mind. If the decision has to be taken before any worthwhile research can be carried out, it may be necessary to consider whether the company:

- takes the decision without any research,
- delays taking the decision,
- does a 'quick-and-dirty' study.

Each of these has its problems, and in making the choice, very careful consideration has to be taken of the cost (in financial and customer relationship terms) of getting the decision wrong, or making a sub-optimal decision. If there *is* time to do the research, then how much time is available will place constraints on the commissioning, phasing and completion of the research.

The objectives of the research

Research objectives spell out what the research is designed to explore, measure, or explain. For research into consumer markets using standard ad hoc or continuous techniques, exploratory research may not be needed. For most business research or for consumer research in unfamiliar markets, an exploratory phase will probably be essential. This will include all work that is preliminary to the main stage of data collection and which is used in shaping the direction, design and operation of the main study, or to check that earlier designs will work satisfactorily.

It is possible to identify five key purposes of exploratory research.

- Diagnosing, analysing and evaluating the real nature, seriousness and urgency of the problem or problems facing an organization.
- Increasing the researcher's familiarity with a topic, with a company, or with a market. Very often the researcher at the outset does not know enough about the situation to be able to design the research or submit a worthwhile research proposal.
- Establishing priorities and objectives of the research. Exploratory work may be needed before it is possible to decide which particular issues require further investigation, and before being able to decide exactly what the research is expected to achieve.
- Providing information on practical problems. It may be necessary, for example, to find out whether certain organizations are willing to co-operate before embarking on a particular style of inquiry. We may need to know certain things about the population before being able to design our sample.
- Generating ideas, gaining insights or suggesting hypotheses that could be tested.

Any of the available instruments of data capture, data collection methods, or the special techniques and applications described in the next chapter may be used for exploratory purposes. A formal, quantitative survey could, for example, be undertaken and used as a preliminary stage for a larger, more comprehensive investigation. By the same token, we could carry out a few informal enquiries with informants or experts in the field and decide that sufficient information had been acquired to make a decision.

The distinction between 'exploratory' and other forms of research may be unclear, and could change as the researcher or the marketing manager reconsiders the role or conduct of the research. Thus a study that began as a 'final' piece of research may be continued so that the results are used as preliminary inputs to further investigation. An inquiry that began as an exploratory study may not be continued, so it becomes 'final'.

For exploratory and descriptive research the objective may simply be to collect the information that has been specified at the earlier stage. Investigative or causal research may, however, need to go beyond simply collecting information and to spell out what needs to be discovered or tested from the data collected. Thus the information required may concern a range of customer demographic characteristics and various measures of the degree of price awareness. The research objectives may be to find out *which* characteristics are most strongly associated with price awareness.

It is sometimes helpful to formulate research objectives as questions that the research is designed to answer, for example:

- What is the relationship between advertising and sales for brands A, B and C over the last five years?
- What is the likely market share for brand Z in three and five month's time?
- How do consumers go about making a purchase of an automatic washing machine?

Notice that the answers to none of these questions will directly make the actual decision that may need to be taken, for example:

- How much should be spent on advertising next year?
- Should we invest in new machinery to make product Z?
- How should we promote our washing machines?

The research provides the information; the manager takes the decision. However, if the research objectives are phrased as a question, then at least it is clear what question or questions the research has to answer – and, when the results are obtained, whether is not it has answered them. Specifying the information required and the objectives of the research should, together, ensure that the right kinds of data are collected and that the appropriate kinds of data analysis can be supported by them.

The research brief

The research brief is a formal document that is, or should be, sufficiently detailed to enable the researcher to formulate a proposal for marketing research that will produce results that can be used effectively for marketing diagnosis, planning and control. Sometimes the company prepares its own brief; sometimes it is prepared with the assistance of a market research agency or business consultant.

The brief will contain a summary of the elements considered so far: a diagnosis of the problem, an assessment of company capabilities, a clarification of the decisions that need to be taken, a specification of the information required, and a statement of the objectives of the research. The brief will also typically contain further details of background information on the company and how the present situation or problem arose, suggestions about the kind and scope of the research envisaged, some indication of the likely budget for

Research Specification

Attitudes to the use of specialized flour in the home

John Ambrose wishes to commission a survey to investigate housewives' attitudes towards the use of specialized flours for home baking.

Background

John Ambrose is a medium-sized, family-owned, flour-milling business which has been in existence for over 100 years. It supplies a complete range of flours to the bakery trade to cover every specialized need. Its customers are mostly small to medium-sized family bakers who have been customers for decades. It does not currently supply to the general public. It has no advertising and only limited sales represetation.

Sales have been falling steadily in the last few years to a point where the company will need to take corrective action to stay in business. Among the alternatives being considered are to supply the general public the same highly specialized flours currently supplied to the trade. These would be more expensive than standard flours.

Research objectives

In order to investigate the feasibility of offering specialized flour for domestic use, John Ambrose needs to know:

- what proportion of households keep flour of any description in stock,
- what kinds of flour are usually kept,
- what other kinds of flour housewives may be aware of,
- what flour is currently used for,
- what are the main kinds of home baking,
- which groups of people are most likely to make use of specialized flour,
- what quantities they are likely to buy,
- would they be prepared to pay a slightly higher price?

Methods

The research should consist of a qualitative preliminary to establish the main dimensions of flour usage in the home, attitudes to home baking, and the possibilities for the use of specialized flour. The main study should be a quantitative survey of about 1200 households to establish the extent of various usages and attitudes.

Qualitative research

Please include a proposal for depth interviews and/or group discussions with housewives of all ages and social classes, and including those who do little or no home baking. The qualitative research should take place in at least two regions. Costing for the qualitative work should be separate from that of the main stage.

Quantitative research

A nationally representative sample of housewives who usually do home baking is required. Would you please quote seperately for the alternatives of random or a quota sample design, discussing their relative advantages and limitations, and giving details of how the design would ensure a representative sample.

The qualitative stage will inform decisions on the content of the questionnaire. At this stage we envisage covering the following areas:

- whether the household currently has flour in stock and what kinds/brands/pack sizes/ quantities,
- how long the flour is usually kept in the house,
- what types/brands of flour housewives can recall,
- how often they buy and the price paid,
- what kinds of baking they do, on what occasions, how often, and what flour they use,
- what they view as their successes and failures in home baking,
- whether they feel that specialized flours could help with their 'failures'.

Timetable

We would like to commission the work at the end of July and to receive an interim report on the qualitative stage for execution of the main fieldwork in November. A full written report is required as soon as reasonably possible after that.

Submission of tenders

Please submit two copies of tenders to John Ambrose no later than 15th June. Meetings to discuss the shortlisted tenders will take place on 26th June. If you wish to discuss the research prior to submission of a tender please contact John Ambrose.

Box 7.1   A research brief

the research, a timescale for when a proposal is required and when the research results will be needed, and whether or not the brief is competitive. There may need to be considerable discussion both within the client organization and between client and agency over details of the brief unless the research is very straightforward or it is repeat business. Very often a company's analysis of its own problems may relate more to symptoms than to underlying causes, so the research executive may need to probe by continually asking, 'Why?' as symptoms or stated problems are described. Such discussions may take place over the telephone, but for unusual or complex briefs will probably be face to face. An example of a research brief is illustrated in Box 7.1.

The research proposal

Like the research brief, the research proposal is a formal document, but it is drafted by whoever is conducting the research. Any organization seeking research from a market research agency will base its commission on such a document. From the perspective of the market research executive, the key objective of the proposal will be to obtain the commission from the client, perhaps in the face of stiff competition. The proposal in practice often has to be drafted on the basis of a less than adequate brief from the client. The research executive may seek further discussion and clarification from the client before submitting a proposal.

The proposal is a formal statement of the methods and techniques that the researcher feels are required in the circumstances, and should contain the following elements:

■ A statement of the background of the research. This should indicate that the researcher has fully grasped the brief and any subsequent discussions about it. It should demonstrate that the researcher fully understands the problem which is the focus of the research, the decisions that have to be taken, and the information required.
■ A statement of the objectives of the research.
■ Definitions of the main concepts, their operationalization into variables, any hypotheses to be tested or models to be used.
■ Details of the actual research techniques proposed. These should include a definition of the population of cases to be studied, the size of the sample, the techniques for selecting cases, the data capture instruments, the data

collection methods, and the specific techniques and applications to be used.

■ The personnel who will be involved in the research, including some indication of their qualifications, experience and background.

■ A time schedule, outlining the dates or periods of time between each phase of the research. Typically, this is done on a month-by-month basis.

■ Details of the data analysis procedures. For survey research, this will outline the procedures for editing, coding, processing and tabulating data.

■ The costs of the research. This would normally be a global sum, but occasionally clients ask for a breakdown of costs.

In planning the methods and techniques to be used, the basic considerations are whether the research should be ad hoc or continuous, and if ad hoc whether it should be qualitative or quantitative. In selecting from the range of market research techniques available, the research executive will need to bear in mind the resources and the time that will be needed for each technique, along with the appropriateness of each for minimizing the risks among the decisions identified as needing to be taken. A checklist of useful questions to consider would be as follows:

■ Will depth interviews with key informants, experts, technicians, colleagues, or suppliers provide sufficient information to take the decision?

■ Will group discussions be needed with consumers to explore issues more thoroughly, and if so, what kinds of groups, how many groups, and how are they to be selected?

■ Will some form of experimental research be appropriate? If so, should it be in the laboratory or in the field?

■ Will some form of survey be required? This is the most expensive, resource-heavy, time-consuming form of research and should be resorted to only when information from other sources is clearly not going to be adequate. Careful thought will need to be given to the size of the sample required, the type of sampling, and the mode of delivery of the questions, for example, face to face, by telephone or by mail.

A company considering commissioning research will normally ask up to three agencies to submit proposals for research in response to a research brief. These would then be evaluated and compared. For large-scale undertakings the agency may be invited to present these proposals in person so that they can be questioned about them. Alternatively, where a client is coming back for repeat business, there may not even be a research proposal – an understanding of what the research is to cover and the cost may be all the needs to be clarified. It would be unreasonable for the client to expect that the agency has done a great deal of work on the problem before the research is commissioned. In particular, it is unlikely that the agency will include a questionnaire even in draft format this stage. An example of a response to the brief in Box 7.1 is illustrated in Appendix 2.

Reporting the findings

While the research, as explained above, is not neutral, it is, or should be objective in the sense that 'correct' procedures have been followed rigorously and systematically, and that bias, as far as possible, has been eliminated; but however valid and insightful the research, the findings will be of little value unless they are communicated effectively to those who commissioned the research and to those responsible for incorporating the findings into tactical or strategic decisions. Reports of research may take either or both of two main forms: a face-to-face presentation and a formal written report.

The manner in which findings are reported will be affected by the complexity of the problems being researched, the audience to whom the presentation or report is to be addressed, and the degree of importance attached by the client to the form of the report. Not every client wishes a face-to-face presentation, but where one is required, it is usually an opportunity for the research executive to give preliminary results and conclusions, and for the client to ask about the research before the final report is written. The presentation is usually given by the research executive who was involved in the initial discussions with the client and who has been responsible for the design and execution of the research. The presentation will normally take place in the client organization, and nowadays the visual aids used can get quite sophisticated with the increasing availability of desk top publishing packages for use with laser printers, some of which can produce coloured overheads for overhead projectors, plus electronic projection systems like Powerpoint. Comments on the methodology need to be very brief. What the audience wants to know are the key findings and the practical implications. The language used needs to be kept free of jargon, and diagrams need to be clear and simple. There are many excellent books on the skills required for giving good presentations, for example Scott (1986) and Vardaman (1981).

The formal report, like the face-to-face presentation, is above all a method of communication, so the author should bear in mind the kinds of people who are likely to read it and what their needs are. Reports will normally be written in management report style. This means clear, concise, grammatical English, free of jargon or complex sentences, and organized in a way that allows the reader quickly to assemble and digest the content of the report. A fairly standard approach is to use plenty of headings and sub-headings, and arranged into a format similar to that suggested in Box 7.2. Wherever possible, graphs, tables, charts and diagrams should be used to illustrate and clarify arguments. Ideally, these should be incorporated into the text, each numbered according to the appropriate section, for example 'Table 4.1.2', and referred to in the text, which gives an interpretation or extracts the key points or lessons to be derived from it. A good report is persuasive and convinces the reader that the conclusions and recommendations make good sense.

The number of copies of the report to be made available to the client is usually specified in the research proposal. Sometimes reports may be available and distributed before the face-to-face presentation; more often the formal report will be submitted afterwards so that the points raised in the discussion of the research can be addressed and included.

The researcher may, at the request of the client, either stop short of making recommendations, or such recommendations may be specifically asked for. The research itself may, of course, be only one input among others that is taken into account when deciding upon some course of action. The client may, for example, have to review the company's financial situation if implementation will require considerable expenditure. Making recommendations, however, is one thing: implementing them is another. It is not usually up to

Title page

This should state:

- title of report,
- who commissioned it,
- who prepared it,
- date submitted.

Contents page

This should:

- systematically number sections and sub-sections,
- list tables and figures.

Executive summary

This is a one-page abstract of the entire report, and may be all that a busy business executive reads. It should:

- explain the terms of reference, the purpose and scope of the report,
- state the key methods and approach used,
- list the main conclusions,
- list the key recommendations.

Main text of the report

This consists of a series of sections arranged under headings and sub-headings that typically would include:

1 Bacground - an analysis of the current situation or problem.
2 Research methodology
   2.1 Objectives of the research
   2.2 Measurement of the key variables
   2.3 The population of cases to be studied
   2.4 Sampling procedures
   2.5 Data capture instruments
   2.6 Data collection methods
   2.7 Specific techniques and applications
   2.8 Data analysis
3 Market analysis
4 Results
5 Conclusions
6 Recommendations

Appendices

This may include:

- any explanatory notes that would clutter up the main report
- tabulations and calculations not included in the text
- references
- copies of questionnaires or visuals used

Box 7.2 A management report

the market research agency to suggest how its recommendations should be put into practice, but if some of the recommendations are carried out, it may be called upon to provide information that will be used to monitor or track the results. Thus advertising tracking studies and various market tracking and market measurement research may be used for this purpose.

Selling research – the agency perspective

The major objective of the research executive in a market research organization in designing research and in offering a formal research proposal will be to obtain the commission from the client. He or she will need to bear in mind the strengths and weaknesses of the agency in terms of styles of research, and its current loading of resources already committed to other projects currently underway. If it is a large company, it will be able to offer the full range of research so that if, for example, it looks as though qualitative research is appropriate to the client's problem, then the client can be passed on to the division or subsidiary company in the organization that specializes in that type of research. In smaller specialized agencies, the research executive will, of course, try to show why the company's particular expertise is just what is needed to help the client.

In reviewing briefs received by potential clients and deciding which ones to offer research proposals for, the agency will need to consider:

- the level of detail in the brief and whether further discussions with the client are needed,
- the kind of research envisaged or that the agency thinks is appropriate,
- how the data are to be used (and by whom, when and how),
- any limitations in terms of time and money,
- the scope of the research in terms of geographical area, size of sample, the information required, the input to research design needed from the research executive, and the end-product – restricted to data analysis, or to include interpretations and recommendations,
- the kind of report required,
- the competition – how may other agencies are quoting.

If the agency decides to offer a research proposal, it will need to consider all those aspects that will affect the design and cost, for example:

- the availability of past research or published data,
- the size, spread and contactability of the sample,
- the data collection method,
- the need for exploratory research,
- the need for a pilot survey,
- the need for personal briefings,
- the length of the questionnaire,
- the number of open-ended questions,
- the need for evening, weekend or holiday time interviewing,
- the scale and complexity of the data analysis required,
- the type and scale of reporting.

Buying research – the client perspective

From the perspective of the manufacturer or other type of organization wishing to purchase research services, the objective will, of course, be to buy good research, that is, research that is good value and which addresses effectively the problems, issues or opportunities that the company faces. Before approaching any market research agency, however, the client first of all needs to consider:

- whether research is needed at all,
- whether a research brief is needed and if so whether the company is able to produce one in-house,
- whether it can do what research is needed entirely in-house,
- whether it wants to commission a 'full' study or just part of the activities required, for example, employing only field and tab assistance, or putting a number of questions into an omnibus survey,

- what companies or agencies to approach for a proposal.
- The client company may decide against doing any research if:
    - the data or information needed already exist or can be purchased, for example from business publishing houses, from market research agencies or advertising agencies, or by subscribing to continuous research services,
    - there is not enough time to conduct research before a decision has to be taken,
    - the cost of getting the decision wrong is relatively low so the cost of any worthwhile research would be greater than the likely payoff,
    - the situation is too complex with too many factors and variables for research to have a significant impact on the decision that needs to be taken.

In choosing what market research companies to approach for a proposal, some clients will have a 'pool' of tried and tested companies that they have a habit of using. Others rely on listings, for example by the Market Research Society handbook, or on recommendations from contacts in other organizations. It would be normal to obtain up to three proposals and to advise the market research organizations that it is a competitive proposal, indicating how many have been or will be approached.

The final selection will be based on some combination of:

- evidence that the research executive has fully understood the brief and the problem to be researched,
- the overall approach suggested, including a clear statement of the research objectives, a definition of the population to be studied, the sampling techniques, the field-work methods to be used and the data handling and analysis procedures,
- the experience of the researchers assigned to the project,
- the quality of communications with the agency so far,
- the cost, usually a global sum, but it should be clear what that sum includes, for example a written report and a face-to-face presentation.

The client may need to bear in mind that the 'cost' of the research includes not only paying the market research agency, but also the opportunity cost of what is not being done as a result of devoting resources to the research, and the indirect costs of managerial time spent on further contact. However, the client may also need to consider whether the research, besides being used as a basis for taking a decision, may also be a useful input to a marketing or management information system, or may be used as 'currency' in negotiating with advertisers, advertising agencies, distributors, retailers and so on. Findings on brand loyalty, interpurchasing and frequency of purchase may, for example, be used to persuade a retailer to allocate more shelf-space to your brand.

A commissioning letter will be sent to the chosen market research agency accepting the proposal as a formal contract. Thereafter, the client will wish to monitor progress to ensure that deadlines are met, and that the questionnaire, when drafted, meets with its approval. The client may wish some degree of participation in the research, for example, attending one or two group discussions, and may request that it be consulted over the final coding of answers when the questionnaire are received.

Finally, it would be wise to evaluate the market researchers in a systematic manner by giving a series of ratings against a number of selected criteria, for example:

■ response to the brief,
■ quality of the research,
■ client service,
■ verbal presentation,
■ written report.

Such ratings can then form the basis for making future research commissions.

Designing scholarly research

In contrast to research for organizations, academic research pursues scholarly objectives, the end-product of which is to add to the stock of publicly available knowledge about the ways in which marketing variables relate and to further our understanding of why marketing phenomena happen in the way they do. It attempts not only to be objective, but to be neutral. It does not take sides, although, of course, the findings may be very useful to one or more organizations. A key feature of academic research is that the findings are generally accessible, usually in published form, for example, in an article in a journal or in a book. Such research may be undertaken from either the positivist or interpretive perspectives outlined in Chapter 1, and this will have implications for the design of the research. However, academic research from either perspective does possess common features that contrast it with commissioned research:

■ there is no client and not necessarily, in fact not usually, one single organization whose problems are being diagnosed as a preliminary to writing a research brief, nor are there strengths and weaknesses to be considered nor decisions and action standards that need to be clarified,
■ reporting the findings is to an academic audience, which will have different expectations and apply different criteria on which to judge the 'worth', 'value' or 'excellence' of the research,
■ there may be no specific recommendations for action, but there will probably be more general implications that organizations may take on board in their decision taking.

Because there is no client, it is usually up to the researcher to decide on the key issues to be addressed, and on the direction and methods of the research. It may, however, be constrained by the need to apply for research funding and there may be a degree of 'grantsmanship' in picking the size and scope of a project that will appeal to the fund-giving body. For the student, there will be a supervisor who approves or suggests modifications to proposals suggested, while the research is more an exercise that demonstrates to the examiner an ability to design, conduct and analyse the results of original research. It will be judged by scholarly standards that relate to the thoroughness of the review of the literature, the development or testing of theory, concepts or models, the originality of the ideas, and the sophistication and appropriateness of the techniques deployed to the stated objectives of the research.

The cost implications of student research are very different from organizational research. Thus students will not be charging themselves for the time spent interviewing, but they will have to pay for travel or postage used in a mail survey. Some forms of research, for example telephone research, may be just too expensive for students to undertake. At the same time there are seldom any cost implications for the use of computer time or advice from supervisors. All these factors affect the design of the research.

Key elements in the design of academic research include:

- a clear statement of the nature, purpose and objectives of the research,
- a justification of why the research is important and to whom it is important,
- a review of the literature relevant to the research objectives, including the general theory, principles and concepts of marketing that are important,
- a selection and justification of an appropriate methodology, including the operationalization and measurement of variables, the selection of cases, and the methods of data capture, data collection and data analysis,
- the presentation of the results in such a way that they have a demonstrable validity, but at the same time acknowledging the limitations of scope and methodology,
- a conclusion that relates the findings to the literature and to the research objectives, demonstrates how knowledge and understanding have been advanced, speculates on the wider implications of the research, and outlines what further research may be needed to continue and deepen understanding of the issues.

The nature, purpose and objectives of the research are decided by the researcher, not by a client. The objectives are more likely to be stated in the form of questions that refer to variables that apply to a range of organizations or marketing situations, for example, 'What diagnostic routines do companies follow for detecting weak products in their range?' or, 'What factors affect consumer price awareness for fast moving consumer goods?'

Since there is no client, the academic is always open to the accusation that what he or she is doing is 'trivial', 'lacks practicality' or is 'irrelevant'. While there are proponents of 'pure' research – research for its own sake – it is at least arguable that in marketing there should be practical outcomes or implications. This is not to undermine the value of theory: on the contrary, there is nothing as practical as a good theory – one that can be applied with successful results in a number of different contexts. The development and testing of theory is, then, a key activity for academic researchers. Pointing to the practical implications of, or who might use, a new concept, a new way of measuring a variable, a new theory, a new hypothesis or a new mathematically specified model is a way of justifying why the research is important.

While commissioned research may utilize what data or statistics are already available, academic research will in addition consider what concepts and theories, variables and hypotheses, principles and models form the background to current thinking on the topic. The researcher may see gaps in the literature, shortcomings of approach or methodology, or the potential to apply an idea in a new context. All this literature will be carefully documented with a commentary on how it has developed and with full references to sources in a bibliography. A client commissioning organizational research is seldom interested in such literature.

The research methodology for academic research is just as constrained by cost as is commissioned research – but the cost implications, as indicated earlier, may be very different. Where an academic is applying for research funds it is, therefore, difficult to justify 'pile-it-high-and-sell-it-cheap' research. Research councils and other official and semi-official funding bodies are likely to favour random probability sampling over quota sampling, even if it is more expensive. Most government-funded research does tend to use this more expensive sampling procedure. Its justification is that if the results, and perhaps the data, are to be available to other users then the sample needs to be a microcosm of the population of cases from which the sample was drawn and representative in all respects, not just in respect of the variables used for quotas.

The results and conclusions of academic research are likely to be presented in person by the researcher at a staff seminar or academic conference. Some conferences publish all or a selection of papers presented. Researchers may seek further outlets in academic journals, contributions to edited books, or as research monographs. In all these situations, the research is subject to peer review, and weaknesses of methodology and research design will – or should be – exposed.

Students sometimes ask if it is necessary to have an hypothesis for their research. On the whole, if the research is quantitative and is aimed at measuring or testing concepts or ideas, then it is a good idea that the hypotheses are spelled out clearly in advance so that they can be subsequently compared with the data collected. If the research is exploratory or just qualitative in nature, then one of the objectives of the research will be to generate hypotheses that could be tested in subsequent research. In this situation, it is clearly not possible or necessary to spell out hypotheses before the research is undertaken.

Summary

Designing commissioned research is rather different from research designed for academic purposes. With the former, there is a client on whose behalf the researcher is working. While such research is, or should be, objective, it is seldom neutral. There will always be the client's particular situation to be diagnosed before a brief for the research can be produced and a proposal written. It is also necessary to bear in mind the differing perspectives of the research agency and of the client. One is a seller of research services and the other a buyer. The ultimate test is client satisfaction with the service offered.

Academic research, by contrast, will be judged by scientific criteria that have to do with establishing clearly the validity of the findings, usually though appeal to the 'correctness' of the methods and techniques used.

Key concepts

commissioned research
scholarly research

action standards
research objectives
research brief
research proposal
research report

Questions for further discussion

1 Draw up a table with two columns listing the contrasts between commissioned research and scholarly research.
2 Re-read the case of Elida Faberge at the beginning of Chapter 1
   ■ Diagnose the problems faced by the company.
   ■ Outline its strengths and weaknesses.
   ■ Clarify the decisions that need to be taken
   ■ Specify the information that will be required
   ■ Draft a research proposal along the lines of Appendix 2 that will enable the company to take the decisions you have identified.

8

Specific techniques and applications

This chapter explains how some of the larger market research agencies combine instruments of data capture, data collection methods and data analysis techniques in particular ways to enable them to diagnose the current circumstances facing an organization, to make predictions about the likely consequences of their marketing decisions, or to monitor the progress made by or success of past marketing activity. The techniques described below are only a selection of some of the more widely used procedures, and serve only as an illustration of the possibilities rather than a comprehensive account of all the services available. Since the techniques have been generated and developed to apply to specific situations, problems, opportunities or issues, it is often difficult to distinguish a particular research technique from the application in which it is normally used. Accordingly, no attempt is made in this chapter to distinguish techniques from applications. One distinction that can be made, however, is between techniques and applications that are primarily diagnostic and those that are predictive or prognostic.

Diagnostic techniques are used to review, measure or monitor the situation as it currently is or has been up to now. Thus marketing managers may require, or feel they require, a detailed anatomy of the size and structure of the markets they are currently addressing with their product offerings, and of the purchasing behaviour associated with them. They may wish to know how current and potential customers use their and their competitor's products and what they think about them, or to track the progress of an advertising campaign or some new marketing mix. They may want to know what kinds of media, and which particular media, customers and potential customers watch, listen to or read before they make decisions about marketing communications.

Predictive techniques may be used where marketing managers want to know how consumers are likely to respond to a new product idea or to product modifications, or how well a new advertisement is likely to perform in terms of consumers being able to recall the brand and the theme of the advertising. They may require a prediction of likely sales or share of market that will be achieved by a new or modified product before deciding whether or not to launch it onto the market.

Some of the techniques and applications are fairly standard and well-known among market research executives. Others have been developed by particular market research agencies, often over a number of years, and which in important respects are new or original. These 'proprietary' techniques commonly have a brand name to distinguish them from the procedures used by other agencies. They often have names ending on 'or' like Sensor, Assessor, Conceptor, Locator or ending in 'test' like Microtest, Publitest or Opti-test.

The sections below review the standard approaches to each technique or application. They then illustrate a selection of proprietary tools currently in use. These details should give the reader a better 'feel' for what is actually involved. Many of the branded procedures or systems amount to refinements, developments or combinations of the standard approaches, so these accounts present what are current 'state-of-the-art' applications. Bear in mind that the distinctions between diagnostic and predictive techniques, and between standard and proprietary techniques are often a little blurred. Diagnosis may constitute a preliminary or input to the process of making a prediction, while proprietary techniques are quite often fairly standard, even though their advocates and supporters in the market research companies may claim otherwise. Some systems offered, furthermore, may be a specific combination of diagnostic and predictive, standardised and proprietary elements.

Diagnostic techniques

Before managers can generate ideas for potential marketing initiatives and then decide which ones are likely best to fulfill the objectives of the organization, they will usually need to diagnose the current situation so that they can, for example, estimate how serious or urgent are the problems, issues or opportunities facing them, and what factors may be affecting the situation. A lot of data may already be available or at least gatherable by undertaking desk research. If, however, as is often the case, more information is required, then managers may consider undertaking, or commissioning market research agencies to carry out on their behalf, one or more of a number of primary research techniques or applications designed to acquire that information. The major diagnostic techniques currently in use may be grouped into four broad categories:

- market measurement,
- customer satisfaction research,
- advertising tracking studies,
- media audience measurement.

As is often the case, these categories do not represent watertight compartments (that is, they do not amount to a mutually exclusive and exhaustive set of categories). There are many overlaps, both in terms of the type of data collected, and in terms of the analyses that are performed on them. What activities agencies will actually include under each heading will also vary. However, for the purpose of exposition, it is convenient to treat them separately.

Market measurement

Market measurement is the recording or estimation of market characteristics on a continuous, periodic or occasional basis. Marketing managers are always interested in the detailed anatomy of the markets to which they sell or hope to sell, and in the dynamics of their development. In particular, he or she will want to know:

- the size, composition and structure of the market for the company's brands, how that compares with competitor brands, and whether any changes are taking place,
- the purchasing behaviour associated with the company brands, competitor brands, and any trends in that behaviour,
- product and brand awareness, product usage and attitudes towards the company brands, competitor brands, plus any changes.

The size of a market can be measured in a number of different ways, but key measures are:

- sales,
- brand shares,
- market penetration,
- deliveries.

At first sight it might seem that measuring the level of sales is fairly straightforward. However, sales may be measured either by the volume (in weight or in units – packets, boxes, vehicles and so on), or by value in currency units (£ sterling, Euros or whatever). It may be sales achieved by a complete product category, by a company's own brand or brand variants, or by competitors' brands. Brands often come in different pack sizes, pack types, colours, flavourings, formulations, models, or with a variety of functions, features or associated services. These are generally referred to in the market research industry as 'brand variants', although some manufacturers will call them 'lines', or 'models' or even 'products'. The set of brands that constitutes all the competing products of a similar nature or meeting the same consumer need may be referred to as a 'product category', a 'product field', a 'product class' or a 'product type', like shampoos. Similar product categories may be grouped together into 'market sectors' like toiletries and cosmetics or drinks and beverages.

Sales may be recorded over different periods of time and in relation to different geographical areas. The period of time over which sales are measured may be annual. This may be all that is needed for accounting purposes, but in today's rapidly changing marketing world, sales by the month are rapidly becoming a minimum standard, particularly for fast moving consumer goods, while weekly sales are produced in some cases. Technically, with the introduction of electronic point-of-sale (EPOS) equipment and the barcoding of products, daily measurements are quite possible. However, a daily perusal of sales figures for firms that make hundreds of brands, brand variants and types of product, would involve too much data to digest and act upon. In any event, it is probably unnecessary for products other than those with a very short shelf life.

Although manufacturers will know what their own ex-factory shipments of products are on a regular or even continuous basis, once their transport and distribution systems have offloaded them to the delivery point, they are unlikely to know the progress of the products thereafter. They will not know the levels of stocks held by distributors and wholesalers, what quantities are being delivered to the shops, what stocks are held in the shops and whether these are on display and accessible to customers, what are the levels of sales in the different retail outlets, and what quantities, brands and with what frequencies consumers buy. Still less will they know any of this information for competitor brands. It is in these circumstances that retail panels, consumer panels or regular interval surveys are needed to make estimates of such quantities on a continuous basis.

Market size, as measured by sales, may, in short, refer to the sales achieved by the client brands or brand variants, or to sales in the product field. Sales may be captured at different points in the distribution system, over different periods of time and over different geographical areas. Sales potential is different again and refers to the levels of sales (in all its varieties) that it is estimated could be achieved if there were 100 per cent penetration of the target market.

Trends in the levels of sales are generally treated by manufacturers both as a benchmark against which company performance is measured, and as a basis for setting goals, targets and objectives for the future. However, the absolute level of sales gives little indication of a brand's performance in relation to that of competing brands. Accordingly, market size is also measured by brand share. This is the proportion of total sales in a product category, either by volume or by value (or both) accounted for by a brand over a period of time. Brand share, however, is a measure that has to be treated with caution since in many markets it is not always obvious which other brands fall into the same product category. Furthermore, brand shares may vary from one area of the country to another, and from one market segment to another. Total national brand shares, in short, usually require more detailed analysis.

The main limitation in measuring market size from brand shares is that it is the share of current buyers in the product field. Current buyers, however, may be only a small proportion of potential buyers. In consequence, manufacturers often use a measure of market size which is also a measure of market potential, namely market penetration. This is the number or proportion of individuals or households in specified categories who are considered to be potential buyers who have actually made a purchase of the brand over a period of time in a geographical area, irrespective of the quantities purchased. Market penetration can itself be broken down by any demographic variable or set of variables, for example, the number or proportion of males in the age category 20-24 who are married and who made a purchase of a particular brand in the last four weeks. A low but rising market penetration indicates considerable potential compared with a situation where market penetration is already very high.

The problem with taking sales, brand shares or market penetration as a measure of market size is that they tend to be known only through the expensive process of subscribing to continuous panel research services, and even then they are usually only estimates. Measuring market size by volume or by value of deliveries to retail outlets may be more direct, particularly where EPOS systems are used. Here, the record will be of total quantities, not just estimates. The difficulty here, of course, is that it is the retailer who captures such information, and it may not be readily available to the manufacturer.

The composition of a market is an analysis of who buys a particular brand or product category. It can be described according to a very large number of dimensions. For consumer markets these may include:

■ geographical characteristics like country, area or region,

- demographic characteristics like sex, age, social grade, income, family size, employment status or education,
- geodemographic analyses like ACORN (see pp. 33–4 and p. 52),
- psychographics or the lifestyle characteristics of consumers (see pp. 51–2).

For business and organizational markets, the composition may be in terms of size of organisation, type of organization, regional location, profitability and so on.

Market structure is the complete array of industry characteristics that directly affect the product or service decisions made by the organization and include the number and size distribution of buyers and sellers, the degree of product differentiation, entry barriers, exit conditions and the level of competition. Economists will use these characteristics to distinguish for example between perfect competition, monopolistic competition, oligopoly and monopoly.

The dimensions used to measure purchasing behaviour depend in the first instance on whether consumer or industrial markets are being considered. For consumer markets, the key dimensions are purchase frequency, weight of purchase, repeat purchase, brand loyalty, interpurchasing between brands, source of purchase and nature or occasion of purchase. The purchasing behaviour of retailers will often be recorded in terms of source and quantities of deliveries, ranges stocked, stock levels, shelf-space allocation and merchandizing activity.

Product and brand awareness and the attitudes consumers have of the brands being researched and of competitor brands tend to be very complex and are not amenable to the techniques of consumer and retail panels. Omnibus surveys and market tracking surveys do sometimes cover awareness and attitudes, but not usually in any great depth. There is, however, a species of survey which is dedicated to the in-depth measurement of product awareness, usage and attitude. These are 'usage and attitude' (U&A) studies, but they are not usually carried out on a continuous or even periodic basis. There are conducted on an occasional basis as and when it is felt they are needed.

The main sources of data for market measurement, then, are:

- retail panels,
- consumer panels,
- omnibus surveys,
- market tracking surveys,
- usage and attitude surveys.

The general methodology of panels, omnibus and market tracking surveys was described in Chapter 5. U&A studies are more of an 'application' than a general methodology, and are described below. What follows are detailed examples of each type of service as offered by one of the major market research agencies.

The Nielsen Retail Index

Nielsen was the first market research agency to establish continuous retail tracking operations in the UK, and it is still the largest operator of retail panels in the country. The Nielsen 'Index' is not an index in the statistical sense (that is, ratio of a current value to a past value expressed as a percentage), but rather refers to a range of continuous sales and distribution measurements derived from retail tracking operations. There are currently 10 separate indexes covering:

- grocery,
- health and beauty,
- confectionery,
- home improvements,
- cash and carry outlets,
- sportswear,
- liquor,
- toys,
- tobacco,
- electrical.

These indexes together measure a large number of sales and distribution variables for over 600 different product categories and over 120,000 brands and associated brand variants. Each index has its own sample of shops selling the products to be included, with sample sizes varying from about 450 to over 1300 shops.

All the indexes include shops that are classified into 'multiples', 'co-operatives' and 'independents'. A multiple is a group or organization with 10 or more outlets. Each shop type is then subdivided by turnover range. Sampling of potential shops for the panel is done on the basis of disproportionate stratified sampling (see pp. 132–3). The strata are shop type, turnover range and region. The number of shops selected of each type for each turnover range in each region (a cell) is not directly proportional to the total number of shops in that cell, but is determined by a formula which, while taking that into account, also includes the universe variation in turnover for shops in that cell, plus a factor that measures the cost of auditing that type of shop. The selection of individual shops for recruitment to the panel is done on a judgemental basis that reflects a fair representation of store locations (shopping centre, town centre, out-of-town complex, rural area and so on) and places within the area. For multiples the number of shops in a named group, like Tesco, is kept proportional to the total number in that area.

Sales data for the major multiples (Tesco, Sainsbury, Safeway and Asda) are collected from their EPOS systems. For other types of shop where EPOS data are not available it is necessary to undertake a monthly audit of stocks and, using data on deliveries, deduce what the level of sales must have been since the last audit. This is established by taking stocks at the last audit, adding deliveries and subtracting stock at the end of the audit to give sales. A separate calculation is made for each brand and brand variant. Data on stocks are captured by auditors from Nielsen using hand-held terminals to enter quantities in various locations in the shop.

Most clients subscribe on an annual basis to the appropriate index or indexes that contain the product categories they require. For most indexes they will receive 12 monthly reports in hard copy containing standard tables and charts along with monthly presentations. The tables give sales, deliveries, stock and price data for each brand and brand variant, and this may be broken down by region and shop type. The large multiples give access to their data and to their stores only on the understanding that the data are not presented to

Table 8.1

A Nielsen table

Source: Nielsen

	Consumer sales £ at RSP	Consumer sales volume (tons)	Deliveries (tons)	Retailer stocks (tons)	Days supply
Product class 2	4115.6	1713.9	1704.5	91.9	1.7
Total all items	100.0%	100.0%	100.0%	100.0%	
Brand A	764.1	307.2	305.4	13.0	1.4
Standard	18.6%	17.9%	17.9%	15.1%	
Brand A	710.5	268.4	267.6	13.9	1.6
Extra	17.3%	15.7%	15.7%	15.1%	
Brand A	1474.5	575.6	5733.0	27.8	1.5
Total	35.8%	33.6%	33.6%	30.3%	
Brand B	314.6	127.7	127.1	8.0	1.9
Standard	7.6%	7.5%	7.5%	8.7%	
Brand B	373.3	141.0	140.1	9.0	2.0
Extra	9.1%	8.2%	8.2%	9.8%	
Brand B	687.8	268.7	267.2	17.0	2.0
Total	16.7%	15.7%	15.7%	18.5%	
All other total	1953.2	869.6	864.3	47.1	1.7
	47.4%	50.7%	50.7%	51.3%	

clients by named groups. Accordingly, data, for example for grocery, are available only in categories broken down into 'key accounts', 'total multiples', 'co-operatives' (large and small), and 'independents' (large and small). An illustrative extract from a typical Nielsen table is shown in Table 8.1. This shows a range of measures on sales, deliveries and stocks for brands A and B, which together constitute product class 2. To show trends and changes since the previous period Nielsen uses charts that show sales, purchases (deliveries) and stocks for the current month compared with the previous two months and the same months in the previous year. From these it is possible to understand what has been happening to sales and distribution on a month by month basis. Increasingly, clients receive their data electronically on databases, in support of which Nielsen has developed a range of data management and analysis software. A service it calls Inf*Act Workstation offers a powerful yet flexible personal computer-based decision-support system.

Taylor Nelson AGB's Superpanel

Consumer panels have traditionally relied on diaries or home audits to collect data, but recent panels are based on in-home scanning. Each panel household is equipped with a hand-held laser scanner or light pen for reading the barcodes on the products purchased. This has revolutionized the consumer panels, obviating the need for consumers to fill in diaries. All panellists need do is run the scanner or light pen over the barcode as they unpack their shopping after each shopping trip. The barcode instantly records the country of origin, the manufacturer and the product and product variant. Other information can be keyed in at the same time using the number keys attached to the scanner, including price, source of purchase, date of purchase, promotions, and who made the purchase.

AGB's Superpanel consists of 10,000 households, covering the purchases of some 30,000 individuals aged 5–79, resident in domestic households in mainland Great Britain and the Isle of Wight, and who live in telephone-owning households. Products included cover groceries, fresh foods, frozen foods, meat, poultry, toiletries and cosmetics. In all, data are provided on over 200 markets.

Panel recruitment uses a multi-stage procedure. First, a large sample of households is screened to identify households eligible for the service and with known demographics. For this purpose, Taylor Nelson AGB uses personal home interviews – some 200,000 annually – carried out for its omnibus surveys (RSGB Omnibus and Taylor Nelson's Omnimas, described later in this chapter).

In the second stage, a sub-sample is selected of those households with the relevant target demographics. Targets are based largely on the most recent Establishment Survey carried out for BARB (see television audience measurement below). Third, the housewife (who may be either sex) is contacted by phone. The Superpanel service is described, together with an outline of the personal tasks involved and the incentives offered. The names of those interested are then passed to recruiters who contact the screened homes by phone to make an appointment for a visit. The scanner equipment is demonstrated to all members of the household and the service is explained in detail. If the household is willing to continue, the necessary equipment is installed and a detailed questionnaire is administered. This collects details of shop usage (for unique store identification) and a full set of household and individual demographics.

Data collection is through a personal data terminal equipped with a laser light pen. The terminal is designed to resemble a digital phone and is kept in a modem linked to the domestic power supply and the telephone socket. Data capture is via overnight polling, that is, the central computer at Taylor Nelson AGB dials each panel number in turn (ringing is suppressed) and accesses the stored data in the modem. The terminal has a small screen which is used for prompts and messages. When switched on it asks, 'Shopping trip?' If, 'Yes' is entered then purchaser and shop name are scanned from a code book that identifies each shop with a unique bar-code. The total amount spent is keyed in, each product in then scanned for the bar-code, and price and quantity are keyed in. Details of non bar-coded products are entered by scanning the code book. The terminal software automatically records days of the week and time of day of data entry, length of time taken for the task, the number of purchase records entered, and the number of product codes keyed in rather than scanned due to poor print quality or difficult pack design. This information is used for quality control purposes.

All the data are weighted to population parameters before being grossed up to the population. Reporting is both weekly and four-weekly. The former is confined to data for the country as a whole and is intended as early top-line data. The four-weekly reports contain the kinds of market analyses described earlier under consumer panel research. In addition, some new services have been developed for the use of Superpanel data for promotional analyses and for measuring advertising effectiveness. Thus it offers Brand Monitor, which allows clients to evaluate their promotional and competitive performance on a continuous basis, to identify payback from individual promotions, where to invest further promotional expenditure, and how to develop promotional strategies.

A Deal/Real analysis provides measures of the extent to which consumers of a particular product category buy brands only when they are price-promoted and classifies them as 'deal' or 'real' loyal. TVSPAN provides single source data (that is, data on both media use and product purchasing from the same individuals or households) by installing TV set meters into 750 Superpanel homes in the Meridian Broadcast region. Purchases of over 320 product fields are identified by brand, quantity bought, price paid, date and location of purchase plus any special offer deals, while the set-meters record minute-by-minute household viewing to all TV channels (including satellite) plus their response to specific advertising spot transmissions. This means that advertisers can test the sales effectiveness of different TV advertising deployments. It can provide television ratings measured against audiences defined by their purchasing behaviour rather than purely demographic information.

Taylor Nelson's Omnimas

Some 2100 adults aged 16 and over are interviewed face-to-face every week on behalf of industry, commerce and government. Sampling is random location sampling, using the Postcode Address File and is based on a master sample of 600 sampling points covering the whole of Great Britain. The sample is stratified, within the Registrar General's Standard Regions, in descending order by the percentage in socioeconomic groups I and II using census data.

The interviewer will have a minimum of 13 interviews to do a week. The only quota set is that the interviewer should obtain either six men and seven women or vice versa. So, there is a control on sex, but everything else depends on the randomness of the sample. Up to four attempted contacts per respondent are made. Interviews are computer assisted.

The Omnimas questionnaire is divided into three sections: a continuous section that includes questions that are asked on every survey and are inserted on behalf of a particular client; an ad hoc section of questions that are included on a one-off basis; a classification section that contains all the demographic questions.

Omnimas does not allow questions on some topics for example on home security (e.g. 'Do you have a burglar alarm in your home?). The usual length of the questionnaire is limited to an average of 25 minutes completion time. It takes an average of 20–30 seconds to administer an average question, so the total number of questions will be not more than 60–70. Occasionally, one client may buy up all the space remaining after the demographic and continuous questions have been accounted for. The usual number of questions clients take is about 6–10.

Most questions will be set-choice, but some clients require open-ended questions and they will be charge up to double the amount per question. If clients require help in framing questions, then this is included in the price. Clients can have breakdowns of each question inserted by any of the demographics, up to 30 cells (e.g. a 6×5 table). The demographics include:

- sex, age and social class,
- marital and working status,
- household size and composition,
- telephone and car ownership,
- region (either Registrar General's or ITV),

■   household tenure.

Pre-coded questions cost between £100 and £800 depending on penetration. Open-ended questions cost between £300 and £1800, again depending on penetration. Optional extras include charts, mini-reports, brand mapping, cluster analysis or analysis by ACORN geodemographics. The figures in the tables are grossed up volume figures, and weights are applied. There is a 72 cell matrix – age within sex within region – that is used to weight responses in each cell. Standard errors are not usually provided, but will be offered at no extra cost if asked for.

Questions need to be with Omnimas two days before the survey begins. Topline results are available two days after completion of fieldwork. As an adjunct to the main service Omnimas maintains a database of previous respondents who have indicated their willingness to participate in further research. This can be used to greatly reduce the cost and time-scale of undertaking ad hoc research among particular minority groups in the population. Omnimas, as explained above, also provides a screened sample of households that may be approached for recruitment to the Taylor Nelson AGB's Superpanel.

BMRB's Target Group Index
In 1969 the British Market Research Bureau (BMRB) launched its Target Group Index (the TGI). This is a regular interval survey that is also 'single-source', that is, it covers both product usage data and data on media exposure. Its purpose is to increase the efficiency of marketing operations by identifying and describing target groups of consumers and their exposure to the media – newspaper and magazine reading, television viewing, and the extent to which they see or hear other media. Being single source means that it is possible to identify on an individual by individual basis both what products they use and what media they are exposed to. Respondents are questioned about:

■   their use of 500 different products covering 4000 brands,
■   their readership of over 180 magazines and newspapers,
■   going to the cinema,
■   the ITV channels they watch,
■   the radio stations they listen to,
■   their exposure to outdoor advertising,
■   their lifestyles based on nearly 200 attitude questions.

The TGI questionnaire is self-completed, but left personally by an interviewer who collects basic demographic data at the same time. This gives some information on the people who refuse or who do not return the questionnaire. The major product fields covered are foods, household goods, medicaments, toiletries and cosmetics, drink, confectionery, tobacco, motoring, clothing, leisure, holidays, financial services and consumer durables. Respondents are asked about product and service usage, ownership or participation – not about purchases made or prices paid. In the case of branded product fields, questions on frequency or weight of use are asked, along with questions on the brands used most often, plus others used in the last six months. For food and household products, it is the family use of the product that is recorded; otherwise it is personal use.

The press media questions are designed to collect responses similar to those obtained by the National Readership Survey and show average issue reader-ship (which is explained below). Television questions ask about day-by-day viewing 'on the average' for that day in 15-minute blocks before 9.30 am and half-hour blocks thereafter. Each channel is covered separately.

The lifestyle questions are in the form of Likert-type attitude statements with which people are asked to agree or disagree on a five-point scale from 'definitely agree' to 'definitely disagree'. The statements cover the main areas of food, drink, shopping, diet/health, personal appearance, DIY, holidays, finance, travel, media, luxury/British goods, motivation/self-perception, plus questions on some specific products and attitudes to sponsorship. Demo-graphics include age, sex, social grade, region, household income, terminal education age, working status, home ownership, household size and marital status.

The current questionnaire runs to 85 pages and takes an average of four hours to complete. The questionnaire is totally pre-coded and adapted for optical mark reading – respondents indicate their replies by marking appro-priate boxes with a pencil. The answers are then read electronically using infra-red sensors. There are three versions of the questionnaire: for men, for housewives and for other women. At the time of placing the questionnaire a financial incentive is provided by BMRB.

Recruitment for the TGI is on the back of BMRB's weekly omnibus survey (which it calls 'Access'). This samples 2000 adults every week, selected on the basis of random location sampling. All interviews are face-to-face. Approxi-mately half of the interviews are selected, on a representative basis, for attempted TGI questionnaire placement. Of these, 12 per cent usually refuse to take the TGI questionnaire, 14 per cent accept, but do not return it, and 12 per cent are rejected by the TGI control unit as unusable due to incomplete data. This results in over 60 per cent response and some 25,000 completed questionnaires during the year. A sub-sample of 1100 male housewives is incorporated. These are men living in all-male households or men living on their own.

Data from the questionnaires are weighted in two stages (see pp. 189–92 for an explanation of weighting):

1 Demographic cell weighting, taking age within region, and social class within region for men and for women who are not housewives. For housewives, weightings are applied for working status and presence of children, again by region.
2 In order to remove the small differences in the estimates of readership levels that would otherwise exist between the TGI and the National Readership Survey, a specially designed rim-weighting system has been developed.

Combined weights of up to 19.9 are used. The figures are then grossed up to the population.

The tables of product usage (see Table 8.2) give four measures or indices of product usage:

■ the total number of product users in each demographic category,
■ the percent down, which gives the percentage in each demographic category,

- the percent across, giving penetration for demographic items and composition for media items,
- an index of selectivity, taking penetration (or composition) in comparison with the universe as a whole.

Each of these indices is broken down by heavy/medium/light and non-users, and, for product fields and for brands with more than one million claimed users (about 1400 brands), are cross-tabulated against a range of demographic variables including sex, age, social class, area (standard and ITV region), and number of children, plus media usage and other selected variables.

Thus in Table 8.2 there are 10,781,000 users of vodka (an estimate derived from people in the sample who had indicated 'Yes' when asked if they ever drink it, and grossed up to the population figure), of whom 5,398,000 or 50.1 per cent are men. The users account for 24 per cent of all adults. Users who are male account for 25 per cent of all males, while adults aged 15–24, for example, were 60 per cent above the average for all adult users (i.e. 38.5 per cent compared with 24 per cent).

Besides the product field information, there are brand usage tables, listing users of the product group who use the brand exclusively (solus users), those

Table 8.2 A product usage table from the Target Group Index. **Vodka**

	Population '000	All users				Heavy users				Medium users			
		A '000	B % down	C % gross	D index	A '000	B % down	C % gross	D index	A '000	B % down	C % gross	D index
All adults	44871	10781	100.0	24.0	100	1631	100.0	3.6	100	3681	100.0	8.2	100
Men	21583	5398	50.1	25.0	104	819	50.2	3.8	104	1828	49.7	8.5	103
Women	23287	5383	49.9	23.1	96	812	49.8	3.5	96	1853	50.3	8.0	97
15–24	8825	3401	31.5	38.5	160	695	42.6	7.9	217	1393	37.9	15.8	192
25–34	7929	2559	23.7	32.3	134	398	24.4	5.0	138	846	23.0	10.7	130
35–44	7612	1948	18.1	25.6	106	254	15.6	3.3	92	541	14.7	7.1	87
45–54	6032	1312	12.2	21.7	91	155	9.5	2.6	71	411	11.2	6.8	83
55-64	5865	826	7.7	14.1	59	84	5.1	1.4	39	247	6.7	4.2	51
65+	8607	735	6.8	8.5	36	45	2.7	0.5	14	243	6.6	2.8	34
AB	7864	1863	17.3	23.7	99	212	13.0	2.7	74	646	17.5	8.2	100
C1	10162	2540	23.6	25.0	104	390	23.9	3.8	106	889	24.1	8.7	107
C2	12453	3233	30.0	26.0	108	488	29.9	3.9	108	1062	28.8	8.5	104
D	8027	1965	18.2	24.5	102	344	21.1	4.3	118	677	18.4	8.4	103
E	6365	1180	10.9	18.5	77	197	12.1	3.1	85	408	11.1	6.4	78
ABC1	18026	4403	40.8	24.4	102	602	36.9	3.3	92	1535	41.7	8.5	104
C2D	20480	5198	48.2	25.4	106	832	51.0	4.1	112	1739	47.2	8.5	103
ABC1 15–34	6541	2297	21.3	35.1	146	410	25.1	6.3	172	907	24.6	13.9	169
35–54	6173	1426	13.2	23.1	96	148	9.1	2.4	66	427	11.6	6.9	84
55+	5313	679	6.3	12.8	53	44	2.7	0.8	23	201	5.5	3.8	46
C2DE 15–34	10214	3663	34.0	35.9	149	683	41.9	6.7	184	1333	36.2	13.0	159
35–44	7472	1834	17.0	24.5	102	261	16.0	3.5	96	525	14.3	7.0	86
55+	9160	882	8.2	9.6	40	85	5.2	0.9	25	289	7.8	3.2	38

who prefer it, but another brand is also used (most often users), and those who are more casual in their use, that is, have used the brand, but use another brand more often (minor users). This facilitates some measure of brand loyalty.

Demographic tables use demographic groupings as headings and include breakdowns of respondents by savings and investments, ownership of durable items, leisure items, motoring, drinking, smoking, DIY, entertaining and holidays abroad.

In all, 34 volumes are published annually in July and August following the completion of the fieldwork in March. Rolling annual data are available on tape in August and January each year. An introduction to the TGI volumes gives a number of nomograms so that clients can calculate their own confidence intervals based on standard errors at the 95 per cent level, and incorporating a design factor of 1.2 to allow for the effects of clustering and weighting.

The TGI gives measures of market penetration and weight of use rather than estimates of market size or market share. It allows conclusions to be drawn about the levels of penetration to a target group among different demographic and media audience groups, and it is possible to see how these differ from the population as a whole and how they differ from other groups.

Subscribers have on-line access to datasets for which they have subscribed, or they can analyse the data on their own personal computers where they are provided on CD or cartridge. It is possible to do special analyses that cross-tabulate anything by anything or break down the data by geodemographic segmentation (such as ACORN areas) or by any of the lifestyle questions. Cluster analysis is often used on the lifestyle data to group respondents into segments similar in terms of such lifestyles. This facilitates the more creative use of the TGI since these groupings can then be cross-analysed by any of the other variables.

Media owners are constrained to purchase the full set of 34 volumes, but non-media clients can purchase TGI data on a volume-by-volume basis, or they can buy data for a product field, or, indeed, on a brand by brand basis. BMRB has developed a separate youth study which asks about product usage and readership of 6000 youths aged 7–10, 11–14 and 15–19. These are recruited from earlier TGI households who are known to have children. There is also a separate study that asks about radio listening it has to be separate because of all the regional variations in the available stations. The data, however, can be merged into the TGI data (respondents go on to complete a TGI questionnaire). The result is single-source data for local radio stations. TGI data are also fused with data from panelists whose television viewing is monitored by BARB (this process is explained later). The process of data fusion is explained on p. 275. For the over 50 year olds there is a procedure for re-contacting people in this age group who have already completed a TGI questionnaire. They are sent a separate questionnaire asking about products directed at the over 50s. TGI Premier provides information on the top socio-economic strata of households. It is again a separate survey from the TGI with its own sample of 5500 interviews with social Grade A and B adults.

Usage and attitude studies
Usage and attitude (U&A) studies, also sometimes referred to as 'market studies', provide the basic building blocks for marketing activity since they are used largely to provide an in-depth understanding of the market in which a

particular brand is being sold. They describe a market very much from the consumer's point of view and will cover:

- brand or product awareness (including advertising awareness where applicable),
- brand or product choice behaviour, for example, trial, adoption, loyalty and brand repertoires,
- brand or product purchasing – frequency, source, prices paid, and quantities and size/style of pack,
- usage patterns,
- attitudes to or beliefs about the brand(s) or product(s),
- the needs that the brands or products do or do not meet as far as the consumer is concerned.

Many of the variables, for example brand choice behaviour, brand purchasing, and usage patterns, are similar to consumer panel data. However, U&A studies, unlike consumer panels, also collect data on brand and advertising awareness, and on attitudes towards brands or products. Furthermore, a more important distinction is that they are ad hoc, both in the sense that they are not usually continuous, and in the sense that they are normally custom-designed for individual clients rather than syndicated.

In the 1960s and 1970s it was fairly common for U&A studies to be carried out regularly, perhaps quarterly or six-monthly, but nowadays they tend to be on an occasional basis, perhaps once every two or three years, or even less regularly. There are two main reasons for this. First, they are in-depth 'dip-stick' operations that go into great detail to provide an understanding of the marketplace at one point of time. Typically there will be between 1000 and 2000 face-to-face interviews in a single study, with each interview lasting up to an hour. In consequence, they are expensive, typically £60,000 or more at today's prices. Second, because of the development of tracking studies and consumer panel data, they are no longer required to monitor changes in the key market variables. Changes could not, in any case, easily be measured in the depth to which U&A studies go. In short, they are not required so frequently. They nowadays do not even seek to replicate earlier studies because a lot of things will have changed in the marketplace in the meantime.

U&A studies are usually conducted using face-to-face interviews, often over a four-week period. Postal questionnaires may be used, although they tend to have too low a response rate, while the use of the telephone is limited because it is usually necessary to present visual stimuli to respondents. Interviews typically begin by asking about brand awareness, for example, 'Which brands of product X can you think of, have you seen/bought/used/seen advertised?' Usually some timescale is attached – typically a week, but may be 'in the last 24 hours', 'in the last two weeks' or just 'recently'. Such questions are unlikely to be prompted, and will aim for 'top-of-the-mind' reactions. The interviewer may then turn to particular brands – perhaps the brand leader and the brand being researched – to ask about purchasing behaviour.

Attitudes towards brands will usually be measured using five- or seven-point rating scales so that the ratings of different people and different brands can be compared. Such ratings may well, however, be in batteries of statements that go for across the brand comparisons, as illustrated in Figure 8.1. It is important that respondents understand the characteristics they are being asked to rate,

Here is a list of drinks that you might find in off-licences or supermarkets.
I would like to know your impressions of these drinks, even if you have
not actually tried them, Which of these brands do you think:
(*You can mention as many or as few as you like*)

	A	B	C	D
Is an everyday drink?	1	1	1	1
Is for weekend drinking?	2	2	2	2
Is a cut above the average drink?	3	3	3	3
Is dull and uninteresting?	4	4	4	4
Is particularly strong on alcohol?	5	5	5	5
Is appealing to older people?	6	6	6	6

Figure 8.1 An attitude battery of statements for an alcoholic drink.

and that such characteristics comprehensively cover all the key areas likely to differentiate between products or brands. Where different types of product are the focus of interest, it is, in addition, necessary to ensure that the product typologies or groupings are made in terms familiar to consumers. The development of these attributes is, in consequence, usually undertaken using qualitative research – group discussions or depth interviews. The questions themselves may be tested in an omnibus survey.

Consumer needs may be tapped by asking about their 'ideal' product, using either open-ended questions or with product features as prompts. Respondents are also likely to be asked about what factors are or were important in choosing a particular brand. In many U&A studies the opportunity is taken to look at other issues like pricing, packaging, reactions to new product concepts, media use, or product ownership. Standard demographics will normally be collected for both structural and analytic purposes. Increasingly, these will include lifestyle, life-cycle and geodemographic variables.

Samples used in U&A studies will usually be of current users in the product field, and may vary in size from about 500 to 2000 depending on the need for sub-group analysis, regional breakdowns, or segmentation analysis. Well-known brands purchased by many people may require smaller samples than minority brands. Booster samples of consumers most likely to use less well-known brands may well be used. Most sampling is quota since probability samples are likely to be too expensive and take too long to carry out. In some cases the research may be extended to look at non-users or users of products in related fields.

The standard analysis of U&A data will typically take the form of cross-tabulating all the usage and attitude variables against all the demographics. A lot of useful information about the brand being researched and its competitors can be derived from basic tables of this kind. However, to derive the full value from the research, more sophisticated analyses will often be carried out. Thus batteries of attitude statements may be factor analysed to see which sets of statements inter-correlate. The factors thus generated may then be used as inputs to a cluster analysis to generate market segments by revealing groups of respondents who are similar in respect of a number of variables. Many U&A studies include questions on preferences for product characteristics. Provided these are ranked, they may be used as inputs to conjoint analysis that generates a utility score for each characteristic and an overall optimum product formulation. Mapping techniques and sensory evaluation may be used where the research is to act as an input to product positioning. Besides their key role in market segmentation and brand positioning, U&A studies may also be used in the longer-term development of promotional strategies and in the targeting of new products or relaunched modified products.

Research International's CONCEPTOR

A problem with many U&A studies is that they are normally carried out in markets which clients have been addressing for some time and with which they are already familiar. If all you do is ask people about their usage and attitude, the data tend to be uninteresting, and the response is, 'Well, we knew all that!' At the same time, markets are becoming increasingly complex, dynamic and segmented into niche markets. The broad-brush approach of the typical U&A study is becoming less relevant. In consequence, some market research companies have developed more refined techniques. Thus Research International has expanded the U&A study to include not just usage, but usage occasions. People tend to have a repertoire of brands that they use on different occasions, so they are asked about the last occasion they used the product – time of day, type of occasion, who was involved, what it was used with, what other products or brands might have been considered on that occasion. They are then asked in similar detail about the previous occasion. In this way it is often possible to establish particular market niches that brands fill.

This approach Research International has turned into a proprietary technique it calls 'CONCEPTOR'. By looking at needs on particular occasions, and how far they are met by the particular brand or product, CONCEPTOR allows the influence of attitudes and needs on usership to be assessed, and enables gaps or niches in the market to be identified. The interrelationships between aspects of use occasion can then be analysed, for example, both need and substitutes considered may be related to type of occasion, to who was involved, and to attributes of the product. Substitution in particular is sensitive to occasion, for example, a possible substitute for a chocolate bar may on one occasion be another brand of chocolate bar, but on another may be a biscuit, an apple or a yoghurt. Asking about potential occasions for use of new product concepts may be of considerable value for helping to position the new product in the marketplace.

The use of market measurement data

Market measurement information is required by both top company executives and by marketing and sales managers for one or more of a number of key purposes:

- to reduce the risks in or to maximize the opportunities from taking strategic or operational decisions in respect of marketing mix variables,
- to monitor changes and developments in the marketplace as they occur,
- to build up a marketing database that can be used as a resource for a variety of analyses,
- to use as a common currency in negotiations with suppliers, distributors, retailers, business customers, advertising agencies or media owners,
- to act as an input to market segmentation analyses.

A marketing manager will often want to know, for example, whether or not a strategy of maintaining a full range is maximizing the firm's competitive advantage; whether, from past experience, adding new brand variants of a product is likely to cannibalize sales from the other variants or will increase overall total sales; whether a new product is reaching its target far market penetration and repeat purchase rate; whether a price reduction is increasing or decreasing total revenue; or whether the last advertising campaign was successful in raising brand awareness.

A company that knows what is happening in the marketplace as it happens is able to react to these changes immediately. Knowing, for example, that there was a significant increase in the number of shops handling your brand who were out of stock last week or last month will alert the company to distribution problems or lack of production volume, and it can take corrective action before sales are seriously dented.

A marketing database will include all back data from market measurement activities and, very often, a customer database. If, for example, a company is concerned about the level of its prices in the shops in relation to those of its competitors, by using back data it can see what happened to sales or market shares or market penetration when price differentials between its brands and the brands of its main competitors were at varying amounts.

Any manufacturer will want to know its market share and how it has been changing when negotiating with retailers as to whether its brands should be accepted as part of their range, what stocks they should hold, and what shelf space they should give it. By the same token, media owners need market measurement data to make a case for an advertising campaign using their medium. Advertising agencies use such data for clients for media selection, creative input, account planning, and to monitor campaigns.

Market measurement data may be used crucially for market segmentation which is the process of dividing up the target market into sub-groups with the idea of aiming at those sub-groups different or modified marketing mixes designed to maximized marketing opportunities in each. Market segmentation is an alternative to mass marketing or product variety marketing in which the manufacturer offers a range of product variations, but these just offer choice and are not targeted at specific groups.

The role of marketing research in market segmentation is to identify market segments, ascertain their size and structure, and the nature of consumer behaviour and attitudes associated with them. In some cases, this amounts to no more than researching the structure of the total market in a little more detail and separating consumers into those with higher and those with lower probabilities of buying a brand or a product; in others, sophisticated techniques are used to determine those characteristics which, singly or in combination, will result in the optimum or 'best' way of segmenting the market in pursuit of specified marketing objectives.

Sometimes market analyses have as their primary objective this process of segmentation; in other situations, segmentation is a spin-off or secondary objective of research that was designed for other purposes. Thus a client wishing to monitor the marketplace on a continuous basis may subscribe to a consumer panel and receive regular four-weekly reports of sales broken down by a number of demographics. In looking at the reports it may become clear that certain groups of customers have systematically different patterns of buying behaviour from others. This may suggest that a policy of segmentation, or further segmentation, may be worth considering. Market analyses that are more strictly directed at segmentation are more likely to use the more complex and sophisticated segmentation techniques.

Customer satisfaction research

Marketing is often said to be all about producing satisfied customers, yet, curiously, even specialized books on consumer behaviour tend to focus on pre-purchase phases of consumption rather than on postpurchase phenomena. Even then it tends to be facet-oriented – focusing on what it is about a product or service that consumers find satisfying or dissatisfying rather than how or why consumers become satisfied. Sadly, the lack of success of some organizations in producing adequately satisfied customers may have less to do with product and service facets and rather more to do with lack of understanding of how consumers actually form satisfaction judgements (Oliver, 1997).

Satisfaction is the pleasurable fulfilment of a desire, need or appetite. Customer satisfaction is consumption-related fulfilment. Fulfilment itself presumes that a goal exists – that there is something to be filled, so it can be judged only with reference to a standard or an expectation. The pleasurableness of the fulfilment is an essential part of satisfaction. If it is unpleasurable, then dissatisfaction arises.

In short, customer satisfaction relates to post-purchase feelings of pleasure or disappointment. These feelings, furthermore, are multi-dimensional, trans-. action-specific, and refer to reactions to the *last* purchase or *last* service encounter. Over time these feelings will accumulate into *attitudes* concerning service or product quality. Customer satisfaction will tend to be the key driver of repeat purchase following the first purchase. Thereafter, for subsequent purchases, it will be a function of perceived quality plus customer satisfaction from the preceding purchase. Thus whether or not I buy the same brand again will be a function of my overall perception of product quality based on my longer-term experiences of the brand plus what happened on my last purchase, which, if it were unsatisfactory in any way, may not stop me from repeat purchase if my overall experiences have been satisfactory.

The measurement of customer satisfaction

We saw in Chapter 2 that measurement may be direct, indirect or derived, and that derived measurement itself may be achieved through summated rating scales, profiling, ranking, or statistical explanation. All of these have been used to measure customer satisfaction. Satisfaction may be measured directly by asking customers who have just purchased a product or experienced a service how satisfied they are on a three-, five- or seven-point rating scale. Such direct measures may be created either by asking customers to give an overall evaluation, or by asking them about their levels of satisfaction with particular product features or service components. However, knowing, for example, that 70 per cent of its customers say they are either 'satisfied' or 'very satisfied' does not tell the company whether it is doing well or badly or what it needs to do to increase this percentage. Direct measures of this kind offer little by way of diagnostic value. If customers say they are dissatisfied or even very dissatisfied we have no idea about why, or what levels of product performance or service are causing the dissatisfaction.

Indirect measures of customer satisfaction might include the number of products that have been returned as defective or the number of complaints received. When the bus company Stagecoach won the franchise to run South West Trains in 1996, its chairman, Brian Souter, paid a visit to his new business. He was amazed to discover that SWT received 40,000 letters of complaint a year from passengers. Stagecoach, apparently received no such letters. Souter summarized his approach somewhat pithily: 'We judge customer satisfaction by the number of bricks we get through the window.'

A more traditional and commonly-used indicator of satisfaction is customer perception of the performance of a product or service. In some cases, satisfaction is seen as the sum of the performance perceptions for individual features. The problem with this approach is that any attempt to measure the contribution of individual features to overall satisfaction becomes tautological – individual features are being used to predict their summation. In other cases, there *is* an overall score, usually, but not necessarily, measuring satisfaction, which is derived independently of the scores of the individual items. It is then assumed that those features that correlate most strongly with the overall score across consumers are the ones that have the greatest impact on satisfaction.

Performance analysis is helpful up to a point, and it may reveal some interesting findings for firms that are just embarking on customer satisfaction research. However, it does assume that the relationship between performance and satisfaction is linear, that the correlation between the two is near to unity, and that performance is the cause of satisfaction or that certain performances are, at any rate, key drivers of satisfaction. Performance analysis does not help to explain *why* consumers think that the performance of any item is high or low. Consumer psychology mediates the impact of performance observations on satisfaction judgements. *How* is unexplained. Measures of customer satisfaction may be neither direct nor indirect, but derived in a number of different ways, for example by:

■ comparing expectations with perceived performance,
■ developing summated rating scales,
■ undertaking regression analysis,
■ using structural equation modelling,
■ using conjoint analysis.

Comparing expectations with perceived performance is often referred to as the 'disconfirmation' or 'gap' model. Customers are asked about first, what their ideal level of performance or service would be, or what they would expect, then second, what they perceive they are getting. According to this model, feelings of satisfaction or dissatisfaction arise when consumers compare their perceptions of a product or service performance to their expectations. If perceived performance exceeds expectations (a 'positive disconfirmation') then the customer is satisfied; if it falls short (a 'negative disconfirmation') then they are dissatisfied. A model which is popular among academics for looking at perceptions of quality and customer satisfaction in the services area is the SERVQUAL model developed by Parasuraman *et al.* (1988). This is based on a 22-item set of Likert-type questions grouped into five dimensions: tangibles, reliability, responsiveness, assurance and empathy. The instrument is administered twice, first to measure expectations and second to measure perceptions of performance. Analysis of the data may take one or more of three forms:

1   An item-by-item analysis of the difference between performance (P) and expectation(E) on each item ($P1 - E1$, $P2 - E2$, etc.).
2   A dimension-by dimension analysis in which performance for the four or five items in each dimension are averaged and from which is subtracted the averaged expectations for that dimension $(P1 + P2 + P3 + P4/4) - (E1 + E2 + E3 + E4/4)$,
3   A single measure of service quality in which all 22 items are summed and averaged for performance and expectations $(P1 + P2 \ldots + P22/22) - (E1 + E2 \ldots E22/22)$. This is the so-called SERVQUAL gap.

This model has been widely used, but also widely criticized (for a review of such criticisms see Buttle, 1996). Much of the criticism centres on the notion of expectation. Following the first purchase, expectations of future purchases will tend to adjust to previous experiences so that expectations in the longer term become the sum of past perceived performances. Thus it has been suggested (for example, by Cronin and Taylor, 1992) that perceptions of performance alone are as good if not better predictors of, for example, purchase intentions. In consequence, Cronin and Taylor (1992) have proposed their alternative SERVPERF scale which takes the original 22-item SERVQUAL scale covering the five key dimensions, but assesses these just against performance, not in terms of gaps between expectations and performance. The authors concluded from a survey of respondents in the south-eastern United States covering four industries – banking, pest control, dry cleaning and fast food – that SERVPERF was a more appropriate basis for measuring service quality than SERVQUAL.

SERVPERF is, in fact, a summated rating scale. In practice, most market research agencies offering customer satisfaction research tend to favour a measure of satisfaction based solely or largely on performance ratings, often derived from the summation of a sub-set of items. Many agencies then go on to relate such measures to the importance of the features as perceived by customers. Cronin and Taylor (1992) have argued that weighting performance by importance adds little to the prediction of purchase intention. However, the agencies are more likely to combine measures of importance with an evaluation of their perceived importance in a cross-classification like Figure 8.2. It is vital, so they argue, that companies focus their efforts on the more important drivers of satisfaction and not waste them on those that are

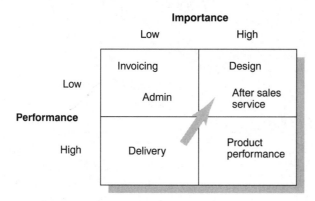

Figure 8.2 Relating performance and importance.

How important is each of these aspects of service?

	Not at all important				Very important
Speed	1	2	3	4	5
Business needs	1	2	3	4	5
Politeness	1	2	3	4	5
Continuity	1	2	3	4	5

Figure 8.3 Measuring importance.

relatively unimportant. Thus in Figure 8.2 customers are highly satisfied with the performance of the company on delivery, but delivery is not seen to be very important. By contrast, design and service are considered to be important, but the company's performance on these is relatively low. Investment in time and resources therefore needs to be moved up and across from delivery to design and service, as shown by the arrow, to improve its performance. Too many resources are probably being devoted to delivery when they should be being used to improve design and service to have the greatest impact on customer satisfaction. Note that if importance had been used simply as a weighting (i.e. P multiplied by I), then design, service and delivery would have received similar moderate scores, and the fact that delivery is high on performance and low on importance rather than vice verse would have been overlooked.

Measures of importance may themselves be direct, indirect or derived. Direct measures ask customers directly how important various aspects of service are from 'Not at all important' to 'Very important' (see Figure 8.3). Such measures are easy and quick to take, but the problem is that people will tend to rate everything as important or very important. What the researcher ends up with is mostly high scores. Usually the items are obtained from qualitative work in the first place, so they are already known to be important

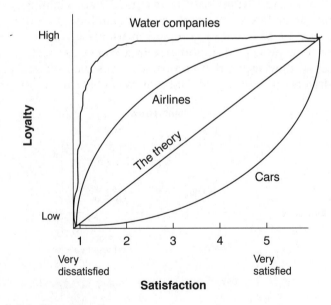

Figure 8.4 Satisfaction and loyalty.

to customers. Indirect measures of importance might include things like the customer's willingness to complain about the features involved. Derived measures will include, for example, the use of conjoint (or 'trade-off') analysis, which establishes importance on the basis of what levels of service customers will trade off against each other.

Oliver (1997) argues that importance is an ambiguous and unreliable concept. First, because it begs the question of importance for what? Second, because importance of individual items is context-specific and will depend, for example, on what features are available from competitors' products. Third, importance often confuses essential with desirable. Having seat-belts in a car is certainly important, but because they are essential, whereas air-conditioning may be important because it is desirable. Fourth, features may be important or unimportant for entirely different reasons. Thus non-smoking policies in restaurants and bars are extremely important to both smokers and non-smokers, but for totally different reasons.

The use of summated rating scales does not require an independent measure of overall satisfaction for their calculation, whereas regression analysis depends on such a measure to assess the contribution each variable or item makes. This means that the 'importance' of each item is generated not from customer perceptions of importance but from the relative contribution each item makes in explaining the variance in overall satisfaction. The problem with such procedures, however, is that they rely on adequate variability in the data. In addition, the top 4 or 5 items may show a relationship with satisfaction scores, but the rest will tend to lack any discrimination. There are also problems of multicolinearity; where variables are highly intercorrelated both partial correlations and slope estimates will be increasingly sensitive to sampling and measurement errors.

Structural equation modelling (SEM) can be traced back to the beginning of the nineteenth century when Spearman developed factor analysis. Later, in 1934, Wright introduced path analysis, but it was not until the 1970s that general SEM techniques became accessible to researchers in the social and behavioural sciences. State-of-the-art computer packages such as LISREL (linear structural relations) and EQS have incorporated many of the traditional techniques like ordinary least squares regression as special cases.

SEM – sometimes called causal modelling – combines path analysis and confirmatory factor analysis into a process that allows the analysis of simultaneous regression equations. It does this by decomposing the direct, indirect and total effects among structurally ordered variables within a specific model. Confirmatory factor analysis is used to test a priori hypothesized, theory-derived structure with collected data. It allows the researcher to cluster observed variables in pre-specified, theory-driven ways, that is, to specify a priori the latent constructs that the observed variables are intended to measure. After estimating the factor loadings (structural coefficients in the regressions of observed on the latent variables) the investigator assesses whether or not the collected data 'fit' the hypothesized factor structure.

Satisfaction and loyalty

Whatever measures of satisfaction are adopted, it must be remembered that they are 'significant' only in relation to comparable measures of the competition. What matters is not, for example, the percentage of customers satisfied or very satisfied, but the extent to which your customers are more satisfied with your products than by your competitor's products. Satisfaction, furthermore, is not necessarily related to loyalty or repeat purchase. The way in which they go together has been shown (e.g. by Jones and Sasser, 1995) to depend on the nature of competition in the industry. In a very competitive industry the difference in terms of loyalty between being completely or 'very' satisfied and just 'satisfied' may be huge (see Figure 8.4). Jones and Sasser (1995) argue that complete and total customer satisfaction is the key to securing customer loyalty and generating superior long-term financial performance. Put another way, any drop from total satisfaction results in a major drop in loyalty. Even in markets with relatively little competition it is important to provide customers with outstanding value. If customers are not totally satisfied they will defect as soon as they are offered a choice. Thus apparently loyal customers will defect as soon as they have exhausted their frequent-flier air-miles programme, or if a market is deregulated. It is the percent of customers in the 'top box' that really counts. The rest, even if they say they are 'satisfied', will readily switch to a competitor.

Dissatisfied customers are probably having problems with the company's core value of its product or service. Often this is a result of shifts in customer need as competitors improve their products or services, as new competitors arrive, or new technologies redefine the game. However, the company has to be sure that it is not just the 'wrong' customers who are dissatisfied, otherwise it may overreact or waste resources. 'Wrong' customers are customers outside the target group and will always be difficult to please. They will continually utilize a disproportionate amount of the company's resources, will undermine the morale of frontline employees, and may disparage the company to other potential customers. Jones and Sasser (1995) argue that the company should actively discourage such custom and make every effort not to attract others like them. They suggest that companies should encourage customers who are 'apostles' or 'loyalists', try to turn switchers into loyalists, and discourage 'misfits' and 'terrorists'.

Approach by the market research agencies

Some agencies offer standardised proprietary techniques while others prefer to tailor their research to individual clients. However, these approaches overlap in the sense that most proprietary techniques are modified to suit individual clients while many of those who do not offer proprietary techniques nevertheless tend to employ standardized components, approaches, or templates.

What follows in an account of the customer satisfaction research offered by three of the leaders in the field: Research International, BMRB and BEM. The first two offer proprietary techniques while BEM does not. The case for both is well argued.

Research International

Research International has developed a proprietary technique for improving customer satisfaction which focuses on levels of service that are provided. The Company calls its technique SMART (Salient Multi-Attribute Research Technique). It identifies which aspects of customer service are the most important, how they impact on a company's brand equity, and how they can contribute towards profits – what is often described as the 'bottom line'. Research

International then gives clients advice on how they can improve their performance and works with them to implement customer satisfaction programmes.

SMART is a micro-model based on conjoint analysis and is a tool for enhancing service, not measuring overall satisfaction. The model discriminates in terms of the attribute importance, it has simulation capabilities and it provides for a needs-based segmentation. It uses semantic scales which are sensitive to attribute performance. These are action-oriented and they can be understood by both staff and customers. Instead of having traditional rating scales of degrees of satisfaction, the semantic scales are behaviourally defined, for example, on the attribute '*Guiding me to the right part of the store*':

- the sales person knows where to find the item and accompanies me to make sure that I find what I need,
- the sales person knows where to find the item and gives me verbal instructions about how to get there,
- the sales person doesn't seem to know where to find them.

These items are derived from qualitative research. Traditional rating scales will often just tell you that most of your customers are satisfied. SMART will tell you what percentages indicate which points of the scale.

SMART is carried out in three phases: qualitative, quantitative and tracking. The purpose of the first is identification, the second, measurement and the third, evaluation. In the qualitative phase SMART identifies various 'moments of truth' (or critical incidents) and the service attributes within each moment. It then generates levels of performance within each attribute. Thus a service experience may consist of:

- order placing,
- receiving delivery,
- invoicing and billing,
- repair and maintenance.

Order placing may, in turn, have several attributes:

- speed of getting through,
- politeness of staff,
- getting through to the right person,
- staff knowledge of the product range,
- continuity of contacts.

Speed of getting through may be identified at four levels:

- answered within 10 seconds,
- answered within 20 seconds,
- takes more than 30 seconds,
- phone is engaged or not answered.

In the quantitative phase perceived performance is measured, for example, by asking 'Which of these statements best describes the service you receive?':

- staff either know or can provide an expert who knows about the entire product range,
- staff have knowledge of the basic products in the range,
- staff lack knowledge of their products.

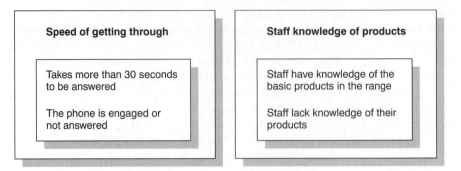

Figure 8.5   Illustration of Research International conjoint analysis.

SMART then determines the relevance of the attributes to the customer by asking, for example: 'How strongly would you feel about each of the following if performance on each aspect were to improve or worsen?':

■ speed of getting through,
■ politeness of staff,
■ getting through to the right person,
■ staff knowledge of their product range.

It is not possible to trade-off every attribute, so the top eight attributes are selected for trade-off. Eight cards, displayed at the lowest level with the next level improvement visible, are then shown to the customer, who is asked which one they would like most to see improved (Figure 8.5). If they would improve speed of getting through, then the next level on that attribute is revealed and the process is repeated. The customer is trading off the attributes one against the other.

The result is the relative importance of each attribute and the relative importance of the levels (see Figure 8.6). The SMART procedure then calculates what proportion clients *could* have achieved in performance that they

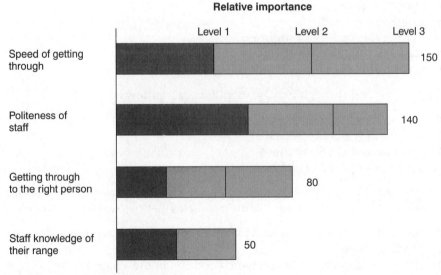

Figure 8.6   Analysis by relative importance.

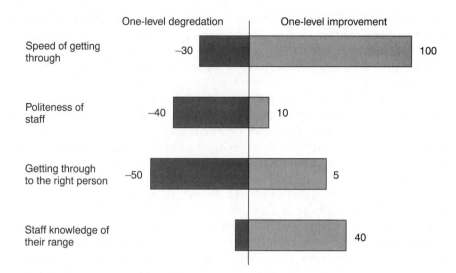

One-level degredation   One-level improvement

Speed of getting through   −30   100

Politeness of staff   −40   10

Getting through to the right person   −50   5

Staff knowledge of their range   40

Figure 8.7 The results of making changes.

actually achieved, weighted by importance. This then tells the client which attribute improvements will produce the biggest improvements in satisfaction. It will also indicate which items will produce the greatest losses if service slips (see Figure 8.7). The results can then be recalculated according to market segment. Attributes may need to vary according to different international markets and different cultures.

In the final tracking phase mystery shopping or survey research may be used. Mystery shopping focuses on hard issues and actual performance. Surveys are better for softer issues, perceived performance and measuring feelings.

BMRB

BMRB has the UK franchise for a particular proprietary technique that was developed by Walker Information in the USA and is now used in nearly 40 different countries. The technique is called CSM (Customer Satisfaction Measurement) Worldwide. Like SMART, there are three phases. In the first phase, exploratory discussions with clients and qualitative research are used to determine client requirements. These requirements are formulated in terms of what actions of customers clients would describe as 'commitment' to the company. Typically this is a combination of getting new customers, customers who are likely to recommend, likely to continue using the company and likely to use other services offered by the company.

In the second phase quantitative research is used to measure what the CSM programme calls relationship outcomes, quality/value perceptions, process evaluations, and performance attributes. These constitute four levels in the CSM process. At level 1, relationship outcomes are derived from the commitment behaviours described in the qualitative phase. These behaviours may be classified, for example, into 'attraction' (getting new customers), 'retention' (keeping customers) and 'enhancement' (for example, recommending to others, using other services offered by the company). These are the relationship outcomes that the client desires. These relationship outcomes, in turn, are driven at level 2 by quality/value perceptions. Thus retention may be driven by perceived value, perceived quality and company image. The various quality/value perceptions are in turn driven by process evaluations at level 3. Thus perceived quality may be a function of ordering, delivery, products and invoicing.

Finally, at level 4 the process evaluations are broken down into performance attributes. Thus products might include performance, reliability and ease of use. Performance attributes are normally evaluated on five-point rating scales. There will be further measurements at levels 1 and 2, for example of propensity to recommend. Image statements with which customers are invited to agree or disagree will include items like 'Uses up to date technology', 'Is easy to do business with', 'Has knowledgeable employees', 'Is proactive'. The LISREL package is used to create structural equation models. The impact of a particular process, for example delivery, might be plotted against performance as in Figure 8.8. The effort needs to go into high impact/low performance items such as 'speed' and 'on time'. An improvement programme can then be developed once the 'key drivers' on delivery have been determined.

In the last phase, recommendations are made, plans are drawn up for company action and deployment activities are agreed.

BEM

BEM is one of the few agencies that specialize entirely in customer service evaluation. It does not offer any proprietary techniques, but claims to offer 'customer relationship research consultancy' that is totally tailor-made for individual clients. However, it has a style of research that usually goes through a number of fairly distinct stages.

The first stage begins with detailed planning for the research – what BEM calls 'alignment'. This involves a critique of the organization – its business objectives, its research objectives and its use of past research. The alignment phase covers what the business goals are, and then tries to put them into 'desired behaviours' – what the client requires from its customers and employees in order to meet those goals. Thus an airline may want loyal customers, which it may, for example, define as using the airline in three out of four journeys, or a producer of software for personal computers wants customers

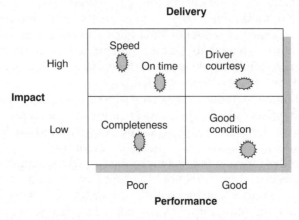

Figure 8.8 Delivery against performance.

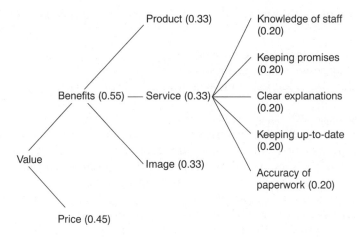

Figure 8.9 Key drivers of satisfaction analysis.

who will recommend them and will register their products and applications. BEM can then design its research around what the organization has to do to get its customers to do the things it wants them to, not just find out what makes them satisfied. Customers might, for example, buy purely on image. Alignment involves a lot of discussion with clients on the whole business, including, for example, employee satisfaction, corporate image and so on. Different customers segments, furthermore, may have different sets of desired behaviours.

In the next phase qualitative research is undertaken to discover what BEM calls key value drivers. Focus groups, depth interviews, critical incident research or projective techniques are used to discover how customers make decisions that cause them to use an organization in a particular way. If the business is not providing value it will loose custom. The qualitative data are then used to build up what BEM calls an intuitive value chain. How customers define their values – benefits and price, or quality and cost – are then evaluated. These are then split down into product, image and services, each of which is then broken down further into its component parts. Thus service may be broken down into knowledge of staff, keeping promises, giving clear explanations, keeping up-to-date and accuracy of paperwork (see Figure 8.9). All this is done with the client.

In the next stage, quantitative research is undertaken to benchmark relative performance. Survey research is undertaken to assess how important the various value drivers are and how well the company is performing on them. A quantitative model using regression techniques is then built up. The model will change as time goes by and as the market changes. The implications of changes can then be calculated.

The final phase is a mixture of research and implementation. There will be a tracking of changes in customer behaviours, a monitoring of changes in the organization, and a decision will be taken on how to take all the data forward in a future strategy.

The focus is very much on the business rather than on the technique. The model is a value-based model rather than a customer satisfaction model. Most of BEM's relationships with its clients are long-term and continuous, not annual or six-monthly. Work is carried out as appropriate and will depend on three things:

- how quickly the market is changing,
- what has happened in the client organization,
- how quickly the client has done something with the data.

Client use of customer satisfaction research

It can be argued that clients using customer satisfaction research go through three stages. In the first stage clients do customer satisfaction research because their competitors are doing it. They are not concerned with what the results do as long as they show the company in a good light. They feel they need a customer satisfaction programme to show that they are customer-oriented. Such organizations will be inclined to see customer satisfaction research as a *cost* which is to be kept to a minimum.

In the second stage clients become more sophisticated, they have some objectives, they are collecting some useful data, but are probably stumbling because they are not sure how to use them. They may be wedded to looking at trends and cannot see how to integrate the customer satisfaction research with business measures. However, rather than seeing customer satisfaction research as a cost, they are inclined to see it as a *budget*.

The most sophisticated group of clients see customer satisfaction research as only one input to the process of developing customer relationships. The key is to look at market perceptions and to understand how customers make decisions about choices of supplier. In this context customer satisfaction research is seen as an *investment* that should have a payoff. Such organizations may be less interested in the techniques deployed and more concerned with the output and how it can be used.

The growing sophistication of clients is something to which all providers of customer satisfaction research need to address themselves. Proprietary techniques themselves are becoming only one input to customer satisfaction research. Clients may otherwise turn to management consultants if agencies do not assist them with being able to make effective use of the data. Some providers of customer satisfaction research focus largely on the service aspects of an organization's offerings to the marketplace; others include the product and its price to the customer and may emphasize the idea of value or perceived value rather than satisfaction as such. Nearly all agencies offering customer satisfaction research cover business customers and private consumers, although, if the research is based on survey research, the structure of the questionnaire may need to be different, for example, business customers may be able to directly compare suppliers whereas private consumers can realistically only be asked for straightforward ratings.

Advertising tracking studies

A key problem with any ad hoc research, even if carried out at regular intervals, is that important features of a trend may be lost. For example, two snapshots or 'dipsticks' of brands A and B taken at time T_1 and time T_2 may well overlook what has been happening to the trend in the meantime, as illustrated in Figure 8.10. Furthermore, such studies will inevitably tend to be timed around the marketing activities of the brand being studied, so it will not

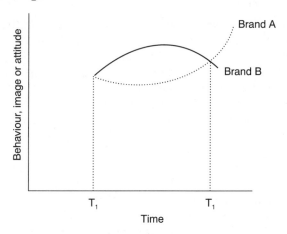

Figure 8.10 Continuous versus ad hoc measurement.

give a clear picture of what competitors are up to since the timings of their activities will be different. It would be easy, but not helpful, inadvertantly to bias advertising evaluation research so that one's own advertising appears in an unrealistically favourable light merely through timing. Furthermore, it would be difficult to know whether any changes out of line with earlier dipsticks were an aberration, or part of a new trend until the next dipstick is taken. In addition, clients are inclined to believe that improved brand measures will remain high rather than slip back to where they started from. A series of dipsticks, provided some are between bursts of advertising, may overcome this to some extent.

Continuous research, by contrast, will reveal trends. Continuous monitoring is particularly important for tracking the impact of advertising over a period of time, and it was largely in the area of advertising that tracking studies have developed. Early campaign evaluations often involved pre-/post-designs that typically took the form of a baseline study carried out before the advertising began followed up by periodic checks once the campaign was under way. A control group, unexposed to the advertising being researched, was often the subject of parallel measurements (Sampson, 1987). The effects of the campaign could then be evaluated by comparing the change over time in the test group with changes that may have occurred anyway in the control group (a before-and-after with control experimental design).

These early studies were thus essentially ad hoc, simplistic in design, and geared to measuring how far the advertising met its objectives. The underlying assumption was that successful advertising would change brand measures regardless of whether the strategy sought to do so. In addition, their timing was always a problem since it would be difficult to determine an optimum point at which to take the post-campaign measurements. Pre-/post-studies are, however, still carried out, for example, because they are cheaper, or because a three-week advertising campaign just before Christmas would be too short for continuous research. The modern tracking study, however, tends to be regarded as synonymous with continuous measurement and planning. It will monitor all the key brands in a product field, usually on a weekly basis, in order to provide the input to improve substantially the understanding of the brand and market being researched. Continuous research overcomes the problem of timing measurements both on the part of the brand being researched and its competitors, and allows trends to be measured both for monitoring purposes and as inputs in making predictions.

What was probably the first modern tracking study in the UK was that carried out by Millward Brown for Cadbury in 1977 (and subsequently continued for 15 years). Cadbury had many advertised brands in the same market and needed to be able to track them all, and to compare their performance with that of their competitors. The tracking study provided an information system for making such comparisons, both across brands and across time. Millward Brown now run over 120 such studies in the UK alone.

The ultimate goal of any advertising is to influence purchasing behaviour and sales. It is often supposed that advertisers can measure advertising effectiveness simply by seeing how many additional sales it generates. Unfortunately, many other factors besides advertising influence purchasing behaviour, for example, availability of the products in the shops, their prominence on the shelves, the use of special offers or coupons, the price, variations in all these for competitor brands – the list is endless. All these will affect product trial, brand choice behaviour and repeat purchasing. For a large established brand the advertising, furthermore, will probably be a relatively minor influence and only needs to produce a very small percentage increase in sales to pay for itself. There has been a lot of interest in trying to model the sales effects of advertising over the longer term. Only relatively recently, however, has it, been possible to do so accurately enough to say that one commercial for a brand is better than another (see Colman and Brown, 1983, for a review).

The majority of advertisers have to be content with determining the probable effectiveness of their advertising by asking people questions. These may be questions about the brand or about the advertising. Brand-related questions will include brand recall (prompted, unprompted, or both) in the product field, respondent images of these brands and attitudes towards them. Questions about the advertising will include respondent recall of the advertisements, the brand they were linked to and the messages conveyed. From the brand questions it is possible to determine whether and to what extent brand awareness increases and attitudes to the brand improve when advertising takes place, and from the advertising questions whether the advertising 'worked' in terms of attracting consumer attention and conveying messages linked memorably to the brand.

Advertising tracking studies always use independent samples rather than panels since it would be inappropriate to ask a panel about their awareness of advertising on a repeated basis. In a typical tracking study there will be independent weekly quota samples of about 100 respondents in the target market for the product field. Typically, 20 or so respondents will be interviewed every weekday, and the interviews each day will be conducted in different geographical locations. The results from any consecutive four weeks are thus nationally representative and comparable with any other consecutive four-week period. Data are normally analysed on a rolling four-weekly basis, so that weeks 1–4 will be cumulated and compared with weeks 2–5, 3–6 and so on. Analysis may be carried out over longer periods, so long as they are multiples of four weeks. So, although the number of interviews in any one week is not large enough to enable weekly analyses, grouping them together in this way still allows weekly comparisons to be made. Since interviewing is normally carried out over 50 weeks in a year (a brief period over Christmas is often left out), over 5000 interviews are carried out annually. This inevitably makes costs quite high, frequently over £100,000 a year – but actually not a lot more than a single one-off U&A (usage and attitude) study.

Most tracking studies are carried out by market research agencies on a client-specific basis, although some are syndicated. The advantage of the former is that the client has total control over the study, particularly the questionnaire. The downside is that such research is more expensive than syndicated research, and it is often difficult to build up a database of all the key brands in the marketplace as a key resource. While syndicated research is cheaper, it is, however, difficult to change any of the key dimensions as you go along in order to meet the changing needs of the company. Some agencies offer both syndicated and client specific tracking research.

The typical tracking study will measure:

- product use in the product field, for example, 'Which of these alcoholic drinks do you drink nowadays?'
- spontaneous awareness of brands, for example, 'What brands of cider can you think of?'
- prompted awareness, for example, 'Which of these brands have you heard of?'
- trial, for example, 'Have you ever tried any of these brands?
- past purchase, for example, 'Which of these brands have you bought recently?
- future purchase intent, for example, 'How likely would you say you are to buy brand X in the next three months?'
- brand images, for example, using attitude batteries like those for U&A studies, but shorter,
- advertising recall, for example, 'Which of these brands of cider have you seen advertised in local newspapers or magazines recently?'
- advertising content recall, for example, 'What can you remember about the last TV ad you saw for brand X?'

Clearly, there is considerable overlap between tracking studies and usage and attitude studies in terms of the information sought from respondents. The key difference lies in the fact that tracking studies are continuous and tend to be used to monitor the effects of marketing activity, especially advertising, on existing brands or recently launched brands. U&A studies tend to be ad hoc and undertaken in pre-launch situations or before proposed changes to the marketing mix are made. Tracking studies are also far less detailed than U&As; an interview will typically last less than 30 minutes.

A key measure used in all advertising tracking studies is advertising awareness, usually based on recall of advertising. There are, however, many different ways of measuring recall, and what characterizes differences between the approaches of different market research agencies to advertising tracking is often the question posed to respondents to measure it. One distinction is between verified or proven recall and claimed recall. The former uses the answers to subsequent questions about the content of the advertising to verify that the respondent did actually recall the correct advertisement and is not confusing it with some other or making false claims. Claimed recall, on the other hand, takes the respondents' claims at face value. It is sometimes argued that the former is misleading since some advertisements are very much easier to describe than others and is in any case biased in favour of long-running advertisements or campaigns. In consequence, claimed recall may be used since this may be a better indicator of the extent to which advertising 'got through' to consumers and associated itself with the brand.

Another distinction is between prompted and unprompted recall. In the former respondents are given a list of brands and asked which of them they have seen advertised, while in the latter they are asked to recall what brands they remember. Millward Brown, the brand leader in market tracking studies and which tracks for 50 of the 100 top UK advertisers, found that very different results are obtained on measures of awareness depending on the question asked. Thus you could ask, 'Have you seen any advertising for brand X on television recently?' or 'What brands have you seen in the last three months?' or 'Have you ever seen a television commercial in which . . .?' Advertising awareness will decay more rapidly between advertising bursts if you ask about advertising seen 'recently', and hardly at all if you ask about advertising 'ever seen'. Millward Brown prefers 'recently' because this relates best to sales effects, and it is possible, if awareness dies away rapidly, to see what happens during the next burst. In addition, advertising awareness accessed through the brand (as in the first question) relates better to other tracking measures than awareness triggered by reference to the advertising. It is important, furthermore, to see how memories or recall of your advertising swings into the brain in association with mention of the brand name.

The proportions mentioning the brand being advertised are usually plotted at four-weekly intervals and compared with the television ratings achieved. These ratings are measured by totalling the percentage of the population watching television each time it goes on air over a week. They are a good measure of exposure to the advertisement and are a better measure than taking the cost of the advertisement, which may vary by time of year, the effectiveness of the advertising agency in buying air time and by target group. How these ratings are measured is explained in the next section on media audience measurement.

Figure 8.11 shows brand X being advertised using two different campaigns over a two-year period. The bottom half of the graph shows the television ratings achieved by each. The top half shows the percentage who recall the

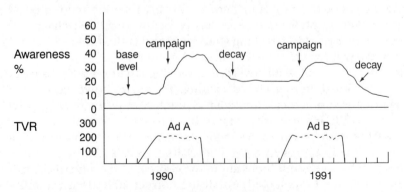

Figure 8.11 Advertising awareness and television exposure.

advertisement using the Millward Brown question. The time scale points are four weeks apart, so there are 13 in a year. Both advertisements were screened more or less continuously over a 24-week period, achieving about 200 rating points. There was a base level of about 10 per cent awareness before advertising began, which will have been influenced by past advertising. The campaign using advertisement A was, clearly, more effective than the campaign using advertisement B. The former raised awareness from about 10 per cent up to nearly 40 per cent. When the advertisement finished, there was a period of decay, but the awareness fell back to only about 20 per cent. Campaign B raised awareness from 20 per cent to 35 per cent, a gain of 15 per cent compared with a gain of 30 per cent for advertisement A.

To compare these gains in advertising awareness directly, however, is to assume that all other things are equal – which they usually are not. The advertising may, for example, be for different lengths of time, achieving different rating points over the campaign. Obtaining a directly comparable measure of advertising effectiveness (in achieving awareness) can be quite complicated.

Millward Brown's Awareness Index

By looking at back data, Millward Brown discovered that, while more advertising results in increased awareness, the amount of the increase associated with a given amount of advertising exposure varies enormously from one advertising campaign to another, depending on how 'good' the advertisement is, the amount of past advertising, and a number of other factors. However, the interesting point is that *within* an advertising campaign, this relationship tends to be remarkably stable; so much so that Millward Brown call it their 'Awareness Index'.

Awareness, as measured by level of recall at any one point of time, is a combination of two factors. First, an underlying base level, which is a residual awareness and is a level to which awareness is assumed to return should the brand not be advertised for a long period. This base changes only slowly over time, and is assumed to be constant over an advertising campaign. Second, there is the short-term awareness which is directly a result of the present advertising. It is this element that the Awareness Index measures and is defined as the increase in television advertising awareness generated per 100 rating points. To calculate this figure it is necessary to know what awareness would have decayed to since the previous week in the absence of the current advertising, and add this to the absolute increase that took place. Awareness, it has been found, decays at a steady rate of 10 per cent per week – in other words, the 'retention factor' is 90 per cent. This makes it possible to calculate decay.

The difference between the decayed and actual awareness is how much is due to the present week's advertising. It is this difference which is related to exposure to work out the extra advertisement awareness per 100 rating points. The calculation is the equivalent to advertising in some theoretical television area which had never been exposed to the advertising for the brand previously. In other words, a comparison is being made between commercials on how they would perform if put on an equal footing. The Awareness Index is thus a pure measure of the efficiency of a given commercial in generating advertising awareness.

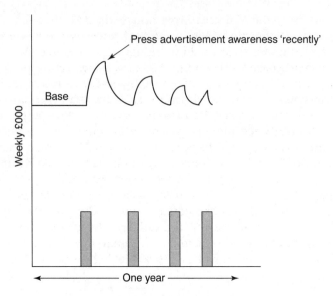

Figure 8.12 Tracking press advertisement awareness.

Tracking advertising awareness for press advertising is in many respects quite different from advertising on television. People tend to get bored with press advertisements over time and stop noticing them. A typical pattern may be as in Figure 8.12. Overall awareness for any one advertisement declines on repeat printing. An Awareness Index for press can measure extra advertisement awareness per £100,000 spent, and this usually declines sharply after the advertisement's first couple of appearances. How much time a reader spends looking at a press ad is up to the reader. People may read or glance at the ad two or three times, but will turn the page once they have 'seen it'. For television this is not the case. A 30-second advertisement is watched for 30 seconds every time it is screened. Furthermore, it will be watched whatever the level of interest in the product itself. When people watch television advertisements repeatedly, they tend to 'home in' on the bits they enjoy watching rather than take in more detail. In short, whereas for press advertisements it is necessary to creatively grab attention, for television attention is assured. But what people remember is what they enjoy, and creativity is needed to link that enjoyment to the brand being advertised.

Advertising tracking is basically diagnostic and retrospective. It cannot be used directly to make a quantified prediction of trial, repeat behaviour, purchase cycles and so on. However, by giving an overall diagnosis of how well an advertising campaign went, the results can feed into the planning of future campaigns. If the advertising has a good Awareness Index and appears to be conveying the right messages, it is doing as well as it can in the circumstances. If a brand is in terminal decline then no amount of effective advertising will do more than prop it up temporarily. It would be wrong in these circumstances to 'blame' poor advertising for not producing better results.

BJM's stochastic reaction monitors

Modern tracking studies, ideally, should be used as strategic planning tools. A total market perspective should be fully integrated into planning and setting performance goals for the future, rather than being restricted to retrospective monitoring. One system that explicitly integrates diagnosis, evaluation, tracking and the planning of marketing strategy has been developed by BJM Research and Consultancy. Called 'Stochastic Reaction Monitors', its objective is to act as a marketing tool that provides fast, continuous, quantified feedback on the cost-efficiency of all marketing activity related to a brand. It is a system for tracking and evaluating the success of marketing strategies in the marketplace relating to brand positioning, advertising and trade activity. The first step is an evaluation of current strategies for branding, advertising, and below-the-line and trading activity. This is then followed by data collection from weekly independent samples of respondents interviewed in-home covering:

- communication,
- behaviour,
- attitude,
- image.

The usual brand questions, 'What brands of product X have you seen advertised recently?' or the prompted, 'Which of these brands have you seen advertised?', according to BJM, tend to confuse advertising awareness with brand saliency. Advertising awareness has more to do with what messages are being communicated by the advertising than with what brand names can be remembered. Consequently, BJM ask respondents simply to describe in words the advertising they have seen in a particular market sector, for example, 'Describe to me the advertising you have see on . . .', and 'What else do you remember?'. They are then asked what brands the advertising was for, and what the advertising was trying to tell them apart from getting them to buy or use the product. This process may be repeated two or three times, for example, 'Now tell me about the next advertising you remember'.

The result is that it is possible to disentangle true awareness of the advertising from whether or not the product is adequately branded. The percentage of respondents who recall and articulate various messages divided by the percentage who correctly name the brand gives an index of the adequacy of the branding. This describes the effectiveness of the communication, which is the extent to which brand-linked messages are being conveyed to target markets. Data on what messages are linked to the brand will reveal how the brand is currently positioned.

On behaviour, the Stochastic Reaction Monitor takes the share of the brand as a proportion of all the brands purchased in the product field on the last occasion. This is a derived measure of market share, not an observed one. However, it does relate reasonably well to data on actual brand shares from consumer panels (where these are available), and does provide a measure of change, even if the absolute level is not totally accurate. Respondents are also asked about the brand itself – whether the last purchase was the first time they had bought it, or had they bought it previously? This gives a measure of trial and repeat purchase. Analysis of these data facilitates answers to questions about market penetration, the effect of marketing activity on trial and brand loyalty, the effects of competitor activity, the impact of advertising on trial, and the impact of attitude change on loyalty.

Attitudes are measured on a seven-point scale of disposition to buy, as illustrated in Figure 8.13. This combines both positive and negative dispositions

1	Those who insist on buying brand X above all others	INSISTORS
2	Those who prefer to buy brand X amongst others	PREFERERS
3	Those who are interested in buying brand X	INTEND
4	Those who would buy brand X under certain circmstances	ACCEPTORS
5	Those who have heard of brand X, but don't know much about it	NO OPINION
6	Those who have never heard of brand X	UNAWARE
7	Those who would never buy brand X	REJECTORS

Figure 8.13   Attitude scaling for BJM's Stochastic Reaction Monitors.

to buy with lack of knowledge or awareness. The objective of marketing activity is to push the brand upwards. For a new brand the aim will be to push awareness into willingness to try it. The share of positive attitudes (1 and 2) is what BJM call the 'stochastic share', which may be calculated for all key brands. It is in a way the share of the consumer's mind which is the result of all marketing activity to date.

Stochastic share is then compared with the actual share to see whether the brand is achieving its potential. If, for example, the short-term share is above the stochastic share, it is a measure of the short-term vulnerability of that brand; it will probably fall or be artificially maintained by marketing activity.

Image is measured with a series of attribute positioning statements supplied by the client or its advertising agency about what the advertising is trying to do and what the communication activity is trying to say about the brand. These are then given to respondents to indicate how important each if these is to them. The analysis will expose discrepancies between actual brand profile and advertising, as well as identifying a brand's strengths and weaknesses and what are the important attributes.

The essence of the system is to infer relationships, not by using a statistical 'black box', but trying to understand patterns of cause and effect. Problems tend to emerge as the analysis proceeds, and the discussion in the presentation of the findings is frequently about the development of future marketing strategy, as well as about the short-term tactical brand issues.

Media audience measurement

In deciding which type of medium to use to communicate with consumers in chosen markets, and in selecting which particular channels, stations, newspapers or magazines will be most effective, it is essential to know what media individuals and households in the target market use, how much they use them, when they use them and how they use them. The purpose of media measurement is to provide both quantitative and qualitative data on media usage by audiences and readers.

The 'media' include all means of communication with large numbers of people in an impersonal manner. The so-called 'mass' media may reach millions of individuals and households in the process, while specialized media, for example, minority magazines and radio programmes, may have relatively small audiences. The concept of an 'audience' is common to all the media, which include:

- the broadcast media – television and radio,
- the print media – newspapers, magazines and books,
- outdoor media – posters, billboards, on buses, on the underground and so on,
- film and video – cinema and video shops.

Manufacturers and other types of organization are normally interested, for marketing communication purposes, only in those media that carry advertising, or allow sponsorship of programmes or printed material. In the UK, this excludes the outputs of the BBC, but very little else, except perhaps books. UK advertisers spend over £3,000 million on advertising on television, in newspapers and magazines and on the radio. It is not surprising, therefore, that the advertising industry (which includes the advertisers, the advertising agencies and the media owners) finances carefully designed and expensive research into the viewing, listening and reading habits of the population.

Detailed information about audience size and structure, and about audience use of and attitudes towards the advertising media and their offerings is required by:

- programme makers, broadcast schedulers, and newspaper and magazine editors who are planning the development of their media,
- media owners selling to manufacturers and other organizations providing opportunities to communicate with an audience through advertising and sponsorship,
- buyers of such opportunities – the advertisers whether in manufacturing, commerce or non-profit-making organizations,
- advertising agencies and market research agencies.

The techniques used for the measurement of particular media audiences is a vast topic which really deserves a book to itself (see Kent, 1994). However, what follows is a brief overview of he current techniques used to measure the size, composition, behaviour and perceptions of audiences to television, radio, newspapers and magazines.

Television audience measurement

It was only with the development of commercial television channels – those supported by advertising revenue – that the demand emerged for detailed and precise information on the audiences achieved. The UK was the first to introduce commercial television in Europe (ITV) in 1955. Other large European countries did not follow until the 1980s (Gane, 1994). The technical characteristics of television lend themselves to the use of electronic meters, which were introduced in the UK in 1956. In France, Germany and the Netherlands, meters were installed in panel households somewhat later, but in advance of commercial television and at the behest of governments. Consequently, their development has tended to be controlled by official organizations.

The original 'set meters' recorded only the status of the set (on or off) and the channel selected. The viewing of individuals was determined separately through self-completion diaries. However, as more and more channels became available and as increasing numbers of households had more than one set – and perhaps a video-recorder – so the demands on meters grew rapidly. AGB, a UK market research agency, was the first to develop a 'peoplemeter' which not only recorded who was viewing, but also allowed for the retrieval of data via the telephone. These were installed in panel homes in the UK and Italy in 1984 and in Ireland in 1985.

By the early 1990s, fully operational peoplemeters were in place throughout Europe (Gane, 1994). There are, however, still considerable differences in the ways the meters are used, for example, whether or not to include people who are on holiday, and whether 'viewing' means present in the room with a television set switched on, present in the room and able to watch, or actually watching. Attempts are being made to harmonize techniques across Europe, but progress is slow.

In the UK a committee was set up in 1957 to represent the interests of both the advertisers and the ITV companies and to award a contract to a market research agency to measure television audiences. This was the Joint Industry Committee for Television Advertising Research (JICTAR). The BBC had its own system, but a joint system was established in 1981. This involved setting up a company jointly owned by the BBC and the ITCA called the Broadcasters' Audience Research Broad (BARB). AGB held the contract to supply the quantitative audience measurement service exclusively until 1991, when BARB split the contract between two research contractors. Television audience measurement depends on peoplemeters being installed in panel homes that are representative of the country as a whole. Panel recruitment and quality control was passed over to a company established for the purpose by RSL and Millward Brown called RSMB. This company was to be responsible for the design and execution of an Establishment Survey, the sample design for the main panel, the design and maintenance of the panel control scheme, the recruitment of panel households, the maintenance of details about panel households, panel household incentive schemes, and the design of weighting procedures. AGB (now Taylor Nelson AGB) was to supply and connect metering equipment, the nightly telephone polling of panel households, data processing and the publication of data to subscribers.

Establishment surveys establish and track reception and viewing characteristics of television viewing households in the 17 ITV regions into which the UK is divided. The information is then used to design, monitor and control the composition of the main panel in each region, and to provide a pre-screened address bank from which homes may be recruited when they are required to meet control targets in their area. Until 1990 the Establishment Survey was carried out once a year over a four-week period on a random sample of about 20,000 households. It was then increased to over 40,000 households and carried out on a continuous basis. The increase was needed because the new panel from 1991 was enlarged to take account of audience fragmentation and the considerable expansion in viewing possibilities. Accordingly, a bigger file of potential households was required.

The Establishment Survey is selected as an annual sample which is then divided into 12 monthly replicates. The design allows for monthly network reporting and for full regional reporting every quarter. The size and geographical structure of each annual Establishment Survey is determined primarily by panel recruitment requirements. Currently, the full annual sample is 43,000 households. Regionally, sample sizes vary from 8000 in London down to a minimum of 1000 (except in the Channel Islands which has a sample of 384).

Households are selected from the postcode address file using systematic sampling within selected enumeration districts. Interviewers try to interview the housewife at all the selected addresses, making at least three callbacks at different times of the day. The average response rate is 75 per cent. The interview covers four different sections.

- Television and related equipment owned or rented by the household, for example, the number of television sets, whether colour, teletext, remote control, video cassette recorder, plus satellite or cable television decoders.
- Reception – what channels can be received. Which actual ITV transmitters the household can receive is established by where it is located. This is important for defining the geographical areas reached by each transmitter and delimits overlap areas served by more than one.
- Viewing characteristics – this is crucial for establishing whether household members are heavy, medium or light viewers. It is based on the number of hours the respondent (who is usually the housewife) says each set in the household is used, and whether for BBC or ITV.
- Household demographics including family size, presence of children, their ages, socio-economic status of head of household and so on.

Information from the Establishment Survey is combined with basic population demographics from the Office of National Statistics (ONS) to produce universe size estimates for panel control purposes and to weight survey results.

The main panel consists of some 4700 households. With an average of 2.56 individuals per household, the sample size of individuals is over 12,000. These individuals aged from 4 upwards are the basis for reporting viewing.

The panel in each region is balanced by size of household, presence of children, age of housewife, presence of working adults, and socio-economic status and educational status of the head of household. These together create a structure that represents stages of the life-cycle, for example, 'pre-family/one-person/ABC1/late terminal education age households', 'pre-family/two-person/ABC1/early TEA households' and so on. There are 24 groups in all. Each combination of characteristics is then checked and held in balance for average weight of television viewing.

The development of television set meters was described in Chapter 3 (under electronic recording devices). The current peoplemeter, which is placed in every panel home, is the AGB 4900 model. This records viewing on a second-by-second basis and has the ability to record up to 255 channels as well as the use of the VCR for time-shift viewing. It can track the viewing habits of eight members of any one household, plus up to seven guests. Demographic data on age and sex of the guests are entered via the handset, following prompts on the display screen on the peoplemeter. Viewers are prompted to check that the correct buttons are pressed every 15 minutes while they view in order to maximise the accuracy of the information being recorded.

The main currency for the measurement of television audiences is the 'rating'. The rating for a television programme is the size of its audience expressed as a percentage of the relevant population size. Thus the adult rating for Coronation Street in the Midlands ITV area is the proportion of all adults in that area who watched a particular episode. The 'relevant' population is those adults living in private households capable of viewing the appropriate station. Audience sizes vary throughout the duration of a programme and is measured for each individual minute. The minute-by-minute ratings are then averaged over the whole of the programme. A rating of, say, 37 per cent would be typical for such a favourite programme. Some advertisers will call this 37 'rating points'. Others abbreviate 'television rating' to TVR, especially for tables (see Sharot, 1994).

Ratings are also calculated for advertisements by taking the minute in which the advertisement begins. Advertisers and their agencies then add these ratings over all the 'spots' (showings) for a given advertising campaign. The total is called either the total TVR or the Gross Rating Points (GRP). The figures will, of course, no longer be a true percentage since it can exceed 100, but it is taken as a measure of the 'weight' of the advertising campaign. If the audience sizes themselves rather than the ratings are added together, it measures total 'impacts' for the campaign, reflecting the actual sizes of the audience rather than the proportion of the total potential watching. Impacts are often the basis for charging differential rates for advertising air-time according to region.

Ratings are used by broadcasters, advertisers, advertising agencies and media specialists. Broadcasters need to know what proportion of the population watch each of their programmes, and the regional and demographic characteristics of each audience. Not all programmes are expected to achieve large ratings, but there is a target depending on the type of programme and its place in the schedule. Commercial broadcasters also need spot ratings (for each commercial) and break ratings (for each commercial break) as a guide for selling air-time to advertisers. Highly rated spots (with large audiences) command a higher price and the broadcaster issues a rate-card giving the price of each spot.

Advertisers need reassurance that their advertising budgets are being spent effectively, so they require information on the size, frequency of exposure and demographic profile of the audience to their advertisements. Equally important is information on the cost per 1000 viewers.

Access to the audience measurement data is largely electronic, although there is a basic weekly report of the viewing figures. Audiences are calculated on a 15-minute programme and 60-second advertising 'spot' basis. Some of the data are available daily (the so-called 'overnight' ratings) and others only weekly. Data processing bureaux can provide on-line access or print hard copy following customized client requests. Data can also be accessed directly on floppy disc, tape, or CD ROM so that companies can analyse the data for themselves.

The UK has what is probably the most sophisticated and accurate gauge of a nation's viewing habits in the world. However, advertising agencies have had to learn new skills in accessing the data in electronic form and in coping with more complicated data. With the rapidly developing use of VCR to time-shift viewing, viewing behaviour is becoming more complex, so there are more ways of measuring ratings. Thus 'consolidated' ratings consist of ratings achieved at the time of the broadcast plus any ratings accrued to the same programme if it has been recorded on a VCR and played back within a seven-day period. This may sound simple, but the combination and permutation of live and playback ratings with household and guest viewing, adult and child ratings, people viewing only fragments of a playback or zipping chunks of it, or viewing it on several occasions, will facilitate vastly more complex analyses when users require them. However, while advertising agencies have full access to the figures, BARB publishes only the consolidated figures in its press releases. While this attempt to establish the consolidated figures as the main currency for buying commercials gives a bonus to the independent television companies since they will be able to charge for the additional playback audiences, the public will no longer know who switches on to see a particular programme.

The current BARB contract for television audience measurement runs out in July 1998. The new contract may well be split again between Taylor Nelson AGB and RSMB since the former has the experience of operating the people-meters while RSMB has developed the Establishment Survey into a refined instrument. What is clear, however, is that the existing peoplemeter system cannot cope with digital compression, video-on-demand, or interactive television. A new meter that measures *what* is being watched on screen is being developed by AGB Television. Passive sensing may no longer be relevant if the issue is identifying what is being viewed rather than simply improving the identification of the individual viewer. Certainly, digital paid-for channels will make different demands on audience research. At the same time, not a lot of use has been made of all the data enhancements, such as time-shift viewing, arising from the 1991 contract. Kirkham (1996) argues that audience fragmentation is causing a progressive decline in the accuracy of current peoplemeter systems. The result is pressure to increase panel sizes. The UK, however, already has one of the largest panels in the world and increasing its size further would not be economic.

By analysing existing viewing data, Taylor Nelson AGB has shown that, for any given time of day, the number of homes viewing varies far more than the demographic composition of the audience, and most of the variation that does occur in audience composition depends on time of day rather than on regional differences. Some 85 per cent of all the variation in category ratings is accounted for by variations in the number of television sets switched on. The existing peoplemeter panel could be more than doubled to, say, 10,000 homes at broadly the same cost by splitting the panels into two component parts, one consisting of about 3000 homes with the current peoplemeters and a much larger panel equipped with only setmeters. These would monitor tuning to all available stations second by second for each television set in the home. Ratings for individuals would be calculated by combining the two sources of data.

A recent development has been the fusion of BARB data with other datasets, for example, TGI data. Thus BARB has a panel of 9000 adults who are on the BARB panel. Each is matched for sex, age, social grade, region, weight of viewing, how many children and whether they have a VCR, against one of 25,000 adults on the TGI. A special algorithm of distance measurements is used that incorporates the weighted importance of 13 variables in all. Each BARB panellist is then described in terms of anything that is available on the TGI, for example by brand and product use.

Qualitative assessment and the evaluation of television programmes was for many years undertaken by the BBC's Audience Reaction Service using a Television Opinion Panel (TOP). This has now been taken over by Research

Services Limited (RSL) which maintains a national panel of individuals with an achieved sample size of about 3000 respondents per week on which the 17 ITV regions are represented according to size. In addition, there are regional boost panels, making the achieved sample in each region up to 500 respondents. Members of the regional boost panels complete a diary once every four weeks and each region participates on a four-weekly cycle. National panels members, of which there are 4600, are contacted weekly and, with a response rate of about 65 per cent, gives the achieved sample of 3000. If people do not respond for two or three weeks they get a letter asking if they wish to continue; otherwise they are dropped. There are 5400 on the regional boost panels.

Panel controls are similar to those for the BARB panel, but weightings are applied to adjust for biases from over- and under-representation of certain groups among those responding. Panellists are given a seven-day booklet which runs from Monday to Sunday and is in three sections:

- a list of all programmes on a day-by-day basis asking respondents to give a score on a six-point scale for each programme seen (see Figure 8.14),
- more detailed questons are asked about selected programmes. Some of these questions are open-ended; others use Likert-type scales,
- questions about series that have just finished, long-running serials or questions of a more general nature.

From the first section an appreciation index (AI) is calculated. This is done by allocating a score out of 100 in each level of response (see Figure 8.14). The AI is the average of all the responses. Most AIs are between 50 and 90, but they are not absolute numbers, rather they facilitate comparisons. These comparisons are made with programmes of a similar type, for example, 'feature films', 'sport', or 'news and current affairs'. Weekly AI reports list each category separately and are broken down by age, sex and social class. The aim is to cover all programmes, but where fewer than 25 responses for a programme have been received, no AI is calculated, and, if less than 50, separate AIs are not calculated for demographic groups.

It has been found that, overall, there is little correlation between AI scores and audience ratings – bigger audiences do not necessarily mean higher appreciation scores and vice versa. However, Barwise *et al.* (1979) argue that if a distinction is made between information and entertainment programmes, then there is a small positive correlation between audience appreciation and size within these types, but that the correlation between the types is negative. Menneer (1987) argues that there is no reason to *expect* a relationship since they measure different things. Audience size for any programme is

		Allocate score
6	Extremely interesting and/or enjoyable	100
5	Very Interesting and/or enjoyable	80
4	Fairly interesting and/or enjoyable	60
3	Neither one thing not the other	40
2	Not very interesting and/or enjoyable	20
1	Not at all interesting and/or enjoyable	0

Figure 8.14 The Audience Appreciation Index.

determined largely by the time of day it is broadcast, and what the competing programmes are, irrespective of the quality of the programme. AIs are a crucial and necessary complement to estimates of audience size in evaluating channel and programme performance. AIs, furthermore, have a useful role in predicting, and later explaining, the audience delivery for a series of programmes.

Radio audience measurement

In many ways the measurement of radio audiences is more complex than for television. First, listeners are not always aware of, or can correctly identify, the station to which they are listening (for television this is automatically recorded by the peoplemeter). Second, radio listening is often casual and undertaken while other activities are being pursued, or it may be used just as background. Although there are problems, as we have seen, over what counts as 'watching' a television, at least presence in the room in which there is a television switched on (and peoplemeter attached) is clearer than the idea of 'presence' when a radio can be heard. Third, listeners tend to be mobile – some 20–35 per cent of listening takes place outside the home, often on radios not owned by or tuned in by the listener. This creates problems either for recall or for diary-keeping. Fourth, radio is a highly fragmented and rapidly expanding service. At present there are over 200 radio stations using the air waves in the UK. This number could expand considerably when digital audio broadcasting begins in 1998. Keeping track of all these developments is more complicated than for television channels, even with satellite television.

Until 1992 the BBC and independent local radio undertook separate radio audience research. In 1992 a new company, Radio Joint Audience Research Ltd (RAJAR), was established to operate a single audience measurement system for the radio industry as a whole. This company is jointly owned by the Commercial Radio Companies Association (CRCA) and the BBC and covers all BBC national and local stations, UK licensed stations and most other commercial radio stations. Detailed discussion takes place and operational decisions are made in a Technical Management Committee. RAJAR research is currently contracted to Research Services Limited (RSL).

While it is, of course, technically feasible to use meters on radio sets, it is far too expensive for the industry to afford. Consequently, it has nearly always been done using either interview survey techniques or self-completed diaries. RAJAR uses a seven-day diary covering Monday to Sunday. Over 165,000 diaries are placed annually in 86,000 households. With an average completion rate of 85 per cent, that gives about 140,000 adults and children who report their radio listening. The diary is in two sections. The first covers media consumption including general radio listening, television viewing and newspaper readership. The second section records actual radio listening (see Figure 3.8 for a demonstration diary page). For any occasion when respondents listen to the radio for five minutes or more, they are asked to record their listening by drawing a line through the appropriate time segment boxes. Respondents are also asked to indicate where they listened – at home, in a car, van or lorry, or at work/elsewhere. The stations that can be received in that area are listed across the top.

All radio stations agree with RAJAR the area that will be covered, usually in terms of Postcode Sectors. Since many of these areas overlap, over 400 segments have been created, each with their own unique listing of stations.

Since each segment has four rotations of station listings (except in areas with few stations), over 1000 different diary lists are needed. This in turn means a complex sample design and a complex printing task. London alone is divided into 11 segments.

The sampling universe is all individuals aged four and over living in private households in the survey area. The sampling procedure is in three stages. First, the adult population of each local or national total survey area (TSA) is divided by the required sample size to produce a sampling interval. Non-overlapping TSAs are created by allocating the overlapping area to whichever TSA has the smallest sampling interval.

In the second stage the number of sampling points is determined. These are based on enumeration districts which are chosen with probability proportionate to population after stratifying in order of distance from the centroid of the non-overlapping TSA. In addition, controls are imposed to represent the ACORN profile of the non-overlapping TSA as a whole.

In the third stage, quotas on age, sex and working status of the Chief Income Earner plus household size, are set for each sampling point based on the household and population profile of the enumeration district. The sampling points are then allocated evenly across all weeks within a quarter.

At each sampling point the interviewer is required to place diaries with all household members aged 4 or more at a total of 10 households. Interviewers are allocated 99 addresses from the Postcode Address File. Every fourth address is designated as forming part of the primary sample. The remaining addresses are used as alternatives if the primary sample is exhausted.

At each household a contact questionnaire is administered to check eligibility. If this is in order and the household is willing to participate, a household questionnaire is used to collect demographic details of all individuals resident in the household plus details of the number of radio sets and car radios owned.

The RAJAR service year runs from September and is divided into quarters for fieldwork and publication of results. The fieldwork is in two elements. A national element is continuous, and quarterly results are published for national BBC and commercial services, BBC national regional services, Greater London and local commercial radio services with an adult population of 4 million or over. All other local services have results published once or twice a year depending on population size. In high quarters which include all stations, the national sample size is over 50,000 individuals. In low quarters it is about 14,000.

All questionnaire and diary data are processed using optical scanning technology and undergo a series of checking procedures. The data are then weighted and grossed up. Pre-weightings are used to correct for geographical distribution and for imbalances according to 'white' and 'non-white' groups, while cell weighting is used to correct the profile for sex, age and social class.

In calculating confidence limits, a design factor of 2.0 is applied for the national adult sample of the RAJAR survey. The results (see Figure 8.15 for a sample page) measure:

■ reach – the unduplicated number of different people listening to any specified service over a period of time expressed as a percentage of the total universe,

QUARTERLY SUMMARY OF RADIO LISTENING						
QUARTER 4/96	23 September - 22 December 1996		*Rajar*			

PART 1 - UNITED KINGDOM
Adults aged 15 and over: population 47,320,000

	Weekly Reach		Average Hours		Total Hours	Share of
	'000	%	per head	per listener	'000	Listening %
ALL RADIO	40197	85	17.2	20.2	813114	100.0
ALL BBC	27103	57	8.5	14.9	403127	49.6
All BBC Network Radio	23773	50	6.9	13.8	327475	40.3
BBC Radio 1	10648	23	2.1	9.5	100974	12.4
BBC Radio 2	8819	19	2.2	11.8	104427	12.8
BBC Radio 3	2581	5	0.2	3.8	9919	1.2
BBC Radio 4	8333	18	1.8	10.4	87051	10.7
BBC Radio 5 Live	4953	10	0.5	5.1	25105	3.1
BBC Local/Regional	8653	18	1.6	8.7	75651	9.3
ALL COMMERCIAL	27885	59	8.3	14.1	392597	48.3
All National Commercial	11423	24	1.7	7.2	82288	10.1
Atlantic 252 *	3621	8	0.5	6.0	21904	2.7
Classic FM	4712	10	0.5	5.5	25849	3.2
Talk Radio 1053/1089 AM	2338	5	0.3	6.5	15213	1.9
Virgin Radio (AM only)	2924	6	0.4	6.6	19322	2.4
All Local Commercial	23099	49	6.6	13.4	310309	38.2
Other Listening	2774	6	0.4	6.3	17390	2.1

Figure 8.15 A sample of RAJAR results.

■ total hours – the overall number of hours of adult listening to a specified service over a specified period of time,

■ average hours – average hours per listener calculated from total hours divided by reach.

Both large and small stations get the same level of detail every six months. Information down to the quarter hour consequently sometimes ends up consisting of pages full of asterisks because the sample sizes are too small to support such detailed analysis. Some radio stations have been unhappy with the research results. One station – GWR – even threatened to sue RAJAR over some figures that were incorrect due to a number of diaries not being delivered. Mistakes do happen in research, but rather than having indemnity clauses, the alternative is for all parties to work together to strive towards excellence to ensure that the research is as good as it can be. Nevertheless, the current £2 million a year RAJAR survey has been accused of being 'unwieldy'. The current contract with RSL is scheduled for replacement in 1999. Demands for more user-friendly data are already being made. The contract is expected to be hotly contested with NOP, Millward Brown and BMRB likely to join RSL as UK bidders along with Arbitron from the US.

The future looks bright for radio, particularly with Digital Audio Broadcasting (DAB) which has the technological potential to revolutionize radio in the same way that CD has transformed the music industry. DAB will offer interference-free reception, CD quality sound, easy to use sets, more services and the possibility of text and data display. The BBC has been broadcasting Radios 1–3, 5 and '5-live' experimentally since September 1995. The first commercially available radio sets should be on sale in the Spring of 1998. There are already 100 million radios in circulation at present in the UK. Replacing these with digital radios will create a lot of business.

In terms of audience appreciation, the BBC had its own Listening Panel until 1992 when it was replaced by the Radio Opinion Monitor (ROM), but it still covers only the BBC's networked programmes. Panel members are recruited from the RAJAR survey. Two panels, each of 2250 listeners, complete diaries once every four weeks. One of the panels is thus active every two weeks. The ROM collects Reaction Indices to each programme based on a 'marks out of ten' evaluation. There are also diagnostic questions that contain in-depth questions about selected programmes or series. The service is currently contracted to RSL.

Newspaper and magazine readership

As in other areas of audience research, the commercial importance of readership research stems from the fact that newspapers and magazines carry advertising and are often dependent – sometimes heavily dependent – on this source of revenue. Budgets for such research run into millions annually. There have been major international symposia on the subject and many specialized seminars; scores of conference papers and journal articles have been written. Yet, for all this activity, experts and consultants around the world continue to debate the merits and drawbacks of alternative approaches and techniques. At the same time, advertisers depend on readership research to determine the allocation of their spend between the many different titles available. Readership estimates have become the currency in which advertising space is traded. The data are also of relevance to editorial and circulation departments.

Measuring readership is quite possibly more difficult than measuring either television viewing or radio listening. Reading can mean anything from a cursory glance to a thorough study. Usually, it means that the reader has 'read' only those sections of interest and skipped or glanced at others.

Most readership research takes a complete issue of a publication as its focus of measurement rather than a section, a page or an advertisement. Personal interviews remain the favoured method of data collection since the number of questions that need to be asked is inevitably very large. In addition it is usually necessary to show visuals of mastheads or logos to help respondents to correctly identify publications. Since readership tends to be highly seasonal and subject to atypical events and circumstances, most readership research will be continuous, while the use of panels tends to be too expensive, so they will often be based on independent samples.

Readerships are usually measured in terms of what is called average issue readership (AIR) – the number of different people who read a single issue, averaged across issues. This measure has attracted some criticism – that it is a very bland measure, or that it seriously inflates estimates. It is based on asking respondents when they last saw a copy of a publication. If they claim to have done so in the last publishing interval, they are added to the AIR. The problem is that if the reader looks at the copy again outside the publishing period, then the reading event may be counted twice. This phenomenon of 'replication' can, according to Shepherd-Smith (1994) seriously inflate the apparent AIR estimate. The AIR estimate assumes that the number of people reading *any* issue of a publication, within a period of time equal in length to the interval between successive issues, provides an unbiased estimate of the number reading any specific issue, averaged over issues and measured across an issue's life. It has been argued (Brown, 1994) that this is true only if it is the *first* time an issue is read, otherwise there will be biases from both replication and parallel reading. The latter arises if somebody sees two or more issues within a publishing period. Under AIR this will count only once and will underestimate the amount of reading. Replication and parallel reading will, argues Brown, thus tend to cancel one another out since they work in opposite directions and the overall model bias is very limited. The matter could be solved by adding another question (to each newspaper or magazine seen) concerning whether it was the first occasion and discounting it if it were not. That, of course, would mean lengthening considerably the existing questionnaire. It would also undermine trend data, while some readerships would go up and some would go down. This could upset some clients, so AIR may well be retained for the next contract.

AIR identifies respondents as either readers or non-readers, but it is also necessary to estimate the frequency of reading. Again, this is very difficult to measure. It is usual to ask respondents about their claimed regularity of reading and to take their answers at face value. But, should we ask about actual past reading behaviour or what people 'usually' do? Should the alternative answers between which respondents must choose be couched in numbers, in verbal terms or in a mixture of the two? An example of a mixture would be: 'About how often do you see *The Economist* these days – frequently (three or four issues out of every four), sometimes (one or two issues out of four) or only occasionally (fewer than one issue out of four)?' There is a tendency, however, for regular readers to overclaim their frequency of reading and for low-frequency readers to underclaim (Brown, 1994). Consequently, it is better, argues Brown (1994), to use the answers only to categorize readers into groups and no more (that is, to restrict the scale to an ordinal one).

Most European countries have regular or continuous readership surveys. In some cases these are organized and administered by an industry body set up to represent the interests of the publishers, the advertisers and their agencies. The UK, Germany, Belgium, the Republic of Ireland, the Netherlands and Switzerland fall into this category. Alternatively, the research may be sponsored by a number of individual companies who may not be representative of the industry as a whole. A third possibility is for a market research agency to propose a readership survey, to be responsible for its design and execution and to sell the data to as many clients as possible. Most countries use the recent reading techniques for estimating average issue readership.

In the UK there is a history of readership research that goes back over 60 years (see Brown, 1994, for details), but the current form of National Readership Survey dates from the early 1940s. In 1968 a Joint Industry Committee for National Readership Surveys (JICNARS) was set up to represent the publishers, the advertisers and the agencies. JICNARS drafted the methodological specification for the NRS and awarded the contract to Research Services Limited (RSL). In 1992 JICNARS was replaced by National Readership Surveys Ltd with a board smaller in size than the earlier Committee.

RSL has, in fact, operated the NRS for nearly 30 years – except for a short break between 1974 and 1976 when it was run by BMRB. The current contract was due to end in 1996, but it has been extended on a rolling 12-month contract until the end of 1999. The NRS is based on some 38,000 interviews a year covering nearly 300 newspapers and magazines. The results give five-day, six-day and Saturday average issue readership for national daily newspapers, and frequency, recency, source of copy and how disappointed data for all publications. It also covers car ownership, holidays, consumer goods, financial arrangements and classification questions.

The universe from which the NRS sample is taken is all adults aged 15 and over resident in private households. The sample is a multi-stage disproportional pre-selected sample design. Social grades A, B and C1 are oversampled using certain ACORN types. The frame for the selection of sampling points is all Enumeration Districts while the frame for the selection of individuals is the Postcode Address File (PAF). Selection of Enumeration districts is made with probability proportionate to size. Within each ED selected, 21 standard and five replacement addresses are selected from the PAF, although there are certain modifications made in some Scottish points. Within each address, one or two persons are selected following specified rules that vary according to the size of the household. The selected sampling points are systematically allocated to month and then start day to ensure a balanced daily interviewing schedule. Interviewers are given seven days to complete a standard assignment, starting on the specified day.

The interview uses Computer Assisted Personal Interviewing (CAPI) to capture readership data. Critical to the measurement of readership are the aids used to prompt respondents. These consist of cards showing a listing of up to six newspaper or magazine titles on the front and on the reverse the same publications shown as 'mastheads' or logos together with the relevant frequency of publication. At the bottom of each card is a scale of reading frequency from 'Almost always. At least three issues out of four' to 'Not in the past12 months'. There are some 50 different cards, each printed in four or eight versions between which the positioning of the titles varies.

The cards are sorted into numerical order and the interviewer says: 'We'd like to find out which newspapers and magazines you've read at all in the last 12 months. It doesn't matter whether it was a copy you'd bought yourself or somebody else's, or how old it was. It counts so long as you've spent at least two minutes reading or looking at any copy in the last 12 months.' The interviewer shows the card pack and says: 'I'd like you to go through these cards for me and if you've read or looked *any* of the publications on a card for two minutes or more in the last 12 months, I'd like you to put it here in the

'Yes' pile. If you're quite sure you've not seen anything on the card in the last 12 months, would you put it here on the 'No' pile.' The respondent then sorts the cards with the front side uppermost. The 'No' cards are then turned over to the mastheads and the respondent is asked to look though these again 'to check whether there are any additional publications you have seen at all for at least two minutes in the last 12 months?' Any cards so identified are then put on the 'Yes' pile. The interviewer then takes all the 'Yes' cards ensuring that they are in numerical order and asks for each publication listed whether or not it has been read in the last 12 months. For each daily title identified the interviewer asks if the respondent read or looked at a copy yesterday, and if not, when they last read or looked at a copy. Respondents are then asked the frequency question, followed by a recency and frequency question for Saturday papers. This procedure is then repeated for each title identified. For regional dailies, weeklies, fortnightlies, monthlies and bi-monthlies, Sundays and colour magazines only the recency and frequency questions are asked. Source of copy and how disappointed is asked of all titles included in an average issue readership claim. The how disappointed question is: 'How disappointed would you be if for whatever reason [title] were not available?' The codes are 'Very disappointed', 'Fairly disappointed' and 'Not at all disappointed'. The interviews on average take 35–40 minutes. Any questions added mean that others may have to be taken out to ensure that the interview does not get any longer.

Following the fieldwork, NRS results are subject to extensive reweighting. Pre-weights are applied to compensate for purposeful departures from allocating an equal probability of selection to each member of the population. These cover unequal sampling factions for respondents within households, the constraint of the number of sampling points per sub-area to be a multiple of 12, and some oversampling in Scotland and in parts of England and Wales. A further stage of weighting corrects for discrepancies between the demographic profile of the achieved sample and that of the population.

In the published reports there are a limited number of types of basic readership data that constantly recur. There are tabulations of readership penetration – average issue readership title by title, shown both in absolute terms and as a percentage of the population. These figures will be further broken down by demographic sub-groups. A second main category comprises the readership profile tables. The data are rearranged so that the total average issue readership of each title becomes the base and the body of the table shows the profile of this total audience across sub-groups of interest. Most survey reports also contain tabular data on reading frequency, so that probabilities of contact with the average issue can be calculated. Finally, there are tables of readership duplication – the proportion of the AIR of publication A who are also in the audience of publication B.

The NRS has sometimes been criticized for not providing enough information on the manner in which different titles are read, so a question was introduced on whether respondents look at particular topics when they are reading newspapers or magazines, for example, 'UK/British news', 'Sport', or 'TV programmes'. This, however, still does not refer to the reading of specific sections in specific issues. Some users are frustrated that the survey does not go beyond 'reading frequency' and 'source of copy' to qualify the average issue readership score. Ideally, users would like to know the numbers and profiles of people exposed to a given advertisement. There is currently nothing on time spent reading, the reading of sections or specific issue readership.

Despite these criticisms the NRS has over the years been seen as the 'gold standard' for survey research, setting the standard not only for readership measurement, but also for demographics. Social grading as defined by the NRS has become the standard for the whole of the UK market research industry. Social grade quota setting and weighting of many surveys is often undertaken with reference to the findings of the NRS.

Predictive techniques

Once the problems of an organization and the circumstances of its competitive environment have been fully diagnosed, managers may wish to generate specific proposals for marketing activity and then predict which ones are likely to be 'best' in terms of fulfilling organizational objectives. They may want to know which ideas for new products are likely to be acceptable to consumers, whether consumers would buy a specific product formulation, whether advertising will convey the right messages linked memorably to the brand, or what sales are likely to result for a new or modified product. There is a wealth of predictive techniques that market research organizations and in-house researchers use, but the remainder of this chapter will focus on just three widely used techniques:

■ testing products and product concepts,
■ advertising pre-testing,
■ volume and brand share prediction.

Testing products and product concepts

Product concept tests
Ideas for product development are evaluated and 'rounded out' using product concept tests. Many companies offer proprietary concept tests, sometimes as part of a wider package which includes product testing and perhaps even with a volume prediction technique bolted on. In product concept testing ideas about potential new products are exposed to a sample of consumers who are then asked questions about them. The exposure may take a number of forms. These were described earlier in the context of stimulus materials for group discussions and included concept boards, storyboards, animatics, narrative tapes and physical mock-ups.

The sample of respondents from the target market should include anybody likely to have any part in influencing a decision to purchase and should not be defined too restrictively. A product developed for a particular market segment, for example, mothers with babies, may be used by other groups. Thus baby shampoo may be used by adults. The test may be administered in a number of different ways and in different types of location. Thus the test could be:

■ in-home by personal call by an interviewer,
■ sent by post with a postal questionnaire,
■ sent by post with a telephone follow-up,

■   in a hall test, van test or test centre.

The concept test may be monadic or comparative. These concepts were explained earlier in the context of experimental research. If there is just one concept to be evaluated, then the test will be monadic. There is a problem here of knowing what counts as a 'good' or a 'bad' result unless comparisons can be made with other concepts similarly tested in the past. Comparative tests may be arranged according to a number of different experimental designs:

■   matched monadic – separate sub-samples are given one concept each and the ratings are compared,
■   paired comparisons – getting respondents to compare concepts by expressing a preference in each combination of pairs of concepts,
■   complete ranking – putting all the concepts in order of preference,
■   trade-off or conjoint analysis in which respondents are asked to choose between all combinations of product attributes,
■   comparison with existing products, for example, against the current brand leader.

The questions that can be addressed to respondents depend very much on the information needs of the marketing manager. It is usually necessary to ask one or more questions about overall acceptability. This may be by way of simple rating questions, for example, 'Overall, would you describe this product as excellent, good, fairly good, poor or very poor?' or by purchase intention, for example, 'How likely are you to buy this product: very likely, fairly likely or unlikely?' Respondents may be asked if they would actually like to buy the product at a given price. Diagnostic questions may follow up particular aspects, for example:

■   understanding the product idea,
■   perceptions of its attributes,
■   its believability (as a possible new product),
■   its perceived advantages and disadvantages,
■   its rating on specific product attributes,
■   when and how the product might be used,
■   how often,
■   what products it might replace,
■   the sort of people it might appeal to.

Responses to product concept tests may be analysed by counting up the proportion who respond in particular ways, or using some scoring system on the rating scales that enable an average and a measure of dispersion to be calculated. These may then be cross-tabulated against demographics, especially age, sex, lifestyle, life-cycle or general attitudes. This may help to pinpoint groups most interested in the concept.

Product tests

The result of the concept test should be to weed out ideas that are non-starters or compare poorly with other ideas. The ideas remaining may then proceed to product testing, which is the evaluation and development of the products themselves from a marketing point of view. This is different from testing the physical functions of products to ensure that they meet technical and safety standards. Product testing means having a physical product to which a representative sample of target consumers may be exposed under controlled conditions and which can be used under realistic circumstances and about which they can express their opinion in a structured way.

The designs of product tests vary considerably and the use of any particular procedure by a company is often the result of some historical evolution, habit, or the researcher's or manager's familiarity or comfort with the chosen procedure. Yet different product test designs will give different outputs and different results, so it is necessary to try to establish the most appropriate designs in the circumstances. These circumstances include:

■ management information requirements,
■ the type of product,
■ the type of market,
■ cost and time constraints,
■ the required comparability across studies.

Management may want a product test to identify the most promising product from a set of candidates under consideration; it may want information that could guide product development to arrive at the best formulation of the product in terms of shape, features, colours, ingredients, materials and so on; it may want to know whether a chosen product idea warrants further investment of time and money; it may want information that would enable it to design a strategy for the introduction of the selected product.

Characteristics of products that are likely to affect the design of testing procedures include:

■ the extent to which the product is assessable on the spot,
■ the extent to which the product is new to users,
■ the extent of information search carried out by consumers in product or brand selection.

Snack-type foods and soft drinks are usually instantly assessable and are suitable candidates for hall tests and van tests. Fragrances (perfumes, eau de toilettes, after-shaves and so on) may also fit into this category. Alcoholic drinks may be too affected by the time of day to be assessable on the spot. Some products require either a longer period of use (for example batteries), or need to be used in the home to try them out, for example, a cake-mix, a floor polish or a shampoo. Some products are not susceptible to re-use, for example a device for unblocking a sink, or are very complex and require users to familiarize themselves with their operation. Highly innovative products or really new products are not amenable to comparison with other products and this will affect the test design. Low involvement convenience goods where information search and brand choice behaviour is limited will require procedures different from high involvement shopping goods. The former need analysis of the selected circumstances that consumers use in brand choice, while the latter require a close analysis of the importance and evaluation of product features.

Product testing will vary considerably according to type of market. Some markets are highly branded with lots of advertising, in which case the test product may well need to be branded and promoted. If the target market consists of children or elderly people then their ability to perform certain tasks may need to be taken into account. Product testing in industrial markets or organizational markets will be very different from consumer markets.

Testing procedures vary in terms of the costs involved and how long they take. Some products, like confectionery, do not require extensive testing since they may be tried out in the real market for a period and withdrawn with very little loss if they are not successful. The development of a new model of car, on the other hand, merits considerable expenditure at all stages in the new product development process. Cost and speed may need to be traded off against the reliability or accuracy of the results.

Testing procedures may be affected lastly by the need for comparability across studies. There are advantages to be gained from the standardization of test procedures across a wide range of products. Researchers will gain more experience of such procedures, the procedures themselves can be refined, performance benchmarks may be established, and the results of different tests are more likely to be comparable.

The key dimensions along which product tests vary and which testers need to decide upon include:

- what kinds of people should act as testers,
- what they are to be asked to do,
- the size of the sample,
- the analysis techniques to be used on the data collected.

The main choices concerning who should act as testers include:

- current users of the brand,
- current users in the product field,
- users in the product field plus potential users,
- a general cross-section of the population.

Decisions about what types of people are most appropriate in the circumstances depend on many factors and it would be difficult to lay down any rules. If a product is completely new then there can be no current users of the brand; there may even be no comparable product field and the selection may have to be of people who in some way are likely to be favourably disposed to the new product. If the objective of the test is to see if people notice the substitution of cheaper ingredients or components, then only current users of the brand need to be involved in the assessment procedure. If the product has been improved, then users of that type of product currently not using the brand will need to be included in the test to see if they can be persuaded to switch brands or at least include it in their repertoire. At the same time sufficient current users of the brand also need to be included to ensure that the changes will not alienate them. For some products, like soap, no amount of improvement will persuade current users to use more, even if they agreed it was a better product, so the focus may be on potential new users. Some products are used by nearly everybody in the population, so a general cross-section may be included in the test. On the other hand, potential users may be a very selected group, for example a new device to help the blind. If the test is of a product function, like how well it cleans a floor, then it may not matter whether the testers are users or non-users of the brand being researched.

As a general rule, the more restrictions placed on the selection of testers, the more expensive it is to obtain a sample. Thus a sample of the population at large will be cheaper than a sample of users in the product field. The most expensive is usually a sample of users of the brand since few brands are used by more than 10 per cent of the population.

What testers are asked to do depends on the kind of test. Following Batsell and Wind (1980) we may distinguish four main kinds of test:

- monadic,
- comparative,
- sequential,
- conjoint.

In monadic testing, each person is given just one product to evaluate and will tend to be used where the product is completely new, or where the product is a line extension and the client already has backdata on the other products in the range. However, monadic testing may be used to compare several products by dividing a sample of testers into as many groups as there are products to be tested. The scores (whether preference ratings, intention to purchase, degrees of liking and so on) for the various groups are then compared, and subjected to a test of statistical significance. If statistically significant differences emerge, the most promising product (or formulation of a product) is selected for further development.

In comparative testing, testers are given two or more products to compare on the same occasion and will typically be used where there is a new product formulation. Where there are three or more products or formulations, then evaluation may take the form of paired comparisons, complete ranking, a rating scale for each, or a constant sum of points which is divided between the products by the tester. The advantage of comparative testing is that the comparisons are made directly by individuals rather than by arithmetic comparisons of mean scores. The downside is that comparisons are entirely internal to the set of products being tested, whereas, so it is sometimes argued, with monadic tests comparisons are implicitly being made with all the other brands with which consumers are familiar. Comparisons may be internal to the company's brands, or may be against competitor brands. The former is more likely where there is a formulation change, and the latter if there is a marketing argument to be won, if the client company is losing market share, or they need to test the competitor's products anyway.

Sequential testing is comparative, but evaluations are made on different occasions. The tester is asked to try one product, wait a specific period of time, try the second, and then give an opinion. This procedure, so it is argued by its advocates, more closely resembles the way in which consumers actually compare products. However, it does, of course, take longer and is more expensive, particularly where in-home placements are required.

Conjoint analysis focuses on product features and instead of simply identifying the single most promising product, it tries to clarify the relative importance of features, thus providing guidance for the construction of new product formulations.

Other choices facing the researcher in terms of what testers are asked to do include:

- whether the products should be branded or blind,

- whether competitors' brands should be included among the products to be tested,
- in comparative tests, the order in which the products are presented,
- whether the test should be on the spot or in use, usually at home,
- the attributes to be tested,
- the length of time testers are given.

The branding of a product is as much part of the total offer as, for example, price, so wherever possible branded tests will be used. However, they tend to suffer from halo effects, that is, testers tend to respond more favourably to a product they regard as 'their' brand. If the main focus of the test is to obtain reactions to product features or new formulations, then blind tests are probably more appropriate. If, on the other hand, the interest is in likely purchase behaviour or it is a straightforward monadic test, then branded tests should be considered.

The inclusion of competitor brands depends, again, on the objectives of the test. If the focus is on future purchasing behaviour, then they should; otherwise, probably not.

Where products to be compared are very different, then the order in which they are presented makes little difference, but where they are similar, there is a tendency to prefer the product tested first. Some system for rotating the order of presentation will certainly improve the reliability of the tests.

As explained earlier, some products more than others are amenable to on-the-spot evaluation. Where in-home placement tests are used there will usually be a recall interview, either face-to-face or over the telephone, typically using five or seven-point rating scales. Some clients have their own requirements in terms of scales, wording of scales and show cards that they are used to. Other factors also intervene, for example, the nature of management information requirements, the speed with which results are required and so on.

Attribute lists are usually managerially derived unless qualitative research has been conducted on consumer perceptions. Managers decide what product features they want evaluated based on their experience and familiarity with the market or with the results of earlier tests. However, de Chernatony and Knox (1990) argue that product testing is presented predominantly as a mechanistic process with minimal consideration of the underlying assumptions about user behaviour, consumer perceptions or consumer psychology. The authors suggest that consumers interpret products as arrays of cues, and that judgements are based on very limited samples of cues that consumers believe to be indicative of product characteristics (for example, assessing the quality of wrapped bread from the feel of the packaging). In this way, information search is very restricted. If researchers are interested largely in different product formulations, then these cues need to be the focus of the inquiry. For fast moving consumer goods particularly, there is limited information search and researchers should concentrate on the few salient attributes deemed important by the purchaser – and this may vary from one purchaser to another. In short, attribute lists should be very short and geared to the product concerned; perhaps even to particular types of consumer. In practice, however, it is unusual to use different attribute lists for different categories of customer. This would have implications for sample size, design and cost.

The length of time testers are to be allowed to use the product is often a problem. The pressures are usually to produce a quick result; at the same time, many products are used infrequently in real life, while opinions do often change after extended use.

In terms of sample size, the cost of a product test increases with the number of testers, but so do the usefulness and reliability of the results. Below a certain minimum number of testers the results may be too unreliable to be useful; above a certain number the addition of more testers will not significantly improve the results. It is difficult to say exactly what these minimum and maximum figures are because a number of factors are involved, for example, the number of products or formulations to be tested, regional variations and so on. However, fewer than 30 testers is likely to be unreliable and more than 1000 will cease to be cost-effective. Typically, for a straightforward monadic test, a sample size of about 200 would be regarded as adequate. Samples in practice are seldom more than 300 or so.

The procedures used for the analysis of the data from product testing depend in the first instance on the type of test chosen. Product tests designed for absolute evaluation will summarize the data by counting the proportions who respond in particular ways or by generating scores on the attributes selected for testing and calculating averages. Confidence intervals may be calculated, but are worthwhile only if the selection procedure was random probability from a defined population. Where there are many attributes, then factor analysis on the attribute scores may be carried out. Product tests designed for comparative evaluation will tend to rely on using tests of significance against the null hypothesis (either the t-test for small samples, or the normal distribution for larger ones) on the differences between groups testing different products in monadic tests, or on the differences in mean scores or proportions on product attributes for comparative tests. Because most testers are selected by quota sample a design factor of 1.6–1.7 should be applied, but in practice, this is often not done.

The Taylor Nelson Opti-test

Most market research companies offering product testing services customize each test for the client. There are, however, some proprietary techniques. One is Opti-test offered by Taylor Nelson AGB. This offers a structured approach to optimizing product formulations for food and drink products and can also be used for home and personal care products. It is based on the idea that while consumers are good at telling you how much they like or dislike a product in general terms, they are not so good at diagnosing why. In fact, any reasons given may bear little relation to actual product ingredient or formulation differences. So, instead of asking consumers about particular product features, for example: 'Do you like the sweetness?', they are asked simply to say which of two product formulations they prefer. Samples of respondents are given at random a particular combination so that all combinations are tested. Since the manufacturer knows how the products vary, it is possible to work out those combinations of features that maximize preferences. Furthermore, they will know the effect of adding or removing ingredients on preferences in taste and texture terms.

The set-up of the test requires discussion with the client about the different ways in which the product can be made, and what are the key factors that they are able to vary. The result is a matrix of product combinations.

Samples of 30–50 consumers are given each product combination. They are asked to give an overall absolute rating of the products plus an overall preference between the two products. This enables consumer to say, for example, 'I prefer A to B, but neither is very good'. Testers are, in addition, asked about likes and dislikes, and to rate the product on the more traditional dimensions such as appearance. These are less relevant to the product designers than to creative advertisement developers who can see which aspects of the product relate to the brand and the words and phrases used to describe it. Analysis of variance is used to identify which variables most influence consumer preferences and evaluations, and which product combinations perform best overall. The results can be used to reposition a product, for market segmentation, for cost saving, for new product development, or for fundamental product research to help understand how to improve product formulations.

Advertising pre-testing

We have seen how advertising tracking is used to diagnose how well an advertisement has performed in the past and in what ways. Such procedures are sometimes referred to as post-testing. Post-testing provides data on what *has* happened, while pre-testing influences what *does* or will happen. It is an activity that takes place before resources are fully committed, and provides data on the likely outcomes of marketing initiatives so that a decision can be taken:

- to go or not to go with a particular idea or product,
- to modify the idea or product to improve its likely performance,
- to select the best of a number of ideas or products.

Advertising pre-testing takes place either before an advertisement is printed or put on air, or just after initial screening. It may be designed to weed out those advertisements that are unlikely to work, to select the best of the remaining candidates for creative advertising development, to predict the performance of the advertisements chosen, to provide early feedback, or to make last minute changes. Pre-testing of advertising has long been associated with the use of qualitative research, but in recent years there has been a growing demand for quantified predictions of likely future performance in real conditions before the costs of screening or printing advertisements are incurred.

The precise measures used in quantitative advertising pre-testing are closely related to implicit or explicit theories about the way in which advertising works. The traditional model, of which there are a number of versions, suggests that consumers begin by becoming aware of a product or brand. They then formulate some attitude towards it or image of it, generate a desire to try it, and finally purchase it. Figure 8.16 illustrates the process.

The result has been a debate not only over the techniques to be used to measure each of these, but over whether awareness, attitudes, image or desire to try should be the focus of pre-testing measures. One school of thought argues that, clearly, the nearer you take your measurement to the actual act of trial or purchase the better will be the prediction. However, this sequence of events has been questioned, and it has been suggested, for example by Brown (1991b), that attitudes and images of products and brands are more likely to be

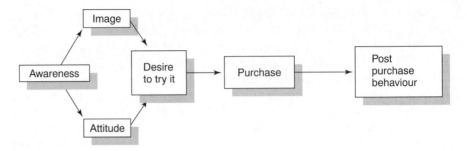

Figure 8.16 A traditional model of consumer behaviour.

formed *after* purchase, so the sequence becomes that illustrated in Figure 8.17.

If this is the case, it is inappropriate to base pre-testing on the measurement of attitudes or images; the best measures must be based on awareness and stated intention to buy or to try. Attitudes towards and images of the products and brands may influence the subsequent repurchase pattern, and this may involve brand switching or inclusion in a brand repertoire, either of which may be with varying numbers of repurchase occasions and lengths of purchase cycle.

While, as we have seen, it is perfectly possible to measure advertising awareness in tracking studies by asking people to recall the brands and the advertising they remember, in pre-testing, once you have shown people an advertisement in a hall or in a van, you cannot within a few minutes start asking them about advertisement and brand awareness and whether they recall which brand the ad was for. The traditional solution has been to substitute the 'stand out' value of an advertisement as a predictor of future recall or awareness. In a reel test a sample of maybe 50–100 respondents are shown a mock up of an advertisement in a reel of six or 10 (which may be in printed form or on a video). The test advertisement has to compete for attention either with advertisements for similar or related product fields. These may be for competing products or they may be other versions of an advertisement for the same product. Respondents are then asked which ones they noticed or recalled, both unprompted, then prompted. Respondents may be asked which advertisements they liked most and least, and their attention is then gradually focused on to the test advertisement and recall of its content or theme. The test advertisement will normally either be in a fixed position in the reel, for example, sixth in a reel of 10, or the order may be rotated.

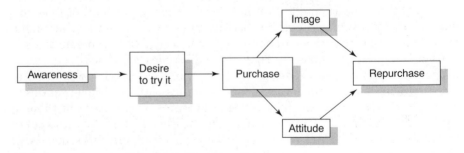

Figure 8.17 An alternative model of consumer behaviour.

The results of such reel tests, however, have been shown (for example by Brown, 1991a) not to tie in well with subsequent measures of awareness in tracking studies. The development of more sophisticated ways of pre-testing advertisements by market research agencies have taken one of two directions: making measures of pre-test recall themselves more sophisticated, or abandoning the idea of recall altogether. Burke Marketing Research has taken the former route and Millward Brown the latter.

Burke's Ad-Visor

Burke Marketing Research offers a refinement of the pre-test recall technique and adds two further measures it calls 'persuasion' and 'diagnostics' into the prediction equation. Burke had already developed a recall technique for on-air advertising by measuring day after recall (DAR) rather than using a reel test. In a new proprietary advertising pre-testing technique called 'Ad-Visor', Burke invites a representative sample of consumers who have already indicated that they would watch a particular programme to view a particular slice of an evening's television schedule at home. Viewing is thus in a natural viewing situation. No particular reference is made to the advertising. The test commercial is screened within this specified period. Recall interviews are conducted the next day by telephone.

In addition, responses from a control group sample are collected the day before screening – so they cannot possibly have seen the advertisement. Both those unexposed to the commercial, and those who demonstrate proven recall of the advertisement are asked their purchase intent in relation to the test brand. The difference between these two measures give an indication of the persuasive value of a commercial. The test design is shown in Figure 8.18.

Using data from Burke's BASES (Table 8.3) on market tracking the raw consumer responses are modelled into realistic purchase probabilities. The difference in purchase probabilities between consumers exposed and

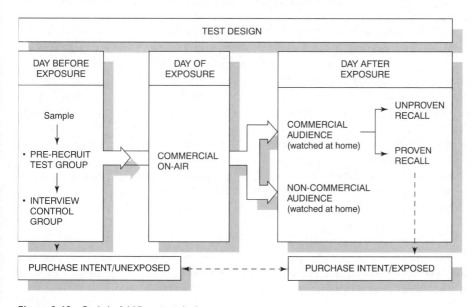

Figure 8.18 Burke's Ad-Visor test design.

Table 8.3
Example of an output from
Burke's BASES

	Plan 1	Plan 2	Plan 3	Plan 4
Awareness (%)				
Year 1	33	35	35	35
Year 2	40	40	35	35
Distribution (%)				
Year 1	50	45	40	35
Year 2	60	55	50	45
Cumulative trial (%)				
Year 1	20	18	15	13
Year 2	27	24	22	1
Sales (000 units)				
Year 1	245	217	210	163
Year 2	565	370	330	270

unexposed to the commercial gives what Burke call its Persuasion Index. This is expressed as a percentile position against all other commercials, so it is not just giving a score, but is related to all the other commercials that have been tested. A persuasion model takes account of the impact of environmental influences such as cultural differences, the structure of the market, brand age and distribution. More than 100 experiments in five different European markets were conducted to parametize the model. Together, recall and persuasion give an effective evaluation of advertising. They are independent parameters and are not necessarily correlated – both could be high or low for the same commercial, so both are required.

Further diagnostic information from those exposed to the ad is added to help explain the recall and persuasion measures achieved. A series of eight open-ended questions probe details of content recall, messages communicated, and specific likes and dislikes. A battery of attitude statements measures perceptions of relevance, involvement, interest, conviction, originality, clarity and appeal.

Ad-Visor thus tests after the first on-air screening, but before all the campaign is put behind it, and before all the media time is booked. Strictly speaking, Ad-Visor is not a 'pre-test'; neither is it a 'post-test' in the sense of market tracking, but lies somewhere between the two. While Ad-Visor entails having a finished ad, it does accurately measure impact – the number of consumers being reached with the commercial. This cannot be done with the standard reel test – the commercial needs to be actively going on air with people sitting there watching it in their own homes. It also means that it is possible to measure, in addition to impact, how much people are being persuaded by the advertisement, what messages the commercial is communicating, and whether or not the brand name is being accurately related to the advertisement.

Millward Brown's link
By looking at a large number of advertisements that worked and those that did not in terms of tracking measures, Millward Brown discovered four key factors of a successful advertisement:

■ it draws attention to the advertisement,

- people enjoy watching it,
- it is easy to follow,
- there is a strong link between the advertising and the brand.

These factors form the basis of a new advertising pre-testing procedure called 'Link'. A sample of 150 respondents is shown the test advertisement along with four other commercials to provide a context. They are then asked to rate the advertisement of one of the other four commercials as a warm up and to act as a bench mark. The four factors are measured on four or five-point rating scales. Thus attention-getting is measured on a four-point scale in response to the question, 'How much will this advertisement make you pay attention each time you see it?'. The responses go from, 'It will definitely make me pay attention' through 'probably', 'probably not' to 'definitely not' pay attention. Enjoyment is on a five-point scale from 'I'll enjoy watching it a lot' to 'I won't enjoy watching it at all'. Ease of following is on a four-point scale from 'very easy' to 'very hard' to follow, and the link on a five-point scale from, 'Nearly everyone will notice the advertisement is for (brand X)', to 'People will probably not realize what it is advertising at all'.

Respondents are then asked to rate the test advertisement using the same scales. The results are then corrected for the halo effect, that is, the more enjoyable advertisements tend to be rated too highly on the other three scales, so these are corrected using responses to the enjoyability rating. The results of these key ratings are then used in a empirically derived model which makes a prediction of the likely Awareness Index (see pp. 267–8). This prediction is further refined in two ways. First, a subset of 100 of those who have undertaken the first stage is questioned about the content of the advertisement, their comprehension of it, and their likes and dislikes. This facilitates a qualitative evaluation of whether the main focus of the advertisement is successfully linked to the brand, and whether it has been understood in the way the advertisers intended. If, for example, the advertisement has been misunderstood, a subjective down-rating to the predicted Awareness Index can be made.

Second, another sub-group of 75 respondents (who may be a subset of those from the first stage, but not the second) are shown a video-tape of the advertisement, and they record their level of interest as it proceeds by moving a lever on a machine which captures electronically the interest on a second-by-second basis. The responses of respondents are aggregated and plotted out on hard copy. Ideally, interest should be high when the brand is being mentioned. If it falls away every time this happens then the key features of the advertisement are not being successfully linked to the brand. The video is stopped at various points and respondents are asked to point to the place on the screen where they were looking. The point is electronically captured as crosses that are overlaid on the still. This may show, for example, that most people are not looking at the point on the screen where the brand is being shown.

By adding in judgement from these qualitative elements, Millward Brown has improved the correlation between the pre-tests and subsequent Awareness Index to 0.9. Furthermore, such qualitative elements provide a diagnosis about *why* an advertisement is likely or unlikely to generate the required awareness. Thus it could well be that the main thing that stands out in an advertisement is unlinked to the brand. Each element of the it may then be separately diagnosed and the likely messages that will be communicated may be predicted. Linking is taking the advertisement to bits to understand the structure of it to see whether the parts that are supposed to be doing the job of linking it with the brand and getting the message over are, in practice, going to work.

While advertising pre-testing procedures such as those described above give an evaluation of advertisements in terms of impact and communication, they cannot be used as a basis for making any prediction of sales that will eventuate. To do that, special techniques have been developed, and it is to these that we now turn.

Volume and brand share prediction

The track record of market research in predicting new product successes or failures has not been a good one. Various empirical studies have shown that between 60 per cent and 97 per cent of new products, whether innovative, line extensions or relaunches of modified products, fail to achieve company objectives. A lot depends, however, on the particular industry. For UK food manufacturers Ramsay (1982) estimated that only 3–4 per cent of new food brands are successful.

It may be argued that this situation is largely a result of lack of research (or lack of attention to the results of research) rather than of inadequate research, but a lot of market research *has* been carried out on behalf of new products, yet the identification of product failure has still been limited. Traditionally, two main approaches to the prediction of the share of market and sales volume that would be achieved by new products have been used:

■   the screening and evaluation of attitudes to new products in product and
     product concept tests,
■   test marketing.

Attitude measurements in product tests that produce a rating on a five- or seven-point scale have, on the basis of past experience, been insufficient to allow accurate predictions to be made about future sales. Just because a high percentage of a sample of respondents say they like a product, or say they will buy it, or say it is good value for money (or all three), does not mean that people in general will necessarily try it, and if they do try it that they will buy it again. There are many other factors that need to be taken into account before such predictions are possible.

As was explained in Chapter 4 in the section on experimental research, test marketing has fallen out of favour. A number of market research agencies began looking at the possibility of laboratory test markets that would simulate a shop as part of a hall test. Others developed the use of concept tests and product tests in which samples of respondents were given statements about the proposed new products on a concept board or, at a later stage, given a mock-up or actual product to try, either on the spot or to take home. Such tests have been used for a long time, but they only gave a score on one or more rating scales, and could not be used to make specific predictions about sales. However, mathematical modelling techniques began to be applied to 'interpret' the answers given in such tests. The idea was to build up a prediction of sales based on the number of people who would try the new products, and the number who would subsequently repurchase.

The models used for volume and brand share prediction have, over the years, been given different names such as 'sales decomposition/recomposition models', 'pre-test market models', 'market-mix testing', but eventually the term now generally recognised is 'simulated test marketing models' or just STM models. All such models use the concepts of trial and repeat purchase, and substitute for simulated or real purchasing behaviour in the marketplace a standard or fairly standard concept test or product test in which a sample of respondents are asked questions about the new product (or existing product being tested) and about their purchasing behaviour. These responses are then used in statistical models of various kinds which weight the replies and produce predictions of a number of variables.

There are, however, significant differences between the models in terms of general methodology, the variables included, the approach to parametization, and the kinds of predicted output. Any manufacturer wishing to compare the advantages and limitations of the various STM models available would have a hard time. The advocates of each particular model will argue persuasively that their approach is best. A start can be made, however, by recognizing the various choices or dimensions along which models vary. In terms of general methodology, the main choices are between:

- comparative or monadic testing, or some combination,
- macro modelling or micro modelling, or some combination,
- whether client inputs, for example concerning distribution, advertising or brand awareness, are modelled or assumed,
- whether various elements that made up the final prediction are modelled separately, thus trial and adoption may be modelled separately, as might switchers and new buyers,
- the samples used for STM models vary from a minimum of about 200 per test up to about 500. It is important to remember that an STM is a test, not a survey, so although sampling is important, no attempt is usually made to obtain a large representative sample. It is, however, necessary to get a regional spread of fieldwork,
- the respondents selected tend to be either product category users, or a general cross-section of the adult population.

In terms of the variables included in the model, while all take trial and repeat purchase as the key variables, the main variations include:

- the number and depth of questions used as inputs to predict trial and repeat purchase. Some models rely on responses to just one question, for example on intention to buy, while others include competitive sets, degree of experimentalism, brand visibility and so on,
- the number and depth of question used as diagnostics to explain the predicted outcomes. These may include the standard demographics, and in addition questions on corporate or brand image, likes and dislikes and so on.

The most long-lived and commercially successful of these models was that developed by Burke Marketing Research.

Burke's BASES

The problem with the simulated store approach is that the research needs to be conducted using finished products, packaging and advertising, involving considerable time and cost. An alternative is to dispense with the simulated point-of-sale element and establish estimates of trial and repeat purchase from survey questions in a consumer survey or in a hall test. These questions might cover:

- intention to purchase,
- product evaluation,
- perceived value-for-money,
- claimed purchase frequency,
- average number of units purchased,
- competitive/substitute product usage.

Answers to these questions are then entered into a mathematical model containing experimentally derived weighting factors to arrive at estimates of trial, repeat purchase, sales volumes and market shares.

BASES was launched in the UK in the mid-1970s. The model was from the outset a volume prediction model and based on a monadic test. Respondents are not asked to compare the test product with other brands in the test itself. It is argued by supporters of this model that it is better for the respondents to evaluate products within their own frames of reference, particularly their own competitive set of brands. In evaluating the test product respondents are, in any case, implicitly comparing it with the products they normally use and in situations in which they normally use them. Comparative tests, by contrast, tend to impose a comparison set. Furthermore, in some markets it may be difficult to put together a comparative set, for example, it is difficult to know what competes with Perrier – soft drinks, milk, fruit juice, tap water? It may, in addition, be argued that monadic tests allow you to ask the respondent which brands the test product would be competing against, enabling some calculation to be made of source of volume.

The model was originally set up by taking about 80 different new products, interviewing people before the product was launched, and then tracking their subsequent purchasing behaviour using consumer panels. This enabled answers concerning purchase intention and so on to be 'interpreted' and corrected for overclaiming and underclaiming. The result was a series of weighting factors that were built into a mathematical model that has subsequently been refined and improved as the results of more studies have become available. Burke Marketing Research now has about 8000 cases on its database.

The two key measures in the BASES model are trial rate and repeat rate. The trial rate is measured by market penetration – the proportion of the total market who buy the brand being researched at least once. The repeat rate is the proportion of trialists who repeat buy. The trial rate is estimated in a standard concept or product test in which consumers are asked both before trial and after trial if they:

- definitely would buy,
- probably would buy,
- might or might not buy,
- probably would not buy,

■ definitely would not buy.

For the trial rate the *pre-trial* intention to buy is used. However, this statement of purchase intent always produces a degree of overclaiming, that is, not all consumers who say they will buy the brand will actually do so in a given period of time. The proportion who, from the historical database of previous predictions, actually did make a purchase in each of the response categories is then used as a weighting for each response in the actual test. Thus if 40 per cent of respondents who answer 'probably would buy' are found in fact subsequently to actually make a purchase, then for the product being tested, if 10 per cent give this response, then 40 per cent of 10 per cent or 4 per cent of those in that response category will, it is predicted, actually buy. Estimates for each response can then be added together.

The calibration from intention to actual purchase is strongly affected by many factors, for example, type of product, the cultural (particularly national) background, the unit price and the age of the consumer. Thus teenagers generally overclaim more than adults; Italians and Spaniards are more likely to overstate than Germans. Using this calibration, the correlation between statement of purchase intent and subsequent actual purchase has been improved to over 0.9. The trial rate estimate is based on this adjusted probability of trial, taking account of clients' estimates of weighted distribution build, advertising plan or brand awareness estimates (which may be from an earlier usage and attitude study), promotional activity and seasonality.

Besides intention to purchase, consumers in both the pre- and post-trial tests are asked about:

■ intended frequency of purchase,
■ purchase quantities,
■ degree of liking,
■ product evaluation,
■ perceived value for money,
■ substitute/competitive usage.

Degree of liking is on a six-point scale, four of the points are positive, one neutral and one negative. Perceived value for money is on a five-point scale from very good value down to very poor value.

Repeat rate is estimated from the number who are still favourably disposed towards the brand after the trial. Favourability is estimated by using multiple non-linear regression techniques based on a combination of intention to purchase *post-trial* (again suitably downweighted for overclaiming), degree of liking score, and perceived value for money score. The conversion rates post-trial tend to be more stable than pre-trial ones. Purchase cycle is based on after-use intended purchase frequency among after-use favourable respondents, adjusted for overstatement and the build of the trial curve.

To obtain estimates of future sales volume (S_t) at time t (the number of weeks since retail availability) the BASES model adds a predicted trial volume (T_t) to a predicted repeat volume (R_t), that is:

$$S_t = T_t + R_t$$

Trial volume, T_t is estimated by taking the cumulative trial rate over the period between now and time t, multiplying by the target market size (the number of households in the target market area) and the purchase quantity (the average amounts purchased at trial). An adjustment is made for trial rate build up over the year. Repeat volume is estimated from first repeat volume plus second repeat volume plus third repeat volume . . . nth repeat volume. The first repeat volume is derived by multiplying the number of triers by the first repeat rate (the number of consumers repeating at least once) and the average quantity. The second repeat volume takes the number of first repeaters and multiplies by the second repeat rate (the number of consumers repeating at least twice) and the average quantity. Subsequent repeat volumes are calculated in a similar manner. The model also builds in a decay rate for people who stop buying after a number of repeats.

The result of applying the BASES procedure, then, is to produce separate estimates of:

■ sales volume,
■ trial rate,
■ repeat purchase rate,
■ purchase cycle.

The output might look like Table 8.3, which shows different estimates of year one and year two trial and sales volume, depending on the assumptions that are made about awareness and distribution. This shows that getting a 60 per cent distribution by year two is crucial for lifting sales. Such tables also enable clients to ask varying, 'What if . . .?' questions. Estimates of repeat purchase rates can also be particularly helpful in gauging the overall likely success of the product since in practice these are related.

BASES, like other similar models that were developed at the time, reconstructs the data that would be provided by a consumer panel, but from a two-stage before and after trial data collection exercise, within a short space of time and before the product is launched – it may be a new product, a line extension or a relaunch. Models like BASES were originally used to make go/no go decisions, but nowadays are increasingly used to determine optimum launch policies. Thus if there is a good trial rate then the focus needs to be on getting repeat.

Burke Marketing Research has developed a family of BASES procedures. BASES I is just the front-end concept test which provides an estimate of year one trial based on samples of 200–300 respondents. BASES II is the full model as described above and incorporates BASES I to provide estimates of repeat purchase and volume sales in addition to trial. Year two and year three estimates can also be made, but BASES II requires a product mock-up for respondents to try. BASES IV is essentially a tracking operation for a product in test market or national launch in its early stages. Standard tracking data are collected on awareness, purchase behaviour and intention to buy. This enables longer-term predictions to be made.

BASES LX is for product line extensions. These are more difficult types of launch to test because it is necessary to take account of brand heritage dilution and cannibalization. Experience and data from the Burke database show that line extensions give higher levels of awareness and have better conversion rates from awareness to trial and from trial to repeat. BASES LX first divides the line extension into one of five types:

- adding new flavour or variety,
- adding a new size or pack format,
- moving the brand name into a new sub-category,
- moving the brand name into a new category,
- moving the company name into a new category.

Each of these has different implications for awareness and ghost purchasing intent, and each needs a different test design. A source of volume analysis shows the likely extent of cannibalization – the sales that are likely to be taken from the parent brand.

Research International's MicroTest

Most of the volume and brand share models are 'macro' models in the sense that they aggregate answers of respondents on a question-by-question basis and analyses are performed on the totals. An alternative, however, is 'micro' modelling, which makes a prediction on an individual-by-individual basis by looking at the pattern of responses to a number of questions, and putting them into a computer algorithm and coming up with a probability that that person will try to subsequently adopt the product or brand under investigation.

Research International has developed a micromodelling technique it calls MicroTest, launched in 1987. This uses a simple product concept test among a sample of the target population to predict trial. Respondents then take the product home, try it and are subsequently reinterviewed and questioned about product acceptability. MicroTest is a volume prediction model based on predicting, individual by individual, the probabilities of trial, adoption, frequency of purchase and quantity per occasion. Trial and adoption are modelled separately. The trial model includes three key factors:

- the predisposition on the part of the consumer to experiment with new products,
- the acceptability of the new product concept to the respondent,
- the visibility of the brand being studied.

It is clear from behavioural and attitudinal data that the probability of trial depends crucially on the level of an individual's experimentalism – the predisposition to experiment with new products. This is measured on a behavioural scale by asking respondents about the new brands they have ever tried. Some people are highly experimental by nature, and if all you do is appeal to them, your sales go up rather nicely – and then come crashing down again.

The acceptability of the new product concept is measured by asking respondents about their attitudes to the proposed price, and their propensity to buy. The concept may be presented in a variety of degrees of sophistication from a simple verbal description through to a finished television commercial.

The visibility of the brand measures the opportunity an individual has to try it. This is affected by distribution, advertising spend and how well-known the brand name is (or heritage). Information on the first two of these is provided by the client. Heritage is included in the consumer interviews. The combined effect of these environmental factors is then predicted using a sophisticated visibility model. A diffusion sub-model predicts the build-up of trial (cumulative penetration) over a period of time.

The adoption model includes two key factors: product acceptability and brand fidelity. Product acceptability is measured by enquiring into purchase intentions and the extent to which the new product meets expectations. This gives a measure of the relationship between pre-trial and post-trial response for each individual.

Brand fidelity is measured by asking respondents which of the new brands they have ever tried they are still using. There are some experimentalists who do show fidelity to brands, while others are just inveterate experimentalists.

Once the probabilities of trial and adoption have been estimated, then volume can be predicted once frequency of purchasing and quantity per purchase occasion have been established. Frequency of purchase for each individual is predicted by asking respondents to project future purchasing of the test product, and 'weight of purchasing' by asking about projected stocks of the product.

The full model is shown in Figure 8.19. The result is a probability for each individual. These are then aggregated and grossed up to the population, whatever that happens to be, for example, mothers with young children. Forecasts are made of sales in years one and two, and the ongoing level thereafter, while sales breakdowns are given between trial and adoption along with estimates for cumulative levels of trial and adoption. Research International use MicroTest to advise clients on 'launch management', for example, what sorts of advertising support they should give. Microtest is performed on samples of respondents in the target population of 200–300. Over 500 Microtests have been carried out, so it is possible to begin applying market validation studies.

MicroTest has subsequently been developed into a family of products. There is MicroTest Concept, which is just the front-end product concept test which can be used at an even earlier stage to predict trial potential. There is MicroTest Laboratory, which is MicroTest with a shop display built onto it. This may be used for more developed products and can represent more real-

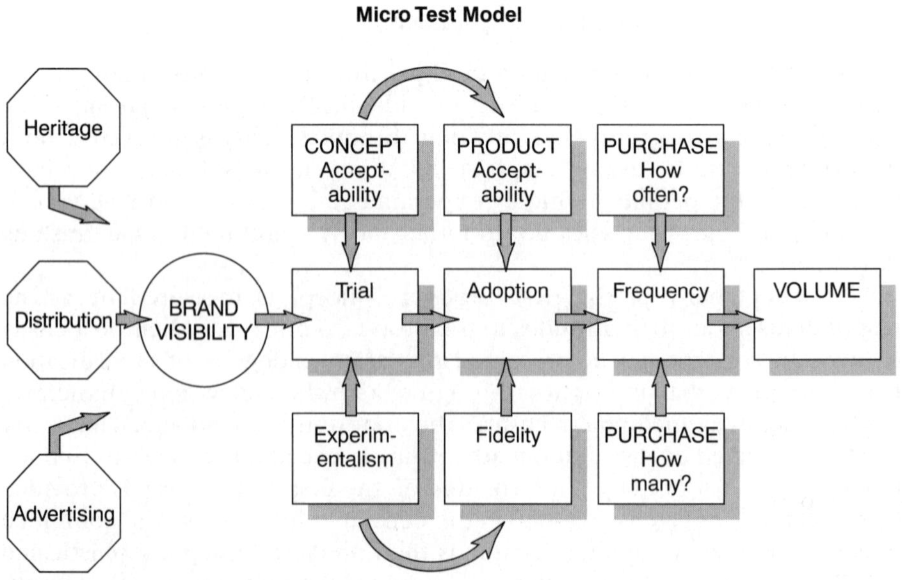

Figure 8.19   Research International's MicroTest model.

world influences such as on-shelf impact, advertising in a competitive context, and actual response from the consumer. MicroTest Market recruits a tailor-made, short-term panel (for about 12 weeks), and the agency does all the shopping for that type of product, for example toilet soaps. Panelists are called upon once a week and the results provide more accurate measures since adoption and frequency of purchase are observed from natural purchasing behaviour rather then being estimated from responses to a questionnaire or from simulated behaviour.

An evaluation of STM modelling

A key advantage of STM modelling is that the risks of launching products that turn out to be unsuccessful are reduced considerably, but without the costs of full test marketing, or even the cost of mini-test marketing. Manufacturers, furthermore, get very precise indicators of the likely performance of the new product. This enables them to generate strategies appropriate to the results. Thus if management have high expectations for a product and the forecast is for increasing volume, then they may decide to go straight for a national launch. If the new product begins from a low base, but will need time to build sales volume, then a test market and tracking operation to test different tactical approaches to boosting sales may be required. If the product begins with a high base, but is not expected to grow, then a national launch with minimum support to maximise profitability may be advisable. Products not expected to move up from a low base, or expected to decline from a higher one, may not be launched at all.

Other advantages of STM modelling are that:

- they can be used at a relatively early stage in new product development,
- they may be used to isolate problems before too much cost and effort have been expended,
- tests which do not use shop displays can be used for products that do not fit into any well-defined market category or product field,
- a wide range of alternative marketing scenarios can be examined by making changes in parameter values, for example, producing estimates on the basis of different assumptions regarding distribution and awareness, launching at different prices or using different promotional expenditures,
- parameters and weights can be validated when historical data on the effectiveness of predictions become available.
- products can be tested without revealing details of the composition or manufacture to competitors,
- they are relatively quick – 8–12 weeks would be a normal time-span for a full STM prediction,
- it is possible to exercise total control over the testing process,
- on the whole, STM systems have proved to be extremely accurate. Sampson (1987), for example, reports that over 8000 tests have been carried out using BASES in 34 countries and across many product categories. By comparing the estimates with what actually happened, typically the estimate is within plus or minus 10 per cent of the actual in 70 per cent of the cases, and plus or minus 15 per cent in 90 per cent of the cases.

One major disadvantage of STMs is that they are complex, and as the sophistication of the modelling grows it becomes more difficult for clients to understand the analysis, which in turn makes it difficult for clients to judge the advantages and limitations of the various models on offer and makes them more reliant on the agency to provide interpretation of the results. Another disadvantage is that it is difficult to give clients access to the data to make their own, 'What if . . .?' simulations because the formulae used for model calculations would be revealed or at least deducible, so agencies normally insist on processing simulations themselves.

The overall trend seems to be away from using STM models to make go/no go decisions and towards launch management that will determine not only optimum launch strategies, but ways of manipulating these strategies to generate extra trial or extra repeat purchase. A further trend is for agencies, having developed a successful basic model, to generate a variety of options for either using only the front-end trial prediction, to enhanced models with additional facilities and measures bolted on. These might include, for example, an optional simulated store test, a brand tracking operation, or models specifically designed to examine line extensions. A third trend is towards the increased use of diagnostic questions that will help to explain why a prediction is poor (or good). Diagnostics may also be used to evaluate an existing brand or brand strategy. These may take into account not only the characteristics of the products and the internal support given to them, but also the circumstances of the external marketplace.

Summary

Instruments of data capture, data collection methods and data analysis techniques are combined in a variety of ways to produce specific research techniques and applications that enable companies to diagnose the situations they face, to make predictions about the likely consequences of their marketing decisions, and to monitor the progress being made by or the success of past marking activity. Key diagnostic and monitoring techniques include market measurement, customer satisfaction research, advertising tracking and media audience measurement.

Instead of looking at the more traditional forecasting methods like time series analysis, which are well covered in books on marketing research, statistics and social research, the focus here is on three currently widely used predictive techniques and applications for the testing of new products and product concepts, advertising pre-testing, and volume and brand share prediction using simulated test market modelling.

Key concepts

diagnostic techniques	Appreciation Index
predictive techniques	average issue readership
market measurement	reach
customer satisfaction research	product concept tests
advertising tracking	advertising pre-testing
media audience measurement	volume and brand share prediction

Establishment Survey   STM modelling
Television rating
Gross rating points

Key services

BEM's customer relationship consultancy
BJM's Stochastic Reaction Monitors
BMRB's Customer Satisfaction Measurement (CSM)
BMRB's Target Group Index (TGI)
Broadcasters Audience Research Board (BARB)
Buke's BASES
Burke's Ad-Visor
Millward Brown's Awareness Index
Millward Brown's Link
National Readership Surveys Limited (NRS)
Nielsen Retail Index
Radio Joint Audience Research (RAJAR)
Research International's CONCEPTOR
Research International's MicroTest
Research International's SMART
Taylor Nelson AGB's Superpanel
Taylor Nelson's Omnimas
Taylor Nelson's Opti-test

Further reading

- Brown, G (1991) 'Response. Modelling advertising awareness', *Journal of the Market Research Society*, Vol 33, No 3, pp 197–204.
- Buttle, F (1996) 'SERVQUAL: review, critique, research agenda', *European Journal of Marketing*, Vol 56, July, pp 1–24.
- Colman, S and Brown, G (1983) 'Advertising tracking studies and sales effects', *Journal of the Market Research Society*, Vol 25, No 2, pp 165–183.
- Cronin, J and Taylor, S (1992) 'Measuring Service Quality: a Reexamination and Extension', *Journal of Marketing*, Vol 56, July, pp 55–68.
- de Chernatony, L and Knox, S (1990) 'How an appreciation of consumer behaviour can help in product testing', *Journal of the Market Research Society*, Vol 32, No 3, pp 329–347.
- Feldwick, P (1991) 'How valuable is the Awareness Index?' *Journal of the Market Research Society*, Vol 33, No 3, pp 179–95.
- Jones, T and Sasser, W (1995) 'Why Satisfied Customers Defect', *Harvard Business Review*, Vol 73, November–December, pp 88–99.
- Kent, RA (1994) *Measuring Media Audiences*, London: Routledge.
- Sampson, P (1987) 'The tracking study in market research', in U. Bradley (ed.) *Applied Marketing and Social Research*, Chichester: John Wiley.

Questions for further discussion

1   The ex-factory shipments of jams and preservatives from a medium-sized, UK based company have been steadily declining over six months, having

been stable for many years. The managing director wants a detailed market analysis to discover exactly what is happening in the marketplace. Suggest key market measurements that will need to be taken to facilitate such an analysis.

2　An airline wants an in-depth understanding of domestic customer usage and attitudes towards the company's services. Suggest the key questions that will need to be included in a U&A study.

3　Review the key measures taken by market research agencies of the 'success' of advertising and suggest what this tells us about what advertisers need to do to create successful advertisements.

4　Measures of television and radio audiences and newspaper and magazine readerships are all based on samples, hence they are only estimates. Review pp. 140–4 on sampling and on-sampling errors and outline the various kinds of error that might arise in estimating media audiences.

5　Review the details of the various STM models described in this chapter and generate a list of factors that manufacturers need to attend to in order to ensure, for a new or modified product, a good trial rate and a good repeat purchase rate.

Useful Web sites

http: //www.nrs.co.uk
http: //www.rslmedia.co.uk

The rise and rise of Cronbach's coefficient alpha

What is Cronbach's coefficient alpha?

Cronbach's alpha is a measure of internal reliability for multi-item summated indexes. The measure was developed by – no prizes for guessing – Cronbach, first published in 1951, so it has been around for 45 years. It takes the average correlation among items in a scale and adjusts for the number of items. Reliable scales are ones with high average correlation and a relatively large number of items. The coefficient varies between zero for no reliability to unity for maximum reliability. The formula subtracts from unity the sum of the variance for each item (σ_i^2) divided by the variance of the scale (σ_s^2) and multiplies by the number of items divided by the number of items minus one.

$$\alpha = \left(1 - \sum \frac{\sigma_i^2}{\sigma_s^2} \right)\left(\frac{k}{k-1} \right)$$

The latter value of course approaches unity as the number of items increases. If the variance for each item is identical, or the variances are converted to Z scores, the formula reduces to the inter-item correlation, r, multiplied by the number of items, k, divided by one plus the inter-item correlation multiplied by the number of items minus one.

$$\frac{k\,r}{1 + r\,(k-1)}$$

Strictly-speaking, Cronbach's alpha is the first of these procedures; the 'standardized' alpha may give a slightly different result (Cortina, 1993 – see end of this Appendix for references).

Alpha has effectively become *the* measure of choice for establishing the reliability of a multi-item scale. According to the Social Sciences Citation Index it has been referenced in over 2200 articles in 278 different journals in the last 20 years (Peterson, 1994). Its availability at the click of a mouse button in survey analysis programs like SPSS has almost certainly meant that it is commonly reported by researchers, but without any understanding of what it means and what its limitations are.

Acceptable levels

Despite its importance, there is little guidance in the literature (and none from Cronbach himself) as to what constitutes an 'acceptable' or 'sufficient' value for alpha to achieve. Most users of the statistic cite Nunnally's (1978) recommendation that a value of 0.7 should be achieved. It is assumed that if alpha for any scale is greater than 0.7 then it's OK. However, all those authors making recommendations about acceptable levels of alpha, including Nunnally, indicate that the desired degree of reliability is a function of the purpose of the research, for example whether exploratory or applied. Nunnnally himself in 1978 suggested that for preliminary research 'reliabilities of 0.70 or higher will suffice'. For 'basic' research, he suggests that 'increasing reliabilities much beyond 0.80 is often wasteful of time and funds' (Nunnally, 1978). In contrast, for applied research, 0.80 'is not nearly high enough'. Where important decisions depend on the outcome of the measurement process a reliability of 0.90 'is the minimum that should be tolerated'. None of Nunnally's recommendations have an empirical basis, a theoretical justification, or an analytical rationale. As with other recommendations, for example by Davis (1964), Kaplan and Saccuzzo (1982) or Murphy and Davidshofer (1988), Nunnally's appear to reflect either experience or intuition. Interestingly, Nunnally had changed his own recommendations from his 1967 edition of *Psychometric Theory* which recommended that the minimally acceptable reliability for preliminary research should be in the range of 0.5 to 0.6.

Peterson (1994) reports the results of a study to ascertain the values of alpha actually obtained in articles and papers based on empirical work. From a sample of over 800 marketing and psychology related journals, conference proceedings and some unpublished manuscripts, he reviewed all alpha coefficients found in each study, resulting in 4286 coefficients covering a 33–year period. Reported coefficients ranged from 0.6 to 0.99 with a mean of 0.77. 75 per cent were 0.7 or greater and 50 per cent were 0.8 or greater. Peterson found that reported alphas were not greatly affected by research design characteristics, such as sample size, type of sample, number of scale categories, type of scale, mode of administration, or type of research. One exception to this is that during scale development items are often eliminated if their presence restricts the value of alpha. Not surprisingly, the alpha coefficients reported were significantly related to the number of items eliminated.

In other respects, however, alpha is relatively robust in the face of differing research design characteristics. Interestingly, while theoretically the larger the number of items in a scale the more reliable it will be, Peterson found that only 10 per cent of the variance in reported alphas could be attributed to the number of scale items. This probably reflects a *decrease* in the average inter-item correlation as the number of items is increased. The conclusion is that to increase the magnitude of alpha, researchers should concentrate on the quality of the items and, as a corollary, the elimination of items that depress its value, rather than focus on adding more items.

Interpreting alpha

Alpha measures only internal consistency. If error factors associated with the passage of time are of concern to the researcher then it will not be the most appropriate statistic. However, since alpha approximates the mean of all possible split-half reliabilities, it can be seen as a superior measure of equivalence, which Cronbach (1951) originally defined as very little variance specific to individual items. It is not, however, as is commonly supposed, an indication of unidimensionality. Alpha can be quite high despite the presence of several dimensions (Cortina, 1993).

It is often forgotten, when interpreting alpha coefficients, that the values achieved are a function of the number of items. Thus for a three-item scale with alpha = 0.80, the average inter-item correlation is 0.57. For a ten-item scale with alpha = 0.80 it is only 0.28. What needs to be kept in mind is that in evaluating, say, a 40–item scale, alpha will be relatively large simply because of the number of items; and the number of items is not exactly a great measure of scale quality. When many items are pooled, internal consistency estimates are inevitably large and invariant, and therefore somewhat useless. Peterson's finding that reported alphas do not increase significantly with the number of items demonstrates this inverse tendency towards low inter-item correlation as the number of items increases.

Alpha, in short, should be used with some caution. It is appropriate only when the researcher requires a measure of internal consistency, and is helpful only then if the number of items used is limited. The value of alpha to be taken as 'acceptable' must be related to the purpose of the research, and even then only used as an indication rather than a 'test' to be passed with a fixed value. Furthermore, if researchers are concerned about dimensionality, then procedures like factor analysis are probably more appropriate. Scales, however, do not have to be unidimensional for alpha to be of use since reliability and dimensionality are different concepts.

References

Cortina, JM (1993), 'What is Coefficient Alpha? An Examination of Theory and Applications', *Journal of Applied Psychology*, Vol. 78, No. 1, pp. 98–104.

Cronbach, LJ (1951), 'Coefficient Alpha and the Internal Structure of Tests', *Psychometrika*, Vol. 16, No. 3, pp. 297–334.

Davis, FB (1964), *Educational Measurements and their Interpretation*, Belmont, Calif.: Wadsworth.

Kaplan, RW and Saccuzzo, DP (1982), *Psychological Testing: Principles, Applications and Issues*, Monterey, Calif.: Brooks/Cole.

Murphy, KR and Davidshofer, CO (1988), *Psychological Testing: Principles and Applications*, Englewood Cliffs, New Jersey: Prentice-Hall.

Nunnally, JC (1978), *Psychometric Theory*, 2nd edn, New York: McGraw-Hill.

Peterson, RA (1994), 'A Meta-analysis of Cronbach's Coefficient Alpha', *Journal of Consumer Research*, Vol. 221, September, pp. 381–91.

Appendix 2

A research proposal: a response to the brief from John Ambrose

ATTITUDES TO THE USE OF SPECIALIZED FLOUR IN THE HOME

June 1997

Prepared for: John Ambrose and Co. Ltd.
Prepared by: Marketing Research in Action, The Research Centre, East Gate, London
Contact: R. A. Kent

CONTENTS

1 Introduction

John Ambrose & Co. Ltd is considering the possibility of offering to the general public the same highly specialized flours that it currently supplies to the trade. The company now wishes to commission research to examine attitudes to the use of specialized flours in the home.

Marketing Research in Action has been invited to present proposals for this piece of research. These have been prepared by our Consumer Research Division. They are based on a written brief received in May of this year and subsequent telephone conversations with John Ambrose.

2 Objectives

A combination of qualitative and quantitative research is required to examine the following questions.

- What proportion of households keep flour of any description in stock?
- What kinds of flour are usually kept?
- What other kinds of flour may housewives be aware of?
- What is flour currently used for?
- What are the main kinds of home baking?
- Which groups of people are most likely to make use of specialised flour?
- What quantities are they likely to buy?
- Would they be prepared to pay a slightly higher price?

The research will comprise two elements. The first stage of qualitative research will provide in-depth information on the main dimensions of flour usage in the home, attitudes to home baking and the possibilities for the use of specialized flour. This will provide the basis for designing the questionnaire to be used in the second stage among 1200 respondents.

3 Preliminary qualititative research

3.1 Discussion

We propose to conduct a mixture of group discussions and individual interviews. Group discussions are most appropriate for a proportion of housewives because:

- groups often produce a more relaxed and discursive review of a topic, and encourage spontaneous comments and comparisons,
- groups are less expensive 'per head',
- differences between consumers are highlighted.

However, depth interviews are often very useful as a 'control' for, or supplement to, groups since they enable individual histories and attitudes to be probed more fully. Furthermore, it is sometimes difficult to get a group of older people together. They often need more reassurance and there are frequently mobility and hearing problems. The majority of such interviews will be with a single respondent; however, we will also seek to include a small number of interviews with married couples.

3.2 Sample summary

We suggest six standard groups of eight housewives aged 18 or more, resident in the UK for at least three years. 'Housewives' are defined as those persons most directly concerned with shopping and cooking for the household. In some cases such a person may be male. Groups will be mixed in terms of age but separated by social class. However, there will be quotas on these two variables in order to ensure that they are represented in the same proportions as in the UK population. Social class will be measured according to the occupation of the head of the household.

Forty depth interviews are proposed, weighted towards the elderly or immobile. The sample structure will be as follows:

6 groups
Social class: $(3 \times BC1) + (3 \times C2D)$
Location: (3)(South) + (3)(North or Midlands)
20 interviews
Sex: all female
Social class: (10)(B) or (C1) + (10)(C2) or (D)
Location: (10)(South) + (10)(North or Midlands)
20 interviews
Sex: all female
Age: 65+
Location: (10)(South) + (10)(North or Midlands)

3.3 Recruiting and moderating procedures

Marketing Research in Action uses interviewers specially trained for qualitative recruiting. We are members of IQCS. We will rely mainly on random street or house recruiting, boosted by recruitment in carefully selected public locations appropriate to the particular sub-groups or respondents being contacted.

The interviews will be conducted in a domestic setting (a recruiter's home). It may, however, be necessary to hold some interviews in respondent's own homes.

All the groups and interviews will be moderated by a member of the Marketing Research in Action research team. All discussions will be tape recorded, and the transcripts of the groups can be made available if required.

3.4 Interview topics and stimulus materials

A detailed discussion and interview guide will be prepared on commission. Currently we envisage focussing on perceptions of the current range of flours available, attitudes to home baking, and the possibilities for the use of specialized flour. Particular attention will be paid to vocabulary, common assumptions, and areas of possible confusion likely to affect the qualitative study.

3.5 Timing

Following commission a period of three weeks will be required for group and individual interview recruitment. Further recruitment will take place concurrently with the fieldwork We envisage a period of about eight weeks will be required for the qualitative phase.

All interim reports should be available by the end of September, assuming commission in July. A full written report could then be produced within four weeks and integrated with the quantitative stage once this is complete.

4 Quantitative research discussion

4.1 Sampling

Option 1: Random sampling
We suggest a three-stage sampling procedure. First, a set of 100 electoral constituencies will be selected with probability of selection proportional to the size of the electorate. Second, an individual elector will be chosen at random from each constituency. The sampling point will then comprise the electoral ward of which that elector was part. Third, every fiftieth name will be selected from the Electoral Register referring to that ward and these will be given to interviewers. Interviewers will determine who is the 'housewife' in the household of the selected elector and asked if they have baked any cakes, scones, biscuits or pastries on the last four weeks. Those who have not are screened out. The interviewer continues until a quota of 12 completed interviews with housewives who do home baking is filled.

Option 2: Quota sampling
Stages one and two will be similar to Option 1. However, for stage three, the interviewer will be free to work wherever he or she liked in the defined areas to achieve a quota of interviews. Quotas will vary by region to reproduce the regional profile of females by age and social class, with non-bakers screened out as for Option 1.

There is the danger that this method will over-represent the 'at-home' population and under-represent working housewives. However, quotas could be applied additionally to working status.

For both Option 1 and Option 2 the achieved sample results will be weighted to the population profile in terms of age, social class and working status.

4.2 Sample size

There is an estimated 23.3 million housewives in Great Britain (excluding Northern Ireland) of which 15.5 per cent (or 3.6 million) are male. It would be unwise to exclude these, so about 180 of the sample of 1200 will be male. Results will be grossed up to this population.

4.3 Screening respondents

Both options will involve a screening procedure based on any baking activity over the last four weeks. Similar research we have conducted recently leads us to suggest that approximately 6 per cent of identified housewives cannot remember whether or not they have done any home baking in that period. We suggest that these, too, should be screened out on the basis that they are unlikely to be frequent home bakers.

5 Quantitative research method

5.1 Contact procedure

For Option 1 the interviewer will continue to call at a selected addresses up to a maximum of four times, varying the time of day and day of the week at each call.

In the case of Option 2, interviewers will be asked to record details of all contacts made and whether there was immediate refusal, non-eligible respondent who refused interview, was extra to quota or whether a full interview was achieved.

5.2 Questionnaire design

The questionnaire will be developed in consultation with John Ambrose and Co. Our costings have allowed for a questionnaire that will take on average 40 minutes to administer. Wherever possible we hope to be able to pre-code questions, drawing on the answers obtained previously in the qualitative research. We have allowed for up to six open-ended questions within each questionnaire. Section 6 describes the procedures for piloting.

5.3 Quality control

All interviewers will be supervised by our regional field directors. Ten per cent of interviews will be subjected to checkbacks. All interviews meet not only the standards of IQCS, but our own additional training ensures a quality of interviewing that few of our competitors can match.

5.4 Coding

We will prepare codeframes for the open-ended questions based on extractions from 100 questionnaires. These will be submitted to John Ambrose for approval before coding begins.

5.5 Manual editing

The objective is to ensure that information is in the correct format for data entry. It includes checks on the presence of leading zeros in quantity fields and full details of sample point. Our policy is to return any questionnaire that lacks key information to the interviewer concerned.

5.6 Data entry

The computer edit is a comprehensive data validation exercise that ensures the logical consistency of information as well as completeness. Any discrepancies it reveals are checked by a research executive against the original questionnaire.

5.7 Analysis

We have developed costings on the basis that 500 pages of computer tabulations will be required. The specification for the analysis will be discussed with John Ambrose before the analysis is run, including requirements for tests of statistical significance. We will supply two bound copies of laser-printed tabulations.

We will need to discuss with John Ambrose the issue of weighting the data. Using the quota approach it will be necessary to weight the data to take account of under-sampling of working housewives. Weights will also be applied to take account of differential response rates.

5.8 Reporting

In addition to the computer tabulations we have allowed for the preparation of a detailed technical report and an interpretive report. The latter will be structured to meet the needs of John Ambrose. It will be illustrated with charts and diagrams drawn from the computer tabulations. Both reports will be submitted in draft and after approval we will supply four copies of each.

We have not allowed for a presentation of the quantitative research findings, but would be happy to discuss this should one be required.

6 Pilot research

We have indicated the additional cost of pilot research in our section on fees. While it is always desirable to pilot questionnaires, we feel that a pilot survey could be dispensed with in this project given our familiarity with the market. However, should one be required we would recommend that the pilot be conducted in three sample points with 12 interviews in each. The procedure for the pilot would be exactly the same as for the main stage quota option given that the main purpose is to test the questionnaire rather than the sampling method.

Interviewers would attend a personal briefing at Marketing Research in Action at our head office. We would produce a brief report on the pilot, suggesting amendments to the questionnaire or survey design for the main stage. The report would also comment on the implications of any changes for the fee for the main stage.

7 Interviewer selection

Interviewers will receive personal briefings at one of six centres nearest to their home. Our regional managers will attend so that they are completely familiar with the survey. The sessions will be conducted by Marketing Research in Action executives responsible for the survey and will last about two hours. Attendance by relevant personnel from John Ambrose will be warmly encouraged.

The main purpose of the briefing will be to ensure that interviewers and managers are totally familiar with:

- the administration of the questionnaire and any question areas of particular difficulty or complexity,
- the type of respondent they will be likely to interview,
- the type of information that needs to be collected.

There will also be a mock interview to highlight the points made during the session.

Interviewers will, in addition, be given a set of written instructions which reiterate in more detail the points made at the briefing session.

Marketing Research in Action has a national panel of about 950 interviewers. Mostly they are self-employed, but they work to standards and administrative procedures laid down by our operating manual. They are organized under a team of 12 Regional Managers, all of whom are full-time employees of Marketing Research in Action.

We are members of the Interviewer Quality Control Scheme, whose professional standards we either meet or exceed. Normal back-checking and accompaniment procedures would be applied to this survey. This, in summary, requires that:

- interviewers should be accompanied at least once in each six-month period,
- 10 per cent of the work will be subject to back-check procedures,
- the back-checking will comprise 10 per cent postal checks; the remainder will be face-to-face or telephone checks.

8 Timing

Our best estimate of how the timing could proceed is as follows:

Weeks 1–7	qualitative research
Week 8	qualitative presentation
Week 11	qualitative report available
Weeks 8–11	quantitative questionnaire development
Week 12	pilot briefing
Week 13	Pilot debriefing
Weeks 14–15	questionnaire alterations and printing
Week 16	main stage briefings
Weeks 17–19	main stage fieldwork
Weeks 18–21	codings and data preparation
Week 22	analysis produced
Week 25	draft report available.

This follows the timetable suggested in the brief and we believe it to be realistic, but it could be amended in the light of further discussions with John Ambrose. Thus if there is no pilot survey the project can be shortened by two weeks.

9 Project staffing

The project will be carried out by the Consumer Research Division of Marketing Research in Action, under its director, Kay Brent, who has had may years experience of consumer survey work. She has specialized in the application of research techniques to the food industry and, before joining the Company in 1982, had spent five years as consultant to the Ministry of Food and Agriculture.

Responsibility for the project would be given to Ken Bray, an Associate Director of the Division. He joined the Company on 1983 and since then has managed a variety of ad hoc projects, several of them in the food sector.

10 Fees

The fees quoted below are exclusive of VAT, and are subject to Marketing Research in Action's standard terms and conditions of contract. The fees are subject to the assumptions contained in these proposals and may have to be amended should any assumptions prove to be incorrect.

Qualitative research	£20,750
Quantitative pilot research	£ 2,500
Main stage – random sampling	£73,900
Main stage – quota sampling	£53,200.

Using SPSS

The Statistical Package for the Social Sciences (SPSS) has been around for a long time. The initial design dates back to 1965 when some 7000 separate computer programs were integrated into a batch/command data analysis system for use on a large mainframe computer. From the outset it has always been a comprehensive set of procedures for data transformation and the production of very sophisticated statistics, but it usually took researchers a long while to learn how to use. SPSS for Windows, however, uses a graphical user interface and is interactive rather than batch, that is, instead of feeding in a complete set of instructions for a 'job' to be run, the user can now obtain instant results as he or she goes along.

   SPSS for Windows is now available in many university computer laboratories and has become something of an industry standard in the market research world, although it has to be said that many agencies developed their own programs many years ago and see little advantage in switching to SPSS at this stage. If you have access to SPSS for Windows try the following exercises once you have logged on to your system and opened the SPSS application. The

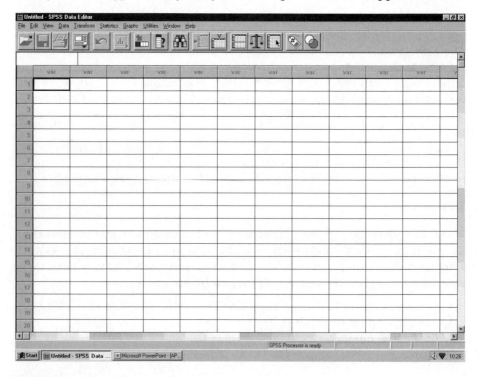

Figure A3.1 The Data Editor window.

Variable name	Variable label	Value label	Code	**Table A3.1**
Sex	Sex of respondent	Male	1	A coding sheet
		Female	2	
Age	Age last birthday		Age in years	
Ban	Attitude to banning advertising	Strongly Agree	5	
		Agree	4	
		Neutral	3	
		Disagree	2	
		Strongly disagree	1	
Sport	Participation in sport	Participated	1	
		No participated	2	
Health	Attitude to health	Avoid fat	1	
		Not avoid	2	
Smoke	Smoking behaviour	Smokes	1	
		Not smoke	2	

illustrations in this appendix show SPSS Version 7.5. In some earlier versions the toolbar and the menu systems are a little different.

Entering data

The first window you will see is the *Data Editor* window (Figure A3.1.) The window is a grid whose rows represent cases (no row should contain data on more than one case) and whose columns will contain the values of the variables for each case. It is thus laid out in the form of a data matrix which was explained in Chapter 2.

Before entering any data it is advisable first to name the variables. These names must not exceed eight characters, they must begin with a letter and must not end with a full stop. There must be no spaces and the names chosen should not be one of the key words that SPSS uses as special computing terms, e.g. AND, NOT, EQ, BY, ALL.

Table A3.1 suggests six variable names for six questions addressed to a sample of 15 respondents. To enter the first variable name (sex), double click on the grey area at the top of the first column. This will obtain the *Define Variable* dialog box (see Figure A3.2). The *Variable Name* text box contains a default variable name, **VAR00001**. *Delete this by typing in* **Sex** and the default will be overwritten. A longer, more meaningful label can, however, be attached to each variable. Click on the *Labels* button in the *Change Settings* subdialog box. This will produce the *Define Labels* dialog box. Type in **Sex of respondent** *in the Variable Label* box. The rules governing the naming of variables do not apply to labels, e.g. there may be spaces, the letters are case sensitive, and up to 120 characters may be used.

Since the variable sex is non-metric, it is necessary to give each value a label, e.g. 1 = Male, 2 = Female. In the *Value* box, type in **1** (the lowest code number) and in *Value Label* type in **Male**. N.B. To move between boxes click on the mouse in the appropriate box (or use the *Tab* key to move to the box below). Click on the *Add* button and **1 = Male** will appear in the lowest box. Now add **2 = Female** using the same procedure and then click on *Continue*.

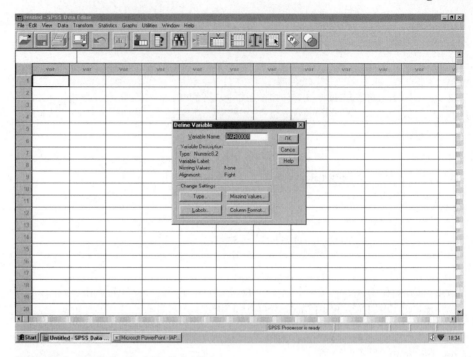

Figure A3.2   The Define Variable dialog box.

Now name the other five variables, adding variable labels and value labels. Note, however, that age is a metric variable and does not require value labels.

   You are now ready to enter the data given in Table A3.2. This will normally be done row by row, that is, case by case or questionnaire by questionnaire. Put the cell highlight on the cell into which you wish to enter a value (begin top left) and simply type the number (always enter the codes, not the value labels!). Move the highlight using the direction keys. Notice that the process of entering is completed simply by moving the highlight to another cell. You could press the *Enter* key instead. The completed data matrix should look like

Table A3.2
Some survey data

Case	Sex	Age	Ban	Sport	Health	Smoke
1	1	23	4	1	2	1
2	2	27	2	1	2	2
3	2	33	1	2	1	1
4	1	56	5	2	2	2
5	2	46	2	1	1	1
6	2	22	1	2	1	2
7	1	48	3	2	1	2
8	1	34	4	2	1	2
9	2	37	3	2	2	1
10	2	34	4	1	2	1
11	1	25	4	1	1	2
12	1	34	1	1	2	1
13	2	23	5	2	1	2
14	1	22	3	2	1	2
15	1	25	4	1	1	1

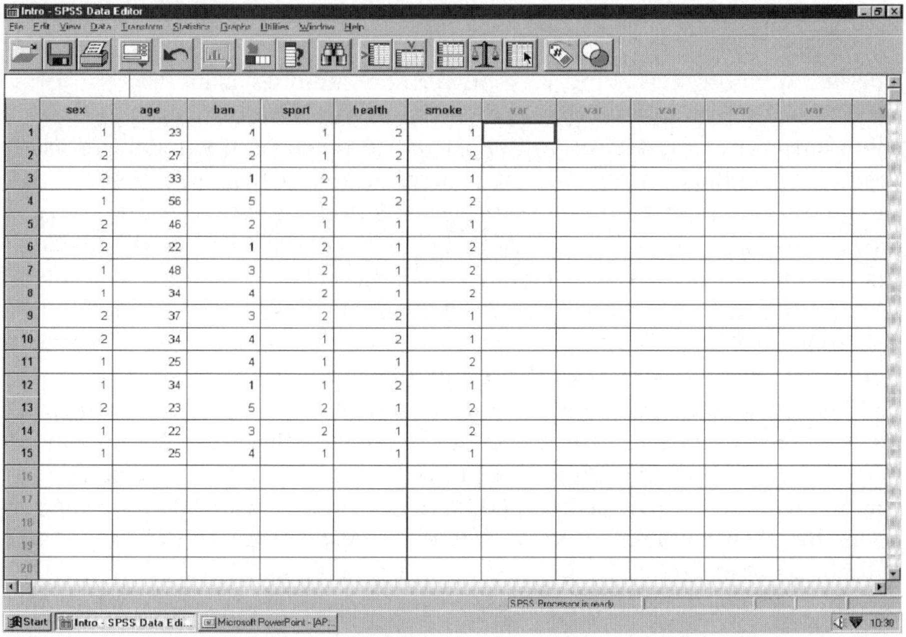

Figure A3.3 The completed data matrix.

Figure A3.3, except that your system may be set up with a default of two decimal places. You can change the number of decimal places for any variable by clicking on the *Type* button in the *Define Variable* window. Click on the *Decimal Places* box and change to **0**, click on *Continue* then *OK*. Alternatively, you can alter the default to zero, but you must do this before you enter any data or define any variables. From the menu bar at the top of the application window select *Edit* and then *Options*. Click on the *Data* tab and change *Decimal Places* to **0**. Click on *OK*.

Notice that just above the grid is a white bar – this is the *Status bar*. This shows your entry as you type it and indicates the cell position on the left. The usual Windows editing functions are available, for example you can cut, copy and paste in the usual way. To change a value in a cell once it has been entered, simply highlight the cell, type in the new value and press *Enter*.

Note that SPSS assumes that all data matrices are rectangular. If you press *Enter* before you get to the end of the second or subsequent rows a full stop is entered in each of the remaining cells in that row. There can be no empty cells. If no value has been entered, the system supplies the *system-missing* value, which is indicated by a full stop.

Saving your work

Remember that SPSS does not have an automatic timed backup facility. You need to save your work regularly as you go along. Use the *File\Save* sequence as usual for Windows applications. The first time you go to save you will be given the *Save As* dialog box. Make sure this indicates the drive you want. Drive a: for your floppy disk, Drive c: for you hard disk or Drive h: if you are on a networked system. *File\Exit* will get you out of SPSS and back to the Program Manager or windows desktop.

Data analysis

SPSS for Windows has some very powerful techniques at its disposal. However, for present purposes only the very basic procedures will be explained. When analysing any dataset you will need to begin by obtaining univariate descriptive summaries for each of your variables, i.e. one at a time. Which summaries are appropriate depends, as usual, on the type of data. For non-metric variables you need the *Frequencies* procedure. This is in the *Statistics\Summarise* drop-down menu from the menu bar at the top. So, click on *Statistics*, then *Summarise*, then *Frequencies*. The *Frequencies* dialog box will appear (Figure A3.4). All variables are listed in the left box. To obtain a frequency count for any variable simply transfer it to the *Variables* box by highlighting it, then clicking on the direction button in the middle. Since all the variables except age are non-metric, highlight all except age in the left box. (NB: hold down the left mouse button while dragging the mouse and you can do them all at once! Click on *OK* and, hey presto, you obtain a frequency count for each variable along with Percent, Valid Percent and Cumulative Percent, as illustrated in Table A3.3 for the variable Ban).

If you click on *Charts* in the *Frequencies* dialog box you obtain the *Frequencies: Charts* dialog box. Simply click on *Bar charts* or *Pie charts* and indicate whether you want the axis label to display frequencies or percentage, click on *Continue* and then *OK*. This will give you a bar chart in addition to the frequencies table. To view the chart you may need to click on the *Chart Carousel* icon.

For metric variables you can also use the *Frequencies* procedure, but in addition you can click on the *Statistics* button in the *Frequencies* dialog box to obtain a range of statistics. Just click the boxes as required. Using the *Graphs* pull-down menu you can obtain a range of graphs. These are mostly

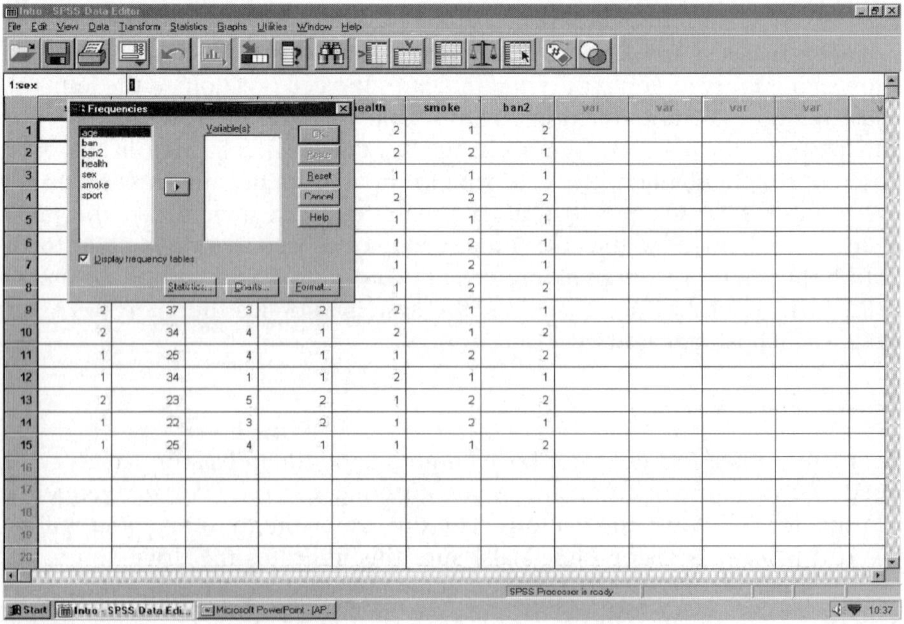

Figure A3.4   The Frequencies dialog box.

| BAN | Attitude to banning of advertising | | | | |
Value Label	Value	Frequency	%	Valid %	Cum %
Strongly disagree	1	3	20.0	20.0	20.0
Disagree	2	2	13.3	13.3	33.3
Neutral	3	3	20.0	20.0	53.3
Agree	4	5	33.3	33.3	86.7
Strongly agree	5	2	13.3	13.3	100.0
	Total	15	100.0	100.0	

Table A3.3
An output table from SPSS

for metric variables. *Descriptives* provides a quick way of obtaining a range of common descriptive statistics, both of central tendency and dispersion – try it on age. Put age into the variables box and click on *OK*. *Explore* contains a large variety of statistics including stem and leaf diagrams and boxplots.

The next stage in any data analysis is to look at the relationships between variables. For example, are men more or less likely than women to agree with a ban on advertising cigarettes? For this you need the *Crosstabs* procedure. This generates contingency tables for non-metric variables. Select *Statistics\Summarize\Crosstabs* to obtain the *Crosstabs* dialog box (Figure A3.5). Enter your dependent variable (Ban) in the *Rows* box so it will appear at the side and the independent variable Sex in the columns. Have a look at what statistics are available for crosstabs by clicking on the *Statistics* button. You will obtain the *Crosstabs: Statistics* dialog box shown earlier in Chapter 6 (Figure 6.5). For nominal variables there is Chi-square, Phi-square, Cramer's *V*, the Contingency Coefficient, Lambda and an Uncertainty Coefficient. For ordinal data there is Gamma, Somers' *d*, tau *b* and tau *c*. For nominal by interval combination there is the statistic Eta. To obtain any of these just click on the appropriate box. Click on *OK* when you have decided what you want. In this example it's really a

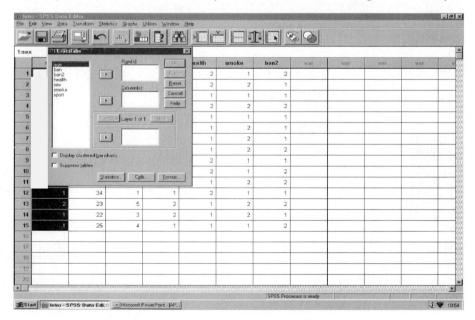

Figure A3.5 The Crosstabs dialog box.

nominal by ordinal combination, so only the nominal data statistics can be used. For a review of these statistics see Chapter 6.

For correlating two metric variables the *Statistics\Correlate\Bivariate* procedure should be used. (NB: strictly speaking there is only one metric variable in this dataset – age. However, treat Ban as a metric variable (i.e. the scores 5–1 are regarded as measures of distance) and correlate Age against Ban. Ensure that the *Pearson* check box is ticked). Graphically, you can obtain a scatterplot with the *Graphs\Scatter* sequence. Where the two variables are rank ordered, e.g. two variables ranked 1–30, then Spearman's rank correlation is a very good statistic. Select *Statistics\Correlate\Bivariate* and click the *Spearman's* check box.

Data transformation

After data have been entered into SPSS it may be necessary to modify them in certain ways. For non-metric data it may be necessary to combine or alter the categories of a variable. This is achieved with the *Recode* procedure.

Recode

Suppose, for the variable Ban, you wish to add together the responses Strongly Agree and Agree to make a new category, and to put Neutral, Disagree and Strongly Disagree into another category (i.e. to create a binary variable). You may need to perform this kind of operation on several variables if the sample size is small and the process of crosstabulation gives too many cells with too few entries, even empty cells. Select *Transform* then *Recode* and click on *Into Different Variables*. This gives another dialog box (Figure A3.6). Click on *Ban* and on > to paste the name into the *Numeric Variable->Output Variable* box.

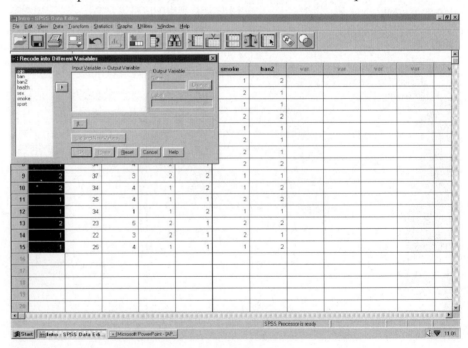

Figure A3.6   The Recode into Different Variables dialog box.

Type the name of the new output variable, e.g. Ban2 into the *Name* box and click on *Change* to insert the name into the *Numeric Variable->Output Variable* box.

Click on the *Old and New Values* box to open the next dialog box. Since the value 1 is to remain unchanged, click on the *Value* radio button in the *Old Value* box, and enter the value **1**. Click on the *Copy old value(s)* radio button in the *New Value box*, then on *Add* in the *Old->New* box. The values 2 and 3 are to be recoded as 1 so click on the *Range* radio button in the *Old Value* box. Enter **2** in the left box and **3** in the right box. Click on the *Value* radio button in the *New Value* box and enter **1** and click on *Add*. Codes 4 and 5 are to be recoded as 2, so return to the *Old Value* box, enter, under *Range* **4** in the left box and **5** in the right. In the *New Value* box enter **2** and click on *Add*. The *Old->New* box will show the transformations that are to take place. Click on *Continue* and then on *OK*. A new variable Ban2 will be added to the worksheet in the *Data Editor* window that contains only the values 1 and 2. Check that these transformations have been carried out.

The *Recode* procedure may also be used to recode ranked and metric variables into coded categories. This will be useful if you wish to crosstabulate these with non-metric variables. Try putting Age into groups of 10 years, e.g. 20–29. 30–39, 40–49 and 50–59.

Multi-response variables

Many questions in questionnaires allow respondents to pick more than one category. For example, the Sport variable could have asked respondents to tick a box against each sport they played. Most statistical and spreadsheet packages are unable to handle these questions since only one piece of information may be entered into a cell. The only solution is to treat each response

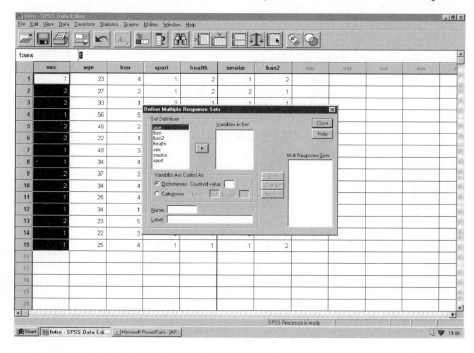

Figure A3.7   The Define Multiple Response Sets dialog box.

category as a binary variable that has either been selected or it has not. SPSS for Windows, however, allows you to treat groups of such variables as multi-responses. This facility is under the *Statistics* drop-down menu. Select *Statistics*, *Multiple Response* and *Define Sets*. The *Define Multiple Response Sets* dialog box (see Figure A3.7) allows you to specify the variables to be included in this set. Simply transfer them from the *Set definition* box to the *Variables in Set* box. Click in the *Dichotomies* radio button in the *Variables Are Coded As* box and enter the value to be counted as part of the set, e.g. if the value 1 has been entered on the questionnaire to indicate that this item has been selected, then enter **1** in this box. Don't forget to give a name to the set. Entering a label is optional. Try the following exercise.

Add three more variables, **foot**, **tennis**, **other**, and for all 15 cases add a zero or 1 at random for each (just to create some fictional data). Select *Statistics*, *Multiple Response* and *Define Sets*. Transfer foot, tennis and other to the *Variables in Set* box. Check that the dichotomies radio button is highlighted and enter **1** in the *Counted Value* box. Give the variable a name (and a label if you wish) and click on *Add*, then *Close*. Reselect *Statistics*, *Multiple Response* then either *Frequencies* or *Crosstabs*.

Several multiple response sets may be defined at the same time. These are then listed in the *Multiple Response Sets* box. The sets so defined may now be used either to show frequencies or crosstabs. Select *Frequencies* or *Crosstabs* from the *Multiple Response* drop-down menu. These allow you to specify which response sets are to be used and what to do with cases to be excluded from the analysis.

Appendix 4
Using PinPoint

Pinpoint is a survey analysis package that allows the researcher to:

- design questionnaires or data collection sheets,
- enter data,
- analyse the data.

There are three main areas in which you will work on a PinPoint 'project'.

- form design and editing,
- form filling,
- data analysis.

Form design and editing

Every new PinPoint project begins with the design of its 'form', or data collection sheet. When you work with a form in PinPoint you work with the Form Editor. The Editor can be thought of as a 'window' onto a form in which you can do several things:

- format the page attributes of your form,
- set up a multi-page form,
- write and edit questions,
- prepare your form for printing,
- import answer data from other PinPoint projects or other applications,
- edit an existing project's form and update the completed answer sheets in its stack,
- 'send' a new form to the sheet editor for completion as the first answer sheet in a new stack.

The Form Editor allows you to describe the data to be collected (write questions), modify them, move them around the paper so they are presented in the required order, and add explanatory text and/or pictures, until you are satisfied.

Using PinPoint, there is no need to sketch out a design for your form and the questions to be asked before beginning in PinPoint, since PinPoint itself provides you with all the tools for sketching. As you are working on the form you can continually refine it by moving, adding and removing work – in many ways it is easier to work in PinPoint than it is to use pencil and paper.

From the File menu, choose New Project. A new form will be created as a single page of the size and orientation as described by the active printer. Try the following exercise.

1   click on the *Pinpoint* icon,
2   click on *File/New project*,

3   click on the *Question tool* (far left on the tool bar – descriptions of the buttons appear on the bottom of the screen as you move the mouse over them),

4   hold down the mouse button and drag down and across to mark out the area into which the question will be placed. (NB: the precise sizing and placement is not important at this stage; these can be changed later),

5   as you release the mouse button the *Question Details* dialog box will appear,

6   type in **Have you purchased a newspaper in the last week**? in the question area box (You can pick any other font by clicking on the *Font* button),

7   click on the *Reference name* box. Delete what is already entered and type **Newspaper**,

8   click on the *Yes/No* radio button in the answer box,

9   click on *OK*,

10 double-click in the area of the question to return to the *Question Details* dialog box and try changing some of the Style options,

11 drag out the area for a new question. Type **In which of the following age groups are you**?,

12 put **Age** into the *Reference name* box,

13 click on *Multiple choice*,

14 click on *Add* and type **Under 20**. Click on *OK*,

15 click on *Add* and type **20–39**. Click on *OK*,

16 click on *Add* and type **40 plus**. Click on *OK*,

17 you can edit or delete any of these items,

18 delete *Left of text* and click on *Justify text to box*. Click on *OK*,

19 click on the pointer. Click on a question and try dragging it about the screen. Try moving the answer boxes,

20 text may be added anywhere by clicking on A and using 'I' to indicate where the text is to go,

21 add a couple of questions of your own,

22 click on *File*, then *Print Form*.

Form filling

A completed or 'filled in' copy of a form is known in PinPoint as an 'Answer sheet'. During answer sheet compilation a copy of the form is always displayed on screen. Answers can be entered directly onto the screen by your respondents, or else answer data can be 'copied in' from a collection of completed paper forms.

Because PinPoint's forms can contain many question 'formats' together with free-form text notes and built-in data entry checks, precise information can entered quickly and accurately.

1   click on *File* then *Save Form*,

2   you will obtain the *Save As* screen,

3   give the file a name, change to drive a:, c: or h: as appropriate. It will be a .ppf file,

4   click on *View*, then *Answer sheets*,

5   complete about 15 forms with fictional data by clicking on a range of

different answers. At the end of each sheet click on *Sheet* then *New*, then *Yes*.

6 now imagine you have 150 forms with 70 questions on each!

Data analysis

A completed set of answer sheets is known as a 'stack'. When a stack of answer sheets has been compiled the sheets are placed into a 'worksheet' for analysis.

PinPoint's worksheets provide the tools for:

- displaying completed answer sheets in tabular form,
- sorting and selecting the sheets,
- performing statistical analyses on numerical (metric) answers,
- the production of graphs, charts and tables,
- under *Save As* one option is to save the worksheet as an SPSS file.

You can add new answer sheets to a stack, and edit or 'update' a project's form and any existing answer sheet(s) at any time.

1 click on *View/Worksheet*,
2 click on *Quick analysis* – you will get the *Quick Graphs* dialog box,
3 click on *All*,
4 choose *Counts* or *Percentages* from the *Analysis* box,
5 select a style from the *Style gallery* – the one far left produces tables rather than graphs; try it,
6 click on *OK* – you will obtain the *Table Properties* dialog box,
7 choose the calculations you want – I suggest *On columns* and *Total*. Click on *OK*,
8 you will obtain a univariate table for each variable,
9 to create a cross-tabulation click on the *Create a cross tab* table icon,
10 you will then be invited to put in the variables you wish as the rows – highlight each variable and click on *Add* then *OK*,
11 do the same for columns. Click on *OK*,
12 in the Crosstab Options box the *Counts* and *Percentages* by columns will be pre-selected. Choose the statistics you want. Click on *Print* – it will not show the table on screen, but will go straight to the printer.

The project

PinPoint stores all project information – the form, the completed answer sheets, the worksheet and all its attributes and any associated graphical presentations – in a single '.ppf' project file.

Copying a project from one machine to another, therefore, is just a matter of copying a single project file into an existing PinPoint installation. From Pin-Point Vrsion 3.1 onwards, it is possible to save as an SPSS file. So, you can design your questionnaire in PinPoint and enter the data. You can then save as an SPSS file and use SPSS data analysis procedures.

Select Bibliography

Assael, H and Keon, J (1982) 'Nonsampling versus sampling errors in survey research', *Journal of Marketing*, Vol 46, Spring, pp 114-23.

Baker, K and Fletcher, R (1989) 'OUTLOOK - a generalised lifestyle system', *ADMAP*, March, pp 23-8.

Barnard, S (1996) 'Driving force', *The Grocer*, 16 March, pp 16-17.

Batsell, R and Wind, Y (1980) 'Product testing: current methods and needed developments', *Journal of the Market Research Society*, Vol 22, No 2, pp 115-39.

Barwise, TP, Ehrenberg, ASC and Goodhardt, GJ (1979) 'Audience appreciation and audience size', *Journal of the Market Research Society*, Vol 21, No 4, pp 269-84.

Belson, W (1986) *Validity in Survey Research*, London: Gower.

Bowles, T and Blyth, B (1997) 'How do you like your data: raw, al dente or stewed?', *Journal of the Market Research Society*, Vol 3, No 1, pp 163-74.

Bowers, D (1996) *Statistics from Scratch. An Introduction for Health Care Professionals*, Chichester: Wiley.

Boughey, H (1978) *The Insights of Sociology: An Introduction*, Boston: Allyn and Bacon.

Brown, G (1991a) 'Response. Modelling advertising awareness', *Journal of the Market Research Society*, Vol 33, No 3, pp 197-204.

Brown, G (1991b) 'Big stable brands and advertising effects', *ADMAP*, May, pp 32-37.

Brown, M (1994) 'Estimating newspaper and magazine readership', in RA Kent (ed.) *Measuring Media Audiences*, London: Routledge.

Brown, MG (1990) 'How to guarantee poor quality service', *Journal for Quality and Participation*, December, pp 6-12.

Bryson, J, Keeble, D and Wood, P (1990) 'Survey of small market research companies: some preliminary findings', *Market Research Society Newsletter*, December, 11. pp 36-7.

Buttle, F (1996) 'SERVQUAL: review, critique, research agenda', *European Journal of Marketing*, Vol. 56. July, pp 1-24.

Chisnall, P (1997) *Marketing Research*, 5th edn, London: McGraw-Hill.

Churchill, G (1995) *Marketing Research: Methodological Foundations*, 6th edn, Fort Worth: The Dryden Press.

Churchill, G (1969) 'A paradigm for developing better measures of marketing constructs', *Journal of Marketing Research*, February, pp 64-73.

Cicourel, A (1967) *Method and Measurement in Sociology*, New York: Free Press.

Colman, S and Brown, G (1983) 'Advertising tracking studies and sales effects', *Journal of the Market Research Society*, Vol 25, No 2.

Converse, J and Presser, S (1986) *Survey Questions*, Beverly Hills: California: Sage.

Cornish, P (1981) 'Lifecycle and income segmentation': SAGACITY, *ADMAP*, October, pp 522-6.

Crimp, M (1990) *The Marketing Research Process*, 3rd edn, Hemel Hempstead: Prentice Hall.

Cronin, J and Taylor, S (1992) 'Measuring service quality: a reexamination and extension', *Journal of Marketing*, Vol 56, July, pp 55-68.

de Chernatony, L and Knox, S (1990) 'How an appreciation of consumer behaviour can help in product testing', *Journal of the Market Research Society*, Vol 32, No 3, pp 29-47.

Dawson, J and Hillier, J (1995) 'Competitor mystery shopping: methodological considerations and implications for the MRS Code of Conduct', *Journal of the Market Research Society*, Vol 37, No 4, pp 225-39.

Diamantopolous, A and Schlegelmilch, B (1997) *Taking the Fear out of Data Analysis*, London: The Dryden Press.

Evans, N (1995) *Using Questionnaires and Surveys to Boost Your Business*, London: Pitman Publishing.

Freeman, L (1965) *Elementary Applied Statistics: For Students in Behavioural Sciences*, New York: John Wiley.

Gane, R (1994) 'Television audience measurement systems in Europe: a review and comparison', in Kent, R (ed.) *Measuring Media Audiences*, London: Routledge.

Goodyear, MJ (1990) 'Qualitative research', in R Birn, *et al., A Handbook of Market Research Techniques*, London: Kogan Page.

Gordon, W and Langmaid, R (1988) *Qualitative Market Research. A Practitioner's and Buyer's Guide*, London: Gower Press.

Griggs, S (1987) 'Analysing qualitative data', *Journal of the Market Research Society* Vol 29, No 2, pp 15–34.

Hague, P (1993) *Questionnaire Design*, London, Kogan Page.

Henry, GT (1990) *Practical Sampling*, London: Sage.

Hunt, S (1983) *Marketing Theory. The Philosophy of Marketing Science*, Homewood, Ill.: R D Irwin.

Irvine, J, Miles, I and Evans, J (eds) (1979) *Demystifying Social Statistics*, London: Pluto Press.

Jones, T and Sasser, W (1995) 'Why satisfied customers defect', *Harvard Business Review*, Vol 73, November-December, pp 88–99.

Kent, RA (1981) *A History of British Empirical Sociology*, London: Gower Press.

Kent, RA (1993) *Marketing Research in Action*, London: Routledge.

Kent, RA (ed.) (1994) *Measuring Media Audiences*, London: Routledge.

Kish, L (1965) *Survey Sampling*, New York: John Wiley.

Kleinman, P (1996) 'A survey of the survey trade', *ADMAP*, March, p 8.

Kotler, P (1997) *Marketing Management. Analysis, Planning and Control*, 9th edn, Englewood Cliffs, New Jersey: Prentice-Hall.

Kirkham, M (1996) 'Measuring the fragmenting television audience', *Journal of the Market Research Society*, Vol 38, No 3, pp 219–26.

Likert, R (1932) 'A technique for the measurement of attitudes', *Archives of Psychology*, No 40.

Menneer, P (1987) 'Audience appreciation – a different story from audience numbers', *Journal of the Market Research Society*, Vol 29, No 3.

Menneer, P (1989) 'Towards a radio 'BARB' – some issues of measurement', *ADMAP*, February, pp 42–5.

Miles, L (1993) 'Rise of the mystery shopper', *Marketing*, July, pp 19–20.

Morrison, LJ, Colman, AM and Preston, CC (1997) 'Mystery customer research: cognitive processes affecting accuracy', *Journal of the Market Research Society*, Vol 39, No 2, pp 349–61.

O'Brien, S and Ford, R (1989) 'Can we at last say goodbye to social class?', *Journal of the Market Research Society*, Vol 46, No 3, pp 289–332.

Oliver, R (1997) *Satisfaction. A Behavioural Perspective on the Consumer*, New York: McGraw-Hill.

Oppenheim, AN (1996) *Questionnaire Design and Attitude Measurement*, London: Heinemann.

Osgood, CE, Suci, GJ and Tannenbaum, PH (1957) *The Measurement of Meaning*, Chicago, Ill.: University of Illinois Press.

Parasuraman, A, Zeithml, V and Berry, L (1988) 'SERVQUAL: a multiple-item scale for measuring consumer perceptions of service quality', *Journal of Retailing*, Vol 64, No 1, pp 12–40.

Payne, SL (1951) *The Art of Asking Questions*, New Jersey: Princetown University Press.

Piercy, N and Evans, M (1983) *Managing Marketing Information*, London: Croom Helm.

Rogers, E and Kincaid, D (1981) *Communication Networks. Toward a New Paradigm for Research*, New York: Free Press.

Ramsay, W (1982) 'The new product dilemma', *Marketing Trends*, Vol 1.

Sampson, P (1987) 'The tracking study in market research', in U. Bradley (ed.) *Applied Marketing and Social Research*, Chichester: John Wiley.

Sargent, M (1989) 'Uses and abuses of qualitative research from a marketing viewpoint', in S Robson and A Foster (eds), *Qualitative Research in Action*, London: Edward Arnold.

Scott, B (1986) *The Skills of Communicating*, London: Gower Press.

Selvin, HC (1957), 'A critique of tests of significance in survey research', *American Sociological Review*, Vol 22, pp 519–27.

Sharot, T (1986) 'Weighting survey results', *Journal of the Market Research Society* Vol 28, No 3, pp 269–84.

Sharot, T (1994) 'Measuring television audiences in the UK', in Kent, R (ed.) *Measuring Media Audiences*, London: Routledge.

Shepherd-Smith, N (1994) 'Something's wrong with average issue readership', *ADMAP*, February, pp 89–94.

Silvey, J (1975), *Deciphering Data. The Analysis of Social Surveys*, London: Longman.

Spector, PE (1991) *Scale Development: Theories and Applications*, London: Sage.

Sudman, S (1976) *Applied Sampling*, San Francisco, Calif.: Academic Press.

Sudman, S and Bradburn, NM (1982) *Asking Questions. A Practical Guide to Questionnaire Design*, San Francisco, Calif.: Jossey Bass.

Sudman, S and Ferber, R (1979) *Consumer Panels*, Chicago: American Marketing Association.

Sykes, W (1990) 'Taking stock: issues from the literature on validity and reliability in qualitative research', *Journal of the Market Research Society*, Vol 33, No 1, pp 1–12.

Taylor, H (1997) ' The very different methods used to conduct telephone surveys of the public', *Journal of the Market Research Society*, Vol 39, No 3, pp 421–32.

Theil, H (1967) *Economics and Information Theory*, Chicago, Ill.: Rand McNally.

Tuckman, WB (1986) 'Developmental sequences in small groups', in A Brown, *Group Work*, 2nd edn, London: Gower Press.

Vardaman, GT (1981) *Making Successful Presentations*, New York: AMACOM.

Ward, J (1987) 'Lifestyles and geodemographics: why advertising agencies shun a single-source approach', *ADMAP*, June, pp 53–6.

Willis, K (1990) 'In-depth interviews', in R Birn, *et al., A Handbook of Market Research Techniques*, London: Kogan Page.

Wimbush, A (1990) 'Clinics', in R Birn, *et al., A Handbook of Market Research Techniques*, London: Kogan Page.

Wolfe, A (1982) 'Sampling error and significance tables for research executives', *IMRA* Occasional Paper, Lichfield, Staffs.

Wolfe, A (ed.) (1984) *Standardised Questions. A Review for Market Research Executives*, London: Market Research Society.

Index